20th CENTURY SOCIAL THOUGHT

20th CENTURY

RAY P. CUZZORT
University of Colorado

EDITH W. KING
University of Denver

HOLT, RINEHART and WINSTON

New York • Chicago • San Francisco • Dallas • Montreal • Toronto • London • Sydney

FREUD
MARX
DURKHEIM
WEBER
MEAD
LUNDBERG
SOROKIN

SOCIAL THOUGHT *Third Edition*

WHITE
MERTON
RIESMAN
MILLS
HENRY
BECKER
BERGER
GOFFMAN
GARFINKEL
DUNCAN

20th CENTURY SOCIAL THOUGHT, *Third Edition*

RAY P. CUZZORT
And
EDITH W. KING

Library of Congress Cataloging in Publication Data

Cuzzort, Raymond Paul, 1926–
    Twentieth century social thought.
    Second ed. published in 1976 under title: Humanity
and modern social thought.
    Includes bibliographical references and index.
    1. Sociology—History—20th century—Addresses,
essays, lectures. I. King, Edith W., joint author.
II. Title.
HM19.C84   1980   301   80-10204
ISBN 0-03-052521-7

Preface to the Third Edition

As we embarked on the third edition of this book, less than three years after the second edition, the state of American society seemed to be in deep ferment. Many abrupt changes were affecting our life styles and expectations. The events of the past several years seemed to call for a more historical orientation and setting for the social scientists presented in this new edition of *Humanity and Modern Social Thought* (now with a title-change to *Twentieth Century Social Thought*). Furthermore, several writers' works that appeared in the first edition, but were not included in the second edition, took on new and important meanings in the light of the happenings of recent years. So our third edition of *Twentieth Century Social Thought* presents the reader with some thought-provoking and differing perspectives on the classical and contemporary social thinkers that appeared in the pages of both the first and second editions of this book.

The crucial impact of World War II on humanism and social thought clearly emerges as we enter the closing decades of the twentieth century. It is this central theme that has shaped the design of our third edition. As in earlier editions, we have chosen social scientists who stand as controversial figures in sociology and in the social thought of Western culture. None of these observers of the modern scene has lacked critics. Each has remained firm against opponents and has defended himself brilliantly and at times persuasively. The material in this book endeavors to show that sociologists are involved with profound problems of both a humanistic and a scientific nature. The writings of these social scientists demonstrate how their scientific concerns led them down some interesting theoretical pathways that were crisscrossed with humanistic concerns. So, as before, the content of this book consists for the most part of discussions of the major works of social scientists who have contributed to social thought and the discipline of sociology. The works of these social thinkers provide the reader with some idea of the diversity of modern social thought. Not every sociologist represented will stimulate the same response from the reader. But we hope that at least one approach will find special favor or meaning for the student of society and social thought.

Earlier we alluded to the current malaise in American life and the central cause of this malaise, the energy crisis, that our final chapter focuses upon. Sociological thought can contribute to a fuller understanding of social problems in the past, in the present, and in the future, as we attempt to demonstrate throughout the book, as well as in the final chapter.

vi   We wish to give thanks for the conception and design of this third edition to our editors at Holt, Rinehart and Winston. Special mention must go to our dear mentor, Everett Hughes, who encouraged us to continue our interpretations of classical and modern theorists during this third edition. We wish to thank our colleagues and students who contributed suggestions and comments once again, so that this new rendering could come into existence.

Boulder, Colorado   R.P.C.
Denver, Colorado   E.W.K.

Contents

Contents

The Sociologist in Anger
The Views of
C. WRIGHT MILLS

12

210

Cultural Dreams and Nightmares
Observations by
JULES HENRY

13

230

Theory and Practice
The Views of
HOWARD S. BECKER

14

249

15

The Use of Sociology as Bad Faith
The Views of
PETER L. BERGER

266

16

Humanity as the Big Con
The Human Views of
ERVING GOFFMAN

286

Accounts, Works, and Ethnomethodology   **17**
HAROLD GARFINKEL
306

Communication, Art, and Victims   **18**
HUGH DALZIEL DUNCAN
327

Overview   **19**
A Coming Crisis in the Social Sciences?
350

20th CENTURY SOCIAL THOUGHT

Introduction

The Nature of Social Thought Before and After World War II

It has become evident in recent years that people have been able to solve a variety of difficult problems in the realms of engineering, medicine, and technology. However, we are still not much better when it comes to solving human social issues than we were two or three thousand years ago. The world is still a place of massive suffering. Starvation is a commonplace fate for millions of people. We seem to be incapable of slowing down what appears to be an inevitable confrontation between the great powers. If such a confrontation takes place, there is no small likelihood that most life on this planet will be annihilated. The United States is far from achieving its ideals of democratic rule, the welfare of its citizens, and continued progress toward a higher form of society. We find ourselves facing crisis after crisis to the point where we feel a growing sense of paralysis as massive social, cultural, and economic forces appear to make any individual effort a mere quixotic tilting with windmills.

We have obtained a kind of mastery over the physical world and, to some extent, over the complexities of biological reality. At the same time, we cannot seem to achieve that kind of wisdom that might enable

1

2 us to make the greatest use of our lives. We become bogged down in racial, ethnic, and political conflicts. We indulge in idle entertainments. We speak of being demoralized. We are not, in a word, capable of dealing with our "simple" social problems as effectively as we are able to deal with "complex" problems such as, for just one example, how to get close-up snapshots of the planet Jupiter.

It is something of a paradox that we are more capable of dealing with the mysteries of the universe than we are with the complexities of ourselves and our social systems. More people probably die each day from problems that come from difficulties in establishing effective economic and social systems than die from strictly "natural" causes. There is also, possibly, something of a paradox in the fact that many people seem to think that it is more important to study those disciplines that deal with technology or "hard science" than it is to study aspects of the social sciences. However, until it is demonstrated that advances in technology have brought about improvements in social relations among people, we shall have to presume that it will be necessary to study society itself as a problematic feature of human existence.

This book presents the reader with overviews of the work of some social scientists and writers concerned with the human condition. We have tried to select writers who we think are interesting and who, at the same time, have been influential. Where we were in doubt, we emphasized the extent to which we thought a particular writer's ideas were engaging and thought-provoking. This book is an effort to present to readers first approaching the discipline of sociology a sense of the excitement and perplexity that can come out of a deeper investigation into the nature of human behavior than our ordinary commonsense understandings bring us to. We designed this book to elicit appreciation for the ingenuity that various social critics and analysts have shown in their effort to promote a better comprehension of what happens when people join together in communities and of the problems that arise from communal living. We believe there is little choice. We must either seek a better understanding of our social and economic systems or suffer the consequences of ignorance.

This book is intended to excite the interest of students of the social sciences. That interest, if it is kindled, will have to lead the reader to the original works of those who are mentioned in this book and to the original works of many other writers before there can be a true understanding of how complex, tangled, and demanding the study of sociology is when it is taken up with any kind of seriousness.

An Aside about Knowing Names

Before we move into the organization and structure of this book, we would like to comment on what we suspect is a prevailing attitude among college students today. The senior author of this book recently administered a surprise quiz to students in a statistics course he was teaching. The quiz consisted of asking the students to list, by author and title, all the sociologically relevant books they could think of in a half-hour period. The students, thirty in number, were all juniors or seniors, and they were all majors in sociology. What was the outcome? It was sad. Several of the students could not think of even a single book or author. A few could think of only one or two. The average, for the class, was a little over six books. Most of these were books with which the students were immediately familiar, such as texts which they had brought into class. It was, all in all, a sorry performance for a group of university-trained seniors. What made it especially interesting, however, was that the students chided the instructor, after the test had been given, and claimed it was unfair to expect anyone to know something as trivial and pointless as authors and book titles. After all, you can always go to the library to obtain such information.

The instructor's reply was that the complaints of the students were a shabby rationalization for ignorance. He went on to suggest that it would surely be most embarrassing for them to tell somebody that they were majors in sociology and then, when asked about books to read on the subject, be unable to mention even one! Knowledge is knowledge of *something*. It is not simply the registering of vague opinions. We suggest, then, that students of social science take the time and trouble to memorize the names of at least some of the authors and books that are mentioned in the pages that follow. Know who Robert Merton is. Associate his name with manifest and latent functions. Know who Emile Durkheim is and associate his name with concepts such as anomie, the collective conscience, and the distinction between sacred and secular events. A student of literature who was not familiar with the names of such writers as Woolf, Milton, Donne, Swinburne, and Emerson, would be considered unworthy of the title of a student of literature. Why social scientists should think they are absolved from knowing the names of leading figures in their own field is something of a mystery to us. Certainly it is important to know the major issues and how these issues have been attacked by different thinkers. But it reveals technical competence and a more sound understanding of these matters for a student to be aware of who was thinking what and when and where and why.

We would also like to make a second comment before we move into the organization of this book. It is our belief that being a good social scientist calls for a broad knowledge, on the one hand, combined with a special or particularly preferred mode of interpretation, on the other. The special preference of the student should, we think, come after some investigation has taken place with respect to the various possibilities that exist.

Varieties of Social Thought

There are many ways of approaching the study of human social behavior. We shall mention only a few at this point to illustrate what we are talking about. There is, of course, the Marxist perspective, which has a large number of followers. There is the structural-functional perspective,

4   which has been strongly influential in American academic social thought. The period following World War II saw the rise of a group of investigators who have attempted to construct mathematical models of the workings of social and economic systems. Quite recently, and in a radically different style, there has been the development of a school of thought known as ethnomethodology.[1] Another approach that has appeared in recent years has been sociobiology. The differences in approach can be quite extreme. The proponents of some schools of thought find it almost impossible to understand what the proponents of another school of thought are trying to do. Professor James Coleman, for example, a leader among those who emphasize a statistical and mathematical approach to the study of social systems, has great difficulty accepting the efforts of a writer such as Harold Garfinkel, the leading exponent of ethnomethodology.

We mention this diversity of approaches because we believe that a person who is considering moving seriously into the study of human social systems should first become acquainted with the variety of possibilities that exist. Perhaps drawing an analogy will make our point a little clearer. A good artist usually experiments with a variety of techniques and styles before eventually evolving the one that is appropriate for his or her talents and artistic development. There is no reason why an artist cannot establish a single style at the outset and stay with it for the remainder of his or her artistic life. This was pretty much the case with Norman Rockwell, and he was a successful person. However, some great artists, such as Picasso, acquire greatness by examining many styles and techniques and being effective with all of them—from the realistic to the most impressionistic and abstract.

We would like to suggest that it is similar for students who are moving into the social sciences. Such students should first attempt to remain as open as possible to the variety of styles, techniques, approaches, and concerns that are recognized in academic centers today. Each approach should be evaluated in terms of its strengths and weaknesses. Become skilled in your understanding of each approach. Only then is it appropriate for the student to select a particular technique or approach as one that is congenial and proper for intensive development. We do not believe that a person should manifest prejudice, contempt, or fear of any particular point of view until that point of view has been thoroughly examined. After all, a large number of quite intelligent people have endorsed, and attempted to promote, the progress of each of the established academic perspectives that are currently a part of the social sciences.

We would like to suggest that the reader retain, as much as possible, an open mind toward the various arguments that the representatives of different schools of thought have made. Open-minded or not, the reader

---

[1] For some idea of the variety of major social theories now being considered by the social sciences, see Don Martindale, *The Nature and Types of Sociological Theories* (Boston: Houghton Mifflin, 1960). A later work is Kinloch, *Sociological Theory: Its Development and Major Paradigms* (New York: McGraw-Hill, 1977).

of social science literature should develop the ability to work within any
point of view and present essays and arguments that show a command
of that point of view. Just as the artist spends a lot of time copying old
masters while developing a sense of craftsmanship, the student of social
science should be able to copy the style and the character of a particular
school of thought in sociology or anthropology or political science. It is
instructive, in this regard, to read Norman Podhoretz's engaging book,
Making It,[2] in which he describes his training as a writer at elite English
schools. Not only were students asked to write essays in the style of
some well-known author, such as Hemingway, Woolf, or Carlyle, but
they were also expected to be able to write a parody of, let us say,
Hemingway, as Thurber would write the parody. Few students in American schools—it has been our experience at least—would tolerate such
an assignment. Yet without making this sort of effort one can gain little
real working understanding of what a school of thought is all about. The
student must attempt to incorporate the style, the perspective, and the
understanding into his or her *work*. Anything less is, to use the vernac-
ular, an intellectual cop-out.

    We have suggested, then, that it is good for a student or reader of
social science to acquire, quite early in the game, a sense of the diversity
of thought that exists in the social sciences. The student should move
within this diversity, examine it, and begin to make some decisions about
which point of view is most acceptable. Two or three years is not too
long to spend in this kind of examination. Professionalism in the social
sciences is, in part, a matter of knowing the range of thinking that exists
concerning social issues and what the strengths and weaknesses of each
position are. The temptation is to latch on to a single point of view and
accept the comfort that singular reasoning offers. We cannot prevent
this, but we think it reveals a lack of intellectual character.

    To be a serious and well-trained social scientist requires, we believe,
a mastery of the extent to which social theories vary in their nature and
types. This book gives a limited overview of the extent of this variety.
We have tried to reveal to the reader the excitement of this variety
without presenting it in such detail that it would ultimately prove confusing. Even though our coverage is necessarily limited, the demands on
the good student are severe. The reader is not only called on to note
that Weber stresses the nature of bureaucratic organization or that
White is a radical cultural determinist or that Garfinkel is an ethnomethodologist, but the reader must also constantly keep in mind how each
of these points of view is highlighted, in various ways, through its contacts with the others. It is not enough, for example, simply to have some
idea of what Freud was talking about at the turn of the century. One
must keep in mind how Freud leads into or away from what Durkheim
was talking about. In sum, the reader must retain a comparative sense.

[2] Norman Podhoretz, *Making It* (New York: Random House, 1967).

6   *Practicality and Social Thought*

At the same time, we would like to think that studying the ideas of the writers included in this book will have some relevance to more than just academic craftsmanship. The question invariably arises as to whether or not such study is "practical." What can it *do* for people?

The question is not an easy one to answer. The practical value of social thought comes out of the extent to which a person is aware of such thinking and can make use of it. The social essay is generally not pointedly practical. A treatise on repairing a bicycle tire, on the other hand, is purely practical. It is written with nothing more than a practical problem in mind. The social essay is rarely as mundane as an instructional booklet on repairing a tire. The social essay usually covers highly abstract and complex situations. It is rarely written with the idea in mind of some sort of immediate practical application. At the same time, almost any social essayist of stature has written about society because he or she believes that such information is important for the society and that it is, in some sense, necessary. Occasionally, the practical implications are made apparent by the author or the nature of the work being done. C. Wright Mills, for example, was concerned with human warfare and how to understand it in a manner that might lead to its cessation. We cannot think of a more practical human concern. At the same time, it is not easy to see some of the practical possibilities in Max Weber's overview of the economic effects of the Protestant Reformation. We would like to spend just a moment or two reviewing the way in which one student at the University of Colorado used Weber to promote his own understanding of a highly practical vocation—the practice of medicine.

The investigator referred to has been concerned for the past several years with the quality of health care in small medical centers in the rural districts of the western part of the United States. He devised procedures for checking the effectiveness of such centers, and his work has been considered to be of a highly practical character. Eventually, however, he became interested in the ideas of Max Weber and decided to write his doctoral dissertation on the history of western medicine as it might be interpreted from Weber's point of view. The result proved to be a pro-vocative work in which the current influence of the Protestant Ethic on patient-physician relationships in America suggests that modern medicine is strongly influenced by a variety of ideological factors. Moreover, this works toward making medicine less effective than it might be.[3] In this example, then, Weber has paved the way for a practical piece of work. But, as this example indicates, the practicality inherent in Weber's writings must be developed by a person who is familiar with that writing. Nothing within it, per se, points directly toward its possible practical applications.

So it is with many of the writers whose essays and concerns are a part of this book. But the practicality, again, does not come simply from

---

[3] Jon Garlinghouse, An Ideological History of Medicine, Ph. D. dissertation, Department of Sociology, University of Colorado, Boulder, Colorado.

reading what these people have to say. No writer presented in this book **7**
offers some kind of instructional manual on how to be a leader, or how
to be happy though married, or how to achieve a great society. Nonetheless, hints for any of these concerns appear in the essays of even the
most abstract theorists. It is for the reader, the intelligent and socially
sensitive reader, to note them and to use them—however that might be
possible.

Social Thought Before and After World War II

We have organized the essays of this book in a roughly chronological
order, beginning with social writers and theorists whose major efforts
took place prior to World War II and ending with those whose work
essentially appeared after that war. There are some broad differences
between those who came prior to World War II and those who came
after.

The Second World War had a profound effect on Western intellectuals. Until that time, there had been a growing optimism about the
future. The century that preceded World War II generated some of the
most exciting sequences of change that people had ever experienced.
Virtually every major invention and innovation that we now think of as
part of our modern technology had its origins at this time. Modern
medicine, aerodynamics, the radio, evolutionary thought, Freudianism,
Marxism, the gasoline engine, relativity, modern forms of mass production, movies—all came out of the late nineteenth and early twentieth
centuries. There was a new hope. The technological successes of the age
were dramatized in great "world's fairs" which attracted millions of
people. The future appeared to be unlimited. The application of rational
thought seemed sufficient to deal with any problem—including those
problems that came out of trying to organize people into effective communities.

So it was that thinkers near the turn of the century began to suggest
that the powerful thoughtways of science should be applied to the
examination of human affairs. The problems of individual behavior could
be examined scientifically through the development of a disciplined
study of psychology. The vagaries of the marketplace would be eventually
understood in terms of the development of a more scientific study of
economic processes. The political arena could be subjected to a more
objective consideration through the development of political science. So
it was reasonable that this optimism should eventually be elevated to the
fullest extent by suggesting that the entire range of human communal
activities could be examined scientifically and that such scientific understanding would enable people to achieve better and more ideal social
structures. The new society would be as radically rational and as well
designed as a modern jet liner. People would achieve greater efficiency
in their social as well as their technological efforts. All that was needed
was the time and the effort to develop the necessary research and theory.

The turn of the century must have been exciting for people who

8 were on the threshold of new knowledge. There was the illusion of advancement. The future was one of progress. Even that most damnable of all Victorian inventions, Darwin's theory of evolution,[4] was based on the idea that progression was something inherently natural. Darwin set the tone, and down to the present time there are still echoes, very strong echoes, of the belief that progress is inevitable. Darwin said:

> The presence of a body of well-instructed men, who have not to labor for their daily bread, is important to a degree which cannot be overestimated; as all high intellectual work is carried on by them, and on such work material progress of all kinds mainly depends, not to mention other and higher advantages. . . . Progress has been much more general than retrogression.[5]

There were those who were concerned about the excesses that had developed during the early periods of the industrial age. Foremost among these was Karl Marx. He was outraged by the cruelties he saw carried out in the name of industrial progress. At the same time, the vision he offered the people of the world was an extraordinarily utopian one. People would achieve not only a new world of technological riches, but they would also come to the point where they would be able to organize themselves into social and economic systems that would abolish class discriminations and the inequities of wealth that were an integral part of the times in which Marx lived. People would no longer exploit each other. There would be no poverty. Struggle and conflict would be reduced to the point where war would be a thing of the past. There is no stronger appeal in the literature of the nineteenth century than that of Marx, and he has had a strong influence on the minds of hundreds of millions of the world's current population.

A Time of Optimism

The optimism inherent in Darwin's and Marx's visions of the world was shared broadly by a great variety and number of people concerned with improving the character of modern societies. The great depression of the 1930s was a bit of a jolt, but, in the final analysis, it only reconfirmed the belief that careful research and the development of appropriate theory could handle anything that posed a crisis for people. Economic leaders, following the theories of John Maynard Keynes, attempted to curb the economic frustrations of the depression, and they eventually began to feel that an economy could be rationally manipulated. While this was taking place in the United States, the Russians were initiating a bold experiment in economic control. It was a time of optimism.

---

[4] Darwin incensed the Victorians, who were shocked and revolted by the idea that they might share a biological affinity with "lesser" creatures, such as monkeys and apes.
[5] Charles Darwin, *The Descent of Man*, 2nd ed, (New York: Wheeler, 1936) p. 137. (Originally published, 1874.)

This optimism carried into, and a little beyond, the drama of World War II. With the return of American GIs to colleges and universities throughout the country, the future seemed bright. Allied forces had gained the victory. A major threat to democracy had been eliminated. Production levels were high. Education of a high order was being democratized through the GI Bill. Thousands who never dreamed of graduating from college were receiving degrees and going on to graduate school. It appeared, at the time, that nothing could stop our progression toward a more highly technological and more civilized world.

Faith in the scientific method probably reached its highest point at this time. The technological wonders that came from scientific research created labor-saving machines and new levels of comfortable living. But there was something still more impressive: *science* had won the war. Science was power. The introduction of science into the study of human behavior and human societies could only bring about more powerful understandings that might lead to better and more powerful forms of society. Science was turned to as a possible means of improving the moral character of humankind.

The Situation in the Social Sciences After World War II

Paradoxically World War II, the very event that had created the great faith in science and the hope for moral progress, was also the event that began to undermine that faith and that hope. World War II had revealed just how powerful modern technology had become. It was an intoxicating time. Thoughtful observers, however, were beginning to reconsider what had happened. The war had shown that modern technology was, indeed, astonishingly powerful. And it also revealed that people were possibly not ready for such power. There was now an absolute demand that people become morally wiser and stronger. If they were not any better, in terms of social understanding, than the generation that spawned World War II, there was little hope for the future. It was obvious to nearly everybody that World War III would mean the end of civilization.

It was clear, then, that it was absolutely necessary to develop a better sense of humanity. It was necessary to create a social system in which leadership would be able to deal with intricately complex systems and not make any serious errors. With each growth in the power of modern weaponry, the consequences of even one serious error were more and more likely to bring the final catastrophic terror. This was the situation the social sciences found themselves in at the end of World War II.

The challenge seemed, at first, to be one that could be met. The challenge of the war had been met successfully. Again, all that was required, so it seemed, was money, time, research, and the constant application of rational and intelligent thought. There was no problem that could not be solved once it had been formulated properly. If the moral order was a problem, then it would be solved. At the same time, it was not merely a matter of solving a complex problem as a test of

10   human rationality. The point had been reached where the moral problem simply *had* to be solved. People could not continue to conduct their economic, social, and political affairs in those old ways that had characterized social and political and economic practices in the past. The lethality of the older systems of rule and organization had been made frighteningly apparent in the ruin and rubble of the aftermath of World War II. A moving memorial to this fact now stands in Coventry, England, where the magnificent new Coventry Cathedral, built after World War II, stands side by side with the bombed, charred ruins of the venerable thirteenth-century cathedral.

But if the war was a lesson, it was to become a most puzzling one. It was there demanding to be understood. What had caused the holocaust? As philosophers, artists, writers, social scientists, and political analysts examined the war, they began to discover that here was a matter of such complexity and of such peculiar character that it could not be understood in any total manner. There was an especially profound effort to understand what had happened in Germany. There were discussions of the "authoritarian personality," the "banality of evil," "frustration and aggression," the desire to "escape from freedom," and other studies.[6] With the passage of time, however, what took place in Germany and throughout the world appeared increasingly difficult to understand.

Worse yet, whatever lessons had been gained from the examination of the history of World War II appeared to be of little value in improving the moral structure of humanity. The very authoritarianism that had been fought against in Germany appeared in America in the 1950s, as repressive actions were initiated by politicians eager to exploit a growing national fear of Soviet imperialism. Then, only a decade or so later, America became mired in the Vietnam War. Confusion of a profound nature came from this experience—here was the most technologically powerful nation on earth being fought to a standstill by people who lived in underground tunnels and who got about on bicycles. America's dream of the unlimited value of technology was checked. It made little point to argue that we could have used the technology to, as one general put it, bomb the Vietnamese into one huge parking lot. We found, when the moment came, that the technology could not be used. Science was not enough. To add to the growing pessimism, quasi-scientific "body counts" and statistics were being grotesquely used to offer an apparently rational interpretation of what, by the end of the war, was obviously a mad venture.

So, at the international and national levels, there were major social and political movements that could not be ignored and that, at the same time, revealed the importance of social science when it came to moving

---

[6] We refer the reader to such books as: T. W. Adorno et al., *The Authoritarian Personality* (New York: Norton, 1969; originally published 1950); Erich Fromm, *Escape from Freedom* (New York: Holt, Rinehart and Winston, 1963); Elie Wiesel, *Night* (New York: Hill and Wang, 1960); Hannah Arendt, *Eichmann in Jerusalem: A Report on the Banality of Evil* (New York: Viking, 1963); and Bruno Bettelheim, *The Informed Heart: Autonomy in a Mass Age* (New York: Avon, 1971).

people in the direction of more rational and certain moral progress. There were some signs, however, from *within* the social sciences that indicated a growing disenchantment with the older dream of a logical and precise science of human social action. If there was to be a science of human social action, newer writers argued, it would have to be a science quite different in form from that which characterized the natural sciences. The natural sciences, for example, assume that the processes of nature are regular and that these regularities can be uncovered and described. Light, for example, can be counted on to conform, in a most regular manner, to the bending effects of gravity. The effect, in this instance, is astonishingly subtle,[7] but it is regular, and it can be counted on to take place anywhere in the universe and at any time throughout the billions of years of existence of the known universe. It is possible to find regularities in human social systems, but the most obvious ones are just that—obvious. The accomplishment of the natural sciences has been to probe ever further into subtle regularities. The social sciences have had limited success in uncovering subtle regularities. Quite often a finding that appears strong in one setting is weak in another. It is much as though a law of physics that operated well enough in England in September worked in quite a different way in Japan in May.

One of the more shocking revelations of the limitations of the social sciences has come to light in the recent inability of modern economics first, to anticipate and, second, to control, the peculiar circumstance of inflation combined with depression. Economics has been, and remains, the ideal social science. It uses mathematical logic and highly rational models, and it can point to empirical methods that are superior to those used in any other social science. It is the only social science whose practitioners are regularly awarded Nobel prizes. Still, with these advantages, the economic behavior of the nation as a whole has been sufficiently erratic to make economic conditions the major crisis of our age.

The late twentieth century, then, has become a time of reassessment in the social sciences. There is still hope, and there is still a serious commitment, but the problems now seem to be greater than they appeared to be for idealistic intellectuals of the late nineteenth and early twentieth centuries. There have been two major responses to all of this. We might refer to one as the conservative response. This response presumes that the older vision was essentially correct, and that whatever errors have come about have been human enough, and that all that is necessary is to work a little harder, apply a bit more effort, research, and thought, and it will still work out. The conservative response still places its faith on mathematical models, the acquisitions of great amounts of empirical data, the use of computers, and rational theorizing employing causal systems, path analysis, and other logical models.

The other response might be called the radical response. It tends to reject not so much the hope of the older idealism but rather the

---

[7] A beam of light aimed at the earth's horizon bends only a third of an inch over a distance of 4000 miles as a result of the earth's attraction. See Nigel Calder in *Einstein's Universe* (New York: Viking, 1979), p. 45.

12 conservative's emphasis on a limited conception of what constitutes science. Where the conservative response views human behavior as intrinsically rational, along with the other basic processes of nature, the radical response claims that people are forced to solve essentially irrational problems. The older "conservative" social scientists rejected moral questions because they could not be dealt with in terms of scientific analysis. Science never raised the question of what, for example, an atom *should* do under certain circumstances. Science only sought to find out what atoms did in fact do. The conservative approach to the scientific study of human social behavior accepted this attitude. It ignored the issue of what people *should* do. It sought to deal with what people in fact did. But what people were doing was solving on their own the critical issue of what they should do. The social scientist, in other words, had bypassed the most crucial of all human problem areas. If the sociologists or economists or political scientists could not assist in making moral decisions, then what could they do? And if they helped make moral decisions, were they really being scientific? It was a dilemma which, by the end of the 1960s, had become painful. The response of the "radicals" has been more open in its espousal of various moral positions and, at the same time, the newer writers have concentrated more on just how people deal with the problem of being "moral."

This rather sketchy overview leaves us with the following observations. Social science came out of the scientific and technological optimism of the late nineteenth century. A strong belief in the rational control of society, as well as of nature, continued through World War II. The massive horrors of the war, coupled with the debacle of the Vietnam War, brought about a tempering of the earlier optimism. The present time finds the social sciences entering a crisis.[8] One response to the crisis has been to reaffirm the older faith in a purely scientific approach to the study of society. The other response has been to argue for a revision of how we should go about studying society.

About the Writers in this Book

The chapters that follow give a rough indication of how this progression has developed. Among the writers we have included from the period before World War II are two men who were overwhelmingly optimistic about the utilization of science and human progress. Karl Marx envisioned a utopian future for the world. That utopia would come from the application of scientific principles to the organization of society. Rather than allow irrational forces such as greed and ownership to dominate human moral progress, people would eventually come to see the advantages of a scientifically ordered and rationally arranged economic and social system. George Lundberg did not envision utopia, but he did believe that if there was anything we could hope for as the savior of a

[8] The possibilities of this crisis have been extensively outlined in Alvin Gouldner, *The Coming Crisis in Western Sociology* (New York: Basic Books, 1970).

potentially doomed humanity, it would have to be science. Science and **13** only science could save us.

Some of the other writers of the time were not so openly optimistic, but even those who were pessimistic about the future—one was Robert Merton—still retained a strong faith in the scientific method as *the* method for dealing with any kind of intellectual problem, natural or social.

The writers who come later take on a different character. C. Wright Mills, for example, was an exuberant man, and he was also the author of some of the most condemnatory commentaries on the American scene of anyone writing in the social sciences. America, to sum up Mills's observations, had become pretty much a mess. Moral "progress" had not taken place. Americans had instead become impersonal and unconcerned. If anything, retrogression was a possibility. Mills felt that Americans were about to abandon the high political and social ideals that had been set forth in the Constitution.

Erving Goffman, perhaps more than any other writer of the postwar period, struck a responsive chord among the new-mode sociologists. There is certainly nothing tightly "scientific" about his work. Moreover, Goffman dotes on the irrational, tricky, deceitful, and dramatic qualities of people. After Goffman, it is difficult to continue to believe that people are interested, really, in being logical or in improving their moral systems according to some rational plan. They appear to be more interested in being dramatic than in being healthy or wise.

Now at the cutting edge of modern sociology, there is a new development—the interest that has been shown in Harold Garfinkel's "ethnomethodological" approach to human behavior. Here is a most peculiar conjoining of the rational and the irrational. Garfinkel seeks to establish a systematic way of studying how people make decisions in situations where there are no especially rational or logical devices available for coming to a decision. Garfinkel seeks—in a manner somewhat similar to the actions of nineteenth-century artists who sought art for its own sake—to deal with pure sociology, a sociology removed from any practical applications; it is almost a sociology for sociology's sake. Certainly it is a sociology that does not have much to do with social reform. In its most recent manifestations it has led to intense examinations of the opening thirty seconds of a conversation or how one learns to play jazz piano. Such sociology opens itself to the criticism that, like the graphic arts, it has moved into a kind of dadaist period. Sociology, having found itself impotent in dealing with the great and vast issues and concerns of humanity has possibly turned inward and is now satisfied with studying the trivial in a ponderously scrupulous manner.

We would like to be able to open this work with a rousing assertion of the necessity for, and the utility of, the social sciences. We do think they are necessary and we do believe they are useful, but the issue is certainly not a simple one. Readers will have to examine and then reexamine the matter and draw their own conclusions. The age of unbridled optimism appears to be dead. But this does not mean we have to enter on a new age of paralyzing pessimism. Ambrose Bierce once said of

14 optimists that the only good thing that could be said about them was that they had a high mortality rate. He was right; there is always a danger in being too optimistic about human progress. At the same time, however pessimistic we may be about the future, we must strive to avoid at least the worst of potential futures—certainly seeking to be as knowledgeable as possible about human social and economic systems can work only toward lessening the possibility of a totally catastrophic future.

We would like to bring this introduction full circle by suggesting that although it is the proper effort of social scientists to be as scientific as possible without being rigid, it is still true that their subject matter consists of people and their communities. This is a subject matter which the social scientists share with artists, philosophers, essayists, religious thinkers, journalists, and others who are not so totally dedicated to science. It has been traditional in sociology and anthropology texts to make much of the difference between people who are scientifically oriented toward the study of society and those who are not. We hope that some of this prejudice and antagonism is breaking down.

This book is not an effort to drive further boundary stakes into the ground of intellectual endeavor in an attempt to specify the lines that separate the domain of the sociologist from that of the humanist. Nor is it an attempt to suggest that sociologists and social scientists are no different from novelists, artists, or romantic philosophers. They *are* different. Moreover, it is a difference that makes a difference.

Though there are considerable differences between the humanistic and the social science perspectives, we would like to see greater recognition of the fact that each has much to gain from the other.[9] It is possible today for a professor of English to bring further meaning to a body of literature by using some of the theories, observations, and concepts of the social scientist.[10] It is also possible for a sociologist to use literary examples very effectively as a way of teasing further meaning out of formal sociological concepts.

Sometimes, in an effort to divorce themselves from their humanistic

[9] The rifts that exist between the humanities and the social sciences are the result of each side denigrating the other. The great humanistic critic Edmund Wilson displayed a haughty contempt for sociological literature. One poet, e. e. cummings, saw scientists in general as "oneeyed sons of bitches." Another, W. H. Auden, wanted to add to the list of commandments: Thou shalt not commit a social science.

On the other hand, social scientists have not always been kind in their appraisal of what they feel to be the fanciful and cheaply bought worlds of the imagination produced by the humanist. Lundberg, for example, was highly skeptical of the value of novels as a means of getting at the truth of human nature.

But the attack on the humanist has taken place at deeper and more seriously wounding levels. For the psychoanalytically oriented anthropologist, literature or art is to be taken as a datum—a revelation of the ego of the author or the ethos of the culture—but it cannot be accepted for what it is trying to appear to be. It is surprising that psychoanalysis, which divests art of its meaning more thoroughly than does any other behavioral science perspective, is more acceptable to the literary humanistic set than is, say, sociology. The reason for this probably resides in the fact that psychoanalysis still permits the cultivation of style, while sociological writing virtually destroys any sense of humanistic style.

[10] A very engaging case in point is the analysis of Victorian pornography by Steven Marcus, *The Other Victorians* (New York: Basic Books, 1964).

origins, social scientists have gone to great lengths to hide from others, and perhaps from themselves, the fact that they are interested in matters which, for thousands of years, have interested philosophers, novelists, poets, or artists. In their struggle to achieve scientific respectability, social scientists have, for example, disclaimed an interest in evil—after all, it is an extremely difficult term to define and it certainly lacks objectivity. They are, instead, concerned with crime and delinquency—defined in strictly operational terms. Rather than show an interest in the "art" of love, they are concerned with family disorganization—measured by divorce rates. Rather than endow people with dramatically heroic or antiheroic qualities—which is the eternal humanistic effort—they seem to prefer talking in terms of bloodless abstractions that remove us, as human beings, from the scene.

But language is often misleading. When sociologists talk about family disorganization they are describing, in their own rhetoric, a process that is terribly human and, no matter how objectively described, painful to those involved. They are touching a subject which they must always share with the novelist and the artist. The clinical studies of divorced women by W. J. Goode are, in some ways, more revealing of the realities of human suffering than is Edward Albee's turbulent description of married life in the home of an associate professor of history.[11]

In this book we have tried to make explicit the implicit humanistic concerns of social scientists. Each of the writers considered in the following pages touches on some problem that has already been deeply examined in humanistic literature, but the social scientist brings a new view. Durkheim, in his own work and in works that later evolved from his ideas, looked at faith—particularly religious faith—and attempted to give it a secular place in human affairs.

Max Weber examined the loci of power and, when he was done, the myth of the hero had lost some of its vigor. The humanistic concerns of Marxism are evident to anyone who has read Marxist literature. Karl Marx was profoundly concerned with the causes and the alleviation of human suffering brought about by the economic exploitation of one group of people by another. Sigmund Freud was concerned with the problem of human suffering brought about by repressive moral beliefs. Freudian theory, in some ways, is pessimistic about the relief of suffering. Even so, it has offered twentieth century humanity a vision of an ideal form of self-awareness in which the person is able to achieve higher levels of consciousness and fulfillment than any ever known in the past. George Herbert Mead was interested in the relationship between the individual and the greater community. Is the state more important than the individual? Is the individual the more important consideration? It is an old humanistic concern and one which Mead resolved in a highly

---

[11] *Who's Afraid of Virginia Woolf* (1962) is an eloquent and dramatic statement of what is involved in the act of loving. But it is Albee's statement. W. J. Goode's *Women in Divorce* (New York: Free Press, 1956) is not so eloquent, but it is no less enlightening. A compilation of the experiences of a great number of people can, if ordered by a competent and thoughtful social scientist, have a different but equally profound impact.

16 innovative manner. Pitirim Sorokin found modern society lost in what he called "sensatism." His observations raise some interesting questions about the possible future of the arts in modern society. C. Wright Mills was concerned with the uses and abuses of power. Above all, he was concerned with the modern drift toward total war. David Riesman shed new light on the problem of conformity in mass society. Jules Henry was interested in madness and sanity and, in this interest, reflected a concern with the old humanistic issue of reason and rationality.

The newer writers included in this book do not, by virtue of their modernness, ignore the older issues of humanistic philosophy. Howard Becker is interested in the complex relationship between those people who are labeled "bad" and those who are labeled "good." Erving Goffman offers one of the most unusual treatments of hypocrisy to be found in modern literature. Harold Garfinkel, more than the others perhaps, seems removed from older philosophical issues. However, one of the central issues in Garfinkel's writing is the problem of the nature of subjective experience and its effect on social interactions. Garfinkel (and some of his students) has not denied the subjective—as have many modern scientists—and, in this alone, his work is relevant to the humanistic thinker as well as to the scientific thinker. Peter Berger is unique among the better-known social scientists of our time in the way he has tried to deal with the problem of freedom. Finally, Hugh Dalziel Duncan presents a point of view that admits art once more into discussions of human social behavior. The traditional stance of American social scientists has been to attempt to deny art a central place in human affairs. Duncan's arguments, when properly understood, make art certainly one of the central human activities—if not *the* central activity.

This quick run-through can only sketch some of the different humanistic themes that these writers have developed in their own way. The list is not exhaustive, and it suffers from the drawback that several writers may deal in unique ways with the same general humanistic concern. In radically different terms, for example, Mead, Berger, Mills, and Becker have something to say about the problem of individual responsibility.

The great concentration on methods that has characterized social science down to the present has caused the sociologist to eschew the nonscientific humanistic approach to problems. Often, in this effort to place barriers between the social scientist and the literary person, the social scientist has lost sight of the fact that actually there is little difference between the central concerns of sociology and those of humanistic literature. This book tries to indicate these common concerns without making any claims that social science is the only way to approach them. We have spent too much time, we believe, trying to resolve the problem of whether social science *or* literature should be turned to for inspiration and guidance in our lives. This way of phrasing the question, so typical of Western forms of thinking, is unfortunate. A more profound question is to ask how we can use both sociology *and* the various humanistic pursuits to improve our condition. Each chapter in the book, therefore, attempts to point up the nature of the humanistic concerns of the social scientists considered here.

We should warn the reader once more, before continuing, that it is impossible in a work of this kind to give any realistic presentation of the richness of thought contained in the works of people like Durkheim, Weber, Mead, or any of the others presented here. We must, therefore, be content with the hope that we have caught something of the "spirit" of any given author. If we were successful in this, then we remain confident the reader will want to find out more about these writers by turning to their original works. Only by going to the source can one understand the full extent to which these theorists displayed the courage and tenacity necessary to remain locked in a struggle with profound questions until the questions began to "give a little."

Problems and Issues

Each chapter of this book concludes with a brief section dealing with "problems and issues." Here we try to develop a questioning attitude on the part of the student or reader. Social science, we think, has been successful not so much in the answers it has offered as in the extent to which it has generated a questioning attitude toward our social lives. Social science seeks to reduce the inclination shared by all of us to accept easy answers. Just as we tend to resist having to engage in physical effort, we also tend to resist intellectual effort. But questioning is the "jogging" of the mind. We think that anyone who is interested in his or her total health will engage not only in physical exercise such as jogging but also in mental exercise such as questioning. In the social sciences, intellectual exercise comes from constant and ever-deeper questioning. We wish we could assert that such questioning leads invariably to sure and certain answers. It does not. Sometimes answers are approached. More often, questioning leads only to further questioning. Eventually, the mature mind understands the frightening limitations imposed on the human intellect. To question, to know the impossibility of final answers, and yet to continue in the belief that it is possible to arrive at better understandings—these are the marks of the strong individual.

The people dealt with in this book have affirmed this quality. They have questioned; they have suggested possible responses to complex issues. They have presented their ideas before critical audiences within the general public and among their colleagues. Their contribution should be viewed not merely in terms of what they thought to be correct solutions to problems but also in terms of what they considered to be the problems of their age and ours. For this reason, then, we have tried to close each chapter not with answers but with questions. These questions are not of the "review" variety, in which the student or reader is expected to go back over the material presented in the chapter. They are general questions, which, we think, are relevant to the life and experiences of every person in this society. They are questions designed to elicit further questioning. For example, if we raise the question, "What is religion?" we have opened the way to a further series of questions. At one time such a question was not proper. People knew what religion was. They knew that they were good, God-fearing people and that everybody else constituted a bunch of barbarians. Today we cannot endorse such a notion. We know that religion is a highly varied set of ideas and practices. Just how varied is "religion"? When we begin thinking about religion in this way we can begin to wonder seriously if there really is something to the idea that modern professional sports have religious elements. If so, how do sports and "real" religion differ? What light can be shed on our understanding of religion through our involvement in activities such as sports, which, at first, appear far removed from the temple?

We are reminded of the comment of a physicist who touched on the problem of constant questioning when he used the metaphor of the "dirty cellar" to describe the process of scientific research. He said that physics is like cleaning out a dirty cellar. You finally get the cellar cleaned out and you begin sweeping the floor. As you are sweeping, you notice a trapdoor. You open it. There are stairs leading down—to another dirty cellar! You begin cleaning the newly found dirty cellar and eventually reach the point where you can start sweeping the floor. As you sweep you suddenly notice . . . another trapdoor!

So the pursuit of questioning is endless. For some this is so frustrating as to be unendurable. It is better to take flight into some faith in which questioning is forever abandoned. Then it is no longer necessary to jog. We subscribe to the belief that for the truly toughminded, questioning is the most sophisticated and civilized of all the arts. It is in this more general spirit that we close each chapter with a set of "problems and issues." We consider this section to be as significant as any other part of the book. It is not, again, to be seen as a "review" of the content of any chapter. It is, instead, meant only as a brief stimulus to lead toward the independent thinking and questioning of the reader.

PART I

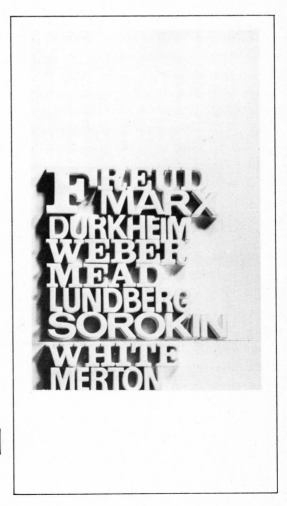

Social Thought
before
WORLD WAR II

The Expression of Modern Individualism

SIGMUND FREUD

. . . our possibilities of happiness are . . . restricted . . . . Unhappiness is much less difficult to experience.

Civilization and its Discontents

BORN: 1856   DIED: 1939

2 The intellectual history of those who live within a Western heritage is saturated with grim and bloody images. Foremost among these, dominating the thought of Western humanity, is the agonized figure of Christ hanging from the cross, His face is tormented by the anguish of solitary pain. These images personify for us the clash between good and evil, purity and sin. They also help perpetuate a conception of humanity that has been influential down to the present time and that even the most liberated modern thinkers draw on for inspiration and insight. This conception, in its essence, sees people as creatures caught between the forces of good and evil, purity and sin. Our lives are ultimately subject to the judgment that we lived as sinners or saints or, in more modern terms, as "losers" or "winners." This judgmental character of human conduct is one of its most significant qualities. We not only judge others; we also conduct ourselves in ways that will, we hope, produce judgments from others that we find gratifying.

Judgments, of course, mean that we must make distinctions. Distinctions, in turn, rest on conceptions of what constitutes a preferred pattern of behavior. Moreover, the distinction between what is preferred and what is not preferred must involve some kind of implicit (or explicit)

22   conflict or struggle between the available alternatives. For example, it would be silly to admire people for having a pulse rate of seventy or for having five fingers on their right hands. We do not, generally, have to struggle to have five fingers on one hand; they are standard equipment.

However, there are some evaluations that people dedicate their lives to attaining. In these quests we find the most dramatic and agonizing of human efforts. Indeed, as we review the innumerable contrasts between those who have been judged great and those who have not, a common theme is that of suffering. Heroes must suffer and, in the conduct of their adventures, risk even greater suffering. To live a life in which one passes from cradle to grave enjoying hedonistic delights while suffering no trials or tribulations is to risk, at least in this society, acquiring a contemptible reputation. It is to risk being judged worthless.

Redemption through suffering is a pervasive idea in Western culture. There is, of course, the possibility of suffering and still not achieving redemption. But the idea of not suffering and yet being allowed redemption is, even in our modern sensate culture, not a readily accepted idea.[1] The dominant theme in all of this is that people are confronted with conflict throughout their lives. Whether we succeed in overcoming our difficulties is perhaps a matter of chance and fortune. However, it is obvious, from this perspective, that we must suffer, and it is not surprising that the sufferings visited on some people become intolerable. They are crushed and destroyed by the struggles into which they are thrust.

Freudian theory rests on the idea of conflict and inevitable suffering. In this respect it is in harmony with the Christian ideology of the broader culture. The unique contribution of Freud, however, was to suggest that conflict and suffering are the natural consequences of human biological nature and the problems that arise when you attempt to transform that biological character into a social being. The result, Freud suggested, was a complex set of conflicts and consequent forms of guilt and anxiety that penetrate deeply into human character. People had known long before Freud that suffering and conflict were part of life. After Freud they became aware that each individual was a battleground, so to speak, where a continuous struggle was waged between the demands of the body and the demands of society. What made Freud's contribution unique was his claim that the individual was generally not aware of the conflict in any clearly conscious manner. Much of the struggle took place at an unconscious level.

---

[1] This is a controversial claim. For the most part, our literature, journalism, dramatic presentations, and art dwell on the theme of suffering. At the same time, we find that when students are asked if it is possible to accomplish something great without having to suffer, they generally reply by saying yes. In one of the authors' classes, 28 students out of 30 said that it was possible to achieve greatness without suffering. Interestingly enough, the two exceptions were students who came from a Japanese-American background.

The Freudian Heritage

The Freudian conception of the psyche took hold in the early twentieth century and quickly became one of the most influential perspectives on human behavior of our time. The Freudian argument is significant in two respects. First, it leans on the premise that there is an unavoidable conflict between individual people and the societies they have created.[2] Conflict, suffering, agony, repression, frustration, and the aggressive response are universal features of human life. In the second place, the Freudian perspective is grounded in observations that came out of Freud's medical and clinical practice. Freud's early investigations into hysteria were investigations of the behavior of people who had, in some way or other, been wracked by the problems of living. The Freudian view, therefore, offers a highly dramatized and possibly exaggerated awareness of the extent to which conflict is a part of our lives.

There was certainly nothing new in Freud's observation that human beings could be crushed by the difficulties of day-to-day living. People had known this for centuries. It was in the elaboration of this theme that Freud brought about his achievement. It was Freud who promoted the discovery of the extent to which conflict was not only taking place at the surface (in such actions as physical combat, argumentation, and economic struggle) but was also going on within deeper, unexplored facets of the personality. Conflict is unconscious as well as conscious. The Freudian heritage brought with it some revolutionary implications.

What was there, in the final summing up, that made the Freudian conception of human behavior so appealing? To answer this question, we must turn to an examination of Freud's work and evaluate it in terms of the sentiments and ideas it so effectively challenged.

The Person in Three Parts

Freud was born of Jewish parents in Freiburg, Moravia, in 1856. He chose medicine as his profession and graduated from the University of Vienna at the age of 25. Before he took up psychology, his writings were devoted to investigations of nervous diseases. As his work in psychoanalysis proceeded, Freud became interested in the use of hypnosis in the treatment of hysteria. He served as a professor of neuropathology at the University of Vienna from 1902 to 1938. The Nazis' rise to power in Germany in the 1930s seriously threatened Freud's life and career. He left Germany for London in 1938 but lived only one more year, dying of cancer in 1939. During his highly productive and radically innovative intellectual life Freud created a model of human behavior which, like

[2] Near the end of this chapter we shall see that this is an overly simple statement. Freud did not consider society to be the exclusively repressive agent in human affairs. He argued in his later works that some aspects of human physiology make frustration and discontent a consequence of the act of living, no matter how we organize our lives.

24 Darwinism, took people away from spiritual forces and saw them, instead, as products of natural forces. Freudian theory was not, for the most part, popular with religious leaders.[3]

We have already suggested that the Freudian model of humanity rests on a premise of conflict between the individual and the community of which he or she is a part. In developing this conception, Freud resorted to a kind of transformation of Judeo-Christian mythology into a form that was in keeping with the more naturalistic philosophies of modern times. The Christian myth views people as creatures born in sin and engaged in a struggle to achieve a state of grace. To be in a state of grace is to be judged favorably by the most important of all judges— God. The judging agent, in this instance, is a spiritual entity removed from any direct communication with people. Sin is relevant insofar as it condemns one to rejection by God.

The whole idea, when taken seriously, is frightening enough in itself. One cannot be certain that one is acceptable to God. Moreover, people are informed that the path to God is hard. To achieve acceptance by God means, according to most Christian doctrine, a denial of the gross appetites that come from one's flesh and from one's carnal nature. The extremes to which this doctrine has been carried are not always recognized by modern men and women. Here, for example, is a brief comment about church leaders of the third century A.D.:

> All the Church Fathers, meanwhile, agreed on one point: half-abstention was only half-emancipation from the evil. The truly pious man must abstain from all sexual intercourse; only so could he achieve inward spiritual peace. This lofty goal could not be reached without sacrifice; thus Origen, one of the greatest and most original thinkers of the Alexandrine School, chose to give mankind an example by emasculating himself. . . . He who would free himself from sin must first purify the spirit, then the body would follow. The best means was to take a vow of chastity.[4]

The interesting thing about this philosophy is the extent to which it has appealed to millions of men and women, who, with surprisingly few exceptions,[5] have not questioned its repressive nature. After Freud,

---

[3] Freud's major writings include *The Interpretation of Dreams* (London: Hogarth, 1900); *A General Introduction to Psychoanalysis,* translated by Ernest Jones and G. Stanley Hall (Garden City, N.Y.: Garden City Publishing, 1943); *Totem and Taboo* (London: Hogarth, 1913); *Beyond the Pleasure Principle* (London: Hogarth, 1942); *Civilization and Its Discontents,* translated by Joan Riviere (London: Hogarth, 1939); *Three Contributions to the Theory of Sex* (London: Hogarth, 1905); and *Collected Papers* (London: Hogarth, 1924). These are some of the better-known of Freud's writings and contributions to the field of psychoanalysis.
[4] Richard Lewinsohn, *A History of Sexual Customs* (New York: Harper & Row, 1959), p. 99.
[5] The Goliard poets of the twelfth century might be an exception. Another notable deviation is the writer Rabelais, whose works, even in this supposedly liberated age, offer some of the most sensible advice and some of the best humor that Western literature has to offer. Rabelais argued that people are both carnal and spiritual and that they risk crippling themselves if they deny either facet of their character. Freud also argued for such a balance of forces and saw in that balance the essence of the healthy person and the strong ego.

repression of the individual, viewed as a negative act, became a central intellectual interest. At the same time, Freud's scheme suggests that it is impossible to have the advantages offered by communal living without having to pay the price of living a repressed life.

The Freudian scheme is simple in its barest outlines. Despite similarities in the conception of people as embattled creatures, the Freudian model is a profound shift away from earlier ideas about the nature of people. Where the Christian model looks on us as creatures of choice, the Freudian model denies us choice. It is a conception in which each and every action, no matter how trivial or apparently accidental, is shaped by innumerable causal influences. Choice is an illusion, and accidents are never accidental. They always make sense, according to Freud, when viewed within the context of their occurrence. This is the rationale behind what is commonly referred to as the *Freudian slip*. In such a case a person says or does something that seems to be a slip or error. Further examination can reveal, however, that the error is meaningful. The woman who, at a restaurant with her date, picks up the menu and says, "It all looks so good, and I'm simply ravished," is communicating something to her escort although it may seem, at the time, to be a simple slip of the tongue. Being ravished, after all, is something quite different from being famished.

Another feature of Freudian thought that separated it from earlier conceptions and set it in conflict with them was the development of the idea that conscious and unconscious forces interact within the individual. Unconscious impulses can give rise to conscious actions in ways that the person may never suspect or comprehend. Earlier views tended to emphasize the rational and conscious level of action.

Still another central feature of Freudian thought is the idea that character and personality are pretty much established by the time a person reaches early childhood. Unlike the above two claims, this one did not conflict with earlier religious orthodoxy, which was also inclined to see character determined relatively early in life.

One of the best-known features of Freudian thought is his tripartite division of the person into id, ego, and superego.[6] In this division the central forces are located within the id and the superego. The *id* (Latin for *it*) is the "animal impulse" or the various biological drives, urges, needs, instincts, or other physiologically determined impulses to act that are a part of the genetic inheritance of the individual. The id is significant in several respects. It can be presumed that, within limits, all people are born with a relatively common set of such impulses. Today this is, among sophisticated people at least, a commonly accepted idea.

If, for a moment, we look at the id as representative of the asocial, egocentric force within us, and if we consider it, in a sense, bad, then we must assume that Freudian thought shares with Christian theology

---

[6] This imagery of the person-in-three-parts is very close to Christian imagery. The id is the devil, the superego is the saintly or angelic conscience, and the ego is everyman and everywoman struggling for salvation, which, if it ever comes, is achieved, in all certainty, after death.

26 the idea that all people are born with sinful inclinations. But where Christian theology offers a hope for redemption, Freudian psychoanalysis claims that we can never rid ourselves of the directives that come from the id. There is no redemption. There is no freedom from the constant urging of the id to engage in asocial actions. Rather, if we are to be acceptable to the rest of society we must find ways to *sublimate* such desires and inclinations. We must transform the raw material of physiological impulse into socially valued forms of behavior.

At this point the logic of Freudian thought leads to a conclusion that places us forever in a state of conflict. The transformation of physiologically grounded impulses into socially acceptable behavior requires us to control or *repress* the pleasure-seeking demands of the id. The Freudian model thus places us in an inescapable bind. If we are to be individuals—if we are to gratify ourselves as physical beings—we must deny our communal commitments to some degree. If, on the other hand, we are to be acceptable to the community, we must deny some of the most compelling and demanding urges that come out of our human nature.

It should be mentioned here that Freud was aware of the peculiarities of this apparently simple argument and observation. Although we are generally inclined to accept this vision of ourselves, it has some drawbacks. Foremost among these is the question of how it could happen that we develop communities that do not represent our "natural" character and are, in many ways, antithetical to that character. How could any community develop to the point where it possesses a force greater than the biological reality of human nature? The problem was sufficiently demanding to force Freud to pay attention to it in several major essays,[7] one of which we shall consider in detail later in this chapter.

The force that represents the directives of the community and limits and constrains the impulses of the id is the *superego*. The superego consists of the acquired ethical and moral standards of the community. It is what we ordinarily refer to as the conscience.[8]

It is in the superego that the sociological significance of Freudian thought appears. The superego is a product of the community and its concerns. With the incorporation of the superego into the self, the individual becomes subject to the directives of the community. Each person is a social being as well as an organism responding to the demands of the id.

Freudian thought inspires more questions than it is able to answer. But the questions themselves offer a form of understanding. For exam-

---

[7] This issue is the central concern of *Civilization and Its Discontents* and is the theme, in great part, of the mythical turmoil described in *Totem and Taboo*.

[8] Freudian thought has emphasized the conflict between the id and the superego. The process whereby the superego is acquired was of some interest to Freud, but he never really examined it in depth. Other writers (notably G. H. Mead) were led to conclude, as they looked into the matter more profoundly, that perhaps the idea of conflict was overemphasized by Freud. From Mead's perspective, individuals, in their social character, are reflected in the demands of the community. From this position, individuals and the society of which they are a part are merely different manifestations of the same thing.

ple, communities characteristically demand leadership. Leadership requires relatively close conformity to the demands of the community—that is, a well-developed and effective superego. However, a highly developed superego tends to promote inhibited, rigid, and anxious behavior. Is it possible, then, that leaders have a unique type of personality that supports a repressive mentality?[9]

The last of the three major elements of the individual is the ego. The *ego* is the part of us that experiences reality and integrates the conflicting demands of the superego and the id. Unlike the id, the ego manifests itself in growth. The superego and the ego develop with the acquisition of moral knowledge. The ego is a realist. It must adapt to the pleasure desires of the id, and it must also be concerned with the moral censorship of the superego. A person with a strong ego is one who is able to accomplish the best, most realistic, compromise between the conflicting demands of the id and the superego. To give in to the id is to indulge in infantile and immature behavior. To be totally at the mercy of the superego is to be rigid and repressive. Between these opposed demands the ego struggles to retain a balance.

The Oedipus Complex

The more elemental concepts of Freudian psychoanalysis do not in themselves reveal the rich possibilities that this system of thought offers for interpreting human behavior. It is generally known that Freudian theory has not always been supported by empirical research and that great portions of it are probably beyond any kind of truth test. Granting this, it is surprising to find that the concepts of psychoanalytic theory still have a strong influence among those who concern themselves with the problem of understanding human behavior—including psychologists, sociologists, anthropologists, political scientists, artists, novelists, and philosophers.[10]

One reason for the continued popularity of the Freudian mode of thinking about human behavior comes out of the unusual possibilities that suggest themselves after one has mastered an understanding of the major concepts. It is as though Freud had created seven or eight basic notes which, in various combinations, produce a nearly infinite[11] set of possible combinations and alternatives. Moreover, once one has a grasp of the basic concepts, the temptation to run off variations of one's own

---

[9] Several interesting efforts to demonstrate the validity of this idea have appeared in recent literature. This work has attempted to probe the character of leaders, from Hitler to Nixon. It is difficult to resist speculating that perhaps the overkill effort of Nixon's supporters to sabotage the Democratic party in the 1972 elections is a confirmation of Freud's observations.

[10] Freudian ideas are especially popular today among French intellectuals, who have relied on those concepts to interpret such diverse matters as cinema and the modern prison.

[11] It is impossible to avoid hyperbole in talking about social theory. The term *infinite* should be used with some care. Here we only mean to suggest a very large number.

28 is nearly irresistible. This is what is meant by "cocktail party psycho-analysis." There is a facile quality to Freudian interpretations that must be guarded against. Freudian thought sometimes seems too easy; within the works of Freud, however, there is a logic that is surprisingly coherent. Nothing, we believe, better illustrates the logic of Freudian thought than the classic psychoanalytic conception of the Oedipus complex.

The *Oedipus complex* arises out of the logic of the relationships among instinct, opportunities for gratification, nature of the family, and fear of the father. We have noted already that the instinctive nature of the person, located within the impulses of the id, is amoral (neither moral nor immoral). The id seeks gratification and pleasure and is not especially concerned with whether these accomplishments come about in a manner that is socially acceptable. It is the superego that imposes a moral sense on the quest for gratification.

As the young male child begins to mature and experience sexual desire, he naturally turns toward the person nearest him who might be a possible source of gratification. This person is usually his mother. Note, again, the logical simplicity of this idea. If the id seeks gratification and is not concerned with social niceties, then efficiency, immediacy, and the heritage of already established pleasurable experiences received at the hands of the mother would make the mother attractive in a primary way. The mother becomes a *logical* choice for the young boy. In a similar way the young girl finds the father an attractive person as she begins to mature sexually. The term *Electra complex* has been used to designate the case where the female child is attracted to her father.

The desirability of the parents introduces, of course, the possibility of incestuous sexual relations, and this is morally intolerable. The censoring functions of the superego militate, in part, against the fulfillment of the boy's desire to possess the mother sexually. But there are even more ominous features to the logic of the Oedipus complex. Not only do the moral standards of the community stand against the young man in his desire to make love with his mother, but he also finds himself wanting to challenge the established and almost godlike power of his father. The father shares the marital bed with the mother while the son is excluded. To attempt to intrude into that domain would be to risk the wrath of the father, who possesses the power to castrate the son.

To make matters more complicated, the id, being an amoral force, does not react to such frustrating situations with a mannerly sense of resignation. The inclination of the id, when frustrated in its desires, is to seek to destroy that which stands between it and gratification. In this situation the father is the barrier to gratification. The response of the id is to seek to destroy the father. Murdering the father, of course, is as repugnant to the superego as the idea of having incestuous relations with the mother.

This, then, is the situation into which the Oedipus complex brings the young child. For the boy it means desiring the mother, being frustrated by the father, and wishing, then, to kill the father. For the girl, it is desiring the father, being frustrated by the mother, and wishing, then, for the mother's death. The logic of the pattern of relations is so compelling that Freud was inclined to see the Oedipus and Electra complexes as universal, something all people in all cultures experienced. Recent studies indicate that this is evidently not the case, although the Oedipal pattern is probably more common than critics of Freud are willing to grant.[12]

This "family romance" is the original setting, or initial testing ground, for the individual's response to innumerable conflicts which will, henceforth, be part and parcel of his or her active social life. It is in the Oedipal moment that we each come of age. The agony of a totally forbidden but nonetheless compelling desire is made apparent. How we manage to resolve this first major encounter with the greater forces of the id and the superego will shape our future destiny. If we remain fixed in the love for the opposite parent and cannot redirect the desire, then we may become relatively inflexible in our social life.

A number of consequences are possible, according to psychoanalytic theory, when the Oedipus complex is inadequately resolved. It can be the source of sexual fears; it can lead to highly compulsive behavior in which the individual attempts to atone for having such base desires; it can help account for people who reject marriage entirely. According to this interpretation, such people have never been able to find anyone who can truly compete with mom or dad as a person worthy of love.

Two further comments should be made about the Oedipus complex before we move into more sociologically relevant features of Freud's theory. The resolution of Oedipal stresses is promoted by two factors. The first involves the boy's identification with his father, who is a social role model. As the relationship between the father and the son is secured through common masculine social interests, the boy is drawn away from his mother. The second resolving factor is the boy's fear of his father's authority, which could lead to punitive retaliation. The boy is thus drawn toward his father by both the positive attraction of the masculine model which the father has to offer and by the fear of the father's authority, which the boy dares not antagonize. The attraction toward the father permits a breaking away from the desire for the mother and, eventually, the freedom to find women who are more socially acceptable.

We have considered the problem of resolving the Oedipal dilemma. Now we will discuss the domain wherein much of this conflict is experienced. This domain, the realm of the *unconscious*, is a truly unique territory that Freud brought before the world. The Oedipus complex, to a great degree, occurs in ways that are not made directly available to conscious thought. Individuals, Freud suggests, are influenced by unconscious forces that affect their waking, knowing, and conscious activities. Psychoanalysis deals with the problem of finding ways to ascertain the things that people do not themselves know. The quest for knowledge of the nature of the unconscious has made Freudian thought seem, to some behavioral scientists, perfectly impossible. The unconscious, according to this point of view, remains beyond empirical observation and

---

[12] For a scholarly treatment of this issue see William N. Stephens, *Oedipus Complex: Cross-Cultural Evidence* (New York: Free Press, 1962).

30 therefore is not a proper subject for scientific investigation. However, to others it is an effort that has to be undertaken because the reality of the unconscious cannot be easily denied. And science is the effort to investigate anything operating within nature.

The Unconscious

The concept of the *unconscious* has put the new and struggling efforts to achieve a science of human beings into a quandary. If we grant the existence of the unconscious, then the methodological problem is to find ways of gaining access to it. But the unconscious, by definition, is not readily accessible to our awareness; it is an elusive part of ourselves. It is intriguing by the very fact that it is inaccessible. On the other hand, if we deny the concept of the unconscious and try to deal with human behavior in terms of what is consciously known, we run the risk of being superficial and of violating a concept that makes too much good sense to be ignored. This is, in part, the impact of Freudianism. It has opened the question of how one ascertains what people are, in fact, intending when they do something.

Even at the dawn of time it must have been apparent that what people say and what they are up to can be two quite different matters. Politics, love, poker playing, and salesmanship are only a few of the human activities that often involve duplicity at conscious levels. But if there is duplicity at the level of conscious action, then how much more involved does the situation become when it includes the possibility of unconscious desires and fantasies?

Freud made people self-conscious in a new way. Before Freud, people believed that human beings struggled to achieve a variety of conditions that they considered to be good and worthwhile. After Freud, any quest had to be reexamined in the light of both its conscious and its unconscious possibilities. Consider, for example, the crime of murder carried out by two young and unusually brilliant students at the University of Chicago during the 1920s. The two were caught, convicted, and sent to prison for their crime. While the killers were motivated at a conscious level by the desire to show their superiority over everyone else, they seemed to have been motivated at a different level by the desire to be apprehended and punished. They did this by leaving a trail that detectives found extremely easy to follow.[13]

The significance of this feature of Freud's thought cannot be too heavily underscored. Before Freud, the task of ascertaining why people did many of the things they did seemed to be relatively easy. From a theological point of view, people behaved badly because they were driven by demons. From an economic point of view, people were driven by a desire to possess the good things of life. From a political perspective, people were driven by a desire for power. Freud muddied the waters.

[13] For an interesting novelistic treatment of this true story, see Meyer Levin, *Compulsion* (New York: Simon & Schuster, 1956).

Human motivations, after Freud, became an extremely complicated problem. Possibly it was Freud's greatest insight and argument to suggest that
not only are other people's motivations difficult for us to ascertain from
outside, but even we ourselves cannot, on our own, have a clear picture
of why we behave as we do. For example, consider the kind of people
who work late at night, apparently driven by the desire to succeed in
business. Their motivation appears clear and evident, both to those who
know them and to themselves. But Freud, as we have said, has muddied
the waters forever. We are now aware that any number of possibilities
may exist and that these must be examined—psychoanalyzed—if we are
to hope to find the most reasonable answer. It might be that such persons
have a repressed but dreadful hatred of their parents. They may, in turn,
have unconsciously directed this hatred toward their spouses, whom
they unconsciously would like to murder. They therefore spend a lot of
time at work—thereby avoiding their families and evading their complex
and conflicting desires and motives.

Freud made it evident that people were not so aware of themselves
as they thought. To obtain self-awareness it was necessary to rely on the
services of an expert—a psychoanalyst—who might be able, if the lengthy
process of examination went correctly, to uncover what people were
"really" doing when they did things. It was as devastating a notion to
the rational Victorian mind as Darwin's evolutionary ideas had been.
Much is made of the shockingly sexual nature of Freudian thought. The
deeper shock was the discovery that individuals were not the masters of
their fates and the captains of their souls. To the contrary, individuals had
little personal understanding of the forces within themselves or external
to them. Such understanding, if it could be had at all, could come only
from an expert in psychoanalysis.

The Superego

We have suggested that the idea of unconscious forces presents some
profound methodological problems for the social sciences.[14] If the unconscious has some kind of influence over the affairs of people, and if
it is lost or remote from the rational and ordinary understanding we have
of the world, then how can the unconscious be approached? Freud
argued that one way to find out about the nature of the unconscious is
to examine it when it has managed, somehow, to slip by the controls or
censoring activities of the superego, when it is, so to speak, asleep at
the switch. During such moments the id can break into overt expression.
This, again, is the so-called Freudian slip. One might, for example, write
the word *sex* when one intended to write the word *six*. An unconscious

---

[14] One problem, which is certainly worthy of consideration but which we cannot go into
here, is the question of the unconscious motivations of those who press toward a neat,
tidy, and "systematic" science of human beings. What kind of authoritarianism might be
lurking in the hearts of these people? Freud actually forced a reexamination of the motives
of behavioral scientists themselves!

32 desire has possibly gained expression during a moment when the superego is not paying attention.

A second form of betrayal of the unconscious reveals itself in the
more serious neurotic and psychotic behaviors of people who have
nearly been destroyed by conflicts between the demands of the id and
the superego. The unraveling of such conflicts is, of course, part of
psychoanalytic therapy. One aspect of Freudian theory features the idea
that becoming aware of unconscious impulses and gaining a clearer
understanding of them can help resolve the tensions that the underlying
conflict has brought about.

A third approach to the nature of the unconscious is through the
analysis of dreams. During the sleeping and dreaming state the superego
is less effective than during the waking hours, and the unconscious can
speak with less likelihood of being censored. Thus the content of dreams
offers an opportunity to meet with the character of the unconscious. But
dreams, of course, cannot be observed directly. They must be described
in terms of conscious recall—and during consciousness the superego
has an opportunity to impose censorship once again. Trying to fathom
the character of the unconscious by means of conscious recall is something like trying to find out about corruption in government by employing a governmental investigation committee. The threat of the committee
leads to a tendency on the part of those who have indulged in corruption
to hide their activities all the more carefully. Nonetheless, a committee
can hope to get partial information, and psychoanalysis relies on dreams
and their interpretation as at least one available means—albeit a crude
one—for probing into the unconscious.

Freudian analysis has led to an attempt to go beyond the apparently
rational acts of men and women. The result has been a series of interpretations of ancient issues that have the stamp of modernity about them.
Among the issues considered are war and crime, madness, the relationship between men and women, growing up, our need for machines, and
the rise of civilization. There really are few areas in which Freudian
analysis has not, at one time or another, intervened and left its mark.
The modern stamp that Freudian analysis gives to these old issues involves a marked lack of moralizing,[15] an extremely deterministic premise,
a tendency to see all people as having essentially the same instinctual
nature, and a conception of conscience and moral action as a product of
human, rather than divine, intervention. At the same time, as the opening
of this chapter suggests, the Freudian model leans heavily on a Christian
vision of people that finds them embattled and struggling to deal with
their "base" nature.

It is when Freudian philosophy moves beyond the level of individual

---

[15] There is a morality to Freudian thought that tends toward a kind of enlightened nineteenth-century domesticity—if one can have such a thing. But this morality is attained after
one has come to grips with and accepted the fact that morality is not good in and of itself.
Nor is one's animal nature necessarily bad. Freudian thought has moved modern society
far down the road toward a position not so much amoral as critical of any morality that
presumes to be of worth simply because it is rooted in tradition.

emotional disturbances into an examination of social issues that it be- **33**
comes relevant to sociological concerns. There is no possible way in
which a discussion as brief as this can consider all the contributions of
Freudian thought. Instead, this chapter will close with a short examination of an engaging intellectual problem and how Freud responded to
that problem.[16]

Civilization and Its Discontents

In 1930 Freud published a work entitled *Das Unbehagen in der Kultur*
(Civilization and Its Discontents). He had originally intended to use the
term *unglücklich* rather than *Unbehagen*. *Unglücklich* means "unhappy." *Unbehagen* is more difficult to translate into English; it is close
in meaning to the French *malaise*. The title implies that there is dissat-
isfaction in the finest of human creations—civilization. However, if this
is so (and there is much current as well as past evidence to suggest that
people have found their civilizations a source of considerable frustration), then how can one say that civilization came out of human desire?

A simple conception of the rise of civilization would be that it
emerged to provide people with greater protection, more freedom, and
a degree of security against the onslaughts of nature. But if civilization
makes us miserable, then why bother with it? Indeed, some recent social
movements within the United States and other so-called advanced countries have been in the direction of moving away from the entrapments
of civilized living.[17]

The question, then, is: How could civilization arise out of the needs
and character of people and yet, at the same time, not enhance or
improve their chances for happiness? A commonsense approach to civilization would see it as leading to an upward spiraling trend in human
happiness. The fact that civilization retains a great degree of discontent
suggests a disparity between people's sociological and psychological
natures. This disparity forced Freud, later in his life, into a deeper consideration of the relationship between society and the individual.

Freud began by taking up the nature of happiness. He saw happiness as a universal human concern, but he considered happiness to be
more difficult to attain than unhappiness. Unhappiness is something that
cannot be avoided. Freud listed three major sources of unhappiness or
misery. The first is found in the simple physiological limitations of the
body, which is subject to decay and dissolution with the passage of time,
regardless of how one struggles to dodge that fate. The second is found

---

[16] We do not subscribe, in general, to a Freudian approach to human behavior. However,
we believe it is foolish not to respect the tremendous opening of awareness—the forced
expansion of possibilities—that Freud brought to the investigation of human behavior. For
a highly sophisticated—and sympathetic—critique of Freud, see H. D. Duncan, *Communication and Social Order* (New York: Bedminster Press, 1962), pp. 3–17.

[17] We cannot go into a discussion here of the success of the "back-to-the-land" efforts of
some young people in this country. We do, however, find the thrust of their concern in
keeping with Freud's observation that civilization has its discontents.

34 in natural catastrophes of various kinds, which, again, are difficult to avoid. The third and, said Freud, perhaps the most unbearable of all, is the unhappiness laid upon us by our fellow men and women.

But what means are available to people for the attainment of happiness? What constitutes the greatest happiness a person can experience? Freud had to deal with this question before he could enter into a treatment of the relationships among humanity, the quest for happiness, and the rise of civilization.

The quest for happiness involves both positive and negative approaches. In the negative approach one attempts to evade the sources of pain; in the positive approach one seeks to enhance the extent to which one is able to experience pleasure. Freud turned his attention to this latter form of the quest for happiness and made the following observation:

> What we call happiness in the strictest sense comes from the (preferably sudden) satisfaction of needs which have been dammed up to a high degree, and it is from its nature only possible as an episodic phenomenon. When any situation that is desired by the pleasure principle is prolonged, it only produces a feeling of mild contentment. We are so made that we can derive intense enjoyment only from a contrast and very little from a state of things. Thus our possibilities of happiness are already restricted by our constitution.[18]

This statement is significant in that it points to a particular characteristic of Freudian thought—its inclination to turn toward people's physiological nature to explain behavior. In this brief comment Freud tells us that the possibilities of happiness are already restricted by our biological nature. Then, when we add the frustrations imposed by communal living, it is a wonder that people are not *more* unhappy than they are.

The Freudian picture of humanity is that of a general state of wretchedness. Not only is happiness attainable only in brief and episodic moments, but the fulfilling of instinctual needs—one form of happiness—can be a threat to communal order. Civilization came about as a result of a precarious balance of payoffs. Freud, like many present-day social writers, reveals an inclination to romanticize primitive people. We can see this in his summary of how civilization might have come into being even though it brought still more unhappiness with it.

> If civilization imposes such great sacrifices not only on man's sexuality but on his aggressivity, we can understand better why it is hard for him to be happy in that civilization. In fact, primitive man was better off in knowing no restrictions of instinct. To counterbalance this, his prospects of enjoying this happiness for any length of time were very slender. *Civilized man has exchanged a portion of his possibilities of happiness for a portion of security.*[19]

[18] Freud, *Civilization and Its Discontents*, pp. 23–24.
[19] Ibid., p. 62. Italics are Freud's.

It is a shaky response to an engaging problem. The shakiness of the response suggests some of the problems with Freud's approach to human behavior. Is civilized humanity actually more repressed? Do primitive people—at least as we know them—live in "free" and instinctually fulfilling circumstances? Is the fulfilling of instinct actually the locus of happiness? Can people sometimes be highly gratified and happy with themselves even as they deny themselves some kind of gratification? There is, for example, a surprisingly happy and exultant quality in some of the diaries of Japanese *kamikaze* pilots who were waiting to go out on suicidal missions in World War II. It would seem that such total denial of the self would produce great unhappiness.

We have raised these questions here because more recent forms of social theory, particularly those developed by Mead and, somewhat later, by Duncan, take a different approach to the interpretation of human behavior (see Chapters 6 and 18). We find that the logic of Freudian analysis is not quite so tight as his more devoted followers see it. In one sense this is unfortunate. It would be nice, after all, to have a definitive statement that would be binding in its understanding. On the other hand, it is good to know that there are some possible ways out of the dilemmas that Freud kept putting us in.

Freud himself was not quite so dogmatic as many of his disciples were. He opened a new set of approaches to the study of human eccentricities, neuroses, and various forms of madness. He placed people in a natural universe in which their bodies and their instincts, in conflict with the powerful demands of the greater community, were viewed as the cause of behavioral problems. The older religious notions of sin, divine intervention, wickedness coming from the proddings of the devil, and other "unnatural" explanations were brushed aside. Freud also claimed that people were destined, even at best, to live lives that were a delicate balance between the growling demands of the id and the imperious censorship of the superego. As we said earlier, it was a dramatic notion. People were destined to live out their days in conflict. The mind was a locus for battle. This interpretation is lively, romantic, and exciting. And many people have come to look upon Freud as a person who had all the answers. Freudianism, for some, has become a religion that can account for anything and everything. But for Freud the situation was much more complex. We pick up this sentiment in the closing sentence of *Civilization and Its Discontents*. Freud was aware, as he wrote this essay, that people had created vast engines of destruction and, given the human instinct toward aggressiveness, were likely to use them to destroy the earth. Perhaps, he argued, the forces of love and the natural urge to live would move into the picture and struggle against the darker forces of aggression, hate, and destruction. Freud then closed his essay with an admission of the fallibility of all intellect: "But who can foresee with what success and with what result?"[20]

[20] *Civilization and Its Discontents*, p. 92.

Freud is generally considered to be a psychologist. His writings, however, have had considerable significance for the interpretation of human social behavior. Particularly relevant are Freud's essays on the relationship between society and the individual. The relationship is primarily one of conflict—conflict between the physiological demands of the body and the moral demands of society. The more "civilized" we become, the more we find ourselves "discontented." What is the evidence for "discontent" in modern society? Is Freud inclined to romanticize earlier or simpler social structures? Americans appear to believe that happiness is possible. Just what is happiness? To what extent has it, in fact, been achieved in American culture? How do the media deal with the problem of happiness?

One of the contributions of Freudian thought is the idea of the "unconscious." Given this idea, we are forced to the conclusion that we can never really understand our motivations unless an "expert" unravels them for us through the interpretation of our dreams. How do we establish our motives? Why are motives important in social conduct? How does Freud approach the problem of motives?

Freud paved the way for a generation of writers and social and political analysts who became engaged in "debunking." That is to say, it became even easier, after Freud, to argue that the reasons people give for doing whatever they are doing are not the "real" reasons. Nixon, for example, claimed to act in the interests of national security. Debunkers claimed he acted because he was insecure, paranoid, anally retentive, or any of a variety of more "real" reasons or motives. Through what means can we establish the truth or falsity of such interpretations? Why do we feel continually impelled to ferret out the true motives underlying actions?

Profit, Greed, and Misery

Social Theory and Karl Marx

KARL MARX

The mode of production in material life determines the general character of the social, political, and spiritual processes of life.

A Contribution to the Critique of Political Economy

BORN: 1818   DIED: 1883

Malthusian Inevitability

The industrial age introduced novel forms of demeaning experience for great numbers of Europeans. In earlier times they suffered from plagues and war. The industrial age brought with it new kinds of poverty and grinding work. The change was too obvious to go unnoticed by intellectuals of the time. What accounted for it? Was it necessary? Could anything be done about it? Would the situation improve or simply continue to get worse? Revolutionaries and optimistic intellectuals of the late eighteenth century saw such misery as merely part of a transitional phase that would lead to a greater and more progressive society. Others were less inclined to be hopeful about the future. Among the pessimists was an eighteenth-century economist and minister named Thomas Robert Malthus.

Malthus concluded that the source of such massive misery was located within nature itself. He argued that the simple laws of supply and demand, coupled with the even simpler laws of procreation and the ability of organic populations to increase in a snowballing manner, led

3

38   to an inexorable bind. Populations, human as well as animal, tended to increase to the point where they exhausted their means of subsistence. At this point population stresses could be resolved only by the wholesale slaughter of warfare, the ravages of disease, and the decimating effects of famine, deprivation, and misery.

We seem to be digressing in this chapter, which is supposed to deal with Marx, by talking about an earlier and much simpler economic argument. However, we would like to stay with Malthus for just a while because the Malthusian argument is so persuasive that to argue against it seems to be the height of folly. Yet we come to understand the great power of Marxism and its tremendous appeal when we counter the optimism of Marx with the dour pessimism of Malthus. So let us simply sketch in a few further comments drawn from Malthus's contentions.

Human populations, said Malthus, have one very interesting mathematical property—they grow in a geometric fashion. In fact, all populations, whether human or not, have this property. Malthus meant by this that organic populations, including populations of human beings, double in size over a given interval of time and continue to double with each succeeding interval.

We might want to stop for a moment at this point. Even if we had never heard of Malthus or of the present concern over the world's population explosion, we could, if we were only slightly arithmetically inclined, trace out some of the implications of this statement. Suppose, for example, that human populations doubled every fifty years. We could begin at the time of Christ with two people and see how long it would take to reach the present world population of roughly four billion souls. The arithmetic is so elementary we could, with pencil and paper and a small amount of patience, determine the answer in a few minutes— sometime during the sixteenth century. By the middle of the twentieth century we would, at this rate, have a world population of over one trillion people—a figure more than two hundred times greater than the present world population.

We can, if we wish, change the interval of time. How many people would we have in the world today if we began with two people at the time of Christ and their numbers doubled every twenty-five years? Malthus made the calculation, and his answer is startling. We would have enough people to place four persons on every square yard of habitable ground on this planet. Even so, there would be a surplus. Enough people would be left over to populate all the planets in the solar system in a similar fashion. And yet there would still be a surplus. We would have enough remaining to place four humans on every square yard of all the planets of all the stars visible to the naked eye at night—assuming each to have as many planets as our own sun. And we would still have a surplus.

This is, of course, a fantastic figure—a purely mathematical fantasy. Nonetheless, it fires the imagination and leads immediately to speculation about what "really" is happening. Since the doubling of human populations every twenty-five years is not unreasonable, what has happened to the large numbers we might arithmetically expect? Obviously something has controlled or checked the growth of population. Malthus concluded that devastating checks on population growth were necessary, natural, and inevitable. Since the checks involved reduction of population through famine, disease, war, and misery, Malthus came to the logical and rational conclusion that misery is our unavoidable destiny. He did not, incidentally, believe that population growth could be effectively checked by contraceptive practices.[1]

The model of the world Malthus offers us is a compelling one. The fateful consequences of Malthusian logic depend, of course, on whether some of the conditions ascribed to the variables used in the model are, in fact, true. For example, do human populations necessarily tend to increase in a geometric fashion until checked by the means of subsistence? Have we today, through the use of sophisticated contraceptive devices, reached the point where population growth will decline to zero and population size will remain constant? We can see that it might be possible to check population growth. However, even our present sophisticated technology looks as though it might be swamped by the problem, and intellectuals still debate whether or not we shall soon experience massive catastrophes throughout the world. Setting such considerations aside for the moment, let us recall that Malthus offered the century that followed the initial publication of his essay in 1798 a gloomy argument to chew on.

The Malthusian picture suggests that poverty is an integral feature of human communities and that it comes out of natural processes that cannot be corrected by any other than the most extreme and distressing devices. The poor and starving will always be among us. Why, asked Malthus, worry about punishing the poor, when nature will do the punishing for us? The world is the way it is and we cannot hope to alter it in any significant manner. Conservative leaders in politics and industry found this argument of the Reverend Malthus quite comforting. But there was a response to the fatalistic implications of Malthusianism, and it gained hundreds of millions of adherents throughout the world. This response appeared in the writings of Karl Marx.

Industrialization and Human Misery

Marx was born in a period when the industrial power of Europe was truly beginning to manifest itself. Marx was the great philosopher of the industrial age. One of the unusual contributions of the industrial age was the appearance of the industrial town. Like few other communities in history, the industrial town offered extreme contrasts in what today would be called life styles. It contained, on the one hand, a small minority

---

[1] Thomas Robert Malthus, *An Essay on the Principle of Population: Or a View of Its Past and Present Effects on Human Happiness*, 7th ed. (London: Reeves and Turner, 1872). Seven editions, each enlarging and refining the original essay published in 1798, attest to the concern Malthus gave his argument and the care he took to meet the criticisms leveled against him.

40 of people who were able to afford and enjoy the new benefits of an expanding technology and, on the other, large populations of workers whose homes and living conditions were miserable almost beyond belief.[2] As we have seen already, one response to the wretched condition of the working population was to attribute the whole business to the cruel workings of a heartless and impassive nature. The other response was to view the tragedy as a consequence of a flaw in the organization of human affairs. Diligent pursuit of an understanding of how people arrange their societies and how this, in turn, produces unanticipated and excessive brutality might eventually lead to the most ideal of all human conditions—a state in which misery coming from adverse forms of social and economic organization would be decreased to a minimum. Few people in the intellectual history of humankind ever dedicated themselves more totally to this fundamental hope for all of humanity than did Karl Marx.

Whether we agree in the final summation with Marx's vision, we must acknowledge that it stands as the most painstakingly rational effort to see through the complexities of entire social systems ever written. Behind the work of Marx was the driving animus of a desire to comprehend the inhumanity of people.

Marxist Sociology

Marx is known, of course, as an economic theorist. His theories, however, have far too many ramifications to be restricted exclusively to the realm of economic analysis. If Marx is an economic theorist, it is only because, in searching for an answer, he became convinced that the manifold forms of political, religious, cultural, and philosophical systems under which people have lived throughout time are to be understood in terms of their relationship to the modes of production that prevail in any community at any time.[3] It would seem obvious that a hunting society, with its attendant forms of production and distribution of goods, must

---

[2] Despite the eulogies bestowed upon the industrial age by those who have benefited from it, there is today a "hidden" population that lives more miserably than most Americans are able to appreciate. Grinding poverty of the variety that appalled progressives of the nineteenth century continues, of course—nicely hidden from the eyes of the indulgent suburban American. A visit to some of the barrios of South America is a searing experience for a person of any sensitivity. For literary descriptions of such poverty see Frantz Fanon's *Wretched of the Earth*, translated from the French by Constance Farington (New York: Grove, 1965).

[3] The major works of Karl Marx include: *The German Ideology*, parts 1 and 3, with Frederich Engels; introduction by R. Pascal (New York: International, 1939; originally written 1845–1846); *The Poverty of Philosophy*, with an introduction by Engels (New York: International, 1963; originally written in 1847); *The Communist Manifesto*, with Engels (New York: Washington Square Press, 1964; originally written in 1848); *The Eighteenth Brumaire of Louis Bonaparte* (New York: International, 1964; originally written in 1852); *A Contribution to the Critique of Political Economy*, translated by N. I. Stone (Chicago: Kerr, 1904; originally written in 1859); *Capital: A Critique of Political Economy* (Chicago: Kerr, 1906; originally written 1867–1879).

necessarily have legal, religious, educational, kin, and other institutional **41** structures quite different from those of a society that relies on an economic base employing the use of landed estates, agricultural systems, and barter.

It was an idea that was to have considerable impact at a time when people were discovering that personal worth could be bought with money. During the feudal period, status was inherited and transmitted through noble blood lines. With the rise of the industrial state a person could begin thinking about purchasing a sense of importance. The bond between social structure (ideology, values, status, belief, and other nebulous, but nonetheless significant, features of society) and the economic order was becoming much too apparent for thinkers to overlook. Money was beginning to have a large voice in human affairs. It became quite apparent that money and ideas were connected. The question to be examined was the extent to which money ultimately led to the purchase of social systems that were inimical to the progress of human welfare.

It is extremely important for the student who is being introduced to modern social philosophy to understand the essential issue raised by Marxist social thought. It is a considerable oversimplification, but it helps us gain an insight into the problems of sociological investigation if we see the central thrust of Marxist doctrine as being directed toward the end of finding a "substance" in social systems.[4] There are, on the one hand, those who believe that social systems are located within a realm of values, beliefs, ideologies, symbols, linguistic systems, moral codes, doctrines, and other "substanceless" forces. Opposed to this position is the argument that the relations which bind people into greater communal orders are sustained by "lower" or more "basic" conditions which have "real" manifestations. According to this latter position, ideologies and moral codes and such other "insubstantial conditions" are a "reflection" or response to the more real conditions that underlie them.[5]

As almost everyone knows today, Marx turned to the economic order as the primal reality that determines the ebb and flow of moral and social structures. People are sustained by the extent to which they cooperate in productive efforts to attend to the individual and communal needs. This primitive and eternal necessity cannot be ignored. If so

---

[4] Marx found his substance in labor and its use and abuse. Labor creates value. At the same time, Marx was quite aware that the value of a particular commodity is affected not only by its labor input but by its socially granted merits as well. Labor in and of itself cannot impose a value. The thousands of hours of labor that might go into the building of a useless machine will not generate as much value as a smaller amount of labor that might go into, let us say, the painting of a masterpiece. This example, though crude, is sufficient to make us immediately aware of the problems involved in locating value exclusively within a labor context.

[5] A recent work by the anthropologist Marvin Harris extends this argument in an even more basic manner. Harris argues that human culture is a response to the quest for protein. Protein, then, becomes the most fundamental substance within the materialistic argument. See Marvin Harris, *Cultural Materialism: The Struggle for a Science of Culture* (New York: Random House, 1979).

42 inclined, one can dismiss the philosophies of the existentialists or the Christians or the Buddhists and not come to any special grief; but one cannot ignore the iron laws of the marketplace. Perhaps we do not live by bread alone, but we must have bread before we can engage in any other form of activity.[6] Ultimately, Marx suggested, it is the manner in which people obtain their "bread" that determines the way in which they will establish their programs of justice, religion, kinship, education, and other social institutions. The power that people gain over each other has its locus in the forces of production.

Marxist sociology, then, is characterized by an effort to interpret uniquely social events in terms of how those events are associated with economic conditions or factors associated with the production and distribution of goods. So Marx, writing in 1859, pointed to the mode of production and said that it determines the general character of the social, political, and spiritual processes of life. Marx argued that it is not the consciousness of people that determines their existence, but, on the contrary, it is their social existence that determines their consciousness.[7]

The ringing and oft-quoted words that begin the *Communist Manifesto* give us a feeling of the inspirational quality of Marx's message:

> The history of all hitherto existing society is the history of class struggles.
> Freeman and slave, patrician and plebeian, lord and serf, guild master and journeyman, in a word, oppressor and oppressed, stood in constant opposition to one another, carried on an uninterrupted, now hidden, now open fight, a fight that each time ended either in a revolutionary reconstitution of society at large or in the common ruin of the contending classes.
> In the earlier epochs of history we find almost everywhere a complicated arrangement of society into various orders, a manifold gradation of social rank. In ancient Rome we have patricians, knights, plebeians, slaves; in the Middle ages, feudal lords, vassals, guild masters, journeymen, apprentices, serfs; in almost all of these classes, again, subordinate gradations.
> The modern bourgeois society that has sprouted from the ruins of feudal society has not done away with class antagonisms. It has established new classes, new conditions of oppression, new forms of struggle in place of the old ones.[8]

Economic interpretations of history are still popular and reveal the extent to which the Marxist influence permeates Western thought. Indeed, a lot of Americans who would be shocked to think of themselves as Marxists nonetheless subscribe to a fundamentally Marxist mode of thinking. That is, they think in terms of economic determinism. Following

---

[6] The humanistic psychologist Abraham Maslow has developed a hierarchy of needs with the suggestion that some needs cannot be fulfilled until others are met. See A. H. Maslow, *Personality and Motivation*, 2d ed. (New York: Harper & Row, 1970).

[7] Marx, *A Contribution to the Critique of Political Economy*, p. 11.

[8] Originally published in London in 1848, in German only, *The Communist Manifesto* was the platform of the Communist League, a workingmen's association and secret society. The document was drawn up by Marx and Engels, who were commissioned to prepare a program for the Party. The first English translation was made by Helen Macfarlane and was published in London in 1850 by G. J. Harney.

are some general examples of the impact of economic interpretations of history and social order.

Charles Beard wrote an interpretation of the founding of America in terms of economic interests and managed to shock a number of Americans who thought American government was grounded in higher ideals.[9] The development of applied mathematics and the growth of science as a unique ideological system have been traced by some writers to the growth of a need for more accurate counting procedures on the part of merchants as commercial expansion took place in the fourteenth and fifteenth centuries. Business still remains a tremendous consumer of computer technology, and in many ways the computer is essentially a business machine. The growth of exploration in the fifteenth century was motivated less by idle curiosity than it was by the need to expand markets and acquire resources for European countries. As a final general example, we ought to mention that most of the popularity of current discussions of socioeconomic class structures owes its impetus to Marxist thought. In sum, the pervasiveness of Marxist thought within Western social philosophy is greater than many people recognize. Anyone who emphasizes the economy as a source of social and ideological change and who views human beings as essentially economically motivated is conceding a central argument to Marx.

Economic Riddles

Compared with social theory, the realm of economic study seems closed, nicely ordered, and a proper subject for rational analysis. To a considerable degree this is the case. There will probably never be a sociological Nobel Laureate, although there have been several Nobel Prize winners in the field of economics. However, the fact remains that economic behavior and the more vague and ephemeral forms of social conduct that resist logical analysis are bound together. Some of the central issues in economic analysis are dependent on a parallel understanding of certain sociological forces for their resolution. We are going to mention two areas of economic uncertainty because we believe they lead nicely into an appreciation of some of the problems encountered in Marxist approaches to social systems. These issues also quickly reveal the interdependent nature of economic and more general sociological forces.

The first area of interest has to do with the problem of production and utilization of economic surpluses. It would seem, at first, that the whole idea of the development of economic surpluses would be a simple matter to explain or account for. We all remember the lesson that comes out of the story of the grasshopper and the ant. The grasshopper fiddled while the ant stored surpluses against the bad times ahead. The value of surpluses is so obvious to us today that the possibility that surpluses are

[9] Charles Beard, *America Faces the Future* (New York: Books for Libraries, 1932); Charles and Mary Beard, *America in Mid-Passage* (New York: Macmillan, 1939).

44 peculiar is difficult to accept. Nonetheless, the economic history of humanity suggests that the acquisition of large surpluses is a unique event. In a sense, true surpluses come about when people are coerced, by some device or other, to produce more than they need as individuals.[10]

The second area of interest has to do with the utilization of surplus forms of wealth. Once conditions of surplus goods and materials are achieved, some means must be devised of separating people from their individually acquired savings so that those surpluses can be employed for the benefit of the community. At this point the crucial connection between the individual and the state is subjected to a searing commentary by Marx. Marx, more than anyone else, posed the moral question of how a person's surplus efforts were to be fairly distributed. We shall return to this issue later. Let us first consider the apparently simple matter of the achievement of surplus wealth.

We are so familiar today with the idea of surpluses that it is difficult to comprehend the extent to which surplus wealth is, as a matter of fact, an engaging economic question. The relationship between need satisfaction and the acquisition of surpluses is not as simple as might at first be presumed. In traditional economies, surplus wealth is meager. At the same time, there is no strong motivation to acquire surplus wealth.[11]

For example, in the film *The Hunters,*[12] bushmen of the Kalahari desert are shown hunting down a giraffe. It takes them over a week to accomplish their quest. They then butcher the carcass, take home the remains, distribute the food, and eat and tell stories until, once more, it is time to hunt. In a world where life is difficult and brief, food hard to come by, and the acquisition of goods a serious struggle, there is reason why work is limited and surpluses relatively slight.

One of the central concerns of Marxist social thought focuses on the nature of surplus wealth. Surplus wealth, of course, has reached the point in our time of being a sort of *reductio ad absurdum* in this society. We not only have surplus wealth to the point where we suffer from "gluts," but we even have "surplus labor." There is a strangeness in the idea of surplus labor. As David Riesman has noted, surplus labor actually refers to surplus people. We live in a surplus economy, and an elementary understanding of the nature and character of surpluses—what they mean for people, how they affect our lives, and the problems they pose—

---

[10] Weber used the term *traditional economy* to refer to cases where people work primarily to fulfill immediate needs. American entrepreneurs sometimes find themselves frustrated in other cultures when they encounter workers who prefer not to maximize their income but instead work just long enough to get whatever income will satisfy their needs of the moment and then stop.

[11] Anthropologists in New Guinea observed that some "primitives" were astounded by the wealth of goods and supplies that they saw coming from ships and aircraft during World War II. The natives were convinced that such supplies were coming from their ancestors and were meant for their consumption and use. Whole cults were built around the idea of receiving such largesse. These "cargo cults," as they came to be known, were not grounded in an idea of excess or surplus wealth. The economy of the natives remained essentially a traditional or subsistence economy.

[12] We strongly recommend this film for undergraduate classes for the insights it offers into a variety of aspects of "primitive" life. It also just happens to be esthetically graceful.

is essential for anyone who seeks to be informed about the affairs of our time. Having raised the problem of surpluses as an interesting question in and of itself, we would like to set it aside for a moment and turn to another aspect of the nature of surplus wealth. This second feature of surpluses is even more interesting, we believe, than the question of how surpluses came into being in the first place.

This question has to do with how individuals are separated from some or all of the surplus goods and services they may produce. Suppose, for example, that you have worked hard and industriously for several years and have managed to accumulate savings of some sort. These savings, of course, constitute wealth above and beyond the demand of immediate necessities. They are surplus wealth. Suppose further that members of the community come to you and tell you that if you give them your savings, it will be to the benefit of all and that you, along with the others, will live in a better world as a result. In this baldly simple form, the problem of the separation of the individual from his or her surplus is dramatically clear. What right do others have to your savings or surplus? If they persist, by what devices can they separate you from some or perhaps most of the results of your effort? It is immediately evident, although in real situations the matter becomes more complex, that two elemental devices are available for achieving the separation. The first of these is persuasion—you might be talked out of your holdings by members of the community who come to you and plead for your help and assistance. They might add, as part of the persuasive effort, a suggestion that if you give some of your holdings to the community, you will be rewarded with nonsubstantial but nonetheless significant honors and elevations in prestige. You can, as it were, purchase a sense of significance. This is one way to be parted from surplus wealth.

The second way others can get your surplus is to take it by force. This, of course, is a time-honored device. Taxation, for example, is a forceful procedure. Two forms of force are commonly employed in the venture of separating people from their available wealth: illegal force and legal force. Both are used toward the same end; the effect is not different. The difference lies largely in the agent making use of force. It is pretty tricky, incidentally, to argue that legal force is good because it works for the benefit of the community and illegal force is bad because it serves the selfish interests of some crook. The state can take surplus wealth and employ it for evil ends, and a poor man can hold up someone and use the stolen money to feed his family.[13]

We are interested, at the moment, in the simple idea of how you go about taking someone's excess wealth and what you do with it if you succeed in getting it. This, in a sense, is one of the more dramatic concerns of Marxist philosophy. What are the implications of the rela-

---

[13] An interesting case in point is the popular bandit who, like Robin Hood, redresses excesses of the state by robbing from the rich and giving to the poor. The subject is not without interest to sociologists and is discussed by Eric J. Hobsbawm in *Primitive Rebels* (New York: Holt, Rinehart and Winston, 1963). See also Robert Nisbet, *The Social Philosophers* (New York: Crowell, 1973), pp. 262–265.

46 tionship between the acquisition of surplus wealth and the application of force necessary for the distribution of such wealth? One central concern of Marxist doctrine is the speculation that force leads to a concentration of wealth in the hands of a few because wealth is capable of being transformed into force. Therefore, those who are initially successful in acquiring wealth will, at the same time, augment the power needed for gaining greater access to existing wealth. At this point we can begin to see that the motivation for the acquisition of surplus wealth might lie in the fact that wealth offers security, in the form of power, to those who have obtained control of the economic process. The question of surplus, then, can be explained, at least in part, as the never-ending need for greater and greater security of those who are in positions of power. And so it is that people, who in traditional economies might have produced enough to meet their simplest needs, were later transformed into creatures whose needs could never be satiated.

The Dialectic

This introduction enables us to move into some of the more original features of Marxist thought. It would seem, from the above discussion, that the dynamics of the relationship between wealth and power would lead to greater and greater concentrations of wealth in the hands of the very few. And there is something to be said for such a view of human social and economic order. There are people whose wealth is so vast that the ordinary person cannot begin to comprehend the magnitudes of power and money that are involved.[14]

Consider, for example, the wealth and power controlled by someone who approaches billionaire status. If it were necessary to escape from some impending catastrophic situation and one could buy such escape at the cost of a hundred dollars a foot, some of us would not be able to get more than twenty or thirty feet from ground zero. To get a mile away would take over half a million dollars. A billionaire would be able to get almost two thousand miles away. The vast difference between the capacities of an ordinary person and those of a billionaire can be dramatized in a variety of ways, but words cannot fully convey the overwhelming force of wealth.

Given the combined forces of wealth and power, one augmenting the other, it would seem that an ever-growing concentration of wealth would be inevitable. And, indeed, some have looked on Marxist thought as advocating just that. The process of history would produce circumstances in which the legions of the poor would increase while the wealthy

---

[14] Anyone interested in the nature and character of great wealth should read Ferdinand Lundberg's *The Rich and Super-rich* (New York: Grosset and Dunlap, 1968).

would become fewer in number but ever stronger and wealthier.[15] It is **47** to the credit of Marxist thought that it does not stop here and, like the conservative thought of the Malthusians, concludes that the fate of most people is to be wretched, miserable, and doomed forever.

Marx was convinced that the historical process would lead, eventually, to a balancing-out of affairs. The very forces that instigate eras of grinding wretchedness will dig their own grave by virtue of their excesses. Marx referred to this process as the *dialectic*.[16] The dialectic consists of a threefold historical movement in which a given condition, referred to as a *thesis*, creates its own opposition, or *antithesis*. The ensuing struggle between these opposed forces leads to a new state, or *synthesis*, which then, in turn, creates its own opposed conditions. The dialectic has been looked upon as a model of cultural and economic change that viewed history as a dynamic and continuous series of confrontations in which a given historical epoch creates the seeds of its own destruction.[17]

So, if the industrial age had produced grinding conditions for the laboring classes, the greater thrust of history would eventually even the score. Industrial capitalism would dig its own grave and do it unwittingly. It would be led by its own logic to create those conditions which would bring about a movement toward a noncapitalist state. The dialectic process meant the inevitable establishment of a classless society.[18]

The Working Day

All of this is rather abstract and generally known, if not thoroughly understood, by most high school seniors. But Marx is famous not for his political rhetoric (though he was a master of invective) nor for the creation of abstract philosophical systems in the older German tradition.

---

[15] There is still much reason to dispute whether or not we are continuing to move in such a direction. Lundberg notes, for example (in *The Rich and Super-rich*), that the relative distribution of wealth in the United States and India is the same. And, of course, at a global level, we are all familiar with the data showing that America, with 6 percent of the world's population, consumes over 40 percent of the world's available energy sources. It is ironic to watch the world's most powerful people groan over the prospect that they might someday have to lose out to others in the race for consumption, when losing would simply mean the achievement of parity in gluttony.

[16] The term was borrowed from the ideas of Hegel, a German philosopher who saw historical change coming about as a result of each cultural epoch creating its own antithetical forces in a constant "dialectical" exchange. See George W. R. Hegel, *Encyclopedia of the Philosophical Sciences* (New York: Macmillan, 1967; originally written in 1817).

[17] Even Weber, a profound critic of Marx, found the dialectic an implicit, if not explicit, model for his study of the paradoxes of Puritanism and capitalism. He could not help noting the ironies to be found in the extent to which ascetic Puritanism brought about the sensate excesses of capitalistic economies.

[18] One can quickly see that if the process is inevitable, there should be no need to promote it. Marx's revolutionary propaganda seemed, to some critics, to be a refutation of the dialectic or at least a possible revelation of a lack of faith in its own vision.

48   Marx established his reputation, in great part, by penetrating into the most picayune, minor, and seemingly inconsequential details available to him. Out of these details, and out of thousands of established and documented facts, Marx began to put together a grand conception of history and of the moment in which he lived. It was the factual, not the abstract, Marx who overwhelmed readers and won adherents by the thousands. Possibly Marx, more than any other single individual of his time, gave hope to people who sought to ground social argumentation in factual observations.

Marx not only theorized over the nature of labor in its more abstract character but he also described what it meant, in concrete terms, to be engaged in labor. Nothing, we believe, better reveals the extent of Marx's concern with labor than his treatment of the working day.[19] Marx's involvement with the working day achieves two effects simultaneously. First of all, it provides an opening for a treatment of the nature and character of surplus wealth. Second, it presents a shocking description of the wretchedness into which unbridled capitalistic practice had thrown most men and women who were forced to live under its sway.

The working day was divided by Marx into two parts. The first consists of the amount of time it takes a worker to produce the materials and goods necessary for his or her subsistence. The second is a variable period during which the worker produces goods and materials above and beyond whatever is necessary for subsistence. On this elemental foundation, Marx was able to build a structure that leads to an inevitable clash between those who purchase labor—the capitalists—and those who must sell their labor—the workers, or proletariat. Furthermore, this clash results from a strictly rational consideration of their interests by both groups. The worker must determine what is a reasonable working day while the capitalist must determine what constitutes a maximum possible working day. Both the capitalist and the worker, operating within the economic dictates of capitalism, are coerced to respond as they do.

From a Marxist perspective, the capitalist seeks to extend the working day for as long as possible. The workers seek to reduce the length of the working day so that it is not beyond their capacities. But the final resolution of this conflict of rational interests cannot be a matter of rational discussion. In the final analysis, the confrontation between those who labor and those who purchase labor will have to be resolved by the application of force.

> The capitalist maintains his rights as a purchaser when he tries to make the working day as long as possible, and to make, whenever possible, two working days out of one. On the other hand, the peculiar nature of the commodity sold implies a limit to its consumption by the purchaser, and the labourer maintains his right as seller when he wishes to reduce the working day to one of definite normal duration. There is here, therefore, an antinomy, right against right, both equally bearing the seal of the law of exchanges. Between equal rights force decides. Hence is it that in the

[19] Marx, *Capital.*

history of capitalist production, the determination of what is a working day, presents itself as the result of a struggle, a struggle between collective capital, i.e., the class of capitalists, and collective labor, i.e., the working class.[20]

In this quotation Marx reveals a variety of conceptions basic to his approach toward the examination of social systems. First of all, capitalists are considered dispassionately as operating within "their rights" when they seek to extend the working day in order to maximize surplus wealth which may, then, be transformed into profit. Second, workers are also within their rights when they seek to bring the working day within what constitutes a "normal" duration.[21] Third, the clash of two evenly balanced rights makes necessary the use of force.[22] Fourth, and finally, the central struggle within humankind exists not so much between nations as between two necessarily opposed classes of people—the workers and those who purchase labor for gain.

There is in this quote, as there is in Marxist doctrine generally, a cold reasoning that sees both the capitalist and the worker as beings caught up in historical forces that demand the working out of competing interests. There is no condemnation of either side. There is, however, the belief that it will be labor which should, and eventually *will*, exercise the decisive historical force.

But Marx's consideration of the working day goes beyond a simple calculation of the problems involved in determining what constitutes a proper duration for the work day. The greater part of his discourse on the working day is a chronicling of the industrial horrors encountered by working men, women, and children of the nineteenth century. One cannot read Marx at any length without comprehending the extent to which his logic was driven by his compassion. Marx comprehended that capitalists were only exercising a right when they attempted to minimize labor costs by extending the working day to its maximum effective limits. At the same time, the cost of such practice in terms of simple human suffering was not to be ignored in the name of rational economic practice. Here, for example, is one case which Marx presents for our consideration when he talks about the working day. It is worth reviewing because it places in perspective the milieu out of which Marxism arose.

In the last week of June, 1863, all the London daily papers published a paragraph with the "sensational" heading "Death from simple over-work." It dealt with the death of the milliner, Mary Anne Walkley, 20 years of age,

---

[20] Ibid., p. 259.

[21] The terminology here is vague. Later in his discussion of the working day, Marx makes clear, by implication, what constitutes a "normal" working day by providing astonishingly detailed observations on the extent to which the working day in industrial Europe was, by any reasonable consideration, abnormal.

[22] Marx is sometimes considered to have advocated violence as a proletarian virtue. The issue, however, is more profound than that. Violence or revolution is unavoidable, for the simple reason that there is absolutely no other device for resolving the confrontation that arises out of the rights of *both* the working classes and the bourgeoisie. Revolution is an unavoidable historical necessity. It is a logically reasonable event.

50   employed in a highly-respectable dressmaking establishment, exploited by a lady with the pleasant name of Elise. The old, often-told story, was once more recounted. This girl worked, on an average, 16½ hours, during the season often 30 hours, without a break, whilst her failing labour-power was revived by occasional supplies of sherry, port, or coffee. It was just now the height of the season. It was necessary to conjure up in the twinkling of an eye the gorgeous dresses for the noble ladies bidden to the ball in honour of the newly imported Princess of Wales. Mary Ann Walkley had worked without intermission for 26½ hours, with 60 other girls, 30 in one room, that only afforded ⅓ of the cubic feet of air required for them. At night, they slept in pairs in one of the stifling holes into which the bedroom was divided by partitions of board. And this was one of the best millinery establishments in London. Mary Anne Walkley fell ill on Friday, died on Sunday, without, to the astonishment of Madame Elise, having previously completed the work at hand.[23]

There was not much new in the fact that there existed in the world people who were poor and oppressed and others who were not. What concerned Marx was the problem of finding the natural source of poverty, the locus of oppression. He found it within the economic structure.[24] Ultimately, according to Marx, poverty was a condition that came out of the ways in which the means of production for any given society were used to meet the needs of the people. Unlike earlier religiously grounded explanations for the plight of the impoverished, Marx's theory neither excused nor condemned poverty as a moral flaw. The poor were not poor because they were lacking moral virtues; nor were the wealthy granted their exalted lives because they were morally superior. In the world of Marx, the distinction between the poor and the wealthy had come about through the operation of impersonal and natural forces that worked within the give and take of economic practices. The moral order rested on the economic structure and was essentially a rationalization of that structure. Therefore, moral action could not be separated from economic action. The day and age of simple moralizing had passed. It was not enough to condemn the poor as people lacking in the moral virtues necessary for a better life. The time had come to deal with moral issues from a broader perspective. The human moral condition was taken out of the church and into the marketplace.

The Marxist Vision

It is too easy to dismiss Marx because some of his predictions about the collapse of capitalistic countries did not come true in quite the manner he anticipated. Prophets in the realm of economic and social affairs,

---

[23] *Capital,* pp. 280–281.
[24] It must be kept in mind that naturalistic philosophy prevailed in Europe in the nineteenth century. It seems obvious today to find the causes of poverty within economic systems. Actually, the causes of poverty are not at all obvious—even within a naturalistic framework. Marx did, however, pretty much kill the argument that poverty is a moral condition and that wealth, in and of itself, is indicative of superior moral fiber.

whether Marxist or capitalistic, have an all too well-known record of miscalculations and erroneous forecasts. If we condemn Marx because he was not perfect in his forecasts, then we must condemn any other social visionary as well.

It is difficult at times to determine why some American industrialists are so anti-Marxist. Most of them, as we suggested before, take an economic approach to history—to the extent they might be concerned with the interpretation of history. Most of them think that money is essentially what makes the world go around. Marx would agree. Most of them are inclined to believe that satisfying physical needs through production, more production, and still more production is the highest thing one can work for in life. In some ways Marx would still be inclined to agree. Where, then, is the cleavage? What is it about Marxist doctrine that is so distressing to many Americans?

The answer, we believe, lies in the vision Marx offered of a world in which people would be judged by the worth of their labor rather than by the more spurious forms of worth that could be obtained through the control of wealth. A person who has inherited a million dollars from a father or mother and who has not, since the inheritance, done a lick of work, is an object of contempt to the Marxist. Such people were looked upon by Marx as parasites. It is good and (we cannot help adding the term here) proper invective. American capitalism, despite demurrers to the contrary, has always been ambivalent about work. It is good. And yet it is something for suckers. But the Marxist vision is grounded in a belief in the value of work and the worth of all forms of human labor. So it is that the Chinese send their intellectuals into the rice paddies to find out about aching backs and muddy feet. Possibly it is this aspect of the Marxist vision that chills the American sophisticate.

Whether this is true or not, there is no denying the impact that the Marxist vision has had on the world. It has produced in our time several major national bureaucracies that are surprisingly free of corruption. It has produced a nearly puritanical morality in social and economic systems that, before being transformed by the Marxist vision, were corrupt and ineffective. We are witnessing today a historical epoch in which the forces opposed to the Marxist vision stand in somewhat the same position as those countries which stood opposed to the Protestant Reformation.

Marxism is an essential part of the studies of anyone who is going into economics, sociology, anthropology, political science, or any of the other areas of humanistic interest. Marx offers one of the finer models of how to cope with a social or economic concern. He was thorough in his examination of the facts. He was broad in his historical perspectives. He developed a theme or theory in which the historical progression of a variety of events could be systematized. These are essential features of any powerful approach to social issues. But there is something else in Marx's writings that gives them special vigor in this day and age of social objectivity. There is a sense of moral dedication and outrage. Marx documented that the nineteenth-century road to progress was paved with decadence, corruption, and suffering. He not only described the

52   social illnesses of his time, he also prescribed what was needed if real progress was to be achieved. No other person in modern times has had as powerful an impact on the course of the world's political, social, and economic future.

Problems and Issues

The controversies and conflicts that have spread through the world because of Karl Marx are legion. No writer in modern times has come so close to the heart of major social issues and expressed them in a way that has divided people so forcefully into one camp or another. The issues are relatively simple and clear cut. One is concerned with the distribution of wealth. There are four ways in which wealth can be distributed: (1) to each according to need; (2) to each according to want; (3) to each according to what is earned; (4) to each according to what can be taken—by whatever means. Most people appear to subscribe to the idea that people should get what they earn. It is a Marxian position. Social injustice constitutes, as its most pernicious form, the exploitation of those who work by those who have the power to exploit them. What is a proper basis for the distribution of wealth? Is the American system of distributing wealth democratic, fair, and just? How is it that someone who picks vegetables and serves the community gets little income, while one who serves no useful purpose—such as a champion golfer—may earn millions?

Another issue arises out of the fact that Marx focused attention on the class structure as no other writer before him was able to do. Instead of idealizing the members of the upper classes, Marx described them as parasites who lived in luxury only because they had stolen from the working classes that which belonged to the working classes. Much upper-class wealth is inherited and therefore is unearned. If you believe that people should only have that which they have earned, how do you deal with the problem of inheritance? This is no simple or light question. American democratic ideals sprang, in part, from the injustices that derived from the feudal system in which power was inherited. In America money is power and to inherit money and the power associated with it is to participate in a social and economic system that is closer to feudalism than it is to democracy. On the other hand, the denial of inheritance does not seem reasonable either. How do we deal with the problem of inherited wealth and power?

Marx dealt with the problem of labor—the exploitation of labor, the value of labor, the idealization of labor. It remains a problem for us today. At first the distinction between leisure and labor appears to be an easy one. Further thinking about the matter reveals that defining the nature and character of work is really rather difficult. For example, is work simply any activity at which one makes a living? If so, then some people would have to be called workers who engage in little more exertion than clipping the coupons on their stocks and bonds. Is a professional boxer really a worker?

What kind of conception of work did Marx offer the world? (We are reminded, in this discussion, of a little lady who asked a young graduate student "Do you work? *Or are you going to school?") What is the American attitude toward work?*

Marx is commonly thought of as a "materialist." That is, he believed that people are basically influenced by how they deal with the problems of the material world. At the same time, we are aware today that people often seek material goods for their "symbolic" or "status" value. What does it mean to be a materialist? In what ways are capitalistic ideologists and Marxists similar in thought? Where do they differ?

The Sacred and the Profane

An Introduction to

EMILE DURKHEIM

Society is a reality sui generis; *it has its own peculiar characteristics, which are not found elsewhere and which are not met with again in the same form in all the rest of the universe.*

Elementary Forms of the Religious Life

BORN: 1858   DIED: 1917

4 The social world is "invisible." That is to say, social relationships are usually not perceived directly by any of our senses; they can only be known by learning the meaning of the relationships to the participants. To a surprising extent, many people, including some who should know better, think they can "see" social happenings. For example, when asked if they have ever seen a family, students in introductory courses quickly, and with few exceptions, reply in the affirmative. Of course they have "seen" families—after all, have they not lived in one for the past eighteen or nineteen years?

Although students think they know a family when they "see" one, they really do not. The point is simple to make, and its implications, as we shall presently note, are quite profound. Suppose we observe a young man walking down the street with his arm around the waist of a young woman; toddling behind them are several children. We immediately think we are looking at a "family." However, this collection of individuals might in no way constitute a family. Perhaps we are looking at an unmarried man and woman who have been baby-sitting for a neighbor; or they might be related or unrelated in a variety of other

ways, none involving kin associations. We have no way of knowing **55**
whether they constitute a family unless we ask them or unless we examine credentials that might certify them as a bona fide family.

Observation of the Invisible

It comes as a mild shock to most people to be told that the entire web
of human social interrelations is founded on many invisible and indirect
meanings that we bestow on various individuals. Not only have we never
seen a family, we have never seen a student or a teacher. Nor have we
ever seen a scientist, a saint, or a sinner. So it is with all socially defined
statuses. We can observe the people who occupy such statuses,[1] but
until we are informed that they occupy a certain status and we are
expected to behave accordingly, we cannot respond in an appropriate
manner.

The social world is, then, largely an invisible world. This constitutes
a major methodological problem for the sociologist.[2] Sociology is supposed to be a science; and science, after all, is based on observation.
What kind of science is it that devotes itself to an examination of events
that are, by their very nature, not directly observable? We shall not
belabor this question for long. Let it suffice, for the moment, to mention
that many sciences (high-energy physics for one) believe that it is valid
to rely on indirect observations. The problem the invisibility of social
identities poses for scientific sociology must be left to weightier methodological treatises.[3] We will pass it by and move into the more engaging
substantive implications of the invisible nature of the social world.

Social Influences: Effects and Interpretation

Let us begin by establishing two fundamental and realistic principles.
The first of these is that social influences, though not directly observable,
may have observable effects. We cannot, for example, directly observe
those ideas and involvements that lead people into wars, but we can
observe the aftermath of a bombing raid. We can say, then, that even

---

[1] Some epistemologists and philosophers would even dispute this contention, but we do
not need to go into such cloudy flights here.

[2] This, of course, is not only a problem for the sociologist; every social scientist must cope
with it. The cultural anthropologist, for example, is concerned as a scientist with the
meanings which different events and things have for people in primitive societies. A true
understanding of these can come only from an extensive "immersion" in the culture. One
cannot merely observe what is happening at a physical or behavioral level and fully comprehend its anthropological value.

[3] Sociology certainly cannot be said to suffer from a lack of investigations into methodology;
it perhaps suffers from an excessive concern with methods. As one writer commented,
sociology is the field with the most methods and the fewest results. If this condition is so,
it is a testimonial to the problems that exist in observing what we think we are observing
when we talk about human social behavior.

56   though social forces remain hidden, they are nonetheless "real." They are real because they are real in their effects. If the invisibility of social forces appears to deny validity to the efforts of social scientists, the real consequences of social involvements give their work a scientific justification. Science, after all, is the serious examination of what is real.

It is necessary to mention this first principle because some people want to deny the reality of social forces.[4] Apparently they go by the old maxim that sticks and stones can break one's bones but social meanings will never hurt anyone. We argue, quite to the contrary, that society, though "invisible" and indirect, is powerfully real—and can be malignant as well as benign. It is real because it is real in its consequences.

The second principle we must develop before going on is that the invisible and indirect nature of the social realm makes it subject to considerable interpretation. Social influences daily confront us with the equivalent of "black box" problems. Black box problems are those given to students in electronics, who observe the electrical energies going into and coming out of a mysterious black box and must determine what is in the box on the basis of this information. So it is in society. We are given various kinds of information and perhaps more importantly, misinformation about people, and we must reach some conclusions about what makes them tick the way they do. This second principle—that social behavior is subject to interpretation—is significant because, paradoxically enough, the form the interpretation of social forces will take comes from society itself. This feature of society gives it a power over the individual that it would otherwise lack.

Here is a brief illustration of what is meant by the statement that society provides the form of its own interpretation. In earlier times, persons who behaved peculiarly were likely to be accused of harboring demonic spirits. This was in keeping with the religious temper of the times. Today we would be more likely to say that such a person is "sick." There is surprisingly little difference between the two interpretations of what is going on inside the black box. Both kinds of interpretations are ways of legitimizing the use of repressive sanctions against the individual. Both interpretations provide society with a justification for imposing penalties on the person who is violating proper standards of conduct. Both interpretations are capable, to a surprising degree, of blinding us to the moral or external or normal features of the behavior of the person we believe to be possessed of the devil or of sickness. In this way we are armed by socially authorized forms of interpretation with a rationale for injuring others in the name of keeping them in their proper social place. The surprising thing is that this occurs in even the most sophisticated and knowledgeable of social orders.

If the fact that the social world is veiled or hidden behind meanings

---

[4] A debate has gone on for years among sociologists as to whether or not society is "real." A very popular technical treatment of this argument appears in a paper by Charles K. Warriner. See "Groups Are Real: An Affirmation," *American Sociological Review* 21 (October 1956), 549–554.

creates problems for the modern social analyst, how much more so must **57**
it generate difficulties for people living in primitive social systems. How
do primitive people respond to the social "black box" problem? How do
they come to grips with complex, indirect, powerful, and invisible forces
of social influence? According to our second principle they must endow
these forces with properties they understand; they must reduce them to
terms that fall within the rhetoric of their culture. Even as we, in a
scientific age, attempt to reduce social forces to the rhetoric of science,
so must primitive people rely on their beliefs, their culturally given
awareness, for social understanding. The end product of the primitive
effort is often a mythology populated by supernatural beings or powers.
The mechanism inside the black box is a spiritual force. This, in a very
brief and inadequate condensation, is the argument made by Emile Durkheim in *The Elementary Forms of the Religious Life*.[5] This book is possibly the best of his works.[6]

Religion as a Form of Sociology

Durkheim claimed that religion is actually a primitive form of sociology;
religion is an interpreter of the social order and, as such, is also its
fountainhead.

> It is a consistent part of Durkheim's conception of religion that a deity
> expresses in a personal form the power of the society, a power clearly felt,
> though not so consciously defined. God is society "apotheosized"; society
> is the real God. This identity is adumbrated in the totem animal, a "sacred
> object"; and more clearly shown in the personal deity, Jahveh, or Zeus.
> The tribal god is, like the totem animal, often confusedly conceived of as
> a member of the group; another evidence of the close relationship between
> group and deity.[7]

Durkheim, despite his agnostic and scientific mentality, held that
no society could exist independently of religious forms of sentiment and
action. Into any social event there will intrude religious forms of expression. Even science, that most secular and skeptical form of human en-

---

[5] Emile Durkheim, *The Elementary Forms of the Religious Life,* translated by J. W. Swain
(New York: Free Press, 1954). Durkheim's other major works, all published by Free Press,
are *The Division of Labor in Society,* translated by George Simpson (1960); *Education and
Sociology,* translated by S. D. Fox (1956); *Moral Education: A Study in the Theory and
Application of the Sociology of Education,* translated by E. K. Wilson and H. Schnurer
(1961); *The Rules of Sociological Method,* translated by S. A. Solovay and J. H. Mueller
(1950); *Suicide: A Study in Sociology,* translated by J. A. Spaulding and G. Simpson (1951).
[6] See Harry Alpert, *Emile Durkheim and His Sociology* (New York: Columbia University
Press, 1939). Alpert's work is one of the better reviews of Durkheim's contributions to
modern social thought.
[7] Charles Elmer Gehlke, *Emile Durkheim's Contributions to Sociological Theory* (New York:
Columbia University, Longmans, Green Agents, 1915), p. 39.

58 terprise, is not immune to religious modes of thought and conduct. Indeed, to the extent science grows and acquires the character of a "community," we might expect to find it incorporating more of the characteristics of a religious institution.[8]

But what are these characteristics? The most essential, in Durkheim's thought, is the quality of sacredness. Every society distinguishes between the sacred and the profane. This distinction is crucial and highly relevant to sociological understanding, for it is essentially a distinction between the social and the nonsocial. That which is considered sacred in a society is given its awesome or sacred qualities by virtue of its capacity to represent values, sentiments, power, or beliefs that are shared in common—the sacred object comes out of and is supported by the total society. The profane object, on the other hand, is not supported in this manner. It may have considerable utility, but it gains its value primarily from the extent to which it is useful to some individual—it has little or no public relevance.

An illustration may clarify what Durkheim was pointing toward. When Babe Ruth was a living idol to baseball fans, the bat he used to slug his home runs was definitely a profane object. It was Ruth's personal instrument and had little social value *in itself*. Today, however, one of Ruth's bats is enshrined in the Baseball Hall of Fame.[9] It is no longer used by anyone in a profane way. It stands, rather, as an object which in itself represents the values, sentiments, power, and beliefs of all members of the baseball community. What was formerly a profane object is now in the process of gaining some of the qualities of a sacred object.

We purposely selected an illustration here that leads us away from traditional conceptions of sacred objects. Durkheim extended the concept of sacredness in such a manner that we come to see the process whereby the profane is transmuted into the sacred in a wide variety of realms. In the case of the bat in the Baseball Hall of Fame, we have a profane object undergoing a mild and limited form of transmutation into the sacred—it changes from a private object to a public object. In the process it becomes distinctive in quite a special way.

The difference between sacred and profane objects has much to do with a comprehension of the nature of religious institutions. The definitive feature of a church or religious institution resides in the fact that the church is an organized body of people concerned with maintaining and responding to sacred objects.

Thus a definition of religion exists: ". . . an interdependent system of faiths and practices relating to things sacred—that is, to such things as are

---

[8] A sociological investigation of science as a community has some pertinent observations. See Warren O. Hagstrom, *The Scientific Community* (New York: Basic Books, 1965).
[9] The introduction of religious elements into a secular pastime provides some insight into the nature of traditionally religious structures. Such "shrines" as the Baseball Hall of Fame take on some of the qualities of parareligious systems.

separate and proscribed, faiths and practices uniting all their adherents in a single community, known as a Church."[10]

We respond to the sacred object with a sense of awe and respect. This response may, on occasion, be so overwhelming that we think our feelings come from the sacred object itself. This, argued Durkheim, would be a mistake. The reason is fairly simple. Anything and everything imaginable has, at one time or other, served the purpose of being a sacred object. An object that evokes mysterious and serious responses in one person can generate laughter in another.

Because an astounding variety of objects may serve as sacred things, the awesome character of the sacred object must come from outside itself. The sacred object represents or symbolizes something—a force capable of inducing submission, awe, a sense of personal impotence, humility, and powerlessness. The force that is capable of achieving this, in relation to the person, is society. Thus, Durkheim came to the conclusion that the sacred object is actually a symbolic representation of social force.

Following in Durkheim's footsteps, a modern sociologist, Guy Swanson of the University of Michigan, carried the argument further.[11] If the sacred object is a representation of society, and if societies differ in the way they are organized, then some of the socially held conceptions of the nature of the sacred should vary systematically with the way in which the society is ordered. Regrettably, we cannot explore all of the ideas and facts that appear in Swanson's work. We can indicate something of its spirit and its connection with Durkheim's thinking, however, by concentrating on how Swanson demonstrated the connection between monotheistic religious beliefs and a particular type of social structure.

God and the symbols associated with God fall in the realm of the sacred. In fact, it is not especially rare to find religions in which the name of God is so sacred it may not be uttered aloud. What accounts for the forms these ideas take? If Durkheim is correct, there must be some association between a given social structure and the conception of God that exists in that society. Swanson argued that religions organized

---

[10] Maurice Halbwachs, *Sources of Religious Sentiment* (New York: Free Press, 1962), p. 23. Halbwachs was one of Durkheim's most brilliant students. In this book he carefully summarizes, mostly in Durkheim's own words, the central thoughts contained in *The Elementary Forms of the Religious Life*. We would recommend that a student interested in this subject read Halbwachs and then turn to the more elaborate discussion by Durkheim.

[11] Guy E. Swanson, *The Birth of the Gods: The Origin of Primitive Beliefs* (Ann Arbor: University of Michigan Press, 1960). Swanson's argument—and, more significantly, his data—reveal the current vitality of Durkheim's thinking in modern sociology. We once gave a talk about Swanson to a church study group and the Episcopalian priest who led it. The conclusions of the work angered some of the audience, who considered them a threat to their beliefs. However, the priest, a man thoroughly trained in Freudian psychoanalytic theory, said, "Very interesting; now I am aware that God works through society as well as through the mind."

60 around the concept of a single God evolved out of societies with particular organizational difficulties that develop as a society becomes more complex.

At this point, before we can begin to understand something of the Durkheim-Swanson argument, it is necessary to introduce a qualification. When we talk of monotheism we must be aware that we are rarely talking about religious conceptions that involve only one God. Usually we are referring to religions that involve a number of gods, spirits, and heavenly beings, with a supreme God or heavenly being standing above this spiritual host. Instead of using the term *monotheism*, Swanson uses the term *high-god religions*. Our own Judeo-Christian religious beliefs provide us with a high-god religion of this type. There is not only a supreme God, but there is Satan, also a powerful god, who rivals the ultimate forces of the spiritual world. More significantly, and more notable to the sociologist, Satan is essentially a disruptive force—a constant threat to the solidarity and smooth operation of the community. The intercession of God Himself is usually required to keep Satan from wrecking the life of any individual and the community that individual serves.[12]

Now we can come back to Swanson's work and rephrase our question slightly: At what point in a society's development does the concept of a high-god begin to appear in that society's religious beliefs and practices?[13] Swanson, again on the basis of an extension of Durkheim's thinking, suggests that a high-god appears when organizational elements within a society begin to conflict with each other and bring about the demand for a higher authority which can resolve these conflicts. Thus, a society organized on a strictly kinship basis, where the family is the principal organizing agency and has no other agencies conflicting with it, will have no conception of a high-god. The character of the society does not require it. Such a society might believe in a diffused spiritual force, sometimes called *mana*,[14] or it might have other religious conceptions, but the idea of a high-god would not appear.

Also, for theoretical reasons too involved to go into here, a society comprised of two major organizational groupings will not have a conception of a high-god. However, when we get into the realm of three or more major organizational groupings, we move into a situation where one of the groupings must become dominant over the other two and must function to resolve conflicts between subordinate major components of the society. Thus, a society organized into kinship units which, in turn, are parts of tribes which, in their turn, are parts of a still higher

[12] We concede that Satan is a more complex personality than we have made him out here. He is not always directly disruptive. For example, in the story *The Devil and Daniel Webster*, Satan offers wealth, position, and a life of happiness for Webster's soul. Presumably Satan may thereby build up his power within the spiritual realm and then prove even more disruptive later on.

[13] We have used the phrase "At what point in a society's *development* . . ." This makes Swanson sound more evolutionary than the specific facts of his study would warrant. We have done this in the interest of making a very complicated point in a relatively brief space. Technically speaking, Swanson's study is cross-sectional rather than longitudinal.

[14] Swanson, *The Birth of the Gods*, pp. 6–10.

level of organization—such as a kingdom or nation—will be likely to have a religion that involves the idea of a high-god. The concept of a high-god is a manifestation of the organizational characteristics of the society.

All of this has been highly speculative and abstract. We are still left with the question: Is there any way of demonstrating whether this is true or not? Swanson's work indicates that there is a way. Moreover, Swanson's demonstration suggests that Durkheim was correct in his speculations.

To test the Swanson-Durkheim theory concerning high-god religions, Swanson obtained data from 39 primitive cultures and examined their social structure and their religious beliefs. With the aid of several assistants, Swanson divided these cultures into those that had religions involving the concept of a high-god and those that did not. The cultures were also divided into those having a "simple" social structure involving only one or two sovereign groups and those with "complex" structures involving three or more sovereign groups.

According to the theory, the idea of a high-god should appear only in the cultures with complex social structures. Cultures with simple social structures should not have high-god religions. When Swanson ordered his facts he obtained the following distribution of cultures (see Table 4-1).[15]

So out of the 39 cultures examined by Swanson, 34 conformed to the theory and 5 deviated. Statistical tests by Swanson indicated that the amount of conformity to the theory was much greater than we might reasonably expect simply by accident. Therefore, the facts do not give us cause to reject Durkheim's general theoretical position.

Swanson, advancing further the theoretical perspectives of Durkheim, investigated such other aspects of religious belief as the idea of a morally concerned God, witchcraft, the existence of the soul, and similar concepts. He found them also to be related to different features of the social structure. We cannot go into these demonstrations here. Exciting as Swanson's research is, we must leave it and return to Durkheim.

4-1 *Social Structure and Religious Belief*

	NUMBER OF SOVEREIGN GROUPS	
High-god	*Simple—1 or 2*	*Complex—3 or more*
Present	2 (against theory)	17 (for theory)
Absent	17 (for theory)	3 (against theory)

[15] Ibid., p. 65. This is a slightly modified version of Swanson's table.

62   *Moral Order and Social Structure*

We began with Durkheim's speculations on religion because they quickly lead us to the heart of his understanding of society. For Durkheim, the only legitimate approach to a comprehension of the nature of social order is by an examination of morality. Because morality and religious thought are so closely conjoined in primitive societies, the investigation of primitive religious thought can be especially revealing to the sociologist. In modern society the relationship between moral order and religious practice is more tenuous, but this does not diminish the value of examining moral force as a means of comprehending human social nature.

> But if there is one fact that history has irrefutably demonstrated it is that the morality of each people is directly related to the social structure of the people practicing it. The connection is so intimate that, given the general character of the morality observed in a given society and barring abnormal and pathological cases, one can infer the nature of that society, the elements of its structure and the way it is organized. Tell me the marriage patterns, the morals dominating family life, and I will tell you the principal characteristics of its organization.[16]

In his doctoral dissertation, published ten years before the above statement appeared, Durkheim presented, at great length, the rationale underlying his claim. This work, entitled *The Division of Labor in Society*, reveals that a superb sociologist can hold views of society as radically different from those of the common man as are the views of physical reality held by the best physicists. We can give some hint of the radical nature of Durkheim's thought by presenting his views on crime.

Crime, Durkheim believed, is a natural consequence of the existence of a collectively supported morality. Crime is therefore a natural part of *any* social order because any social order requires a collectively supported morality. In itself this thesis does not seem radical or inventive—but it quickly leads to a more comprehensive understanding of the nature of criminal action than we can arrive at through biological or even psychological approaches to criminal behavior.

One of the perplexing aspects of criminal action noted by Durkheim is the fact that it is often behavior that does not appear to be directly harmful to society or to any individual. As Durkheim wrote,

> What social danger is there in touching a tabooed object, an impure animal or man, in letting the sacred fire die down, in eating certain meats, in failure to make the traditional sacrifice over the graves of parents, in not

[16] Emile Durkheim, *Moral Education*, p. 87. In 1887 Durkheim began his distinguished 30-year-long career at the University of Bordeaux. This was the first time a French university offered a course in social science. Five years later he moved to the Sorbonne—the University of Paris—where he spent the remainder of his life. Durkheim taught not only social science but pedagogy, and he taught these subjects jointly throughout his career. (See Alpert, *Emile Durkheim and His Sociology*, p. 43).

exactly pronouncing the ritual formula, in not celebrating certain holidays, etc.?[17]

We cannot, then, simple-mindedly define crime as behavior that is directly injurious to the physical safety of the members of a society. There are too many exceptions to such a definition. Even more notably, there are many cases of crimes which, though physically injurious, are less seriously punished than crimes that violate an exotic code—and Durkheim makes much of this fact. A modern example of what we are talking about is the fact that a white man, in the United States of America, who kills a black man is likely to be less severely punished than a black man who rapes a white woman.

We have to give up the whole idea that crime is a simple form of injury to society when we consider further that some actions that are capable of completely disrupting the entire society often carry no criminal onus at all. A stock market collapse, for example, can disorganize the social body overwhelmingly—but it is not viewed as a criminal act.[18] A man may give serious consideration to an action that he has some reason to believe might result in the deaths of thousands of people and yet be applauded as a hero rather than a potential criminal of fantastic magnitude.[19] Crime is not, then, something actually or potentially physically harmful to society. Marvin Harris answers Durkheim in an interesting manner. In his book, *Cows, Pigs, Wars and Witches,* Harris disagrees with Durkheim.[20] Durkheim asks:

> Shall we say [in modifying our conception of crime] that criminal acts are those which *seem* harmful to the society that represses them, that penal rules express, not the conditions which are essential to social life, but those which *appear* such to the group which observes them?[21]

This would seem to be an easy way out of the matter—but Durkheim refuses to accept the gambit. There is more to it than that. This solution, appealing though it is, does not really get us anywhere because it does not tell us why societies have introduced rules that are apparently use-

---

[17] Durkheim, *The Division of Labor in Society,* p. 72.
[18] Ibid. This is Durkheim's example. The objection might be raised that a market collapse does not involve intent to engage in crime. Durkheim would reply that in all probability most societies have not, throughout history, been concerned with intent in reacting to criminal action.
[19] We are thinking, here, of the following news item, which appeared in the May 13, 1967, issue of the *New York Times:* "Washington, May 12.—It may have sounded ominous, but to the White House it was just a regrettable coincidence that no amount of explanation could overcome . . . . What had been for months President Johnson's personal story . . . suddenly broke into print today. . . . On the women's page of the *Washington Post*—a staple in the news diet of every foreign diplomat here—[a news item] read, 'President Johnson told his daughter, Luci, last June, "Your daddy may go down in history as having started World War III. . . ."' He felt he had no alternative, he said . . . and he felt he had taken all possible precautions to limit the effects, but there was reason to worry."
[20] Harris, Marvin, *Cows, Pigs, Wars and Witches,* New York: Vintage Press, 1974.
[21] Durkheim, *The Division of Labor in Society,* p. 73.

64 less. The important thing is to find out why various rules are considered vitally necessary—even when no direct connection between the rules and the viability of the society can be ascertained. Why, for example, was the medieval church so morbidly interested in sexual delinquency? Anthropological studies have revealed numerous societies that sustained themselves admirably with sexual patterns the church would have condemned as highly perverse and disruptive.[22]

The problem is resolved if we can comprehend the extent to which Durkheim is able to distinguish between the form and the content of social action. Though many rules seemingly have little connection with the efficient operation of a society, they may, through the possibility of their violation, remain as standards of the effectiveness of the moral force of the total society. In this respect, it makes little difference what the rule might be. Indeed, the more powerful the moral force of the total society, the more arbitrary the rules of the system can be and still serve as standards of the strength of that force.

This kind of reasoning enabled Durkheim to make an unusual observation concerning the nature of crime. He asserted:

> We must not say that an action shocks the common conscience because it is criminal, but rather that it is criminal because it shocks the common conscience. We do not reprove it because it is a crime, but it is a crime because we reprove it.[23]

Murder is a classical illustration of Durkheim's argument. Murder receives whatever criminal status it acquires according to the extent to which it is reproved by society—not because murder in itself calls for its own evaluation as a moral affront. There are occasions, even in our own contemporary society, where murder, broadly defined as taking the life of another against that person's will, is not reproved and is not, therefore, criminal. Police have, at times, beaten prisoners to death without arousing any great sense of moral indignation in the community they served.

Criminality, therefore, does not inhere within the specific form of an illegal action but rather in the content of that action when viewed in terms of the affront it offers to the moral conscience of the entire society. Curiously enough, according to Durkheim, the stronger the moral conscience of a society, the more likely we are to find murder less reproved than are acts against the body of rules that exist as the moral authority of the society. Durkheim states:

> Thus, in lower societies, the most numerous delicts are those which relate to public affairs, delicts against religion, against custom, against authority, etc. We need only look at the Bible, the laws of Manou, at the

---

[22] Mead and Calas cite a study which reports the marriage of a Chuckchee shaman to another male in the tribe. The institutional incorporation of homosexual relations did not destroy Chuckchee society. See Margaret Mead and Nicolas Calas, *Primitive Heritage* (New York: Random House, 1953).

[23] Durkheim, *The Division of Labor in Society*, p. 81.

monuments which remain of old Egyptian law to see the relatively small place accorded to prescriptions for the protection of individuals, and, contrariwise, the luxuriant development of repressive legislation concerning the different forms of sacrilege, the omission of certain religious duties, the demands of ceremonial, etc. At the same time, these crimes are the most severely punished. Among the Jews, the most abominable attacks are those against religion. Among the ancient Germans, only two crimes were punished by death according to Tacitus: treason and desertion. According to Confucius and Meng-tseu, impiety is a greater crime than murder. In Egypt, the smallest sacrilege was punished by death.[24]

Crime is behavior that has its meaning only because it violates the moral sentiments of society. It is a threat to the integrity of those sentiments and, as a consequence, produces a reaction. It is in the reaction that Durkheim comprehended the distinction between collective force and the nature of the individual. The general reaction to crime is punishment; but the significant thing about punishment is the extent to which it is carried out.

Capital punishment is a case in point. If criminals were to "pay society" for their misdeeds by giving their lives, then it would seem sufficient merely to take their lives in the simplest and most direct manner possible. But this is not done, even in modern and presumably enlightened cultures. There is an institutionalized form of harassment that goes with taking a criminal's life. There are demeaning actions that seem to have the purpose not only of taking the criminal's life but of taking the criminal's humanity as well. Individuals may, for example, have to spend their final hours in a cell which is lighted twenty-four hours a day. They may have to remain in the continuous presence of a guard. Their heads may be shaved. They may have to wear shabby clothes and experience other forms of humiliation. The taking of life is not enough.

A Durkheimian view suggests that our judicial system possibly errs on the side of oversentimentalism in some matters. There is a peculiar illogic in taking people convicted of the same crime and placing some of them in a hospital because they are "insane" and others in a prison because they are "normal." What we are doing in such instances is confessing that, since an individual is normal, what brought about the commission of the crime is not evidently an inherent serious defect in character. It must, therefore, have been something else, and the only other reasonable thing left is social circumstance. But social circumstances cannot be held culpable, and it is necessary to assess culpability. Therefore, one can be guilty of being normal. The sane person may be executed while the insane person is sent to an asylum.

It would seem, if we were being reasonable about this matter, that a person's normalcy would stand as the greatest argument for not punishing that person. Current thinking is evidently based on the idea that a presumably normal person who violates the existing social code threatens, more so than an insane person, the viability of that code. Our

[24] Ibid., p. 93.

66 reaction is not concerned with the welfare of the person who broke the code. Instead, we are concerned with the welfare of the code itself. To the extent the violator is considered normal and yet is subjected to punishment, he or she must be seen as a sacrifice for the welfare of the many. Durkheim would suggest that this is characteristic of all societies.

For Durkheim, extreme and "irrational" qualities of punishment were a clue to the nature of collective sentiments. People are not only concerned with making criminals "pay" through punishment but they are concerned with making criminals an embodiment of suffering that balances some affront to the moral order.

> It is certain that at the bottom of the notion of expiation there is the idea of a satisfaction accorded to some power, real or ideal, which is superior to us. When we desire the repression of crime, it is not we that we desire to avenge personally, but to avenge something sacred which we feel more or less confusedly outside and above us. This something we conceive of in different ways according to the time and the place. Sometimes it is a simple idea, as morality, duty; most often we represent it in the form of one or several concrete beings: ancestors, divinity. That is why penal law is not alone essentially religious in origin, but indeed always retains a certain religious stamp. It is because the acts that it punishes appear to be attacks upon something transcendent.[25]

The power of the moral order comes from the fact that it is a collectively held set of beliefs. That is to say, it is a set of strongly held beliefs shared in common by a large number of people—it lies within the public as well as the individual domain. It is essential to understand that it is the collective nature of the moral order which gives it tremendous influence and which elevates it above any single individual. Indeed, the moral order acquires a solidarity *sui generis* (of its own kind). For this reason, crimes are more than an affront to the individual. They are a threat to the solidarity of the moral order, and the reaction is beyond anything which might seem reasonable to a dispassionate observer.

Thus it is that we, from our present disengaged vantage point, can feel a sense of horror when we read the punishment prescribed by the ancient Germans for damaging a tree:

> Sacred groves were common among the ancient Germans, and tree-worship is hardly extinct amongst their descendants at the present day. How serious that worship was in former times may be gathered from the ferocious penalty appointed by the old German laws for such as dared to peel the bark of a standing tree. The culprit's navel was to be cut out and nailed to the part of the tree which he had peeled, and he was to be driven round and round the tree till all his guts were wound about its trunk.[26]

---

[25] Ibid., p. 100.
[26] Sir James G. Frazer, *The Golden Bough* (New York: Macmillan, 1922), p. 127. Note the discrepancy between Frazer's comment and Durkheim's reference to Tacitus cited earlier. According to Durkheim, only treason and desertion were punishable by death among the ancient Germans.

Whether anyone actually had to suffer this dreadful punishment we do not know. Certainly history offers us countless examples of people who were made the objects of obsessive punishments. Even if no one actually experienced this gruesome punitive measure of the ancient Germans, it exemplifies what Durkheim was trying to say. From a modern perspective it seems unthinkable that anyone could want to disembowel a man merely because he damaged a tree. And that is Durkheim's point! The reaction hinted at in this old punishment transcends a rational, objective, and individualistic consideration of the matter. The threat is not to an individual sentiment but to a collectively shared sentiment—and the reaction stems from that collective source, not from an individual source. So it is that we must come to understand crime and punishment as actions and reactions taking place at a collective level.

Durkheim's considerations of crime are actually a means of entering into a greater matter—an examination of the changing nucleus of social order. Repressive punishment occurs when the solidity of a society comes from its collective commitment to a moral order of some kind. By sharing similar beliefs, traditions, and moral sentiments people are kept together. But this form of social integration is in the process of being supplanted by another. The key to this is the fact that repressive punishment has been steadily declining in severity. Taking its place is punishment more concerned with the attainment of restitution than with making an example through torture.

The Division of Labor and Social Structure

If this is so—if we are witnessing the decline of social organization based on moral consensus—then what is the basis of the newer forms of social order? The answer, says Durkheim, is social order based increasingly on a complex interweaving of highly specialized and discrete units which, together, make up an organic whole, somewhat as the separate and specialized organs of the body make up an individual.[27]

Such a society, organized on the basis of the division of labor, acquires an increasing amount of differentiation between its parts.[28] As this division occurs, the moral basis that forms the common sentiments underlying the society grows broader but does not cease to exist. The violent forms of reaction which characterize its existence in primitive

---

[27] Durkheim was careful to probe further than a simple physiological analogy would suggest. Indeed, he went to great lengths to show the limitations of a biological model for the analysis of society. Durkheim stated: "The division of social labor is distinguished from the division of physiological labor by an essential characteristic. In the organism, each cell has its defined role, and cannot change it. In societies, tasks have never been so immutably distributed." See *The Division of Labor in Society*, p. 329.

[28] Some idea of the extent of this differentiation in the modern United States can be ascertained by a quick reference to the *Dictionary of Occupational Titles*. It currently lists more than 35,550 job titles.

68 cultures give way to reproval of a more feeble sort. A congressman who violates the codes of ethics of Congress, such as they are, is not drawn and quartered and his head placed on a pike for all to witness. He may receive a censure or, at most, be ousted from office. Of societies organized on the basis of a division of labor, Durkheim said,

> even where society relies most completely upon the division of labor, it does not become a jumble of juxtaposed atoms, between which it can establish only external, transient contacts. Rather the members are united by ties which extend deeper and far beyond the short moments during which the exchange is made. Each of the functions they exercise is, in a fixed way, dependent upon others, and with them forms a solidary system. Accordingly, from the nature of the chosen task permanent duties arise. Because we fill some certain domestic or social function, we are involved in a complex of obligations from which we have no right to free ourselves. There is, above all, an organ upon which we are tending to depend more and more; this is the State. The points at which we are in contact with it multiply as do the occasions when it is entrusted with the duty of reminding us of the sentiment of common solidarity.[29]

The division of labor, specialization, the integration of highly differentiated parts—this is a later basis of social solidarity that comes out of and moves alongside the older moral basis. The division of labor is a second ring of force in a nucleus which has the moral order at its core. This theme, the reality and force of the collectively supported moral order, is dominant in Durkheim's thinking and appears throughout all his work. It provides the foundation for his masterful investigation into the nature of suicide. So brilliantly did Durkheim execute this combination of theory and research that it is even today lauded as a model of investigation in social science—though Durkheim published the work in 1897.[30]

Suicide and Its Relation to Social Forces

But why would Durkheim, a man interested in the nature of social organizations, be concerned with something as individualistic as suicide? The answer is that suicide provided Durkheim with a subject matter that permitted him to carry off a tour de force. If Durkheim's sociological perspectives permitted him to bring new understanding to that most individualistic of all acts—suicide—then sociology would be forcefully

---

[29] Durkheim, *The Division of Labor in Society,* p. 227.
[30] Durkheim, *Suicide.* For a work published in 1897 concerning human social nature, this book is astonishingly sophisticated. One need only compare it with more run-of-the-mill social research conducted at the time to see how advanced Durkheim's thought was. This does not mean, however, that Durkheim did not make some serious methodological errors. For a balanced review of Durkheim's effort see Hanaan C. Selvin, "Durkheim's *Suicide:* Further Thoughts on a Methodological Classic," in Robert A. Nisbet's *Emile Durkheim* (Englewood Cliffs, N.J.: Prentice-Hall, 1965), pp. 113–136.

established as a perspective for examining other features of human behavior. How did Durkheim accomplish this demonstration?

It would appear, from a commonsense perspective, that people who have killed themselves have engaged in an act that is about as private and as removed from social approval as can be imagined—and in some instances this is probably so. For Durkheim, however, the issue was whether or not the intrusion of social influences could be found even here—in this most personal and final moment. If the intruding social forces could be found, then a nice case would be made for seeing people as more than the sum of their biological and psychological natures; they would have to be viewed also as captives of social forces extending beyond them and shaping their private fate.[31]

Durkheim began his argument by suggesting that perhaps suicide is such an individualistic act it might not be of interest to a sociologist. Anything which would make suicide demonstrably a result of individualistic conditions would, therefore, negate a sociological consideration of the matter. So, it was necessary at the outset to consider all individualistic factors to determine whether or not they could account for self-inflicted deaths.

> But is [suicide] of interest to the sociologist? Since suicide is an individual action affecting the individual only, it must seemingly depend exclusively on individual factors, thus belonging to psychology alone. Is not the suicide's resolve usually explained by his temperament, character, antecedents and private history?[32]

Note here that Durkheim began by recognizing the theoretical position he intended to oppose. He was aware that he had to develop it thoroughly before he could enter into a discussion of the social perspective he endorsed.

The first psychological argument he took into account was the possibility that suicide is a product of insanity, of mental imbalance, of some derangement of a person's abilities. To refute this argument, Durkheim obtained data from hospitals for the mentally ill. He observed that the proportion of women in such hospitals was very slightly greater than the proportion of men. This being the case, he argued, we ought to expect suicide resulting from insanity to occur as often among women as among men. Suicide rates indicated, however, that men are three to four times as prone to commit suicide as are women.[33]

Durkheim then examined the extent to which the incidence of insanity varied among Protestants, Catholics, and Jews, He found that

---

[31] Durkheim is often viewed as an "anti-psychological" writer. This is not entirely correct. It is more fair to say he was concerned with getting people to recognize the value of social as well as biological and psychological factors in human affairs.

[32] Durkheim, *Suicide*, p. 46.

[33] Durkheim relied to a great extent, in this study of suicide, on what are today called "ecological" correlations. These are very tricky measures of association. See W. S. Robinson's article, "Ecological Correlations and the Behavior of Individuals," *American Sociological Review* 15 (June 1950), 351–357.

70   Jews were more likely to experience mental disorders than were Protestants and Catholics. However, despite this, the Jewish people had
lower suicide rates. From this Durkheim concluded that suicide varies in
inverse proportion to psychopathic states rather than being consistent
with them.[34]

But insanity is only one individualistic possibility. There are others.
Perhaps, suggested Durkheim, alcoholism is a factor in suicide. Durkheim quickly discounted this by comparing maps of the distribution of
suicides in France with maps showing the distribution of prosecutions
for alcoholism. There was no relationship between the two.

If abnormal psychological conditions and alcoholism do not account
for suicide, perhaps there are yet other nonsocial influences which do.
Race, for example, might have an effect on suicide. Durkheim did not
have much racial variation among the nationalities he studied, but he
showed great ingenuity in his analysis of the facts that were available at
the time. Taking the Germans as a racial type[35] he observed that in
different Austrian provinces the proportion of Germans varied from very
high to very low. If the racial factor were important, Durkheim said, then
suicide rates should vary along with the proportions of Germans in the
provinces. But the suicide rates behaved very erratically in conjunction
with Durkheim's racial factor. For example, provinces with very high
proportions of Germans had both high and low suicide rates. Provinces
with very low proportions of Germans also had high and low suicide
rates. Durkheim concluded that race did not affect suicide.

Yet another class of nonsocial influences remained to be considered. Perhaps the physical environment had an effect on suicide. Possibly
climate or weather might determine or at least be associated with self-
destruction. Here Durkheim ran into a problem because the facts did
support a relationship between seasonal changes in weather and the
occurrence of suicide.

> The monthly variations [in the incidence of suicide] obey the following
> law, found in all European countries: Beginning with January inclusive, the
> incidence of suicide increases regularly from month to month until about
> June and regularly decreases from that time to the end of the year.[36]

But any number of other social activities follow the same law. Railroad
receipts are greatest in the summer and lowest in the winter. Accidents
increase in the summer and decline in the winter. Crime increases in the
summer and decreases in the winter.[37] Durkheim admitted there was a

---

[34] This is Durkheim's wording. See *Suicide,* p. 72.
[35] Durkheim is using what would today be considered an ethnic or national type and not
a racial type. Germans are part of a broader Caucasian racial grouping which includes most
of the people of Europe who were included in Durkheim's data.
[36] Durkheim, *Suicide,* p. 111.
[37] Someone once observed that sex crimes were associated with ice cream consumption—
that is, the more ice cream consumed in a community during a month, the larger the
number of sex crimes. The explanation, of course, is that both ice cream consumption and
sex crimes are associated with warmer weather.

relationship but then discounted its significance by claiming that weather is simply associated with human activity in general. Because suicide is one form of human activity, it happens to vary with the weather.

Finally, Durkheim considered the possibility that suicide is a product of imitation or of mass contagion—one commits suicide because it is a fad. The evidence and arguments Durkheim used to dispense with this suggestion are too lengthy to dwell upon here. However, he made a comment that sums up his rejection of imitation as an explanation of suicide:

> Certain authors, ascribing to imitation a power it does not possess, have demanded that the printing of reports of suicides and crimes in the newspapers be prohibited. . . . Actually, what may contribute to the growth of suicide or murder is not talking of it but how it is talked of. Where such acts are loathed, the feelings they arouse penetrate the recital of them and thus offset rather than encourage individual inclinations. But inversely, when society is morally decadent, its state of uncertainty inspires in it an indulgence for immoral acts frankly expressed whenever they are discussed, and which obscures their immorality. Then example becomes truly dangerous not as example but because the revulsion it should inspire is reduced by social tolerance or indifference.[38]

What Durkheim has said is that people do not blindly imitate actions that occur around them. Instead, they are more likely to follow or to imitate behavior that is highly valued. But this changes the character of the problem. If this is so, then we must ask why societies come to value some forms of behavior and not others. We must also consider the position of the individual with respect to the possibility of attaining valued forms of social behavior. What happens, for example, when a man endows his life with meaning in terms of some code of conduct and then is not permitted to live in the manner he has come to feel is important to him? If, under these circumstances, he commits suicide, it is certainly not imitative. It may, to the contrary, be a reaction to a denial to conform to a socially prescribed code.

We have not, in the above paragraphs, done justice to the patience and thoroughness of Durkheim's consideration of views which he felt were in error. We have, through his example, made one point, however. In the examination of human social conduct it is necessary to be as aware as possible of all existing relevant arguments and know the evidence that supports them.

Having considered positions contrary to his own, Durkheim went on to develop his sociological interpretation of suicide. He believed that the cause of suicide lies somewhere in the relationship existing between the individual and the moral order constituting the society of which he or she is a member. This relationship can vary in nature and, accordingly, the individual is variously subject to inclinations toward suicide.

First Durkheim considered the case where the individual is related

---

[38] Durkheim, *Suicide*, p. 141.

72   to the moral order in a normally binding way, but the moral order itself
contains within it ideas that make one see oneself as separated from it.
For example, it is possible for some forms of moral order to place greater
reliance on the individual—to make the individual responsible for his or
her own affairs. In this event, the people do not have recourse to the
community when things go wrong. They are personally accountable.
Such people, said Durkheim, will be more likely to commit suicide than
will those who believe they can turn to the community for support when
they make errors. Suicide coming from this sense of individualism—of
a belief in freedom from the constraining moral order—he called *egoistic*
X   *suicide*. Durkheim felt he had evidence to support this position by observing that suicide rates were higher among Protestants than among
Catholics. The former religion placed people more on their own—freeing
them from institutional constraints to a greater extent and making them
vulnerable to the limitations of their own ego.

A second kind of relationship between the individual and the moral
order that Durkheim considered was one in which there is an intense
binding of the individual to society. In this instance one is so closely tied
into the social group and is so much a part of the moral order that one
is willing to give one's life for it. Suicide of this kind, Durkheim noted,
still exists in the army and in those cultures that impose ancient forms
of obedience. The rite of *hara-kiri* exemplifies this form of suicide. Durk-
X   heim used the term *altruistic suicide* to refer to this phenomenon.

The best example we can relate of altruistic suicide is a celebrated
incident in Japanese history which occurred early in the seventeenth
century and is known as the "Tale of the Forty-seven *Ronin*." This incident involved forty-seven *samurai* warriors who cunningly avenged the
death of their master, a minor lord, who had committed *hara-kiri* after
being insulted by an official in the *shogun's* palace. The *samurai* retainers
of the *daimyo* killed the official of the *shogun* and then, according to
their code, met together in a grove after the assassination. There each
of the forty-seven men killed himself.

The distinction between egoistic and altruistic suicide is not always
a clear one, yet it seems necessary. The suicide of a man who feels
despondent and guilty because he believes he personally has done a
wrong and there is no absolution seems different in kind from that of
the *samurai* warriors who found honor in death.

Finally, Durkheim isolated a third form of suicide, which he called
X   *anomic suicide*. Anomic suicide, described in quite unacademic terms,
is suicide resulting from the pain or disorientation that comes when we
are pushed out of whatever social rut we have fallen into. As a person
matures within a society he or she comes to develop a social character
that is comfortable and acquires a conception of the moral order that
gives stability and meaning to the person's life. Various things can disrupt
this. A poor person, for example, might suddenly fall heir to great wealth.
Rather than finding the riches a blessing, the person might feel alienated
from former impoverished friends while remaining unacceptable to the
established rich—the classical Eliza Doolittle bind. This condition Durkheim referred to as *anomie*—a state of normlessness, of being pushed

into a realm where the rules are either ill-defined, contradictory, or lacking. In such circumstances a person, torn away from the regulative influences of society, finds life unbearable. The result is anomic suicide. Durkheim felt that the higher rate of suicide during times of economic crisis and among divorced persons supported his contention.

By relating suicide to social systems, Durkheim validated the sociological perspective in an almost sensational manner. He was wrong in many particulars, but the tour de force was accomplished nonetheless. After Durkheim it became impossible to view the individual as an autonomous being or society as merely the individual's biological nature extended over the landscape. Society had peculiar qualities which came about from the nature of social organization itself. Society was a condition *sui generis*. While society was, in general, beneficial to people and had enabled them to survive and achieve a dominant state on this planet, it still exacted a cost. Society enabled the majority to live, and, paradoxically, was the cause of death for a minority.

Durkheim in Perspective

Durkheim worked at the end of a century of magnificent scientific achievements, two of which should be mentioned here. Above all, the end of the nineteenth century was the age of Darwin and, as a result, it was an age when humanity was being placed in truer biological perspective. But the obsession to divest people of their angelic origins led to excesses until virtually every feature of human endeavor was believed to have its origins in strictly biological conditions. Durkheim's contribution is, then, all the greater when we recognize the extent to which he was moving against a scientific perspective of great respectability. If Durkheim seems excessive today, it is perhaps because he was attempting to counter another excess—that of biologism.

The second scientific feature of Durkheim's era was the value given to observable facts. The scientific ethic of the time was moving radically toward getting people to "put their money on" whatever could be demonstrated to be observably true. Durkheim's contribution is all the greater, therefore, when we understand he was working within and against the handicap we mentioned at the beginning of this chapter— the fact that the social world is not directly observable. By taking observable forms of behavior, such as suicide or crime,[39] and revealing their connection with social identities, Durkheim gave sociological investigation a new basis in fact—and, at the same time, laid a course for social investigation that has continued down to the present.

The humanistic implications of Durkheim's work are not easy to assess. To an age that idealistically extolled democratic virtues and the autonomy of the individual, Durkheim gave the tempering concept of

---

[39] We cannot really observe a suicide or a criminal directly either. But Durkheim was working with data that revealed some of the relatively more concrete effects of social force.

74 anomie—the price of individualism might be anxiety and death. Individuals require social regulation and order. Anomie is the other face of freedom.

In a century that saw the church being rudely elbowed aside by science, Durkheim further undermined the sanctifying rationalizations of religion by saying God was simply a personification of social force. Yet, at the same time, he also provided the greatest justification for religious doctrine ever granted by a social scientist when he claimed that all societies must have religious commitments. Without religious dedication there is no social order.

For the humanist concerned with the problem of evil, Durkheim offered little hope. Even a society of saints, he suggested, would identify among its body of holy men some who violated the high standards of that saintly group. Social organization, a necessity of life for human beings, has as one of its properties the differentiation of its parts into the moral and the immoral. As there cannot be a success without those who fail, there cannot be a good without those who are evil. The moral order which is the nuclear force binding society together creates, in itself, the evil that is necessary to sustain it. Durkheim's message to the humanist concerned with evil is to recognize that somehow we all share in the process. To the extent we are human, we are social. To the extent we are social, we share. Though the judge who condemns an evil man to die cannot legally condemn himself as well, he should never lose sight of the greater matrix of involvements that brought about the evil and in which we all participated and conspired.

Durkheim devoted his life to the endeavor that people should not lose sight of that greater matrix which he called the moral order or the collective conscience. For that reason, if no other, humanists as well as social scientists will long be indebted to him.

Problems and Issues

Durkheim was very much aware of the extent to which social forces are both powerful and, at the same time, invisible or indirect. We cannot "see" society directly. We must always infer it from what little we do see. At the same time, people make inferences about the social character of both themselves and others and have a strong sense of "certainty" about what they are doing. One way in which they achieve this is by developing abstract religious concepts that function as mythical "maps" of the social order. We tend to think, today, that rulers who refer to their "divine" rights are from another age. However, the ties between leadership and religion are still strong. Is it really possible to be a powerful leader and not at least imply some kind of "divine" right?

The effect of the modern secular intellectual quest, particularly in the sciences, has been to destroy myths. The great debate in Victorian England over Darwin's theories centered on the myth of creation. Most secular

thinkers of our time accept the belief that the organisms of the modern
world have evolved from earlier forms rather than having been created by
a historically recent act of God. "Myth" has become a term of invective for
ideas repugnant to empiricists. Durkheim suggests, however, that society
requires myth. What myths are common to American culture? Why is it
often difficult to be aware of the extent to which myth dominates our
thinking? What is myth, anyway?

One of the great issues raised by Durkheim was that of the human
inclination to engage in complex, elaborate, and intense forms of punishment. Human beings, with few exceptions, might be defined as punitive
animals. (Even the mild and peace-loving Zuni Indians of the American
Southwest would on occasion hang someone by his thumbs.) Americans
are certainly not exempt from the punitive motive. We have a history of
punishment—from lynch mobs to firing squads. Our literature and mass
media are saturated with the vicarious delight of observing punishment.
What is involved in punishment? Is it possible to have a society without
punishment? Are there possible relationships between the punitive imagery
of Christianity and the American inclination to indulge in punishment? Is
human punishment merely a manifestation of "human nature"? If so, why
are some people excessively punitive and others not?

Durkheim shocked people at the turn of the century by suggesting
that crime is a natural part of any social order. This sounds cynical. He
argued that a society must create criminals in order to sustain some notion
of what is "good." Is there an analogy between what takes place in the
greater social order and what takes place in college or university? That is to
say, is there some possibility that a university is required to create a kind
of "criminal" person (worthless, threatening, no-good, stupid, anti-intel-
lectual, and so forth) in order to establish its higher standards (students
who are good, bright, intellectual, and possessed of "honor")?

Finally, let us draw on Durkheim's concept of "anomie" as a take-off
point for further questioning. Durkheim found that people who are "anomic" have a significantly greater inclination to give up on life. But anomie
implies that one is "free" of social obligations and restraints. Do people
really want "freedom"? What are people really talking about when they talk
about being "free"? If people were totally free, would society be possible?
Is the concept of freedom merely an illusion? How is the term used politically by men and women of power? What have been the possible social
effects of having freedom as a political ideal? That is to say, what has a
belief in freedom done to the family, business practices, the school, the
military system, the political structure, and other manifestations of the social
system?

Power, Bureaucracy, Money, and Religion

The Views of

MAX WEBER

Like war and piracy, trade has often been unrestrained in its relations with foreigners and those outside the group.

The Protestant Ethic and the Spirit of Capitalism
translated by T. Parsons

BORN: 1864   DIED: 1920

5 Modern American sociology has been strongly influenced by the work of Emile Durkheim and Max Weber. Possibly only Karl Marx has offered a stronger influence. Certainly these three figures stand as giants among the many European thinkers whose writings affected American social thought. Let us first consider Weber's time as it related to Durkheim's career. Weber's reaction to Marx will be discussed later.

Durkheim was French; Weber was German. Both were born at about the same time: Durkheim in 1858 and Weber in 1864. Each reached the height of his active career in the years just preceding World War I. Durkheim died in 1917. Weber died in 1920.

Despite their different national identities, Weber and Durkheim had much in common. Both men gave paramount significance to religion as a historical and human force. For Durkheim religion was a logical necessity. One is forced to recognize and accept its existence not only because religion is a historical fact but also because it is logically a social necessity. For Durkheim the argument went, essentially, "If society exists, then religion must exist." Beginning with a logical consideration of the matter, Durkheim then investigated religion from a logically preestablished point of view. Weber, with the German scholar's regard for history, approached religion by studying its historical forms in great detail until he reached the point where he could begin to develop synthesizing generalizations.

If Weber is less exciting than Durkheim, he is more versatile. Durkheim was more narrowly dedicated to sociology. Weber's comprehension ranged across economics, sociology, political science, anthropology, history, and philosophy. Even so, the differences between the character and intellect of the two men are less significant than the similarities. Both were thoroughly committed intellectuals and both were extremely contemptuous of simplistic answers to human affairs. More significantly, both turned to the moral order as the fountainhead of social analysis. Both saw religion as a key institution in the understanding of the social order.

Weber was concerned with the specific political and economic consequences of religious doctrine. He concluded, in what is generally recognized as his most popular work,[1] that capitalistic economic practice is an outgrowth of ideas contained within Protestant religious doctrine. Weber examined the pervasive effects of religious thought within the social structure and traced in great detail the many unanticipated consequences of particular religious beliefs.

Weber's career is all the more remarkable when we note that he spent nearly twenty years of his adult life disabled by emotional disorders which at times left him so enervated that he would sit by the window for hours picking his fingernails. He would tell his wife it felt good to do nothing.[2] The contradictions in Weber's nature and the complexity of the man are summarized in the following quote from Gerth and Mills:

> Throughout his life, Weber was a nationalist and believed in the mission of the *Herrenvolk*, yet at the same time he fought for individual freedom and, with analytic detachment, characterized the ideas of nationalism and racism as justificatory ideologies used by the ruling class, and their hireling

---

[1] Max Weber, *The Protestant Ethic and the Spirit of Capitalism*, translated by Talcott Parsons (New York: Scribner's, 1930). Weber's publications are numerous. The following references indicate the breadth of Weber's interests and studies and, at the same time, might be of interest to students who want to pursue Weber's ideas further. *Ancient Judaism*, translated and edited by Hans H. Gerth and Don Martindale (New York: Free Press, 1952); *Basic Concepts in Sociology*, translated and with an introduction by H. P. Secher (New York: Citadel, 1964); *The City*, translated and edited by Don Martindale and Gertrude Neuwirth (New York: Macmillan, Collier Books, 1962); *From Max Weber: Essays in Sociology*, translated, edited, and with an introduction by H. H. Gerth and C. Wright Mills (New York: Oxford University Press, 1946); *Max Weber on the Methodology of the Social Sciences*, translated and edited by Edward A. Shils and Henry A. Finch (New York: Free Press, 1949); *The Rational and Social Foundations of Music*, translated and edited by Don Martindale, Johannes Riedel, and Gertrude Neuwirth (Carbondale, Ill.: Southern Illinois University Press, 1958); *The Religion of China*, translated and edited by Hans H. Gerth (New York: Free Press, 1959); *The Religion of India*, translated and edited by Hans H. Gerth and Don Martindale (New York: Free Press, 1958); *The Sociology of Religion*, translated by Ephraim Fischoff (Boston: Beacon, 1963); *The Theory of Social and Economic Organization*, translated by A. M. Henderson and Talcott Parsons (New York: Free Press, 1964).

[2] Gerth and Mills (eds.), *From Max Weber*, p. 12.

publicists, to beat their impositions into weaker members of the polity. . . . He was proud of being a Prussian officer, and yet asserted in public that the Kaiser, his commander-in-chief, was something of which all Germans should be ashamed. . . . A model of the self-conscious masculinity of Imperial Germany, he nevertheless encouraged the first woman labor official in Germany and made vital speeches to members of the woman's emancipation movement of the early twentieth century.[3]

Weber's scholarship is as complex as his character. Any brief attempt, such as this, to outline the significant ideas in his writing must preface the effort with an apology. Yet it is necessary to make the attempt, for modern sociological thought is grounded, in large part, in the numerous writings of Weber.

Weber lived in a time and place dominated—or at least strongly affected—by the theories and writings of Karl Marx. There was the hope that just around the corner lay a new Utopia—founded in material plenty and a classless society. A politically astute person had to know and had to react to Marxist thought—and Weber was a political man. Much of his thought flowed from his reaction to the writings of Marx. It is certainly an oversimplification, but it is also an aid in reading Weber, to view his writing as an attempt to refute the emphasis Marx gave to material economic concerns. Where Marx saw the church as the apologist for capitalistic exploitations, Weber saw the church as the matrix of ideas from which capitalism was to evolve. Marx claimed that without capitalism the church was not necessary. Weber argued that without a particular type of religious thought capitalism could not have come into existence.

Relationship between Economic and Religious Systems

It is apparent, in this day and age, that both Marx and Weber viewed the historical process too narrowly. Religious and economic systems are not perfectly distinct entities. They are merged and their boundaries are ill defined. It is not really possible to say that one "determines" the character of the other. They both influence each other and, further, they are both simultaneously affected by changes taking place in the other institutions that make up society. Even so, it is instructive to examine Weber's work; it stands as an antidote to the popularity of materialistic interpretations of history.[4]

Weber began his speculations on the relationship between economic and religious systems by considering observed differences in economic productivity in Protestant and Catholic districts of Europe. If the

[3] Ibid., pp. 25–26.
[4] Materialistic interpretations of history are sometimes thought to be the unique eccentricity of Marxists and, more specifically, Russian Marxists. Yet it should be apparent that such interpretations of history and humanity are also very popular in America. When General Electric says "Progress Is Our Most Important Product," it is equating the elevation of humanity with the distribution of a product. Such crassness cannot be claimed to be the unique *Weltanschauung* of either the Russians or the Americans—it belongs to both.

former were more productive, he argued, it was not because they had been "freed" by the Protestant Reformation. Quite the contrary, they had been placed under closer religious control. Moreover, it was not possible to say that the Protestant districts were more economically industrious because they were more materialistic and less "ascetic" than the Catholics in their interests. There were too many exceptions. Some Catholic districts, in France and Italy for example, revealed a lusty interest in life and its enjoyments. Protestant groups, such as the Mennonites in Germany, were possessed of an austere other-worldliness. It was, said Weber, too simple to say that economic effort was influenced by simple religious acceptance or rejection of asceticism.

Yet the economic picture remained clear—the Catholic areas were less economically progressive. One could not readily forego the idea that religion had something to do with economic effort. The problem was to find the hidden connection. To do so required an intensive examination of the nature of capitalist doctrines and Catholic and Protestant philosophy.

To summarize the nature of the capitalist spirit Weber turned to the writings of Benjamin Franklin. Here was capitalism in its most naive and open form of expression—an economic spirit which Europeans found repulsive. One European of the time, writing of Americans, said, "They make tallow out of cattle and money out of men."[5] But the important thing in Franklin's expressions of the spirit of capitalism, Weber held, was to see the *moral* nature of his economic advice. In capitalist economies the making of money takes on the character of a purpose rather than a necessity. It becomes a value rather than something that happens by chance or something that wells out of the avarice of a particular individual. There develops a collective "spirit" which advocates the idea that each of us is called upon to make the utmost of our life and, furthermore, that the form this should take is devotion to industry in this world. Weber examined such statements of Franklin's as the following:

> For six pounds a year you may have the use of one hundred pounds, provided you are a man of known prudence and honesty.
> He that spends a groat a day idly, spends idly above six pounds a year, which is the price for the use of one hundred pounds.
> He that wastes idly a groat's worth of his time per day, one day with another, wastes the privilege of using one hundred pounds each day.
> He that idly loses five shillings' worth of time, loses five shillings, and might as prudently throw five shillings into the sea.
> He that loses five shillings, not only loses that sum, but all the advantage that might be made by turning it in dealing, which by the time that a young man becomes old, will amount to a considerable sum of money.[6]

Weber's point, as he examined the writings of Franklin, was that

---

[5] Ferdinand Kürnberger, quoted by Weber in *The Protestant Ethic and the Spirit of Capitalism*, p. 51.
[6] Benjamin Franklin, quoted by Weber in *The Protestant Ethic and the Spirit of Capitalism*, p. 50.

80 here was something new. There have been wealthy men in the past and there have been men of ambition and avarice. But Benjamin Franklin set forth a moral treatise that took the individual to task for not tending to matters of business. To tend one's groats is also to tend to the interests of one's soul. Western religion had not advocated this prosaic sentiment prior to the Reformation. Indeed, as Weber commented, such a state of mind in the medieval period would have been viewed as the lowest kind of avarice and usury.

Weber established an important point, and we must understand it if we are to appreciate the subtlety of his observations. First of all, capitalism must not be viewed simply as the desire to make money; such a desire in some individuals, Weber claimed, is as old as the history of man.

> The *auri sacra fames* is as old as the history of man. But we shall see that those who submitted to it without reserve as an uncontrolled impulse, such as the Dutch sea-captain who "would go through hell for gain, even though he scorched his sails," were by no means the representatives of that attitude of mind from which *the specifically modern capitalistic spirit as a mass phenomenon* is derived, and that is what matters. At all periods of history, wherever it was possible, there has been ruthless acquisition, bound to no ethical norms whatever. Like war and piracy, trade has often been unrestrained in its relations with foreigners and those outside the group.[7]

Capitalism must be understood as a mass phenomenon. It is a culturally prescribed way of living; it is a complex of ideals; it is a change in the older moral order. Weber's first point, then, is that we must see capitalism as a moral prescription, widely binding on all members of the society, to advance their individual material interests.

The second important feature of Weber's argument is that capitalism must be seen as a massive encroachment on what might be called a traditionalistic sense of effort or the value of work. It is worth noting that Weber was well aware, before American industrial psychologists documented the matter further, that workers are not always motivated to produce in terms of self-interest. Instead, they will often accept a traditionally given standard as sufficient and produce only enough to meet such a standard. Weber summarized the matter nicely:

> A man does not "by nature" wish to earn more and more money, but simply to live as he is accustomed to live and to earn as much as is necessary for that purpose.[8]

So it was that Weber revealed himself to be concerned with a specific form of a broader problem that has interested anyone seriously involved in the social sciences: How does social and economic change occur? How do the massive forces of culture come to be modified? Like

[7] Weber, *The Protestant Ethic and the Spirit of Capitalism*, p. 57, emphasis added.
[8] Ibid., p. 60.

other modern social scientists, Weber concluded that the answer lay **81**
within the nature of the social order itself. To understand social and
economic change we must consider the preexisting social and economic
order. It is the social order that changes itself.[9] Any existing social and
economic system contains not necessarily the seeds of its own destruction but rather forces that change its character to the point where it is
almost no longer recognizable.

From Weber's perspective, the growth of capitalism as an economic
system was also the growth of capitalism as a moral system. To recapit-
ulate briefly, the problem of the capitalistic transition was (1) to make
the acquisitive motive more than a personal eccentricity—it had to be
elevated to a moral principle; (2) to destroy reliance on traditional forms
of economic satisfaction and replace those forms with the rational calculation of returns coming from the investment of given amounts of
labor and capital. So the question is raised: How was capitalism able to
arise out of a preexisting moral order that held the acquisitive motive to
be base and vulgar and that accepted traditional standards of consumption and production? This was Weber's concern.

Behavioral Implications of Protestant Thought

To resolve the problem, Weber turned to an examination of some of the
behavioral implications of Protestant thought. Protestant thought arises
out of, and is quite literally, a "reforming" of doctrines long held by the
Catholic Church. Weber presumed that if people took their religion
seriously, then to some extent at least their behavior would be affected
by it. If this were so, an examination of the moral directives of religion
could help us understand how certain kinds of behavior came into being.
What, then, were the implications of Protestant thought in its relation to
capitalism? Weber turned first to an examination of Luther's concept of
the "calling."

Luther set forth the idea that individuals should accept their "calling," their position within temporal society, so long as the calling is
legitimate. The idea of the calling served one major purpose. Prior to
the Reformation, those activities which most magnified humans in the
eyes of God were efforts which, essentially, involved a withdrawal from
the world. In the exercise of monastic asceticism and priestly celibacy,
the individual found closer identity with Christ and with God. Luther
suggested, to the contrary, that all legitimate enterprises were equal in
the eyes of God and that individuals could enhance their own state of
grace by meeting the demands of their temporal or worldly callings.
Luther was, in a sense, paving the way for the value which we, today,
give to professionalism. Weber was concerned with the extent to which
this theological concept and religious argument would have conse-

[9] This position, in different forms and versions, is endorsed by a number of modern social
writers. Among those appearing in the present book who subscribe to this view are Pitirim
Sorokin, Jules Henry, Robert K. Merton, Lester White, and, of course, Emile Durkheim.

82 quences for the economic realm. He suggested that what Luther did was to bring work into the secular realm; after Luther, worldly duties were no longer subordinated to spiritual or ascetic ones. It was the necessary first move toward capitalistic morality. Weber said:

> The effect of the Reformation as such was only that, as compared with the Catholic attitude, the moral emphasis on and the religious sanction of, organized worldly labour in a calling was mightily increased. . . . Everyone should abide by his living and let the godless run after gain. . . . But in the concrete calling an individual pursued he saw more and more a special command of God to fulfill these particular duties which the Divine Will had imposed upon him. . . . The individual should remain once and for all in the station and calling in which God had placed him, and should restrain his worldly activity within the limits imposed by his established station in life.[10]

Luther provided a justification for involvement in worldly affairs, but he did little more than that. To see the more profound connection between Protestant thought and capitalistic enterprise it is necessary to turn to the writings of Calvin.[11]

Calvinism, following the momentum established by Lutheranism, continued the process of providing religious justification for worldly concerns and effort. Luther supplied the concept of a calling. Calvin supplied an interest in predestination. If people were placed on this earth as God's creatures, and if God stood infinitely beyond their limited intellectual capacities, then it would be foolish to presume that any kind of effort on their part would place them in a state of grace with God. Only God would know, and God, being far beyond anyone's mind, would not tell. Thus, one's fate was predestined in the sense that it was out of one's own hands and in the hands of God. Just as one could not know the specific nature of one's own worldly demise—the form of death—one could not know, in advance, the form of one's relationship with God. At the same time, Calvin claimed that some—a few—would be among the saved. The rest would fall among the damned.

Thus, Calvinism provided the world with a new variation on the older Christian notion of damnation and salvation. Calvin carried the

---

[10] Weber, *The Protestant Ethic and the Spirit of Capitalism*, pp. 83–85.

[11] It is necessary to introduce an antidote to the oversimplifications that characterize any attempt to summarize Weber's work in a brief space. Weber was not saying that Protestantism, and only Protestantism, is the necessary condition for capitalism. Rather, he was concerned with the extent to which some kind of religious moral order is necessary for the development of particular kinds of economic order:

> we have no intention whatever of maintaining such a foolish and doctrinaire thesis as that the spirit of capitalism. . . . could only have arisen as the result of certain effects of the Reformation, or even that capitalism as an economic system is a creation of the Reformation. . . . On the contrary, we only wish to ascertain whether and to what extent religious forces have taken part in the qualitative formation and the quantitative expansion of that spirit over the world (*The Protestant Ethic and the Spirit of Capitalism*, p. 91).

idea of an omnipotent God to its extreme and concluded that salvation
was already determined by God and there was nothing the individual
could do about it. More importantly, there was nothing the church could
do about it. The complete elimination of salvation through the sacra-
ments of the church formed the absolutely decisive difference between
Calvinism and Catholicism.[12] Weber then went on:

> The great historic process in the development of religions, the elimina-
> tion of magic from the world which had begun with the old Hebrew
> prophets and, in conjunction with Hellenistic scientific thought, had re-
> pudiated all magical means to salvation as superstition and sin, came here
> to its logical conclusion. The genuine Puritan even rejected all signs of
> religious ceremony at the grave and buried his nearest and dearest without
> song or ritual in order that no superstition, no trust in the effects of magical
> and sacramental forces on salvation, should creep in.[13]

Not only were magical means useless in the attainment of salvation,
but so were any and all other means. It then becomes a curious matter
to determine how such an ethic, such a religious point of view, could
come to be associated with the worldly, acquisitive, and accumulative
spirit that characterizes capitalism. The principal effect of this idea, said
Weber, was to throw people into a state of brooding individualism. Torn
from the security of the church, of traditionalism, of magic and ritual,
the individual stood alone before God, more vulnerable than ever before. Ignorance was a source of torment. One's fate was unknown. Thus
it was that individualism became a common affliction and not a specific
eccentricity.

But if this idea were carried to its *reductio ad absurdum,* it would
produce unbearable anomie. Rather than stimulating communal development and economic order, it would produce a highly disruptive disengagement of the individual from the affairs of the community. Something had to balance out the individualism of Calvinistic Puritanism by
retaining the individual within the communal order. Weber resolved this
problem by considering the Calvinist's conception of the ultimate purpose of life.

> The world exists to serve the glorification of God and for that purpose
> alone. The elected Christian is in the world only to increase this glory of
> God by fulfilling His commandments to the best of his ability. But God
> requires social achievement of the Christian because He wills that social
> life shall be organized according to His commandments, in accordance
> with that purpose.[14]

Weber's picture of the Calvinist is that of a man tormented with a
concern over his fate. He stands alone, yet bound to the community by

---

[12] Ibid., pp. 104–105. This is a slightly modified version of Weber's statement to the same
effect.
[13] Ibid., p. 105.
[14] Ibid., p. 108.

84 his sense of God's omnipotence. He cannot distinguish the saved from the damned and he cannot rely on any device to assure his own salvation. Yet there remains a very dim light in this ideological darkness. Though Calvinists cannot achieve salvation, they can, through the extent to which they are able to manifest God's glory, convince themselves of their own membership in the elect. They can seek external signs of inner grace. These signs cannot assure them of salvation, but they can help convince them they are among the saved.

The achievement of Calvinism was that it explicitly brought the religious struggle into this world. No longer need fully dedicated, religious persons retreat into monasticism to test their commitment. They could test it in their work, in their calling, in their daily activities. Weber commented that the effect of the Reformation was to make every Christian a monk for life.[15] More significantly, one was a monk who lived and dwelled within the community, within industry, within the school and the family. These and other institutions were to be affected accordingly.

It remains, now, to make the connection between the asceticism of Protestant ideology and the development of capitalism as an economic practice flowing from the greater moral order. The connection is not obvious, because Protestant asceticism, reflecting the more pervasive asceticism of Christianity in general, was inclined to view the acquisition of wealth as morally suspect. One's dominating concern should be the Kingdom of God, not the acquisition of wealth. However, the fear of wealth coming from Protestant asceticism does not come from the belief that wealth itself is corrupting but from the belief that it promotes a moral relaxation. If one can remain dedicated to the principles of good works and the fulfillment of the glory of God and not be tempted into leisure, then wealth is in no way evil. Indeed—and this is significant—it may function as a sign of success in one's calling.

It is not wealth which is evil but rather the waste of time which is the true evil.

> Waste of time is thus the first and in principle the deadliest of sins. The span of human life is infinitely short and precious to make sure of one's own election [into the ranks of the saved]. Loss of time through sociability, idle talk, luxury, even more sleep than is necessary for health . . . is worthy of absolute moral condemnation. . . . [Time] is infinitely valuable because every hour lost is lost to labour for the glory of God. Thus inactive contemplation is also valueless, or even directly reprehensible if it is at the expense of one's daily work. For it is less pleasing to God than the active performance of His will in a calling.[16]

Thus, Protestantism, with its derivations rooted in early ascetic Christianity and Judaism, latched onto work as an ascetic exercise. In this respect it differs from almost all other monastic rules the world over,

---

[15] Ibid., p. 121.
[16] Ibid., p. 158.

according to Weber.[17] Work was elevated to a moral principle and, moreover, a principle binding on all who aspired to the Kingdom of God. Work was made a direct expression of religious fervor. Still more significantly, not all work could satisfy the demands of the Protestant Ethic. Only that work was acceptable which directly served the glory of God—and the glory of God was manifested in the ongoing community and its legitimate interests.

Furthermore, work which was sloppy and ill conceived, even though taxing and tiring, was not sufficient. It might have tried the soul, but it could not work for the glorification of God. That work was best which was conscientiously planned, thorough, and methodical. In a word, work was given *a rational* quality through an irrational process; the religious mysticism of Luther, Calvin, and other Protestant leaders generated the idea of rationality in work. The foundations were thus laid for capitalistic modes of thought. Capitalism, if it meant nothing else, meant the rational use of wealth and the rational use of labor. People had sought wealth before and had worked before—there was certainly nothing new in this. But with capitalism people were set to the task of calculating gains. In determining the worth of an enterprise, rationalism achieved the level of a socially supported value. How, said Weber, could capitalism have come into being unless some kind of moral basis had been laid for it in advance? Because this moral basis was lacking in the religions of other countries—even though they were rich in resources and labor—their economies did not and could not move toward the capitalistic form.[18]

What has happened to the Protestant Ethic? Observers of the present scene find it laboring under the crushing weight of its own successes. It is ironic, if Weber's thesis is correct, that capitalism not only became independent of its Protestant origins but eventually reached the point where it could challenge values dearest to the heart of the Puritan individualist. The challenge, when it came, had its origins in two sources. One of these was the rise of the large organization—the development of modern bureaucracy. The other was modern science. In many ways science is the most rational and possibly the purest extension of ideas contained in the Protestant Ethic.[19] At the same time, it stands as the most secular of human institutions and the greatest barrier to a collective

---

[17] Ibid., p. 158.

[18] Some writers have speculated that the code of Bushido in Japan was influential in promoting the technological and industrial modernization of Japan. We are indebted to Professor Joyce Lebra of the University of Colorado for bringing this to our attention.

[19] Robert K. Merton has attempted to show the relationship that exists between Protestant religious thought and the rise of scientific thinking in Western culture. If Protestantism promoted rationality in business, it seems reasonable to conclude that it promoted rationality in other spheres of human activity. Essentially, the argument is that if God is all-rational and if God made the world, then the rationality of God will be found in His works. Early scientists of the seventeenth century were, according to Merton, predominantly Protestant and, by virtue of religious training, more congenial to the idea of finding rationality within nature itself. This thesis is explored at some length in a later chapter.

86 return to religious mysticism.[20] In any event, as Weber conceded, once the process leading toward capitalistic morality had begun, it eventually reached the point of being an autonomous system—a system no longer reliant on the older morality that brought it into being.

The Nature of Bureaucratic Organization

Weber was concerned with the subtleties of the connection between religious and economic moralities. He was also concerned with the consequences of social organization. In particular he was involved with questions concerning the nature of bureaucratic organization. No sociologist today can discuss this topic without paying his respects to Weber. Indeed, Merton claims that Weber may properly be regarded as the "founder of the systematic study of bureaucracy.[21] Weber was interested in bureaucracy because it represented another facet of the process of rationalization—a process which seemed to him to characterize modern society in contrast to "traditional" forms of society. A rational ordering of the economy brought along with it a rational ordering of social relations. The efficiency that came to characterize the productive process also came to characterize social organization. In their social lives, people were processed as impersonally and as efficiently as the material resources that were also necessary for production.

Capitalism solved the problem of tearing people away from traditionalistic economic motives[22] and traditional patterns of production. Bureaucracy, in essence, solved the problem of breaking people away from a reliance on traditional modes of power. To see this, we need to consider briefly Weber's conception of the nature of power in its traditional forms and in its bureaucratic forms.[23]

Power, very broadly defined as the probability of having a command obeyed by others when they are resistant, can be dealt with in two very distinctive ways. First of all, power can be seen as having its locus in the person or individual. By this Weber meant only that certain features may give a person a commanding appearance and cause others to accept the person's dictates as necessary ones to follow—the individual is felt to be

[20] It is interesting to note, in this instance, the bad press which the "hippie" movement received in recent years. The hippie emphasis on subjectivism and mysticism stands more as a threat to the institution of science than it does to the values of the American middle classes. If science is often ignored in discussions of power in the modern world, it is probably because science is held to be beyond the mundane and arbitrary value interests that are so integral a part of the political scene. This, of course, is a mistake. Science, per se, is a political force, and it is as politically significant in our time as the Holy Roman Catholic Church was in its time.

[21] Robert K. Merton et al., *Reader in Bureaucracy* (New York: Free Press, 1952), p. 17.

[22] This is relative, of course. Modern America, for example, though less traditionalistic than, say, Egypt, in its labor practices, is still not 100 percent efficient in this respect.

[23] The concept of power is extremely difficult to define in a social context; no one has achieved a truly satisfactory definition. If we define power as the capacity to make people do things they do not want to do, we have to establish the fact that they do not want to do what we are demanding of them.

blessed with extraordinary powers. Power that emanates from such a **87**
source he called *charismatic* power. The individual having such power is
believed to be divinely inspired, possessed of sacred qualities, capable
of prophecy, and otherwise set apart from the ordinary run of people.[24]
A second form of power has its locus not within the person but within
the office or status the person occupies.

Charismatic Power

Charismatic power, as Weber considered it, is reliant on the expressive
qualities of the individual. It resides in the flashing eye, the powerful
voice, the jutting chin, or some other sign that identifies its possessor as
a "born leader." Because charismatic power rests, ultimately, on the
unique impressions of the individual, it has an arbitrary and eccentric
quality about it that makes it a potential source of disruption to more
rational forms of power utilization. The charismatic leader, as Weber put
it, is not congenial to the idea of routine. To the contrary, because that
person's power is lodged within personal qualities, he or she exists as a
threat to routine and to the established order.

The unstable, eccentric, and individualistic character of charismatic
power must be regulated somehow if a permanent and stable power
system is to be developed within the community. Weber held that purely
charismatic power exists only in the originating moments of new social
forms. The need for stability leads to the regulation or, as Weber put it,
the "routinization" of charisma.[25]

The necessity for stabilizing power based on the eccentricities of
the individual can be quickly seen. If the followers of a charismatic leader
are dependent on that person for guidance, how are they to cope with
the problems that arise when the leader dies or is incapacitated? How is
the quality of charisma to be given continuity beyond the life span of
the individual who possesses it? How is the magic of charisma to be
retained when the magician has gone? The problem thus becomes one
of somehow taking the power-giving qualities of charisma out of the
ephemeral nature of the individual and bringing them into the stable and
continuous structure of the community. Sources of power that were
once the property of a charismatically endowed individual must become
the property of the community; they must somehow be incorporated
into the routine of communal living. This is the process Weber referred
to as the routinization of charisma.

The problem of routinizing charisma can be solved in a variety of

---

[24] From the extent to which intelligence is idolized in America, we would suggest that it is
a modern form of the quest for charisma. However, the intelligence test has routinized
this form of charisma. In fact, it has gone so far as to lead a number of people with high
intelligence quotients to organize themselves into a group known as Mensa. Weber, we
like to believe, would have been amused.
[25] Weber, *Theory of Social and Economic Organization*, pp. 364–373.

ways. Weber listed the following as among the more common and significant ones:

1. A search can be initiated for persons who possess signs of charisma similar to those possessed by the leader. If the leader had a cleft between the teeth, then perhaps people with cleft teeth will also possess some of the charismatic qualities with which the leader was endowed. Weber referred to the search for the Dalai Lama as an example of this kind of solution. In this instance a search is initiated for a child with characteristics that identify him as a reincarnation of the Buddha.

2. The new leader can be sought through divine judgment, revelation, oracles, or the casting of lots. In such instances, the selection procedure is given a legitimacy—an acceptance by the community—and the person who is thus selected is endowed with charismatic qualities.

3. A very simple and common solution to the problem is to rely on the judgment of the charismatic leader and have that person select a successor. The magician is the person best qualified to select the magician who will follow.

4. A new leader can be established through selection by a council qualified both to determine the charismatic leader and to endow him or her with qualities of leadership by means of special ceremonies. Legitimacy of power rests, in this instance, on the acceptance of a charismatically qualified council and on the impressive and ritualistically correct procedures of ceremony.

5. Another means of routinizing charisma exists in the simple assumption that it can be biologically or hereditarily transmitted. Therefore, the charismatic leader can be replaced by his or her offspring, who will be possessed of similar qualities. It should be noted here that such an assumption functions to solve a social problem in the transfer of power and that it has only a very tenuous connection with reality. The community may possess any number of people who are better qualified, in terms of talent and energy, for the tasks of leadership than is the present leader's offspring. However, to ascribe such qualities to the offspring simplifies what otherwise might prove to be a communally disorganizing process of attempting to rediscover "true" charisma.

6. Finally, the problem of stabilizing charisma can be met by ritualistic transmission:

> The most important example is the transmission of priestly charisma by anointing, consecration, or the laying on of hands; and of royal authority, by anointing and by coronation.[26]

Charisma, which is individualistic, disturbing, revolutionary, and eccentric, cannot long remain the organizing force within a community. It calls for routinization; but routinization—whether of a traditional form

[26] Ibid., p. 366.

or a more modern bureaucratic form—introduces a conservative, stable, **89** and collective structure.

Bureaucratic Power

Whereas the above forms of routinization of charisma are attempts either to find someone who is charismatic or to transfer charisma to someone who is not, bureaucracy solves the problem by investing not the person but the office with power. This relatively profound accomplishment of bureaucratic forms of organization provides bureaucracy with both its stability and its capacity to maintain consistent control over its member-ship. The powerful person no longer needs a flashing eye or a booming voice; he or she needs only the credentials that qualify for a particular position of authority.

Weber was concerned with the ideal forms of bureaucracy: What are the essential features of a rational, large-scale, and efficient social organization?[27] Weber saw bureaucracy as a form of social organization that constrained the personal and eccentric qualities of charismatic lead-ership. But how does bureaucracy operate? In essence, suggested Weber, bureaucracy depends on the relationship that exists between a set of formal regulations and a set of offices. The offices are so organized as to maximize the controlling efficiency of the regulations.

To see what this means, we need to turn to Weber's listing of the essentials of bureaucratic organization.[28] Because Weber's formulations are extremely abstract, we have attempted to illustrate them with ex-amples drawn from the realm of higher education in the United States— a realm that is now well bureaucratized and is also familiar to the student. Bureaucracy, as seen by Weber, involves the following interdependent ideas.[29]

1. *"Any given legal norm may be established by agreement or by imposition, on grounds of expediency or rational values or both, with a claim to obedience at least on the part of the members of the corporate group."* The important qualification in this statement appears in the use of the term *expediency.* Thus higher learning, as a bureaucratic process, comes to abound in "legal" rules and regulations which specify the form—and to a considerable extent the content—of education. It be-comes expedient to differentiate, in a legalistic sense, the study of psy-chology from the study of literature; and it becomes expedient to distin-guish the study of literature from the study of anthropology. So it goes.

[27] For a penetrating statement of Weber's ideas concerning charisma and bureaucracy, the student should read Reinhard Bendix, *Max Weber: An Intellectual Portrait* (Garden City, N.Y.: Doubleday, 1962).
[28] This list is set forth in *The Theory of Social and Economic Organization.* The particular quotations presented here were taken from Merton et al., *Reader in Bureaucracy,* pp. 18–27.
[29] It is necessary to mention that Weber viewed bureaucracy as a form of organization that has appeared in a variety of historical settings. It is not uniquely or specifically modern.

90 Moreover, whatever one is studying, it is expedient to study the subject in terms of an intellectual bookkeeping system that assigns credits for what amounts, on the student's part, to maintaining a sense of bureaucratic propriety. That is, if the student functions according to the norms binding on a proper bureaucrat, he or she will be moved through the career system.

Critics who are concerned with the extent to which students are motivated by expediency perhaps miss the point. From Weber's perspective, a student who recognizes the need for expediency will be conforming more to the character of the educational bureaucracy than will the student who does not.[30] Such a student will be highly rewarded by the bureaucracy—at least in terms of the intellectual bookkeeping system which doles out grades to those freshmen and sophomores and upperclassmen who retain some sense of their bureaucratic nature. The freshman bureaucrat who recognizes the value of expediency will be resonating to a sentiment that is dominant within the greater organizational structure.

2. *Within bureaucracy "administration of law is held to consist in the application of . . . rules to particular cases; the administrative process is the rational pursuit of the interests which are specified in the order governing the corporate group within the limits laid down by legal precepts . . . "* Weber's point here is perhaps the most profound among the many he made concerning the character of bureaucracy. The effective bureaucrat is, from the perspective of Weber, a person who pursues the interests of the corporation as these appear in legal precepts. As a consequence, in specific instances, the individual is dealt with legalistically rather than personally. Actions are measured against the interests of the corporate group and are thereby evaluated. The legal system that makes up the structure of the bureaucracy's interests is accepted as given.

It is this feature of bureaucracy that has resulted in much criticism from existential novelists such as Camus and Kafka.[31] In the clash of the person and the structure, it is the person who is evaluated against the background of the legal system of the structure. For example, in the late sixties, student protesters at the University of Colorado demonstrated against the appearance on campus of a Central Intelligence Agency recruiter. In the application of the general rules to the specific action, virtually no discussion took place concerning incongruities between norms of scholarship or intellectual activity and the morality underlying the activities of the CIA. Instead, university administrators moved quickly and suspended the protesters—thereby protecting the "image and rep-

---

[30] The student motivated by expediency is the eternal concern of the pedagogue. Jacques Barzun commented to the effect that, granted the nature of graduate school organization today, students motivated by expediency are superior to their idealistic counterparts. A very ingenious discussion of the transformation of idealism into technical competence by forcing the student to be expedient appears in Howard Becker, E. C. Hughes, and B. Geer, *Boys in White* (Chicago: University of Chicago Press, 1961).

[31] Franz Kafka's *The Trial* (New York: Knopf, 1937) is one of the better-known fictional depictions of the point being made here.

utation of the university." Weber's point is that in bureaucratic administration, the administrator identifies with and protects the interests of the bureaucracy and does so in a relatively uncritical manner.[32]

3. *Within the bureaucracy "the typical person in authority occupies an 'office.' In the action associated with his status, including the commands he issues to others, he is subject to an impersonal order to which his actions are oriented."* The concept of "office" is important in grasping a deeper understanding of the nature of bureaucracy. It enables us, perhaps, to see professors somewhat differently if we recognize them as intellectual officials, or, to put it another way, as officials who are intellectuals. College students acquire a different character when we view them as minor officials—junior bureaucrats within the educational bureaucracy.

Because an office requires relatively uncritical acceptance of one's official duties, and because being an intellectual demands a critical sensitivity, the college professor of any intelligence sooner or later experiences the conflicts that come from the opposing demands of bureaucratic passivity on the one hand and intellectual rebellion on the other.

Professors who are good bureaucrats will, with considerable pride, boast to their students that they have eliminated all personal allusions and anecdotes from their lectures. In such an instance, the professor is openly recognizing the prior claims of office over any other kind of experience—especially the more disorganizing and less legalistic experiences that arise from one's personal encounters with life.

4. *"The person who obeys authority does so . . . only in his capacity as a 'member' of the corporate group and what he obeys is only 'the law.'"* The educational bureaucracy runs into more problems with this aspect of bureaucratic structure than just about any other. Weber is merely pointing out that bureaucracy has a tendency to restrict performance to the demands of the office. What people do on their own time is their own business. This, again, characterizes an "ideal" bureaucracy. If, for example, the chairperson of the physics department is one of the greatest physicists in the world, then why should it concern anyone that he or she spends off-duty hours passing out ban-the-bomb leaflets or conducting experiments in the application of certain tenets of a philosophy of free love?

A more aggravating problem arises from the extent to which this feature of bureaucracy, within an educational setting, produces "compartmentalization." Students—who, generally speaking, make very good bureaucrats—are all too willing to function as members of a corporate

[32] Though this statement is severe, it is warranted. There is a tendency for the critical evaluations of the administrative official to take the form dictated by the interests of the bureaucracy rather than the interests either of the individual or of broader moral issues. Thus it is that a federal court supported the employment of loyalty oaths for teachers in Colorado—with the assertion that such oaths promote a recognition that this is a nation of laws and not of people. It strikes us as peculiar that the judges were not willing to make explicit the possibility that this is a nation of laws *and* people. Presumably a complete dedication to law has an administrative cleanness that a dedication to humanity does not have.

92 group. When this means they must study English 101, Chemistry 201, Sociology 111, and Modern History 202, they do so. Each course is taken, the requirements met, and the credits entered in the bookkeeping system. The possibility that there might be a connection among all four courses and that each could be profitably examined from the perspectives of the others is rarely considered. Reality reflects the offices of bureaucracy and is subordinated to them, despite the resulting strain.

5. *"Members of the corporate group, insofar as they obey a person in authority, do not owe this obedience to him as an individual but to the impersonal order."* Weber suggested that within a bureaucracy allegiance becomes more abstract. College students might, for example, assert their willingness to do or die for old Siwash, but they would consider it absurd to be willing to do or die for President Jones of old Siwash. In 1966, over a third of the students in our social science classes were unable to identify Ho Chi Minh when asked to do so in tests. He was referred to variously as "a Chinese leader," "a South Vietnam political leader," and "an oriental." The enemy is no longer personalized. Instead, the enemy is looked upon as an abstract condition located somewhere in a misty "they." "They" are held to believe in an equally misty and ill-understood set of ideas called "communism," or "capitalism," or some other "ism," which "they," in a manner never well defined, will somehow impose on all the mistily "free" people of the world. Weber, had he lived in present times, would have been interested in the extent to which human conflict has become an abstracted process.

6. Within a bureaucracy *"the organization of offices follows the principle of hierarchy; that is, each lower office is under the control and supervision of a higher one."* This is a fairly obvious comment and does not require, in this context, much further elaboration. Whether it is a military, political, industrial, educational, or religious bureaucracy, the fact of hierarchy is evident. There are points in the hierarchy, however, that produce interesting situations. Graduate students, for example, stand between the student body and the faculty in the academic hierarchy. They are not really faculty members, and yet they are very close. This poses a problem for the graduate students. Should they treat their teachers as colleagues or as professors? They can easily seem either too formal or too casual. Some students, to avoid the problem, elect to greet their teachers with a noncommittal "Hi" or "Good morning" rather than to commit themselves with a "Hello, Professor Johnson" or a "Howdy, Jack."

7. *"Only a person who has demonstrated an adequate technical training is qualified to be a member of the administrative staff of [a bureaucratically] organized group, and hence only such persons are eligible for appointment to official positions."* The role played by technical competence in bureaucracy is an especially significant one and arises from the more pervasive concern given to the rational pursuit of the organization's ends. It the organization is to attain its goals, then its personnel must be as efficient and as competent as possible. Their efficiency is dependent on the extent to which they possess technical com-

petence. The consequence, in an ideal bureaucracy, is personnel se- **93**
lected on the basis of examinations.

Within the bureaucracy of higher learning, it is hardly necessary to
point to the prevalence of examinations as a means of determining the
right to continue in a career. However, some interesting observations
have been made concerning the manner in which people are selected
for positions in universities when their records are equivalent. Under
these conditions, extraneous features are allowed to sway the choice.
Usually these features will take into account the extent to which the
"personality" of the candidate will be such as to assure a "smooth"
operation of the department.[33]

8. *"In the rational type [of bureaucracy] it is a matter of principle
that the members of the administrative staff should be completely separated from ownership of the means of production or administration. . . .
There exists, furthermore, in principle, complete separation of the property belonging to the organization, which is controlled within the sphere
of office, and the personal property of the individual, which is available
for his own private uses. There is a corresponding separation of the place
in which official functions are carried out, the 'office' in the sense of
premises, from living quarters."* Weber touches here on a property of
bureaucracy that has far-reaching ramifications. He is suggesting, albeit
somewhat indirectly, that Marxist doctrines concerning the social employment of property may be only the ideological reflection or aftereffect
of a process that had already been established by the bureaucratization
of society.[34]

This point, though very profound, hardly needs elaborate documentation or illustration here. It is of more interest to pursue some of
the possible implications of the point. For example (still within educational bureaucracy), what are some of the effects of this on the political
and social ideology of professors? Is there a liberalizing effect? Does lack
of ownership bring about a lowered sense of identification with the
institution and a greater willingness to function as a more cosmopolitan
intellectual? Does the complete, or nearly complete disengagement of
the student, *qua* student, from ownership and the acquisition of goods
produce a feeling that what he or she is doing is not concrete or personally meaningful?

---

[33] This has been documented by Theodore Caplow and Reece McGee, *The Academic
Marketplace* (New York: Basic Books, 1958). At one point in the interviews carried out by
McGee a faculty member said, "He played the recorder. That was the reason we hired
him." [Interviewer]: "Because he played a recorder?" [Respondent]: "Yes, we thought that
would be nice." There is a strong hint here that the respondent, rather unbureaucratically,
was pulling the interviewer's leg.

[34] A particularly interesting treatment of this theme can be found in Adolf A. Berle, Jr.,
Power without Property (New York: Harcourt, Brace & World, 1959). See also James Burn-
ham, *The Managerial Revolution* (New York: Day, 1941). Galbraith points out that the
meaning of property, where large-scale industrial concerns are involved, is extremely
complex. Governmental and industrial interests are so interrelated it is difficult to establish
where the public domain begins and the private ends. See John Kenneth Galbraith, *The
New Industrial State* (Boston: Houghton Mifflin, 1967).

94   9. *"Administrative acts, decisions, and rules are formulated and recorded in writing, even in cases where oral discussion is the rule or is even mandatory. This applies at least to preliminary discussions and proposals, to final decisions, and to all sorts of orders and rules. The combination of written documents and a continuous organization of official functions constitutes the 'office,' which is the central focus of all types of modern corporate action."* Weber is discussing here what Mills referred to as the "enormous file." Not only does the bureaucracy record actions taken and the resulting consequences; it also keeps records of policies formed, and it keeps carefully preserved the rules and regulations that give form to the system. All of this constitutes the "file."

While such files, records, and formally expressed legal definitions of the regulations defining each office provide for a high degree of continuity, they also introduce an impersonal and rigid element into the conduct of office. Paradoxically, it becomes a mark of the good bureaucrat to know how and when to violate the demands of the formal system.[35] An interesting case in point is the following solution to a vexing bureaucratic problem by a professor at a Midwestern university.

The situation consisted, for the professor, of having to teach classes in an old wooden building that had been used as a military barracks during World War II. The building was a fire hazard, and the classroom itself, with a single exit, was a serious potential catastrophe. The instructor was reasonably concerned. He sent several letters to administrative officials who stood above him in authority. His request that something be done to alleviate the situation was ignored. At the same time, the demands of office called for this professor to teach his class three times a week for a period of fifty minutes each time.

Instead of lecturing, the professor instituted a program of training in fire drills and fire safety. He spent ten to twenty minutes of each class period taking his students outside the building to a safe place and then returning. This activity was sufficiently disorganizing to call for action on the part of the administration. They could have done several things—one being to chastize or otherwise bring sanctions against the instructor. However, because he was engaging in an action obviously designed to promote the safety of the students,[36] the administration was forced to capitulate. The episode ended happily with a set of fire escapes being constructed for the classroom.

We will have to bring this discussion of Weber to a close at this point. Weber has been criticized for presenting what, in the final analysis,

---

[35] This point has been amply documented by sociologists. See Alvin W. Gouldner, *Patterns of Industrial Bureaucracy* (New York: Free Press, 1954), and Erving Goffman, *Asylums* (Garden City, N.Y.: Doubleday, 1961). We understand that postal workers in Britain go on strike by following, to the very letter, every regulation required of postal employees; the resultant mess is sufficient to foul up the delivery of mail. We have also heard the same story told of French bureaucrats.

[36] Alvin Gouldner, in *Patterns of Industrial Bureaucracy* (p. 197), points out that administrative officials deal seriously with safety regulations. Gouldner says, "In the main, however, management felt that the most convincing justification for a safety program was the interdependence of safety and production. . . . the *major* legitimation of safety work . . . was its usefulness to production."

amounts to broad historical speculations and hypotheses. He has been **95**
accused of using such general and ideal conceptions that we are made
unwarrantedly secure in our feeling that we understand. (For example,
when we get down to the specifics of a particular bureaucracy we may
find that it deviates considerably from the picture given us by Weber.)
But even if we grant the validity of these criticisms, they still do not
detract from the stature of Weber or the value of his work. Weber
remains a significant beginning point for the humanist or social scientist
who is seriously concerned with understanding the character of modern
society. Few other writers—if any—have so magnificently comprehended
the workings of religious, political, economic, and social organizations.
Readers should note, as they continue through this book, the extent to
which many contemporary sociological writers have been influenced by
Weber. Only to the extent that we perceive this influence can we have
a basis for evaluating the fullness of Weber's contribution to social
thought.

Problems and Issues

*Many observers of the American
scene have commented on the extent to which we are inclined to think of
being impoverished as an indication of some kind of failure on the part of
the individual—usually some kind of moral failure. How does blaming the
impoverished person for being morally derelict influence the problem of
poverty? Poverty is also thought of in terms of economic factors. Weber
suggests that the economic and moral systems are interlaced elements of
a more complete social structure. What problems are created by our modern
tendency to deal with economics as a separate and isolated matter of
markets, labor, and money? Do you think that economic practice is also a
matter of moral choice? How would you define the economic morality of
modern America?*

*Weber was interested in the issue of power—as are most people who
have questioned the nature of human social systems. But "power" is an
extremely difficult term to define. What is power? The President of the
United States, often thought of as the most powerful person in the world,
is very much at the mercy of powerful and competing interests. His life is
public. He cannot control the press in any significant manner. He is expected to represent the interests of the people. Wherein does power lie?
Is a "powerful" individual simply a personification of the power of the
organization he or she represents? Is it possible to be a powerful person
without representing some powerful organization? If not, then power is
latent within the organization and not within the individual. Americans
personalize power and indulge in what have been referred to as "cults of
personality." Is power more properly viewed as a sociological than as a
psychological quality? What are the implications of the way one resolves
this issue?*

96   *Weber is known as one of the foremost students of modern bureau-cratic structures. Bureaucracies are seen as bumbling organizations and bureaucratic workers as ineffectual morons. If you were designing an ideal social system, could you do so without incorporating most of the major features of a bureaucracy—hierarchy, rationalism, officials, tests, communal property, and so on? When you get angry with "bureaucracy" are you angry because it was being bureaucratic or because it was being unbureaucratic? Most students, for example, do not want professors to be especially "personal." What they really want is for teachers to be "likeable." These are quite different matters. A bureaucrat can be likeable without being personal. What are the characteristics of an "ideal" bureaucrat?*

Weber outlined the diverse effects of Protestantism on Western culture and society. He particularly noted the ways in which Protestantism led toward a capitalistic morality. Weber suggested that it is not possible to achieve a real separation of the church and state in other than a legalistic sense. How successful do you believe we have been, in the United States, in achieving this kind of ideal? Do you think we should struggle toward such an ideal? Currently the American Civil Liberties Union is attempting to get American schools to stop the practice of singing Christmas carols, because this violates the principle of separation of church and state. Do you think this is going too far? Why? What are the deeper issues beneath this potential conflict of church and state?

Weber helped bring us the idea of the "charismatic" leader. Most of our celebrities are charismatic "leaders." How do they compare with governmental leaders who occupy positions of official or routinized authority? What are the advantages and disadvantages of each form of leadership?

Symbolic Interactionism and the Work of

GEORGE HERBERT MEAD

"Consciousness" is a very ambiguous term.
Mind, Self, and Society
BORN: 1863   DIED: 1931

The Problem of the Individual and Society

Social theories have a tendency to get entangled in the problem of the primacy of the individual over society or society over the individual. At first the question of this relationship seems like an idle form of speculation—an empty argument similar in character to the ancient riddle concerning how many angels can dance on the head of a pin. Perhaps it is unfortunate, but we cannot dismiss the individual-versus-society question in the same way we seem to have dismissed the old problem of the angels and the pin. The proper nature of the relationship between the individual and society (or the state, culture, or community) still constitutes one of the more exasperating and contentious of all humanistic concerns. It has been the ideological fracture line for great masses of people who turned against each other, at least in part, because of the stand they took on this issue. There are those who believe society should reflect the nature and character of the particular men and women who make it up; society is, according to this view, properly subordinated to the individual. On the other side are those who believe that individuals

6

98 must reflect the nature and character of the society of which they are a part; from this perspective the person is properly subordinated to the society or state.[1]

Another form of this issue appears in the interest that a lot of people give to the matter of whether a person should be a conformist or a nonconformist. To be a conformist, of course, is to give in to the demands of the state. It means burying one's own identity within the corporate identity of thousands of others who speak the same language, wear the same clothes, share the same style of haircut, live in the same kind of house, drive the same kind of automobile to work, and eat the same kind of dinner from the same kind of table when they come home at the same time in the evening to the same kind of family. The dismal portrayal of the conformist that is now so popular in Western literature does not need to be stressed here. We are all familiar with it.[2]

If being a conformist is a dismal moral fate, then the fate of the nonconformist, or deviant, is hardly any better. True deviants are those persons identified by other people as being sufficiently individualistic to attract attention, concern, notoriety, and the threat of—or imposition of—constraint. If deviants continue to assert themselves, they are subjected to constraining sanctions.[3] The assertion of self is, by definition, an act against society. Even relatively minor forms of self-assertion, such as bargaining with store clerks, are beyond the capacities of many Americans.[4] True forms of individualistic conduct exact a great price on the

---

[1] Ayn Rand, for example, does not equivocate in the resolution of this issue. For her the individual is paramount, and the greatest person is the one who is able to force his or her will upon the state. See, for example, *Atlas Shrugged* (New York: Random House, 1957) and *For the New Intellectual* (New York: Random House, 1961), or any of the other works of Rand. On the other hand, until recently at least, academic anthropology has tended to give strong emphasis to the argument that the individual is an almost helpless agent of the state or "culture." The most extreme form of this thinking appears in the writings of Leslie White, who sees the individual as a relatively passive conductor of culture—somewhat like a wire conducting an electric force—no matter how great or unique the person might appear to be. Geniuses, from White's point of view, are only better conductors of the cultural force.

[2] This suggests the ironic impasse, of course, of having a conformistic conception of the nature of conformity—part of being a conformist in Western society, particularly America, is to appear to be a nonconformist.

[3] This is not a technical definition of deviance—a difficult term to pin down when examined closely. We are excluding here unusual but accepted persons such as state governors or best-selling authors. They are in a statistical minority and, in this sense, deviant, but they are generally highly conformistic. We should also mention that the number of devices society is capable of employing to promote conformity to established standards is considerable. They range from the use of violence to the modification of belief systems. They are generally effective enough to induce high degrees of standardization among people. See, for example, Peter Berger's discussion of social control in Chapter 15.

[4] Harold Garfinkel, of the University of California, Los Angeles, had his students attempt to bargain for items in stores. It was common for students to reply that they experienced difficulty telling a clerk they would offer less for an item than its established price. Some students found it impossible. Those who were able to bargain, however, discovered that it became easier with practice. Some eventually concluded, after gaining several surprising bargains by doing their homework for the course, that they would never buy any item priced over ten or twenty dollars without first offering a lower bid. See Harold Garfinkel, *Studies in Ethnomethodology* (Englewood Cliffs, N.J.: Prentice-Hall, 1967).

part of the person who is willing to engage in such assertion. Even **99**
outwardly acceptable behavior, such as exercising one's right to remain
unmarried, will evoke sanctioning activity and negative labeling by those
who look on marriage as a proper form of living. In a society that extols
marriage, trying to remain single for any great length of time can be a
modest adventure in individualism.

At the moral level, then, the problem of the relationship between
individuals and the state is a profound one, centering on the extent to
which individuals, by losing their identity through conformity, have, in
effect, sold their personal soul for a mess of collective pottage. To
conform or not to conform is a daily matter calling for personal judgment.
At the same time, it is a question that becomes as abstract, complicated,
and impossible of precise resolution as the ancient riddle of the angels
dancing on the head of a pin we referred to at the beginning.

We began this chapter on the work of George Herbert Mead with
a brief consideration of the problems contained within the alternatives
offered by conformity or nonconformity. This was done to highlight
moral aspects of the problem of the relationship between the individual
and society. But there is another way of dealing with this issue. Instead
of asking if the individual *should* conform to the demands of the state
or if the state *should* conform to the demands of the individual, we can
ask: To what extent does a person, in fact, conform, and to what extent
is that person, under the best of circumstances, able to express his or
her individuality? This shift in the character of the question moves the
problem from the moral realm to the more empirical realm of observation. Even so, the question, in its modified form, remains difficult and
probably can never be resolved with any degree of accuracy. This, however, should not deter us. The question, though difficult, must be pursued because it is central to the development of both a personal understanding of our own lives and better approaches to political and social
action. We have considered this issue briefly here because it is at the
heart of the thought and concerns of Mead, who was interested in the
nature of the bond that exists between the individual and the community.

Mead's Approach to the Society-Individual Problem

George Herbert Mead taught philosophy at the University of Chicago
from 1893 to 1931. His ideas were especially influential in the development of a form of sociological and social-psychological theory now
known as *symbolic interactionism.* As was the case with other turn-of-
the-century social theorists, such as Durkheim and Weber, Mead found
himself working within an intellectual milieu deeply affected by the work
of Darwin on the one side and Marx on the other. Social Darwinists,
taking the speculations of Charles Darwin far beyond what Darwin himself would have considered reasonable and proper, were advocating the
proposition that the individual shapes the state—that a society composed

100 of biologically inferior people can only be inferior itself.[5] Marxists, on the other hand, were advocating the position that the state shapes the individual. People of superior biological quality, if forced to spend their lives in an inferior society or culture, can only reflect the qualities of that inferior state.[6]

Granting the existence of these two clashing sentiments in nineteenth-century Western thought, it would seem that the only theoretical position one could possibly take would be to espouse either some form of Social Darwinism or some form of Marxism. One of the interesting features of Mead's thought, we believe, is that he did neither.

In his consideration of the nature of the individual and society, Mead arrived at a complicated middle ground in which the individual and society are welded together as integral parts of a common process. Mead argued, in essence, that the old problem of the relationship between the individual and society is a false one because it tries to separate society from the individual—and that cannot, in fact, be done. Society is, Mead argued, prior to the individual. However, the greater and prior force of society nonetheless rests on people who have a good awareness of themselves as individuals. In a sense, the individual and society are different sides of the same coin. True enough, heads and tails on a nickel are different. However, when one is making a purchase, it makes little difference whether one puts a coin on the counter with the head or tail facing up.

The idea that society and the individual are different forms of the same phenomenon gives a new twist to the old problem that opened this chapter. After reaching an understanding of Mead, it is no longer easy to subscribe to the simplistic notion that you must contend with *either* society *or* the individual. Mead presents us with a comprehension of the extent to which individuals, and their personal and social consciousness, emerge out of society. Just as significantly, however, society, in turn, emerges out of the capacity of individuals to acquire complex forms of consciousness and self-awareness. Each must have the other. They are, in a sense, simultaneous happenings.

Peculiar Properties of the Self

Any introduction to Mead has to deal with the idea of "self." The concept of self was central to Mead's observations and arguments. It would seem, at first glance, that the nature and character of self is rather obvious. We

---

[5] This statement obviously is a horrendous simplification. Social Darwinism, as an intellectual movement within American culture and Western culture more generally, is an elaborate and many-splendored thing. In different forms and guises it still counts millions among its adherents.

[6] Again, in the interest of getting on with a discussion of Mead, we have indulged in a simplification that will horrify some Marxists, especially the academic Marxist idealists who tend to concentrate on the utopian features of Marxist thought and not on its empirical economic analysis. We do not intend to convey here the impression that Marxist programs of action are geared toward destroying individualism. We simply want to emphasize the environmentalism inherent within Marxism.

are whatever we are. We talk about ourselves and to ourselves. Others talk about us. We have a definite sense of being certain about what we are experiencing as we move through the world, and we relate ourselves to those experiences. Yet the character of self has some "strange" and not especially obvious features.

One of the more peculiar features of self comes out of what appears to be a dualism or twofold nature. We are referring, here, to the simple fact that people have the ability to comment to themselves about their own behavior. When we do this we take on a twofold action. We are the communicator, as it were, and we are also the individual receiving the communication. People, evidently unlike other creatures on this planet, refer to themselves. They judge and evaluate themselves. When they do this, they are both the judge and the individual being judged.

This is such a simple beginning point that it seems, at first glance, to be a truism. Certainly it does not appear to hold much promise for constructing a more elaborate conception of the nature of the relationship between the individual and society. For Mead, however, it is a primary observation whose value is enhanced by its simplicity and universality. It is practically true by definition that a human being is a creature capable of referring to and making judgments concerning itself.

The peculiarity of this, again, lies in the fact that when we do make references to ourselves we are, at one and the same time, that which is referred to and that which is doing the referring. So when I say, for example, "I am a terrible failure," I have engaged in an act that is, on the one hand, simple and common; on the other hand, it is an act unique among all the behaviors of the inhabitants of this earth. In such a statement, I function as both judge and judged. I convey to myself the fact that I am a failure and in doing so I act as the agent working, as it were, against myself.

Another peculiarity in such behavior is the abstract nature of it. In order for me to function as judge and judged, I must possess devices for complex forms of communication. When Hamlet, for example, talks to himself in soliloquy and ponders the business of whether to be or not to be, he reveals the dualistic nature of humanity in its most dramatic form.[7] Suicide, an act peculiar to humans, is an event wherein the person plays the dual roles of executioner and victim. We cannot resist adding here that no one has, to the best of our knowledge, ever observed a dog, horse, cat, or other animal brooding pensively at the edge of some cliff as it wonders whether it should be or not be.[8] Engaging in such internal forms of communication requires being possessed of and possessed by quite abstract conceptions of the world. These conceptions depend on our ability to employ symbols as a form of reality.

[7] Hamlet, of course, is a fictional creature, and social science is supposed to deal with that which is real. One of the better features of Mead's thought, we think, is its capacity to tolerate the fact that men and women live, as humans, within symbolic realms and that these realms are, ultimately, grounded in varieties of fiction. Literature is a device by means of which we obtain the most valued symbolic understandings our culture has to offer.

[8] Contrary to myth, lemmings do not engage in "mass suicide." See the brief note on this in *Psychology Today*, June 1968.

102   Symbols are the foundation stones of Mead's approach to human
social order. Where others have relied on biological drives, economic
interests, quests for power, or the need to survive, Mead presses into
an examination of the symbolic nature of humankind.[9] Symbols, language, and communication, he argues, must be examined if we are to
gain any understanding of our uniquely social nature.

Of special significance is the relationship between symbols and the
construction of conceptions of the self. These constructions of the self
give humans an especially complex and variable form of social character.
Without self there can be no society; without society there can be no
self. Because of this particular emphasis on the self-concept of the individual, the theories of Mead are relevant, of course, to the interests of
psychologists. At the same time, Mead's awareness of the close relationship between self and society has made his work pertinent to the interests of sociologists and cultural anthropologists.

Mind, Self, and Society

Mead's theories were delivered largely through his lectures at the University of Chicago. The several books published under his name were
compiled by his students and are flawed by repetition and thinly sketched
ideas.[10] Nonetheless, these works provide the basis for what is now
commonly accepted as a discrete school of social theory known as symbolic interactionism.

One of the best known of Mead's works is *Mind, Self and Society*.[11]
In this work Mead turns his attention to the general nature of the social
act. His theory provides an understanding reader with a complex interweaving of the individual and society. In the end one discovers the
integral character of self and society. Although Mead believed society,
in a primitive sense, was necessary for the formation of individual selves,
neither was, to him, distinct from the other.

The route that leads to this conclusion is involved, and we cannot
undertake a consideration here of all the subtleties that appear in Mead's

---

[9] Mead is not alone in this concern. Philosophers before him and after him have recognized
the significance of language and symbols. Mead's contribution is especially valuable, however, in its ability to bring together symbolic communication and human communities as
integrated parts of each other.

[10] The major writings of George Herbert Mead are: *The Philosophy of the Present* (La Salle,
Ill.: Open Court, 1932); *Mind, Self and Society* (Chicago: University of Chicago Press,
1934); and *Philosophy of the Act* (Chicago: University of Chicago Press, 1938).

[11] One writer says of this title that it would be more correct to reverse it so it reads "society,
self, and mind" because of the primacy given to society by Mead. This is an error, we
believe, and a misreading of Mead's basic ideas. Mead's theory specifies that *both* society
and self are emergent from the ability of individuals to refer to themselves as objects and
evaluate themselves accordingly. This is a mental act, covert and subjective, and within the
domain of "mind." Society is as dependent on the "mind" as the "mind" is dependent on
society. See Bernard N. Meltzer, "Mead's Social Psychology," in Jerome G. Manis and
Bernard N. Meltzer, eds., *Symbolic Interaction*, 2d ed. (Boston: Allyn & Bacon, 1972), pp.
4–22.

thought. It will suffice to begin with a consideration of the nature of **103** social constraint as it operates in the form of "social conscience" or "a sense of propriety" or "a feeling of moral obligation or duty." It is easy to dismiss an abstraction such as "social conscience" with the attitude that it properly belongs in theological discussions and is not especially "real." So it is essential, at the outset of a consideration of Mead's thought, to keep constantly in mind an awareness of the fact that the constraints imposed by conscience are able to surpass even biological urges and physical demands in their forcefulness.[12] Once we recognize this, it is reasonable—indeed it is absolutely necessary—to wonder about the source of the coercive power of belief, where belief exists as a form of symbolic meaning.

The first step in beginning to comprehend the coercive nature of symbols is to recognize that symbols can, in fact, construct a reality of their own. This contention was one of the central thrusts of Mead's argument. Mead did not have the advantage of being able to refer to research that later demonstrated, in dramatic ways, the extent to which human perception can be influenced by symbols. Researchers such as Muzafer Sherif and Solomon Asch later provided some of the clearest demonstrations of the capacity of language to influence perception and thereby "create," as it were, a unique reality. Having noted this, it will help to explicate Mead's argument if we take a brief aside and quickly sketch in the general character of the work of Sherif and Asch.

All Sherif did was have people sit in totally darkened rooms and observe a stationary pinpoint of light placed in front of them.[13] People, under such circumstances, see the light as moving in an erratic and random manner. This is referred to as the autokinetic or self-movement effect. Sherif, however, told his subjects that they would see the light move in a straight horizontal line, and they were to inform him of the extent of the movement. So informed, the subjects did, in fact, see the light move in a straight horizontal line, drifting slowly back and forth. The subjects then orally informed the experimenter how far they had seen the light move.[14] Sherif found that when people who saw the light move large distances were placed in communication with those who saw it move small distances, and each group communicated its perceptions

[12] However one responds to Freudian theory, it is difficult to deny the fact that what Freud referred to as the "superego" is often capable of suppressing the animal impulses of the "id." Thus we have the interesting situation where an abstract condition, namely social conscience, arising out of the social training of the child is able to coerce and frustrate more "primitive" or more "real" biologically grounded impulses. For Mead, social conscience is as real as any other form of reality and the problem is to find out why something as apparently insubstantial and abstract as social commitment can assume such force over the individual. The coercive power of belief is, for Mead, one of the most elemental concerns for the development of an understanding of human social systems.

[13] This discussion is based on Muzafer Sherif, *Psychology of Social Norms* (New York: Harper & Row., 1936).

[14] Sherif, interestingly enough, did not comment on the extent to which his own suggestion of apparent horizontal motion was a coercive symbolic construction of perception. Some researchers have found that subjects, told that the light would move in a circular manner and that they were to estimate the radius of the circle, saw the light move in a circle.

104   to the other, the result was a modification of perceptions in such a way as to approach a common mean. That is, those who saw it move large distances reduced the distance when told by others that it was not moving as far. And those who saw it move small distances increased their perceived distance of movement. It is particularly important to comprehend that perceptions actually changed. People who participated in the demonstration saw actual increases or decreases in the distance the pinpoint of light apparently moved.[15]

There is one important aspect of this study that must be mentioned. Such high susceptibility to suggestion comes when the situation confronting a person is without any apparent external structure. Such situations are sometimes referred to as *unstructured* settings. Asch was able to demonstrate that even in structured settings there are ways of convincing individuals to deny the evidence of their own eyes. Asch placed subjects with people who were to disagree with the subject about the length of two sticks. In such situations the subjects tended to agree eventually with the majority and say that the shorter stick was longer.[16]

From the work of Sherif and Asch we can formulate a conservatively stated principle that offers a profound basis for the more elaborate theories and ideas of Mead. The principle is: *In unstructured settings the introduction of symbolic structures can order perception so that the symbolic order is perceived as a real event.*

This proposition requires some comment. It implies that what we often think of as "merely" symbols are, in fact, an integral part of what we think of as *reality*. Virtually any real event a person encounters will be given some kind of symbolic interpretation; and almost any kind of symbolic construction will have implications for how people respond to what we generally think of as reality. Consider, for example, something as real and as concrete as a mountain. Depending on the kinds of symbolic environments from which a person comes, a mountain can be seen as a romantic wonder, a manifestation of the majesty of nature. A mountain might also be viewed, as the Alps were at one time, as a kind of imperfection in nature, a jagged mess of rocks. Or mountains, to a geologist, might be seen as repositories of mineral wealth. In other words, reality responds to the ways in which we define it. The point we wish to emphasize is that the definitions have real consequences. Physical reality, then, is somewhat subject to symbolic modification. Where there are no external constraints on our perception, symbolic modification can become the total reality. A person literally responds to the symbolic definition of the situation and acts accordingly.

Examples of this are common enough. Studies have shown that people are much more likely to give assistance to someone in trouble who is well dressed than to someone who is not. People respond to the symbolic meaning of attire. The "reality" of the character of the person

---

[15] It is easy to demonstrate this in a classroom. All that is necessary is a room that can be *totally* darkened. A flashlight with a small tinfoil cover that allows only a point of light to appear can serve as a light source.

[16] See Solomon Asch, *Social Psychology* (Englewood Cliffs, N.J.: Prentice-Hall, 1952).

beneath the clothes is not directly apparent. It does not have an overt or easily perceived "structure." Character is, then, established, in part, through the symbolic means of clothing or dress. A "good" person in "bad" clothes will immediately be perceived as "bad." A "bad" person in "good" clothes will immediately be perceived as "good." This is not to say that one cannot have altered perceptions as a result of developing longer-term relationships. This phenomenon of changing one's opinion about someone else is something most of us have experienced. It can be dramatic at times. It is dramatic because what we thought was "real" at an earlier time is eventually perceived as not having been "real" at all. A person we once admired is seen later to be despicable. A person we despised we come to see as being admirable. Usually it is the same person throughout the period in which we undergo our "change of heart." Our perception is influenced by the way we come to modify our symbolic impressions of the other person.

We are all vulnerable to this aspect of symbols. When we confront a stranger we are faced with the task of discovering what that person "really" is. But the reality does not exist in any physical form. It is rather obvious, then, that the quest for "true" identity involves symbolic exchanges, and the identity will be grounded in some kind of convincing story. We find out what a person is as we are told stories about that person's character. Such stories become a serious form of reality, as many a martyr has found out. Continuing with this line of thinking leads to the suggestion that literature and storytelling are essential acts for the creation of human character and that human character is, ultimately, grounded in the "fictional realities" within which we live.

Coming back to Mead, we are now ready to move into a consideration of the social nature of self. We have seen that when individuals are confronted with an "unstructured" setting or event, they are extremely vulnerable to symbolic forms of suggestion. Moreover, these suggestions have *real* effects on perception. It is axiomatic to Mead's thought (and that of most social scientists in Western culture) that at birth an individual is not provided with any inborn self-concept or socially structured self-awareness. This is something the person must, in large part, learn. Mead accepted this notion but pushed the issue further by raising the question of how the learning takes place. What is the process that results in self-conceptions that come to be so profoundly learned and accepted by most of us?

The beginning moment for the development of self and society comes with the acquisition of symbols that permit the person to identify himself or herself as an event that can be separated from the rest of the world and referred to as an object much like any other.[17] In our symbol system we have self-referent terms such as *I, me, mine, myself,* and our

---

[17] This raises the empirically interesting question of whether there are cultures in which people do not have well-defined self-referent terms. If so, then it would be a weakening of the Meadian position. We do not know of such a social or cultural system. Along with class structures, the communally given identity of the individual seems to be a cultural universal.

106 personal identifying names. In the use of these terms we are able to achieve the social bond—the force that binds the individual and the community together. Curiously enough, the use of self-referent terms cannot occur without bringing up some aspect of communal concern.[18]

This is most obvious in the case where a person reveals a social identity in the use of a self-referent term (for example, when someone, in response to the question, "Who are you?" says, "I am a Catholic" or "I am married" or "I am a student" or some other obvious conjoinings of self-referent terms with communal status systems). Unless there is a self-referent term—an awareness of one's own individuality—this form of conjoining of the person and society cannot occur. We are able to interact with the community by virtue of the fact that we have at least two primary sets of symbols that permit the interaction to occur. We have, on the one hand, the self-referent terms and, on the other, terms for various communal statuses. This, in part, is what symbolic interaction is about. Society and the person are generated together in those moments when people develop conceptions of themselves by virtue of symbolic interactions with others.

Other forms of the relationship between self-referent terms and communal concerns can be more remote and subtle, but the pure expression of self, independently of communal relations, appears to be impossible. Self is always connected symbolically with others, and in that sense it is always associated with society.

The concept of self is acquired with the acquisition of language. Modern symbolic interactionists are inclined to agree with Mead that self-conception is not inherent at birth. The acquisition of self-concepts comes through a process now referred to as "socialization." The most significant feature of the process of socialization is the development of a particular set of conceptions about the self. One of Mead's better known formulations was his discussion of the stages of development of self-awareness.

Stages in the Development of Self-Awareness

The acquisition of self-awareness is, paradoxically enough, tied in with the extent to which the individual comes to be aware of the complexity of human social interactions taking place. Until this occurs, the person is separated from others and, by virtue of that separation, is not able to

---

[18] This is virtually a tautologous statement. The late Professor Manford Kuhn of the State University of Iowa developed a "twenty statements test" in which people were asked to make twenty responses to the question, "Who am I?" Categorizing responses to this question enabled Kuhn to probe the ways in which people modify their conception of themselves as the character of their relations with others changes. In one study, for example, he found that people who had been socially "clobbered" (we would use the phrase *put down* today) tended to change their responses to the "Who am I?" question in a way that made greater use of "mystical" concepts. See Manford Kuhn and Thomas McPartland, "An Empirical Investigation of Self-attitude," *American Sociological Review* 19 (February 1954), 68–76.

comprehend the meaning of himself or herself as a social being. The development of a conception of self, then, is essentially a matter of the growth of social sensitivity. It is a matter of coming to understand the community. However, a good understanding of what Mead is talking about requires that the student not just see these "stages" of development of the self as a simple progression of sophistication in the person as he or she moves from infancy to maturity. It is a concise formulation of the intimacy of the bond between the individual and the community. It is a statement that reveals the extent to which both are dependent on each other. Self-consciousness, from Mead's point of view, is, strangely enough, a matter of community consciousness. To have a self one must at the same time have a knowledge of the moral order of the community. And in order for the community to exist, the individuals within it must be possessed of a sense of their individuality and the relationship of that individuality to the community.

Mead's stages of self-development fall into three broad stages:

1. *Preparatory stage.*[19] This is a period extending from infancy up to the point where children are able to begin dealing with themselves from the perspective of others. The essential feature of this stage is imitative behavior, in which children often reveal a capacity to mimic others who are engaged in real role performances. A good example of what is being referred to here takes place when a child who happens to see his or her parent reading a newspaper, picks up part of it and starts "reading" it too. The only thing that gives the child's performance away is that the paper is upside down. Such mimicry or aping of adults or older children prepares the child for a fuller social life as an adult.

2. *Play stage.* In the play stage children begin to reveal a capacity for seeing themselves from the perspective of someone else. This is a most important development and is associated with "mind" and the development of self-awareness. In this stage children literally "play" with social roles of a great variety. They are able to construct and formulate roles in a general way, and even more interestingly, they are able to play by themselves as social beings. In such play they assume different roles and then relate one role to another. Children are a sort of one-person band at this point. We should add that if the children are one-person bands at this stage of development, they become intricate and elaborate orchestras by the time they are adults. When we refer to children as one-person bands, we mean they are able to play out a scene against themselves. This might occur, for example, when a particular child, playing alone, pretends to steal a cookie. He might then assume the role of mother and admonish himself, and he might stand in the corner until, as his mother, he permits himself to go play once more.

The ability of young children to look at themselves through the eyes

[19] We are using Manis and Meltzer's description of the first stage, which is, as they point out, only implicitly developed in Mead's books. See Manis and Meltzer, *Symbolic Interaction*, p. 8.

108 of others in a sustained and involved way places them on the threshold of being human. They are nearing the point where they can begin to function as integral members of the community. They have acquired a sense of their own individuality and worth (or lack of worth) even as they have become laced into a larger social unit. Self and society are different sides of the same coin.

The most significant feature of the play stage is the involvement of the children with a variety of social roles. They are not merely little Carolines playing astronauts and Martians or little Rogers playing cops and robbers. One minute the child might be playing mother, another minute firefighter, another minute grocery clerk, another minute explorer, and so on. Children put on and take off roles as though the roles were elaborate symbolic wardrobes of possibilities. The roles might not be systematically related, one to the other, but children develop an awareness of their character through play. And the play operates within the development of the symbols that enable the children to acquire a sense of the nature of the roles.

3. *Game stage.* The currently popular metaphor of "life as a game" shows up in the writings of Mead. However, where the present-day ordinary use of this notion is moderately pejorative (as, for instance, in the phrase, "Don't play games with me, you so-and-so"), Mead looks on games as an integral part of the process of socialization. They are particularly significant for children as a device for locating them within a systematic ordering of roles. Children must come to view themselves in terms of their location within a network of roles, and they must perceive themselves not simply in terms of how they are related to some other single person but in terms of how they are related to large numbers of other people. Moreover, the other people may be related to each other in various ways, and the form of their relationship will affect the child's own significance. It is quite an achievement. The game offers one of the simplest means of entry into this system of relationships.[20]

In the game situation, a new feature is added to the abilities of the child to relate, symbolically, with others, for it is in this stage that the child acquires a sense of what Mead referred to as the *generalized other.* Mead developed his argument by using as an example the game of baseball. Consider, for a moment, the actions of the pitcher on the mound. A casual consideration of his behavior makes it seem as though the pitcher and the batter are locked in a duel and the pitcher's behavior is a simple response to the hitting habits of the man at the plate. From

---

[20] Keep in mind that role and status networks are, in themselves, quite complicated and abstract matters. In modern social systems, they have become sufficiently complicated to call for the employment of a new group of specialists who have the task of attempting to understand them better. These specialists are called sociologists. Every child born into this society must gain at least sufficient awareness of the system to be able to work and live within it. Games promote this awareness. Mead's arguments suggest that children who have difficulty in games will have difficulty in locating themselves in the community of adults in later life.

a Meadian perspective, however, the situation is more involved, less physical, and more symbolic than the ordinary fan in the stands is likely to appreciate.

When we see the pitcher as a person who is simply responding to the problem of the batter confronting him, we tend to think of him as involved with one other person.[21] Mead observed that what seems more reasonable is that the pitcher is actually relating to a large number of people at any one time. An interesting case in point is when a runner gets to first base. The pitcher obviously relates both to the batter at the plate and the runner on first. But Mead sees the pitcher as more highly involved than this. Not only is the pitcher necessarily relating to the runner at first and the batter who stands before him; he must also relate to the catcher, the infield, the outfield, the manager, the fans in the stands, the press, the coaches, the umpires, members of his family, and many others.

Mead termed this broader association with others the *generalized other*. The generalized other, achieved through the imaginative symbolic act of relating one's self to innumerable other people, becomes the incorporation of the community within the individual. It is, in a sense, the source of social conscience. Children encounter it and learn it through play experiences in which they are related to others who are themselves related to each other. The whole process depends on interaction and the ability to elaborate and expand that interaction by means of symbols.

Signs and Symbols

When people interact in terms of symbols, they are engaging in an activity that is quite unique. We must be constantly wary of thinking that we can understand human symbolic behavior by referring to the behavior of nonsymbolic creatures.[22] Such creatures are able to interact in terms

---

[21] We are relegating to a footnote the still popular "looking-glass self" formulation of Charles Horton Cooley. This concept is often mentioned in introductions to social psychology and is similar to Mead's ideas. However, it is much simpler and somewhat misleading in its simplicity. The "looking-glass self" suggests that people see themselves in terms of others by (1) imagining how they appear to others, (2) imagining how others judge that appearance, and (3) responding accordingly. Cooley's statement has the strong virtue of emphasizing that a person's conception of self involves both imagination and some kind of relationship with other people. It has a tendency, however, to leave students with the belief that self is located in encounters with specific other individuals, taken one at a time. Mead's point of view suggests a capacity on the part of individuals to locate themselves within a system of other persons at any point in time. In other words, people respond to a community of others and, ultimately, to the community itself as they have experienced it, heard and read about it, and imagine it. See Charles Horton Cooley, *Human Nature and the Social Order* (New York: Scribner's, 1922).

[22] Mead was inclined to be critical of some contemporary behavioristic psychologists, such as Watson, who wanted to ignore the trickier aspects of language—a feature of behaviorism that continues down to the present time. Behaviorism, Mead argued, must include a consideration of the nature of symbolic action if it is to have any value for the further development of the understanding of human social conduct. Behaviorists are all too willing to bring over into the human realm proofs for arguments that have as their sole support findings obtained from rats or other laboratory animals.

110 of signs but not symbols. People can interact in terms of both signs and symbols. Mead distinguished between signs and symbols by suggesting that signs always elicit a given response. Symbols, on the other hand, do not elicit a particular response but must, instead, be interpreted by those engaged in a symbolic exchange.

One of Mead's most popular observations concerns the character of interaction between two fighting dogs. In such a moment the animals might circle each other while making threatening gestures. Each dog is responding to the other in terms of an immediate stimulus, and the stimulus elicits relatively fixed responses. When the stimulus is withdrawn, the behavior is modified.[23] In such instances the organism is responding to the stimulus as a sign (or signal) to respond.

As we have pointed out, with signs the response is relatively fixed. When, for example, a lion roars in peace and contentment upon awakening, other animals may run away in fear even though the roar has no threatening meaning behind it. The roar is a sign that produces a given response. With symbols an added element is called into play—the necessity of shared meanings. This aspect of symbolic behavior, to the degree we consider it significant, implies that human social conduct will always be, to some considerable extent, immune to exact analysis. If there is a sharing of symbolic content, then interaction is relatively ordered or easy. Where symbolic content is not shared, then interaction is considerably inhibited, although it can continue at "lower" levels. Anyone who has tried to associate with a person who does not speak the same language has found how difficult a social relationship can be. This is an elementary kind of observation. At the same time, it is an important one because it is so basic and because it is so easy for people to confuse signs and symbols. The use of symbols presumes the existence of a social and cultural system—a network of values, meanings, interests, concerns, and labelings that are wrapped up in the elaborate form a language can, in itself, take. The use of signs does not require a social and cultural system.

Symbols, Reality, and History

One problem which the symbolic interactionist school of thought keeps encountering is the argument that symbols are not "real." Human social order and individual consciousness are located in something less ephemeral and more tangible than symbols. This has led, in turn, to a quest for

---

[23] A chimpanzee, for example, when in the presence of another chimpanzee in distress, will behave with evident signs of fear or distress of its own. However, as soon as it is removed from the sight of the suffering comrade, the chimpanzee will immediately resume normal activity. There is evidence suggesting that the human capacity to suffer over the misfortunes of another for any length of time (after that person is out of view) is a function of our capacity to translate that person's condition into a symbolic presence which then is able to stand for the reality of the other person's suffering. Empathy, in other words, rests on a symbolic base. See A. R. Lindesmith and A. L. Strauss, *Social Psychology*, 4th ed. (Hinsdale, Ill.: Dryden, 1974).

the "real" locus or foundation of human social order. One approach has been to look for it in kin systems and the bonds of sexuality. Another has been to seek it in economic relations and the necessity of labor and exchange. Still another approach has used the argument that communities arise out of the survival needs of people—that the community is essentially a defensive structure. These efforts have tried to locate the real foundations of the human community in the family or the marketplace or the military. They share a tendency to reject symbols as a basis for community. Symbols are something that came afterward and that remain, somehow, insignificant when pitted against the more fundamental forces of sex, labor, and conflict.

Mead, of course, was not unaware of the significance of such matters as sexual bonding, the power of the marketplace, or the demands of defense. For Mead, however, these are not forces that in and of themselves account for the extremely elaborate and continuous forms that human communities can give to these activities. An important word here is *continuous*. In order for continuity to exist within human communities, the community must have some kind of history.

History, however, is an almost bizarre accomplishment. It transforms into a "real" and present condition something that occurred in the past and therefore no longer exists and is not "real." By producing and sustaining histories, symbols are able to retain pasts. Mead considered this ability of symbols to be especially important for the formation of communities. In a sense, history offers the community a mirror in which it can view its collective self. Just as the concept of self is significant for the individual and provides the means whereby the person and the community are conjoined, histories enable entire communities to develop a sense of identity or self.

From a Meadian point of view, time and symbols are integral features of each other. Without symbols, people would have no sense of time. Symbols provide us with a past and a future that can be discussed in the present moment. Other animals respond to time in terms of physiological mechanisms that enable them to adjust to seasonal changes and the need to procreate. They probably lack, however, any elaborate conception of their past or concern for the distant future. Through language we are given a communal history or, to use an equivalent term, something anthropologists call *culture*. Through language we are also given a personal history or what social psychologists call *personality*.

Symbols, then, are at the very bottom of what it means to be a human being. They offer us a means for examining ourselves, and in the process we acquire self-awareness. With self-awareness comes consciousness and the ability to reflect on our worth or sense of worth—which influences our ability to relate with others and is therefore a social factor as well as a personal factor. Symbols also give us a sense of history. We become aware of our own past and the past we share with others. We can also construct imagined futures toward which we respond in the present.

In the works of a subtle philosopher like Mead, the symbol becomes a form of reality with implications that far transcend common and or-

112   dinary notions of what it is to be a symbol-using creature. Language does more than simply transmit culture; it is more than a "tool" that early people developed to solve their material problems. Language has been the agent through which people have become aware of themselves even as they become more aware of their physical surroundings. And as they do so, they are able to form the most elaborate and unusual social and cultural systems on the face of the earth.

Problems and Issues

In the 1950s Americans became extremely sensitive to the problem of conformism. Possibly this was a reflection of the fear of authoritarianism that followed World War II. To conform implied the presence of some kind of authority. Freedom from authoritarianism could be measured only by the extent to which one was able to avoid conforming. To what extent are we free to assert ourselves? Is the effort to assert the self actually only another form of conformism? This is not intended as sophistry. If Mead is correct, the self and society are simply different manifestations of the same set of conditions. A society that promotes individualism will be made up of people who see themselves individualistically. If nothing else, Mead makes clear the extent to which we are permeated by social experience. If we wish to improve the individual, we must improve the society. If we are to improve society, we must consider the individual. This seems to be a simple enough observation; however, many social philosophies become one-sided in their emphasis on either society or the individual.

The term "symbolic interactionism" was coined by Herbert Blumer. It nicely summarizes Mead's perspective. The connecting link between the individual and the greater community has to be some kind of communication system. This is as true of the social insects as it is true of human beings. Bees communicate through fixed responses to gestures from other bees, and chimpanzees and baboons have communal organizations that involve relatively elaborate communication systems. So it is with people. The communication system, grounded in symbols, is effective because the system is not precise. If, for example, we tell you that Jane is a student, we have not said anything especially precise. Indeed, we have told you very little. If this is so, then how does language operate to develop social systems? What is the role of language in the development of culture and society? Why is modern society so "noisy"? That is, why are we inundated by messages that come from a variety of sources? Even presumably "alienated" people can be seen with portable radios clapped to their ears, listening to the messages coming from them. What is the role of the symbol in our personal affairs? Particularly significant, in thinking about Mead's ideas, is the nature of "self." To what extent are we the creations of beliefs about ourselves? Mead uses the term "mind." Many modern philosophers, particularly those subscribing to a rigidly behavioristic point of view, would like to get rid of the concept of "mind." After all, you cannot deal with it scientifically. But "mind" does exist as a symbol; one we rely on in common discourse. If someone tells you that you are "out of your mind," what is being said? Must there be some scientific "object" or "referent" in order for such statements to have implications for your own behavior? A concept such as "mind" or "consciousness" is, as Mead points out, extremely ambiguous. Such terms become quasi-religious. They refer to that which is not apparent to the senses. They are extremely abstract. Is it possible to eliminate such terms from our vocabulary, as some people—those given to purely logical or scientific approaches to human behavior—would like?

Mead suggested that people become social, paradoxically enough, at the very moment when they become "selfish," that is, acquire a conception of self. What happens when the individual acquires a sense of self? Why should this seem to offer a more elaborate process for controlling the individual and developing a more complex social being?

How much of the social interaction you participate in each day involves symbolic interaction? How much of it is grounded in purely physiological concerns? Symbols do not have real properties as do physical objects. For that reason, this culture tends to ignore symbols as a part of that which influences and gives shape to our lives and our institutions. What evidence, of a solid variety, can be offered in support of Meadian theories? What evidence would appear to make Mead's ideas less tenable?

Sartre once observed, somewhat in line with Mead's arguments, that young men often "find themselves" or acquire a sense of self by becoming involved with highly authoritarian social organizations such as football teams, the Marines, street gangs, and so on. For Sartre this was something of a paradox. Do you agree that authoritarian social systems often provide a heightened sense of self? What is the appeal of authoritarian systems? Why do young people often find social organizations that grant them great independence and freedom intolerable? What evidence can you find to support or contradict these observations?

Can Science Save Us?

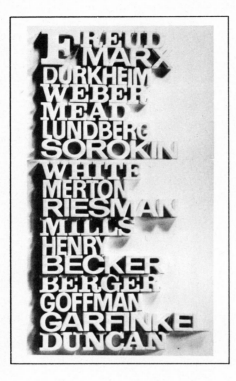

The Question of

GEORGE A. LUNDBERG

The invention and perfection of instruments for the more accurate and precise observation and recording of social phenomena must be regarded as among the most important developments in the social sciences.

Can Science Save Us?

BORN: 1895   DIED: 1966

7 The English essayist Charles Lamb once wrote, "Nothing puzzles me more than time and space; and yet nothing troubles me less, as I never think about them." Our social behavior is, in a way, like time and space. If we stop to think about it, it gets to be a puzzling business that quickly boggles the finest intellects of modern civilization. On the other hand, whatever society is, it manages to work sufficiently well, so most of us really do not bother to think all that much about it. Even when things go awry and we believe that we are forced to think seriously about social reality, we get caught in a peculiar bind. The bind comes out of the fact that we are likely to think about our social environment in a manner that is socially acceptable. For example, when it was fashionable to conclude that bad luck was caused by sin, the inclination to think about one's bad luck as being a result of sin was, in itself, a kind of socially induced thoughtlessness. This is why thinking about society boggles the greatest of intellects. It calls for a kind of "getting outside" the society in order to be able to look in on it. This is a lot like trying to hoist yourself to the moon by tugging on your bootstraps.

To understand society you must get "outside" it. However, if you

get outside it (to the limited extent that might be possible), you find **115**
yourself becoming quite inarticulate and, for want of a better word, mad.
It is a classic form of what Joseph Heller referred to as Catch-22. The
task of the good sociologist is a delicate one—a matter of fine balance—
in which he or she must acquire a quite literally strange mentality that is
capable of standing aside for a while in order to gaze dispassionately on
the passing scene. However, before this habit becomes too ingrained
and produces an intellectual monster in the name of sociological objectivity, the sociologist must return to his or her society and discuss, as
would any other involved and absorbed member of the community, that
which has been seen.

In sum, is there a better way to acquire social knowledge than we
have relied on until now? Must we, by the nature of social reality, rely
on blind faith and tradition? Is society grounded on delusion? Are various
forms of intellectual bigotry the only way to avoid confusion and mean-
inglessness? Or, is there an alternative? Is it possible that science, which
had generated so much optimism during the nineteenth and early twentieth centuries, could be used to examine social reality as effectively as
it had proved to be in the examination of physical reality?

It was this issue that George A. Lundberg attacked and attempted
to resolve. Lundberg sought to provide us with an approach to human
problems that does not lean on emotional surrender to an established
ideology; nor does it force us to respond with a hopeless shrug of the
shoulders as we retreat into a modern cult of despair. Quite simply,
Lundberg suggested that we acquire faith in a form of reasoning that is
itself constantly skeptical of faith. We can be confident only of the
method we use; we can never be confident of our conclusions. This is
the paradox of the position taken by the modern social scientist—and it
is one we shall examine through Lundberg's writings.[1]

Only science, suggested Lundberg, possesses the ability to bring
order into disorder without having to rely on myths and delusions. It has
done this in the physical and biological realms. Now we must accept the
logic and general analytic procedures of science and apply them to our
psychological and social natures. Anything else will result in deception,
error, and confusion. Because this position is so fundamental to the
social sciences—anthropology, economics, political science, social psychology, and sociology—we must give it some attention here.

Lundberg begins by suggesting that of all the different ways of
coming to grips with nature people have tried so far, the most successful
has been science. Science, after a rough and often bitterly vituperative

---

[1] The following brief bibliography of George A. Lundberg's works refers only to his major
writings. *Sociology* (New York: Macmillan, 1939); *Leisure, A Suburban Study*, with Mirra
Komarovsky and Mary A. McInerny (New York: Columbia University Press, 1933); *Social
Research, A Study in the Methods of Gathering Data*. 2d ed. (New York: David McKay,
1942); *Can Science Save Us?* 2d ed. (New York: David McKay, 1961). This chapter is based
primarily on materials appearing in *Can Science Save Us?* and extracts are reprinted by
permission of David McKay Company, Inc.

116 struggle for survival among ideas, won out over religion, magic, and tradition as a means of bringing nature under our control. It has not yet, however, won out over these less effective thoughtways when it comes to an understanding of people. In this realm preference is still given to customary forms of thought, to religion, or even to reliance on magic. When we can see how successful science has been in bringing about control over physical reality and, to a lesser extent perhaps, over biological reality, why do we not apply it directly to human political, economic, and social concerns?

The reason we do not allow science to enter human affairs more extensively, says Lundberg, is that most people feel they already know the answers to problems of social relations.[2] The person who places faith in the slower but more certain logic and rigor of science is at a disadvantage in the human realm because here one must compete with a variety of charlatans who provide quick and superficially reasonable answers. Lundberg sees the social scientist in a position similar to that of honest physicians who were at one time disadvantaged in their competition with snake oil practitioners.[3] The snake oil practitioners in the human realm are the astrologers, fanatics, and lonely-hearts columnists who, though they give enough occasional good advice to remain successful, rely in the final analysis on their own prejudices. The major distinction between idealistic charlatans who are ignorant of the limitations of their knowledge and the old-fashioned snake oil quacks is that at least the snake oil quacks knew they were frauds.

But is it not equally a form of ignorant and idealistic faith to rely on science as the savior of humanity? Only, says Lundberg, if we force science to give us quick and ready answers.

> I know that the method I propose is scoffed at in some quarters on the ground that, while it may be the solution for the long run, life is a short run. Whose life? Human life in its collective aspect stretches backward at least a million years and may reach much farther into the future. Throughout the ages it has been regarded as the mark of the intelligent and the civilized man that he has the power to feel and plan beyond the immediate situation. In any case, what choice have we? The proximate and immediate solutions which all desire are themselves dependent upon the development and use, in however modest degree, of scientific knowledge. Whether we look at it from the long or the short perspective, certain social problems have arisen as a result of science, and in our struggle with these problems science alone can save.[4]

Lundberg tells us, in this passage, that we really have little choice in the matter. The development of a social *science*, regardless of the extent to which such an endeavor falls short of pure scientific ideals, is necessary and inevitable. Now what we must do, says Lundberg, is come

[2] Lundberg, *Can Science Save Us?*, p. 5.
[3] Ibid., p. 13.
[4] Ibid., p. 16.

to a full understanding of what this means for all of us. Lundberg entreats the layman, on the one hand, to develop greater understanding of and patience with the behavioral scientist. On the other hand, he takes social scientists to task for not being sufficiently dedicated to science as a way of life or, at least, as a way of developing knowledge. Although social scientists cannot be as rigorous in their work as chemists, physicists, or biologists, they are nonetheless morally called on to act as scientifically as possible and not to relax in this effort.

Lundberg does not equivocate in his defense of the social sciences as sciences. They are, in his estimation, legitimate sciences in every respect. The ideal social scientist is an objective observer and writer whose own values and emotions do not intrude into the quest for decisive facts—facts that will either lend further support to a theory or weaken it to the point where it is no longer acceptable. The scientists Lundberg describes are detached, dispassionate, and thoroughly rational intellectuals. They offer no panaceas. They do not plead for some reform or social movement. They can tell you with equal effectiveness how to stimulate a race riot or operate a bakery. Their duty is not to tell you where to go; only how to get there.

> My point is that no science tells us *what to do* with the knowledge that constitutes the science. Science only provides a car and a chauffeur for us. It does not directly, as science, tell us where to drive. The car and the chauffeur will take us into the ditch, over the precipice, against a stone wall, or into the highlands of age-long human aspirations with equal efficiency. . . . the scientist who serves as navigator and chauffeur has no scientific privilege or duty to tell the rest of the passengers what they *should* want.[5]

For Lundberg, social scientists can, with some accuracy, make conditional statements about the outcomes of given policies—but they may not themselves formulate the policy. They can say, with all of the neutrality of an electronic computer, " . . . at the technical level alone, exemplary central nuclear attacks offer significant advantages. The problems of command, control, and communications, which are very great in sustained high-intensity nuclear wars, are much reduced in slow-motion exchanges that are limited and deliberate."[6] One must not, however, if one follows the ideal described by Lundberg, indicate any personal preference for one alternative over the other.

The "Scientific" Social Scientist

This characterization of the social scientist that Lundberg draws for us is not especially attractive. After all, many people come into the social sciences because they are discontented with the way things are in the

[5] Ibid., p. 38.
[6] Herman Kahn, *Thinking about the Unthinkable* (New York: Holt, Rinehart and Winston, 1965).

118 world today. They want to improve conditions—and this desire for reform means that one is permitting an intrusion of values into one's work
as a social scientist. Yet one does not become a criminologist in order
to amass knowledge that may be sold with equanimity to police officials
or gangsters. We do not devote our lives to the development of theories
of conflict only to have them, when published, used by national or
community leaders as a means of suppressing an exploited population.
But Lundberg has a reply for this kind of warmhearted approach to social
science.

In the first place, argues Lundberg, the desire to reform people or
impose our values on others interferes with the validity of our scientific
findings. Social science can be respectable in the eyes of the world only
if its findings are as accurate and as unemotional as it is possible to make
them. One of the things that makes the quotation from Kahn just cited
as sobering as it is, is the fact that Kahn maintains an attitude of not
caring. If he were a pacifist, people would be inclined to discount his
statement—thinking, perhaps, that he was writing satire. If he were a
militarist, people might wonder whether he was trying to whitewash the
use of thermonuclear devices in warfare. But Kahn has the virtue of being
able to maintain a disinterested attitude. Lundberg claims that only by
this kind of dispassionate presentation of arguments can the findings of
social science come to have any effective application in the attainment
of whatever values we hold dear.

In the second place, says Lundberg, the cold objectivity of the
scientist does not mean that values and sentiments are to be done away
with. To the contrary, only by having scientists assume this cool and
detached attitude can we hope to maintain some semblance of a democracy and avoid a dictatorship of pseudoscientific frauds. Scientists
may legitimately attempt to ascertain the prevailing values of their society. They might, for example, poll people and determine how they value
equality of opportunity for all people in the United States. Once the
values are ascertained, they can then suggest ways of efficiently achieving
them. In a word, Lundberg advocates a democratic system of determining
values through scientific means. If, for example, polls indicated that the
majority of the population wanted to destroy some minority, then—
though perhaps personally disagreeing with this policy—the scientist
who wishes to continue to function as a social scientist, is obligated to
seek the most efficient ways available for achieving this end. Lundberg's
social scientist begins to look like Dr. Strangelove—with the addition of
a heavy trace of Adolph Eichmann. If we dislike this characterization, we
must consider the alternative. The alternative is a world in which scientists themselves establish values. But there is nothing in science that
gives it moral insight—it is fraudulent to pretend science can provide us
with moral directives.

If we are to avoid situations in which the masses of people become
dedicated to inhuman values, we cannot do it by giving the scientist
moral power. We can do it only by giving greater freedom to people
whose task it is to concern themselves with human values—writers,
theologians, philosophers, artists, poets, and politicians. Scientists dare

not step into the moral arena; the moment they do so, their scientific character becomes blemished. Facts become suspect. Arguments and writings are directed not toward scientific truths but toward what one believes ought to be, or what one would like to think is the human condition.

The radical quality of Lundberg's proposal appears most explicitly in the following quotation. In reading this quotation, keep in mind it is being made by a man who is a liberal advocate of democratic government; moreover, he is presenting this argument to colleagues who, almost unanimously, are of similar political persuasion.

> The services of *real* social scientists would be as indispensable to Fascists as to Communists and Democrats, just as are the services of physicists and physicians. The findings of physical scientists at times also have been ignored by political regimes, but when that *has* occurred, it has been the *regime* and not the *science* that has yielded in the end.[7]

As Lundberg views it, the only way social scientists can increase their utility and enhance their status as scientists is by sticking to the job *as scientists*. Whether they operate within a fascist, communist, or democratic regime, scientists should tend to the development of scientific knowledge and ignore the broader issues of values and policy formation. Lundberg reduces the central tasks of the social scientist to three general concerns.

> Social scientists, as scientists, had better confine themselves to three tasks: First and foremost, they should devote themselves to developing reliable knowledge of what alternatives of action exist under given conditions and the probable consequences of each. Secondly, social scientists should, as a legitimate part of their technology as well as for its practical uses, be able to gauge reliably what the masses of men want under given circumstances. Finally, they should, in the applied aspects of their science, develop the administrative or engineering techniques of satisfying most efficiently and economically these wants, regardless of what they may be at any given time, regardless of how they may change from time to time, and regardless of the scientist's own preferences.[8]

Although superficially it seems prosaic, this is nonetheless a daring manifesto and an extremely controversial one. Behavioral scientists are still not agreed on it, and every person who considers entering the social sciences as a profession should seriously come to his or her own conclusions concerning the merits of this proposal. The most controversial proposition in the above statement is the one suggesting that the social scientist should develop techniques for satisfying the wants of the masses economically and efficiently regardless of what those wants might be at any given time. If we refuse to do this when we cannot agree with the desires of the masses, are we violating our commitments as social sci-

[7] Lundberg, *Can Science Save Us?*, p. 57.
[8] Ibid., pp. 59–60.

120 entists? If one accepts Lundberg's arguments literally, the reply to this question has to be affirmative.

The Character and Division of Education

Now let us consider another feature of this discussion. If science is the hoped-for savior of modern humankind, education is the medium within which a proper scientific spirit is sustained. Lundberg examines the character of education in modern society and concludes it may properly be divided between the arts and the sciences. The humanities should be incorporated into one or the other of these two central divisions. Philosophy, for example, is one of the humanities. It must, however, be taken apart, says Lundberg, and its different pieces should be placed either within the sciences or within the arts. For example, logic is more a scientific concern than a humanistic one; therefore we ought to place the study of logic within the sciences. Also, those portions of philosophy that deal with ideas about people or nature belong in the sciences so long as they represent historical efforts to achieve valid forms of understanding. But when philosophy is concerned with esthetics, it belongs among the arts. It has been extremely confusing, argues Lundberg, to lump diverse intellectual efforts together in a fusion of arguments that become tangled simply because people are unwilling or incapable at times of distinguishing between scientific and artistic thought.

In his proposal Lundberg does not give priority to science over art. Indeed, he claims only to seek to free both for the fullest achievements of which they are individually capable. He makes this clear in the following comment:

> A reasonable content for general education today, then, seems to me to be as follows: First, a command of the principal linguistic tools essential to the pursuit of either science or art. Second, a familiarity with the scientific method and with its principal applications to both physical and social problems. And third, appreciation and practice of the arts, including literature. Furthermore, these three fields should be so integrated toward a common purpose that the question of their relative importance would not even arise. One does not ask which is the most important leg of a tripod.[9]

The Middle Ages were able to unify education through theology. No such unifying principle exists today unless it is science. But science is not, as students so often believe it to be, a particular subject matter. It is, instead, a method of study, and it is applicable to the study of humankind as well as to the study of nature. If science as method can become a unifying theme within education, then many of the ills of contemporary education may be resolved. But what is this scientific method that Lundberg speaks of? He gives a relatively clear and brief statement. Science, says Lundberg, is a form of behavior having four

[9] Ibid., pp. 74–75.

parts. It consists of the following:

1. Asking clear and answerable questions
2. Making pertinent observations in an unprejudiced manner
3. Reporting these observations clearly and accurately
4. Revising previously held assumptions and beliefs in the light of our reported observations.

If we approach the study of people from this methodical base, then we must revise the curricula of our schools. Many educators believe the best form of education is one that begins with the old established classics and works its way into the problems of modern times. Lundberg is extremely skeptical of such a procedure and suggests that it might be better to ignore the classics for a while and first concentrate on contemporary events; then, when one has established via science a sufficient understanding of modern problems and the contemporary situation, one may be ready for the classics. The classics are not relevant to modern problems because they are located in the past. More significantly, they must be examined with great caution because they are often the fascinating and unwitting fables of people who were capable of telling lies with incomparable genius.[10]

We ought to note here that Lundberg dismisses the classics by using a very nonscientific device—the testimony of a famous man. He quotes Jefferson's opinion of Plato in which Jefferson says, "His foggy mind is forever presenting the semblances of objects which, half seen through a mist, can be defined neither in form nor dimensions. Yet this, which should have consigned him to early oblivion, really procured him immortality of fame and reverence"[11]

It is difficult to avoid the feeling that Lundberg, in his defense of science, is using a number of nonscientific devices to achieve the effect he is seeking. We shall want to keep this in mind when we evaluate his efforts more broadly near the end of this review. At the moment, we will simply make note of the fact that Lundberg is behaving like the representative of any faith—that is, he is relying on authority, rhetoric, tradition, and, perhaps, an essentially personal hope to generate the argument that science is the way we *should* develop an understanding of ourselves.

Lundberg is opposed to displays of reverence for established bodies of work that have been elevated to the status of classics. Science, however it is defined, always retains a high degree of skepticism—and in the social sciences this skepticism must be directed against official, traditional, accepted, or "classical" interpretations of human character. The story is told of two scientists who were riding through the countryside and, in the course of their tour, passed by a flock of grazing sheep. One of the scientists commented to the other that it seemed the sheep had just been sheared. The other laconically replied they did in fact appear to be sheared—at least on the side he could see. This degree of skepti-

[10] Ibid., p. 85.
[11] Ibid., p. 86.

122   cism is required of all scientists, but we should especially reserve such skepticism for observations having to do with people. Yet, obtusely enough, people generally seem more willing to direct critical skepticism against the findings of the social scientist while accepting the more casually developed generalizations of the novelist or armchair philosopher; a factually supported generalization is no more likely to be accepted than any other kind.

Science and Art

Will science supplant artistic, literary, and spiritual ways of life? If it does, says Lundberg, then the cost of science has been great—certainly greater than he would be willing to bear. Is the physical or social scientist a barbarian incapable of any "real" feeling? Is he like the man in e. e. cummings's poetry who appears in the lines

> While you and i have lips and voices which
> are for kissing and to sing with
> who cares if some oneeyed son of a bitch
> invents an instrument to measure Spring with?[12]

Does science deaden esthetic and spiritual sensitivity? Lundberg replies persuasively. In brief, Lundberg says that without scientific understanding we cannot have a heightening of esthetic and spiritual sensitivity. How does he make his point?

First of all, says Lundberg, some people claim that spiritual sensitivity is created by a sense of mystery. They further argue that science reduces the mysteries of nature and thereby robs people of enjoyment of its beauties and spiritual qualities. A knowledge of astronomy takes from us the ability to wander into the "mystical moist night air, and from time to time, look up in perfect silence at the stars." This is an unfortunate notion, because there is nothing in astronomy that prevents a person from achieving an emotional appreciation of the stars. If anything, an astronomer can see more to be awed by than can an ignorant person. Who is more awed, the person who believes, in a primitive manner, that the stars are light shining through holes punched into the umbrella of the sky; or the person who is aware of the magnitude of intergalactic distances and the forces that radiate throughout space? Lundberg sees no reason why the first person should have greater spiritual or esthetic strength than the latter. Science does not reduce spirituality by reducing mystery, because science is as capable of generating mystery as it is of reducing it. Even as science resolves certain questions, it raises an even greater number of other questions—and the process is endless.

In the second place, says Lundberg, some people believe that scientific sophistication overly commits one to analysis. As a result, people

---

[12] From *Poems 1923–1954* by e. e. cummings. Reprinted by permission of Harcourt, Brace & World, Inc., Publishers.

lose their appreciation of esthetic, ethical, literary, and artistic concerns. A physicist who gives a discourse on the physics of an especially beautiful sunset may be pitied because the audience feels that a scientist who is so busy analyzing the event has little chance to appreciate it. People may wonder if someone who knows as much about the physiology of sex as, let us say, Johnson or Masters,[13] can enjoy love. Lundberg dismisses this attitude toward science in much the same manner as he dismisses the first.

> Ask the musician if his study of harmony and counterpoint has decreased his enjoyment of music and he is likely to go to the other extreme and assure you that without these studies you can't *really* enjoy things musical. But he may feel quite concerned about the esthetic life of our physicist and almost certainly about the esthetic experience of the botanist and the sociologist.[14]

It is, perhaps, true that ignorance can generate a certain kind of reaction to an event that sophistication cannot offer. A person who, for example, is ignorant of how to fly an airplane will find the first experiences at the controls more thrilling than those which come after several hundred hours in the air. In a similar fashion, a person's ignorance of an ethnic or religious or racial group can produce a sense of excitement— the kind of thrill that comes with feelings of fear and uncertainty. The acquisition of sound and reliable knowledge is likely to change this.

Lundberg spends time with this issue because it is important and because it is, despite the seeming obviousness of a plea for knowledge, an extremely difficult argument. There is strong resistance to the idea that knowledge is worth the effort it takes to obtain it. This is the "I like what I have now, why should I change?" kind of attitude. How can one answer this? How can one demonstrate—how can one convince another—that the accumulation of knowledge can improve one's life? We grant a certain value to knowledge, but usually it is a cash value—a college education means more money in the bank. Or we evaluate knowledge in terms of the extent to which it can be translated into technology. The pragmatic test of knowledge is whether we can do something with it, earn something with it, build something with it, or, in a military state, destroy something with it.

Lundberg's plea for social science is at bottom a pragmatic one. He says we can engineer society closer to our desires if we emphasize the accumulation of better social knowledge, that is, more scientific knowledge. However, it is not easy to sustain this argument. It is possible, when it comes to human social organizations, to make as much pragmatic use of a myth or a lie or common sense as it is to make use of scientifically valid knowledge. Santa Claus is not without utility—and Madison Avenue has shown that mythical imagery sells more products than symbolic logic

---

[13] See William Masters and Virginia Johnson, *Human Sexual Response* (Boston: Little, Brown, 1966).
[14] Lundberg, *Can Science Save Us?*, p. 99.

124　ever could. Charlie Brown in the comic strip *Peanuts* has been more influential than many college professors.

The value of good knowledge, whether social or physical, is ultimately a matter of personal recognition, mature taste, and a matter of faith. All one can do who has the knowledge is reiterate that it means something—it is valuable. If you have mastered musical theory, you know its value for the appreciation of music, but you cannot communicate this value to a person ignorant of the theory. So too, the social scientists would like to communicate the value of their knowledge to the ignorant, but it cannot be done. One has to be willing to find for oneself whether the game is worth the candle.

Lundberg asserts that the knowledge we acquire about ourselves must be valid knowledge. We cannot achieve understanding and mastery over the world around us and over ourselves if we indulge in delusions. He cites the case of a British social scientist who doubts the validity of cinematic depictions of social mobility in America by referring to novels that reveal a different picture. Then Lundberg goes on to say,

> . . . while most people in Europe get their ideas about America from the movies, this "social scientist" is not so gullible. He checks on the reliability of the movies by reading novels. In short, if we really want to know how things are at the bottom of a rabbit hole, read a work by Lewis Carroll for the report of an eyewitness named Alice. Or, if you want to check the reliability with which the English novel portrays English life, visit the English movies.[15]

We must reject the distortions of society brought to us by people whose job it is to entertain us. These people are spinners of myths and masters of deception. We must rely, for serious work, on science and reason. This appeal to reason, this request for faith in scientific procedures, lies at the heart of modern social science. And it places the social sciences in a peculiar position. After all, the social sciences deal with a subject—humankind—which has been the traditional subject of humanistic studies. At the same time, they attempt to employ a method—that of science—which has become the hallmark of the natural sciences. This situation has made the social sciences particularly vulnerable to criticism. If they succeed as sciences, then they are apt to be scorned by humanists; on the other hand, if they succeed as humanistic studies, they are apt to be scorned by the scientist. This vulnerability cannot be overcome simply by protesting greater faith in science. Instead, we must, as social scientists, attempt to evaluate as honestly and as completely as possible what a subscription to science has meant for the social sciences.

What does faith in scientific method mean for the social sciences? William Stephens deals with this question more openly and specifically than others have. Stephens, to an extent not developed by Lundberg or any other positivist, wrestles with the problem of truth in social and psychological studies. He concludes that propositions which can be val-

---

[15] Lundberg, *Can Science Save Us?*, p. 103.

idated most completely are, at the same time, of least social or human value. If we put all of our money on scientific skepticism, as Lundberg would have us do, we might find ourselves in the position of having to live on the basis of validated knowledge which is of little utility to us. This is a messy paradox for social scientists and one which we do not yet know how to handle. The problem, in a word, is to balance probably valid trivia against possibly delusional profundity.[16]

Let us illustrate what is being discussed here with two quotations. One is taken from a social science journal and the other from the writings of an astute humanist.

> There is a very high correlation, as might be expected, between intimacy of family life and fondness for the parents, although the correlation is not quite as high as was found to prevail among a sample of University of Minnesota students. (From an article appearing in *Child Development*.)

Compare the above statement, made by a social scientist, with the following, made by a humanist.

> When I first read D. H. Lawrence's novels, at the age of about twenty, I was puzzled by the fact that there did not seem to be any classification of the characters into "good" and "bad." Lawrence seemed to sympathise with all of them about equally and this was so unusual as to give me the feeling of having lost my bearings. Today no one would think of looking for heroes and villains in a serious novel, but in lowbrow fiction one still expects to find a sharp distinction between right and wrong and between legality and illegality. The common people, on the whole, are still living in the world of absolute good and evil from which the intellectuals have long since escaped. (From an essay by George Orwell.)

The point is not so much that one statement is based on a careful and extensive collection of scientific data and the other is not. The point is that Orwell's comment offers us greater insight. We can fit Orwell's observation into a number of contexts and acquire at least the illusion of understanding. For example, Orwell sheds some light on the popularity, in America, of Batman. His observation, taken from literature, also seems to apply to the simple romances and adventures that make up most of the entertainment offered by daytime television. The social scientist offers us a more carefully validated statement—we can be more confident. At the same time, it is not an especially exciting statement. That is to say, once one is given this information, one finds it difficult to

---

[16] Stephens puts it yet another way: "The proper scientist finds, when he leaves his laboratory, that well-documented hypotheses will not take him very far. In his everyday activities and in his private thoughts—outside the laboratory—he must be almost as credulous and superstitious as the rest of us. Likewise, the more sophisticated speculative writer has some understanding of scientific procedures and the demands of evidence. He can, perhaps, temporarily suspend this awareness, in order to free himself to speculate. But this awareness, no matter how it is handled, must be with him, and it must affect the way he feels about his work." From William N. Stephens, *Hypotheses and Evidence* (New York: Crowell, 1968), p. 209.

126   do much with it. Lundberg seems to overlook this sometimes very glaring difference between fact and utility.

Lundberg gives us the impression, although he probably would not endorse this idea, that any scientifically established proposition is superior to any nonscientifically asserted proposition. For example, the scientifically demonstrable fact that white populations have longer life expectancies in the United States than do nonwhite populations is superior to the proposition that Santa Claus uses LSD. However, as obvious as this argument seems, when we get into the realm of human behavior the situation is not so clear as it looks at first.

Let us consider, for just a moment, the use of astrology as a means of finding oil wells and as a means of attending to personal affairs of the day. In the first instance we are likely to find that, compared with scientific procedures, astrology is not competitive; scientific methods work better when it comes to oil wells. But what happens when we use astrological procedures for our personal affairs? Suppose the stars "tell" us that today we will be in an unusually social mood and we should take advantage of the "fact" to make friends and influence people.

In this case the astrologer is not only providing us with a means (sociability) but also with the end toward which the means should be employed (making friends). If we follow the statement provided by the astrologer, it is likely to work. We have a kind of self-fulfilling prophecy here which acts to validate the statement. After following the astrological advice we have received, we are able to validate it. Thus, astrology can work in the field of human affairs to an extent not possible in the physical world. We must add that we are not attempting to justify astrology as a way of handling social problems. We merely want to point out that astrology can be relatively more useful in human social affairs than in the physical domain. In other words, astrology can compete more effectively with psychology and sociology than it can with geology or physics.

The Blending of Ends and Means

It is possible, then, when working with humans, to blend together ends and means. The reason that lonely hearts columnists, politicians, writers, demagogues, or any other nonbehavioral science figure can be effective in persuading others of the "rightness" of their assertions is that the assertions have a self-validation built into them. If, for example, I say, "You're great!," I have not only made a statement concerning a goal toward which you might aspire, but the statement itself helps serve the attainment of that goal.

We have, then, a situation in which quite nonscientific assertions may have a degree of social utility and thereby prove competitive with the assertions of social science. On the other hand, we find that some of the facts of the social scientist may contain an implicit, if not explicit, moral commitment.

When we add to all of this the fact that there is considerable debate among social scientists themselves regarding the extent to which social science should be objective and value-free, we have come back to the point where we began this discussion. What are we to do? Once more we are subjected to a confusing clamor of contradictory claims and opinions. There are people who want to underscore the word *science* and people who want to underscore the word *social* when we talk about the social sciences. Despite this confusion and debate, there is, within all the social sciences and among most of its leading representatives, a common set of aspirations that give unity to their efforts. We discussed these common factors—naturalism, generalization, an emphasis on social causation, and objectivity—in the first chapter of this book and do not need to elaborate on them further at this point. Whether or not the dedication that social science has given to these ideals will result in a "superior" knowledge of human nature remains to be seen. Certainly large-scale organizations cannot be run by the stars and survive for very long. The demand for social science comes out of the needs of big social organizations. Whether social science is useful to the individual is a more difficult matter. Many people survive with only the most minimal awareness of the findings and arguments of the social scientist. Personally, we believe a knowledge of social science is able to reduce fears and to expand awareness and understanding. It is, therefore, of value to the individual. But this belief is largely a matter of faith grounded in our own experiences. Each of us must find out individually whether or not science is able to save us.

Two Implications of the Social-Scientific Ethic

Before we leave this topic we must consider at least briefly, the broader implications of the social-scientific ethic. We think there are two issues worth mentioning. One of these has to do with the place of faith in human affairs. The other has to do with the conflict between scientific and humanistic interpretations of people and their nature.

It is difficult to examine Lundberg's writing or that of the writers who preceded him, like Comte and Spencer, without recognizing that a plea is being made for the acceptance of a new faith. Any human activity must be grounded, in the final instance, in beliefs which are not, in themselves, subject to any form of test. These beliefs we take at face value and endorse them and act on them without critical examination. Often the elements of faith become so thoroughly a part of our intellectual and emotional baggage that we come to believe they are instinctive features of people in general—they are simply human nature. We may take on faith the idea that progress is good. We might accept on faith the idea that sex is dirty. Faith may lead us to believe that work is a test of an individual's spiritual worth. We may, through faith, become followers of those who range in thinking from the fundamentalist evangelism of a Billy Graham to the racial vituperations of a George Lincoln Rockwell. It is a matter of faith.

But if faith is a necessary and central feature of being human, what happens when an idea appears on the scene that tells us to reject faith

128   as a basis of action? As we said before, the paradox of scientific thought is that it claims you must be faithful to skepticism. But skepticism is a rejection of faith. This sounds like a clever trick—if it can be done. What have been some of the consequences of people's attempts to live within a skeptical ideology whose force cannot be ignored and which, at the same time, deprives them of the comforting illusions of older faiths?

One response has been to perceive nature as "meaningless" and people as a puny and insignificant element within it. As skepticism has torn away many of the ancient conceits people gave themselves, it has led some of us to react with a moan of anguish and self-pity. Others have attempted to replace the old conceits with new ones even more arrogant and irrational. The current vigor of racism, for example, seems to be historically associated with a decline in the salience of a number of Christian moral doctrines.

Another kind of response to skepticism—one which both social scientists and humanists have hoped for—is a recognition of the freedom and the responsibility it gives the individual. Skeptical and knowledgeable people—sophisticated people—are freer to do with themselves what they will. Those who are aware of many of the subtle forces brought to play on them by society have an advantage the unaware person lacks. Knowledgeable persons have the potential for using rather than being used by the social situation in which they find themselves. In this sense, then, we can agree with Lundberg when he suggests that science can save us. It can free us from the binding constraints of blind tradition. We have been saved insofar as we have been freed. But, in our freedom, we must find in our own way the best use to which we can put our lives—and in this effort science cannot help us. Here the responsibility is ours alone and we cannot blame physics, psychology, economics, or any other science if we fail.

The second humanistic concern we wish to touch on, before leaving the subject of faith in science, is the one that has to do with the rivalry between humanistic and scientific conceptions of human beings. We have already alluded to this with a quotation from an eminent humanist, e. e. cummings. Scientists, as cummings sees them, are myopic and sickly characters who try, all too often, to measure things that are better not measured. Measurement and quantification seem to be at the heart of the issue between the humanist and the scientist. When the social scientist attempts to measure marital happiness or group morale, the humanist can be heard snickering in the background. But when social scientists attempt to develop a measuring instrument of this kind, they do so with the end in mind of furthering communication between people. We can discourse reasonably with each other only if the terms we use have some kind of common meaning. A measuring instrument provides this commonality. A measuring instrument is not, as e. e. cummings sees it, something that takes the spring out of spring and the life out of living. Indeed, it is something of a paradox that humanists who shout most loudly for better communication between people can, at the same time, deride a certain kind of communication—the scientific measuring instrument.

We have tried, in this chapter, to make the student or the general **129** reader aware of some of the pervasive problems that appear when one argues for a science of humankind. We have not been able to present any clear answers to these questions because we do not believe there are any. A commitment to science is a personal thing—not too distant in nature from a commitment to religion. We have seen too many steely-eyed people of faith in both science and religion, however, to want to present a one-sided argument for science. This chapter will have been successful in its intentions if it causes the reader to examine further and steadily the personal implications and the social values of science in our time. Lundberg stated the question simply: Can science save us? Let us think a while longer before we try to answer with a muted yes or no.

Problems and Issues

Lundberg's thesis is essentially a simple one—we must become more rational or we shall fail to survive. Rationality is viewed in terms of being scientific. The more scientific we become, the more rational we become. Is this true? Is it possible to be scientific and, at the same time, highly irrational? The problem, of course, is that in order to be logical and scientific we must choose certain goals that we can then work toward in the most efficient manner possible. If we want large quantities of energy, then science can help us. Is it rational to want large amounts of energy? To what extent are resources in America today being consumed for rational activities and to what extent for irrational activities?

Lundberg suggests that if the leaders of a society are antidemocratic and seek to implement certain policies, the social scientist, exclusively in the role of social scientist, has the task of implementing those policies in the most effective, efficient, and expeditious manner possible. Only in this way can the social sciences hope to function in a purely scientific manner. Do you agree? What kinds of problems are suggested here with respect to the utilization of social science as a science? If you believe that science cannot deal effectively with human social issues, with what would you replace it? What does this suggest with respect to the limitations of science?

Extreme supporters of science within the social sciences, and also within the natural sciences, are usually impatient with the arts. Lundberg thought the arts were pleasant lies concocted by ingenious liars. Are there several forms of "truth," such that one form is better represented through science and the other through art? How do you identify such forms, if this is so? When an artist tells us of "A savage place! as holy and enchanted/ As e'er beneath a waning moon was haunted/ By woman wailing for her demon-lover" we cannot consider this to be a "scientific" description, but can science provide a better description of a haunted scene? Can one develop any kind of scientific description of haunted events? Why not? Are scientists justified in spending money to prove that obviously mythical ideas such as the Bermuda Triangle are just that—myths? Even more significantly, are they wasting their time when they censor venturous and almost certainly false ideas such as those advanced by Velikovsky, who claimed that many Biblical legends were true and were the result of large astronomical bodies passing close to or colliding with the earth in ancient times? Is science, a human enterprise, any more free of human vices than other institutions? Is the modern tendency to accept the word of the expert on nearly any issue a new form of blind faith? How might Lundberg have responded to the current controversy that has developed with respect to the employment of nuclear energy? Has science been able to resolve the issue? If the issue is resolved, how do you think the resolution will come about? What will be the role of science in the resolution—great or small?

What do you think would be the consequence if you attempted to resolve every personal problem you encounter in life with scientific procedures? To what extent is some kind of "scientific" thinking essential as a part of day-to-day existence?

The Crisis of Our Age

The Views of

PITIRIM A. SOROKIN

In most of the great social revolutions, reforms, and reconstructions it is sociology of this or that kind which has been the leading ideology and guide.

Society, Culture and Personality

BORN: 1889   DIED: 1968

Professor Pitirim Sorokin stands as one of the most prolific and controversial of modern sociological writers. Few sociologists have been referred to with such a diversity of terms as "Old Testament prophet,"[1]
"severe and sarcastic,"[2] "renowned,"[3] "bullheaded,"[4] "moderate,"[5]
"unexcelled powers of penetration,"[6] and "philosophic."[7] Friendly or

---

[1] David R. Mace says, "The book [Sorokin's *The American Sex Revolution*] does, indeed, convey the atmosphere of grave concern and urgent warning that we find in the writings of some of the Old Testament prophets." See *Pitirim A. Sorokin in Review*, edited by Philip J. Allen (Durham, N.C.: Duke University Press, 1963), p. 141.
[2] Alexandre Vexliard in *Pitirim A. Sorokin in Review*, p. 179.
[3] Lucio Mendieta y Nuñez in *Pitirim A. Sorokin in Review*, p. 319.
[4] Sorokin cites some of his critics as claiming him to be idiosyncratic, bullheaded, and deviationist. See *Pitirim A. Sorokin in Review*, p. 35.
[5] Arnold J. Toynbee in *Pitirim A. Sorokin in Review*, p. 73.
[6] Othmar F. Anderle in *Pitirim A. Sorokin in Review*, p. 121.
[7] Joseph B. Ford in *Pitirim A. Sorokin in Review*, p. 39.

132 unfriendly, the readers and critics of the works of Sorokin[8] are forced to recognize the exceptional energy, imaginativeness, and involvement of the man who wrote them. Two colleagues paid Sorokin a tribute which, we believe, aptly sums up the quality and extent of his work.

> We can, in fact, imagine that the sociologist of the future may well complain, much as a frustrated successor to Plato once did, "Whenever I go anywhere in my attempts, I meet Sorokin coming back"[9]

Sorokin's life career spanned nearly two-thirds of the twentieth century. It was a career marked by adventure, controversy, astounding scholarly productivity, and laudatory recognition from professional societies and the general public. He was born in northern Russia in 1889.[10] In 1918, during the Bolshevist revolution, he was arrested and thrown into prison. Of this experience he commented, at the time,

> Well . . . I have been a prisoner of the Czar and now I am a prisoner of the Communists. From this varied experience I should emerge a practical as well as a theoretical criminologist.[11]

He was released, again imprisoned, and awaited execution. He was, however, released by order of Lenin.[12] In 1922 he left Russia, and in 1923 he arrived in America to begin life anew. He quickly attracted students and continued to write at a pace which, as he noted, enabled him to accomplish in three or four years an amount of publication which many sociologists would be happy to leave behind as a lifetime's effort.

---

[8] An incomplete listing of Sorokin's works covers ten pages of printed material. We cannot list the nearly forty books and several hundred editorials and essays he has published. Among his more important works we can mention *Leaves from a Russian Diary* (New York: Dutton, 1924); *Sociology of Revolution* (Philadelphia: Lippincott, 1925); *Social Mobility* (New York: Harper & Row, 1927); *Contemporary Sociological Theories* (New York: Harper & Row, 1928); *A Systematic Source Book in Rural Sociology*, with C. C. Zimmerman and C. J. Galpin, 3 vols. (Minneapolis: University of Minnesota Press, 1930–1932); *Social and Cultural Dynamics*, 4 vols. (New York: American Book, 1937–1941); *Crisis of Our Age* (New York: Dutton, 1941); *Man and Society in Calamity* (New York: Dutton, 1942); *Sociocultural Causality, Space, Time* (Durham, N.C.: Duke University Press, 1943); *Russia and the United States* (New York: Dutton, 1944); *Society, Culture and Personality* (New York: Harper & Row, 1947); *The Reconstruction of Humanity* (Boston: Beacon, 1948); *Altruistic Love: A Study of American Good Neighbors and Christian Saints* (Boston: Beacon, 1950); *Social Philosophies of an Age of Crisis* (Boston: Beacon, 1950); *S. O. S.: The Meaning of Our Crisis* (Boston: Beacon, 1951); *The Ways and Power of Love* (Boston: Beacon, 1954); *Fads and Foibles in Modern Sociology and Related Sciences* (Chicago: Regnery, 1956); *The American Sex Revolution* (Boston: Sargent, 1957); *A Long Journey: An Autobiography* (New Haven: College & University Press, 1963). This is only a partial listing. The more complete list from which this partial listing was taken can be found in *Pitirim A. Sorokin in Review*, pp. 497–506. Even this partial listing makes one aware that to read the entire works of Sorokin would, in itself, constitute quite a sociological education.

[9] Matilda White Riley and Mary E. Moore in *Pitirim A. Sorokin in Review*, p. 224.

[10] Sorokin, *A Long Journey*, p. 11.

[11] Ibid., p. 142.

[12] Ibid., p. 171.

Sorokin's View of Cultural Patterns   **133**

The richness and variety of his personal experiences, his Russian background and training, and his migration to another land and another academic setting made Sorokin a person ill inclined to accept provincial or narrow conceptions of humanity. The work for which he is most famous in this country is his four-volume investigation of cultural patterns, *Social and Cultural Dynamics*.[13] It is a work that attempted nothing less than to take in the changing patterns of human societies and cultures across the globe and down the reaches of historical time. It is a work that has been held by some to be too vast in scope to yield valid or worthwhile results. It has also been criticized because of its obvious contempt for the "sensate" character of modern civilization. Yet, granting its strengths and limitations, it is a powerful and intriguing work. It is, to use Sorokin's own term, one of his most fascinating "yarns."[14]

Sorokin made use of the fact that if we examine, in a comprehensive way, the culture and society of any people at any time, we begin to acquire a sense, however vague, of a relationship between the disparate parts of the culture. Mythology, art, law, philosophy, morality, family structure, the conduct of war, architecture, music, religion, economics, sense of time, logic, science, mathematics, humor, and leisure pursuits seem to be associated with each other. For example, in a culture such as ours, where affairs of the marketplace appear to be dominant, a wide variety of cultural habits and practices are related in their mutual support of the business ethic.[15] The cultural practices of the Pueblo Indians, on the other hand, appear to be related to religious practices and concepts associated with the problem of bringing rain to an arid land.[16] Sorokin stated the problem clearly:

> Is every culture an integrated whole, where no essential part is incidental but each is organically connected with the rest? Or is it a mere spatial congeries of cultural objects, values, traits, which have drifted fortuitously together and are united only by their spatial adjacency, just by the fact that they are thrown together, and by nothing more? If it is the first, then what is the principle of integration, the axis around which all the essential characteristics are centered and which explains why these characteristics are what they are and why they live and pulsate as they do? If the second, then how did it happen that in a given area one kind of conglomeration of cultural objects and values took place, while in another area a different kind occurred? How and why did it happen that in the course of time one

---

[13] It is recommended that the student read *The Crisis of Our Age* before turning to the four-volume work.
[14] In the conclusion of his autobiography, Sorokin says, "Therefore I scarcely have reason to complain of being 'a forgotten man' or a 'has-been scholar.' If anything, the world seems to be paying my 'yarns' attention far beyond their merit." See *A Long Journey*, p. 319.
[15] Jules Henry discusses this matter at some length (see Chapter 13).
[16] Ruth Benedict, *Patterns of Culture* (Boston: Houghton Mifflin, 1934). Sorokin cites Benedict but disagrees with some of her conclusions.

134   conglomeration moved in one direction while another changed in a way that was wholly diverse?[17]

Sorokin approached this problem by presuming that a culture would be profoundly affected by the manner in which it defined the nature of reality. Such definitions are pervasive and may, as a consequence, influence a great variety of behavior, ranging from art and leisure to law and science. As Sorokin saw it, there are two approaches to reality. We may, on the one hand, think of that which we can sense through our bodily organs as illusory—the real reality is held to be supersensory or spiritual.[18] The other approach to reality is to limit it as much as possible to that which is immediately apparent to the senses.

Ideational Versus Sensate Culture

To locate reality within the supersensory or spiritual realm is characteristic of what Sorokin called the *ideational mentality* or the *ideational culture*. To locate reality within that which can be sensed directly through our organs of perception is characteristic of *sensate mentality* or *sensate culture*. The concepts of ideational and sensate cultures became the core terms whereby Sorokin was able to explore further the problem of the integrity of cultures. Ideational and Sensate cultural mentalities are the axes around which the various essential characteristics of any culture are centered. Sorokin stated his case clearly in the preface to the second volume of *Social and Cultural Dynamics:*

> When a culture passes from, say, the Ideational to the Sensate type, or vice versa, all its art, philosophy, religion, science, ethics, and law undergo the same profound transformation. From this standpoint . . . what a given society regards as true or false, scientific or unscientific, right or wrong, lawful or unlawful, beautiful or ugly, is conditioned fundamentally by the nature of the dominant culture. In the Ideational culture, Ideational science, philosophy, religion, law, ethics, and art triumph, and their Sensate forms are rejected as false, wrong, unlawful, sinful, heretical, and blasphemous. Contrariwise, in a dominant Sensate culture—such as we are now living in—Sensate forms of science, philosophy, religion, ethics, law, and

---

[17] Sorokin, *Social and Cultural Dynamics*, vol. 1, p. 3.

[18] A very dramatic insight into this kind of mentality is offered by Herman Melville. Captain Ahab says of Moby Dick, " 'Hark ye yet again,—the little lower layer. All visible objects, man, are but as pasteboard masks. But in each event—in the living act, the undoubted deed—there, some unknown but still reasoning thing puts forth the mouldings of its features from behind the unreasoning mask. If man will strike, strike through the mask! How can the prisoner reach outside except by thrusting through the wall? To me, the white whale is that wall, shoved near to me. Sometimes I think there's naught beyond. But 'tis enough. He tasks me; he heaps me; I see in him outrageous strength, with an inscrutable malice sinewing it. That inscrutable thing is chiefly what I hate; and be the white whale agent, or be the white whale principal, I will wreak that hate upon him.' . . . 'God keep me!—keep us all!' murmured Starbuck, lowly." From Herman Melville, *Moby Dick*.

art become dominant; and their Ideational forms are branded as superstition, prejudice, ignorance and the like.[19]

Before applying the concepts of sensate and ideational culture mentalities to more specific features of society, we should expand them further. Table 8-1 presents, in brief, some of the significant differences between the two types of mentality.[20]

Sorokin stacked the deck in his distinction between the two kinds of culture mentalities by including in his definition of the mentalities some of the characteristics he intended to explain with them. This is like defining a priestly mentality as one which abstains from marriage and then explaining priestly celibacy by saying it is a product of priestly mentality. But this is a criticism that dotes too much, perhaps, on the technical problems of explanation. If we grant the validity of this criticism, it still does not seriously detract from the vision Sorokin offers us. To comprehend this vision, let us take the culture mentalities and apply them to a specific concern—the ethical and moral structure of societies. It is in these applications that Sorokin displayed best the orchestral nature of his scholarship.

Ethics under Ideationalism and Sensatism

A culture dominated by an Ideational mentality has a particular form of ethical system. In such a culture, ethics cannot be placed in the service of promoting sensual happiness, comfort, pleasure, or utility. These conditions are imaginary or illusory and therefore cannot be the final concern of Ideational ethics. Medieval Christianity from the fifth to the thirteenth centuries typified a culture dominated by Ideational ethics. The summons of the monastery was a call to better things, and to everyone the monastic life represented the highest goal on this earth.[21] Sorokin wrote,

> Seclusion from the world, holiness, devotion of the whole life to God, the vows of obedience, poverty, chastity; contempt, often torture, of the flesh; suppression of carnal needs—these were the traits of monastic Ideational ethics, whether for hermits or for monks living in monasteries. . . . Monasticism and asceticism compose the main pattern of the medieval ethics even outside of the monks.[22]

[19] Sorokin, *Social and Cultural Dynamics,* vol. 2, p. vii.
[20] Ibid., vol. 1, pp. 97–99. The comparison presented here is a highly modified and very abbreviated version of the one presented by Sorokin. Sorokin included in his discussion a cultural mentality type that is between the Ideational and the Sensate. He called this an "Idealistic" system. We have, in the interests of brevity, omitted this middle category.
[21] The phrasing here is essentially that of F. J. Foakes Jackson, who is cited by Sorokin in *Social and Cultural Dynamics,* vol. 2, p. 495.
[22] Ibid.

Table   *Ideational Versus Sensate Mentality*
8-1

Ideational culture mentality	Sensate culture mentality
1. Reality is seen as eternal, spiritual, and transcendental to the senses.	Reality is seen as located in material "things." It is immediately apparent to the senses.
2. The main needs of the individual are spiritual. Physical desires are curbed.	The primary needs of the individual are physical. Sensory indulgence and gratification should be maximized.
3. "Progress" is achieved through self-control.	"Progress" is achieved through control of the external milieu.
4. There is belief in "Being," and an indifference to transient values.	There is belief in "Becoming." Values are transient. There is endless readjustment.
5. The sensual person and self are repressed.	People are dedicated to "self-expression" and to sensual fulfillment.
6. People are introvertive and subjective in character.	People are extrovertive and objective in character.
7. Truth is based on mystical inner experience. Intuition, faith, and relevation are used.	Truth is based on observation, measurement, and experimentation. Logic is used.
8. The moral code is imperative, everlasting, and unchangeable.	Morals are relativistic, changeable, and oriented toward the provision of pleasure and happiness.
9. Art is symbolic and directed toward religious values.	Art is directed toward entertainment.

Our first point, then, is that the Ideational system of ethics cannot promote happiness of an earthly kind. A second feature of such an ethical system is that its commands are absolute. The ethical system is geared toward bringing its adherents into unity with supreme and transcendental powers. It may not, therefore, be tampered with. It is binding on all, and its moral imperatives are unchanging. Such a brief statement conjures up a static morality and a frozen world. This would be an error. We can get a more realistic understanding of the nature of an absolute morality from the following description of medieval European life by Herbert Muller:

The famed unity of the Middle Ages is not a mere fiction. There was a practically universal agreement on the basic ideas by which men professed to live. Catholicism was not only the one Church but the primary inspiration of art, the main source of education, the accepted basis of all philosophy, science, political theory, and economic theory. Medieval men all knew the same absolute truth about the human drama, from the Creation to the Last Judgment. There was also an underlying similarity in social institutions. The world of chivalry was much the same everywhere, and everywhere rested on the hard work of villein or serf; the same literary and art forms were employed all over Europe, or even the same legends of Charlemagne, Alexander, and King Arthur; Latin was the Universal language of educated men. There were no strict nationalities, no fixed boundaries, no armed frontiers, no passports. Merchants, students, minstrels, buffoons, pilgrims, pedlars, friars, masons, scribes, pardoners, cheap-Jacks—all wandered freely from place to place, to give the medieval scene everywhere the same gaudy variety.[23]

Finally, the ethical commandments of an Ideational culture emanate from God or some other supersensory source. The point Sorokin was concerned with here was that the locus of the Ideational ethical system comes from a point outside this world. It is, to use a term of Max Weber's, "other-worldly."

In contrast to the Ideational ethical system, that of the Sensate culture reflects a radically different set of premises concerning reality and people's relationship to that reality. First of all, Sensate ethics are concerned with moral conduct geared to promote human happiness, comfort, and pleasure here on this earth during the person's lifetime. Compare, for example, the Ideational sexual codes of St. Paul with the Sensate sexual ethic of Hugh Hefner, editor of *Playboy* magazine. St. Paul, attempting to divine the nature of the divine, reached the point where he was concerned with whether or not a virgin girl commits a sin if she marries.[24] Hugh Hefner, on the other hand, promotes a sexual ethic which permits the widest latitude in sexual gratification—constrained primarily by the limitation that it should not be damaging to other people. The significant thing to note in Hefner's case is that ethical constraint has its locus in this world rather than in some supersensory realm.

A second characteristic of a Sensate ethical system is its relativism. It is subject to changing times and it changes along with them. Some contemporary intellectuals are of the opinion that the modern world may reach the point where morality will become largely a matter of style.

---

[23] From Herbert Muller, *The Uses of the Past: Profiles of Former Societies* (New York: Oxford University Press, 1953), p. 239.
[24] See First Corinthians, Chapter 7. Paul's famous statement reads, "Art thou bound unto a wife? seek not to be loosed. Art thou loosed from a wife? seek not a wife. But and if thou marry, thou hast not sinned; and if a virgin marry, she hath not sinned. Nevertheless such shall have trouble in the flesh: but I spare you."

138 Today one reads and discusses the sodomistic experiences of Genet and takes LSD; next month the style will be to read and discuss Ralph Waldo Emerson and drink hot chocolate. I ought to point out here that Sorokin was entirely in disagreement with such a point of view. As we shall see a little later, Sorokin argued that Sensate ethics, and Sensate culture more broadly conceived, have reached what he referred to as an "over-ripe" stage of development. The thrust of the future will be in the direction of a reestablishment of Ideational values.

Finally, Sorokin observed, Sensate ethics are patently human rules. If they serve the purpose of happiness, they are justified. A nearly perfect illustration of what Sorokin is saying appears in the writings of A. E. Taylor, who in 1899 wrote a dissertation, published in 1901, which argued that the meaning of morality is to be found in the individual and not in the Absolute.

> The first law of moral action is, Know what you really want, and the second, like unto it, See that you are not misled into accepting a spurious substitute. . . . Only before you embark on the profession of a harlot, it is your duty to find out all you can about the life to which you are committing yourself, and to make sure that a career of prostitution ending in a Lock Hospital will really give you what you want. If you decide that it will . . . you are morally on the same level as the missionary who chooses to end a career of self-devotion by dying alone and untended in a leper-settlement; that the world in general does not recognize the resemblance is only another proof of the world's ample stupidity.[25]

The quotation from Taylor is all the more significant because Taylor was an Assistant Lecturer in Greek and Philosophy at Owens College, Manchester. It would be a trying task to find a medieval moralist who argued that an individualistic ethic could be used as the justification for entering harlotry as a career.

Economics under Ideationalism and Sensatism

The differences between an Ideational and Sensate system of ethics seem clear enough. What about some of the other characteristics of a socio-cultural system? What about economic activities, for example? The differences between Ideational and Sensate cultures with regard to economic practices are as definite as they are with respect to ethics. Both economics and ethics, Sorokin claimed, are enmeshed in the domination of the Ideational or Sensate point of view. In an Ideational culture the attempt to amass wealth and to concentrate on wealth-for-the-sake-of-wealth is considered a sin. Wealth is subordinated to greater ends. Business and economic conduct is a tolerated necessity, not an activity meriting the exclusion of an individual's other interests. For this reason, medieval society—a highly Ideational system, according to Sorokin—

---

[25] Quoted in Homer Smith, *Man and His Gods* (Boston: Little, Brown, 1953), p. 423.

punished those who sought wealth beyond what was necessary for a modest living. Moneylending for interest could and did result in expulsion, excommunication, and other severe measures.[26]

The role of wealth and the importance of the economic life are, of course, elevated considerably in the Sensate culture. Benjamin Franklin put it baldly and succinctly when he said, "Honesty is useful because it assures credit; so are punctuality, industry, frugality, and that is the reason they are virtues . . ."[27] Because it is of this world, because it can promote temporal physical pleasure, because it can augment worldly power, and because it is a visible and measurable sign of worth, wealth assumes greater importance in a Sensate culture than in an Ideational culture.

Art Forms under Ideationalism and Sensatism

Sorokin argued, then, that ethics and economics shared one kind of fate in an Ideational culture and a quite different kind of fate in a Sensate culture. But this shared fate takes place with various other aspects of the culture as well, the arts, for example. Sorokin was intensely interested in the nature and character of the arts. In this respect he differed from many other social scientists of the time who were inclined to be disdainful of the arts. Let us turn our attention, now, to what Sorokin had to say about the fate of the arts in Ideational and Sensate cultures.

Whether it is in the form of paintings, sculpture, music, drama, or literature, art is also enmeshed in either an Ideational or Sensate dominating culture. Ideational art forms exhibit a concern with spiritual or religious topics. The ambition of the artist is to "penetrate" the external characteristics of the subject and present a rendition of "eternal" or "absolute" qualities. Style tends to be more formal and symbolic. Medieval paintings of the Madonna, for example, pay careful attention to poses that, in themselves, have special meanings. Or, as a further example of such symbolism, a picture might show the Madonna with an egg, suspended from a string, hanging directly over her head. Ideational art is ascetic or, to use a current term, "dry." It has a nonerotic quality. Finally, the Ideational artist is directed toward God as a subject. Ideational art is filled with saintly figures, superhumans, gods, and demigods. There is pathos and tragedy, but there is always the triumph of the eternal, the spiritual, that which lies beyond the decay of the flesh and the dissolution of matter.

Sensate art—and modern art illustrates this form, according to Sorokin—moves in the direction of worldly rather than spiritual topics. The ambition of the artist is to portray the subject dramatically, to catch a moment of sensual reality, to impress the viewer or reader with an art

[26] Sorokin, *Social and Cultural Dynamics,* vol. 2, p. 501.
[27] Ibid., p. 506.

140 object that has impact.[28] Style is neither formal nor dry. The artist is concerned, whether in the graphic or literary arts, with achieving visual impressions. The subject is dealt with in terms of its "fleshly" character. In graphic art the Sensate movement means the development of nudism. In literature it means an increasing emphasis on the physical lusts of the writer's characters. As Sensate art forms develop, they increasingly take as their subjects nonheroic, everyday, commonplace people. Eventually, stage center of Sensate art is occupied by pathological individuals engaged in bizarre and pathological actions. In its "overripe" period, Sensate art produces works like Henry Miller's *Tropic of Cancer,* or William Burroughs' *Naked Lunch.* Painting moves toward dazzling the senses, as is the case with "op" art.

Commenting on Sensate art forms Sorokin made clear his attitudes toward them and left himself open, at the same time, to the objection raised by so many of his critics—his lack of objectivity and his "deck stacking" against modern views. Sorokin said of visual or Sensate art,

> Criminals, prostitutes, courtesans, ladies of easy virtue, beggars, street urchins, ragamuffins, exotic Oriental personalities and scenes, "the poor," "the oppressed," "the poverty-crushed persons," the social derelicts of all kinds, the socially and mentally maladjusted, the bloody, the greedy, the gluttons, the sick, the pathological—these and similar types of human beings become more and more favored topics of such an art and mentality. And the art of our days (just as we shall see, in its literature, its science, its politics, its ethics, its philosophy) is filled with such types and events. The "physiodirty" stream of interpretation of man in the so-called science and philosophy of our days ("psychoanalytic," which reduces man to a bag filled with sex—and dirty sex—only; "the economic," which reduces him and his culture to a stomach only; the "behavioristic," which tells us that man is a mere combination of reflexes—conditional and unconditional; the biological and evolutionary, which makes of him a mere animal; the mechanistic, which assures us that man is merely a mechanism and so on) is the same phenomenon that we meet in our art.[29]

Statements such as this reveal Sorokin as a vehement critic of modern culture. There is almost a quaintness about his revulsion. His claim that psychoanalysis reduces the individual to little more than a sex-filled bag—and dirty sex at that—is downright funny. If there were nothing more, we could consider such ranting as only the harmless barbs of a twentieth-century academic Don Quixote who had his head and heart somewhere back in the ninth century. But there is more to it than this. Sorokin was a critic, yet he was a critic who had the scholarship of more than fifteen volumes of his own effort as a basis from which to judge. If

---

[28] This Sensate art form has its ultimate current expression, perhaps, in advertising appeals to movies which inform the prospective viewers that the film will make them "blow their mind." We gather, from this expression, that the highest Sensate experience one can aspire to is having one's mind "blown." Since the actuality of a "blown" mind is almost incomprehensible, art forms exist which offer a safe and relatively limited version of this sought-after Sensate excursion.

[29] Sorokin, *Social and Cultural Dynamics,* vol. 1, pp. 499–501.

Sorokin was critical, we should not dismiss him with a simple-minded condemnation that he was not objective. We should, instead, look at the evidence on which he based his thinking.

The evidence consists of four volumes of historical data. These volumes cover every kind of social and cultural activity and perspective from art forms to space-time concepts. In Volume 1 of *Social and Cultural Dynamics*, for example, over a hundred thousand paintings from Italy, France, Central Europe, Hungary, Poland, Czechoslovakia, Germany and Austria, the Netherlands, England, Spain, Russia, and Islam are evaluated in terms of Ideational and Sensate characteristics. The time span ranges across three thousand years.[30] Sorokin had, therefore, a wide perspective on which to draw as a critic. When Sorokin criticized, it was not, we believe, because he was caustic or because he was suffering from some kind of reactionary "hang-up." Rather, the historical view which he possessed made him sensitively aware of the excesses to which we have gone in modern Sensate culture. It is not so much that Sensatism is "bad" but that the exhaustion of such an orthodoxy calls for someone to point it out.

We have, so far, established the distinction between the Ideational and Sensate forms of culture mentality. We have noted that ethics, economics, and art are some of the features of a culture that seem to conform to these dominant motifs. We have also noted the critical use to which Sorokin put these concepts.

Cultural Trends

Before going on to other features of Sorokin's work, we need to consider one further aspect of these two views of the world. If we grant that a culture can be defined as Ideational, how does it come about that a particular culture, such as our own, moves from the Ideational form to the Sensate? To put it crudely—how did we get from St. Paul to Hugh Hefner? If it is possible to answer this question, can we anticipate future cultural trends? Sorokin asserted that he had at least a general answer. In brief, a given cultural mentality—whether it is Ideational or Sensate—creates the conditions for its own downfall. If we are now in a Sensate period, the trend for the future will be in the direction of a new form of Ideational culture. And so the grand sweep of history consists of a constant ebb and flow across the centuries from Ideational cultures to Sensate cultures and back again. These historical tidal movements are measured in centuries.

The principal reason for this ebb and flow is that neither Ideational nor Sensate approaches to truth are perfectly correct. If the Sensate form, for example, were the final answer, then, once it came into being, it would remain dominant forever. But this cannot happen. By virtue of its weaknesses, which become more apparent as the Sensate form as-

[30] Ibid., p. 505.

142 sumes dominance, it is led into excesses. The corrective is to move in the Ideational direction. Similarly, the Ideational society is also fallible and also subject to excesses that are eventually corrected by a move in the direction of a Sensate form of culture.

Thirty years ago Sorokin cast his eye on modern Sensate culture and predicted its downfall—or, more correctly, its reform. From his vantage point in 1937, when the first volume of *Social and Cultural Dynamics* was copyrighted, Sorokin foresaw the necessary conditions for the fall of Sensate culture. He made thirteen forecasts.[31]

1. Because of its materialism and its objectivity, Sensate culture will increasingly lose its sense of the distinction between right and wrong, beautiful and ugly, and the more abstract human values. As a consequence, moral, social, and esthetic anarchy will become predominant.

2. People will be debased. They will be increasingly interpreted in mechanical and material terms. The spiritual—and lasting—basis of human worth will be lost sight of.

3. With universal values lost, there will be a loss of binding and pervasive consensus. Instead, there will be a multitude of opposed opinions.

4. In Sorokin's terms, "Contracts and covenants will lose the remnants of their binding power. The magnificent contractual sociocultural house built by Western man during the preceding centuries will collapse."

5. Force and fraud will be required to maintain moral order. Values will be ineffective as agents of control and we will be led into an age of "might makes right."

6. Freedom will be constrained and used as a myth of control by an unbridled dominant minority.

7. Governments will become more unstable and more inclined to resort to violence.

8. The family will, under the decline of universal values and the intrusion of overripe Sensate values, continue to disintegrate.

9. The Sensate culture will tend to become shapeless, as undigested but sensually appealing cultural elements are dumped into the market.

10. "Colossalism"—the idea that what is biggest is best—will replace the values given to quality. Those with "gimmicks" will be valued over those with genius, and the creativeness of the system will wane. Because valuable things are not, by any means, necessarily negotiable in our society, what is negotiable will win out while what is valuable will tend to be ignored.

11. Because of increasing anarchy and decreasing creativeness in the Sensate culture of today, depressions will grow worse and levels of living will deteriorate.

[31] Sorokin, *Social and Cultural Dynamics,* rev. and abr. (Boston: Porter Sargent, 1957), pp. 699–701. The list presented here is a slightly reworded version of Sorokin's list.

12. There will be declining security of life. Suicide, mental disease, **143** and crime will grow. "Weariness will spread over larger and larger numbers of the population."

13. The populace will divide into two parts. On the one hand will be the gluttonous hedonists who seek indulgence and pleasure. On the other will be those who withdraw and become antagonistic to Sensate values.

These forecasts form an engaging feature of Sorokin's work and thought. They indicate his concern for the future and his courage in being willing to attempt, at least in a general way, to fathom its possibilities. They stand at the conclusion of his major effort and, in a sense, leave to the future the vindication or rejection of his imposing argument. They also leave the reader to draw his or her own judgments.

From a vantage point of more than forty years later, we can see that some of the forecasts missed the mark—at least in American culture. We have not, as yet, been subjected to lower levels of living. But, then, perhaps more time is needed. Or, possibly our levels of living are lower, but we are not aware of it. As we speculate in this fashion we begin to see some of the weaknesses as well as some of the strengths of Sorokin's vision. It is a grand and sweeping vision—of this there can be little doubt—but it is also a vision that is slightly out of focus. We know that we are seeing things on a breathtaking scale as we tour through history and humanity with Sorokin, but when we attempt to isolate a certain detail, we sometimes find it difficult.

For example, when Sorokin says the "creativeness" of the system will wane, we may be inclined to go along with him. But the term *creativeness* has so many varied meanings we can never be certain just what the forecast is referring to in specific terms—in concrete details. Sorokin can, in a sense, fit the present, or the future, to his prognostication merely by assigning to a term like *creativeness* meanings that will back up his predictions. Yet, even as we mention this criticism, we are loath to carry it very far. Despite a lack of focus, it is better to see vaguely than not to see at all. And, though every reader will interpret the thirteen forecasts somewhat differently, it seems, at least to us, they are more often right than wrong. Though Delphic in many places, Sorokin's probe into the future still provides a means of broadly interpreting a variety of modern events, ranging from the once flourishing subculture of communes to the noisy wasteland of current American commercial television.

Fads, Foibles, and Faults

Sorokin's vast and roving scholarship is impressive. He directed it toward an understanding of broad patterns of historical change and development. As we have seen, he also directed it toward a critical examination of modern Western civilization. Sorokin, like C. Wright Mills (see Chapter 12), expressed his love for humanity by poking—and not too gently—

144 at its ugliness and shapelessness. If he could not exorcise its faults, he could at least try to make others painfully aware of them. When Sorokin moved from a global examination of the entirety of humanity down to more specific and local events, his critical reflections became more pointed and devastating. Sorokin was not only concerned with humanity in general but with the specific means people have established for observing and thinking about themselves. Among these means is what we today refer to as sociology. Sorokin took a look at sociology—a field to which he devoted a long and intelligent life—and appeared to throw up his hands in horror.

Sociology, as Sorokin saw it, is overrun with any number of faults.[32] It suffers from what he called the "discoverers' complex." This consists of forgetting that others have already observed or commented on what the sociologist has observed—and often the earlier observer has done a better job. Having conveniently forgotten or overlooked that others have already covered the same terrain, the sociologist can then shout, "Eureka, we are onto something hitherto unheard of!" Sociology also suffers, said Sorokin—and he is not the first, nor will he be the last, to make this point—from involuted language and "sham-scientific slang."

He went on to examine with an extremely critical eye a variety of other fads, foibles, and faults in the repertory of the sociologist, psychologist, economist, political scientist, or anyone else he happened to come across. He picked at nearly every weakness known to exist in psychological tests, and he used pungent language in the process.[33] He referred to our present "testomania" and to the twentieth century as an age of "testocracy." The quest for quantification in the social sciences he dismissed as "quantophrenia."

Moreover, Sorokin did not hesitate to attack the very core of modern sociological belief—the idea that our knowledge of the social world should be grounded in "empirical" fact. This notion, Sorokin argued, is both faulty and senile. Intuition plays a very important role in the development of scientific understanding and we cannot limit ourselves merely to the "empirical" realm of the senses. Indeed, social behavior is, when properly understood, beyond the direct observation of the senses. Furthermore, any number of fictions—in the strongest meaning of that word—play a most important role in scientific work, whether it is in physics or in sociology. The square root of minus one or the concept

---

[32] He lays out these faults in *Fads and Foibles in Modern Sociology and Related Sciences*. In his biography he complains, at one point, that C. Wright Mills wrote to him and said that he had used much of Sorokin's critique as a basis for his own book, *The Sociological Imagination*. Sorokin then wryly commented that nowhere in Mills's book is his effort cited.

[33] A later criticism of psychological testing, which is more comprehensive and deals specifically and only with the problem of testing, is Martin L. Gross, *The Brain Watchers* (New York: Random House, 1962). This book, published four years after Sorokin's, led to an investigation of psychological testing by Congress. According to the publisher, this investigation led the Civil Service Commission to withdraw, voluntarily, the use of psychological tests.

of infinity defies any empirical observation,[34] yet science would be seriously inconvenienced without them. Sociologists are fooling themselves when they think they can observe directly certain units of action or role behavior.

Worse yet, for all of their emphasis on empiricism, sociologists, like the worst gossip mongers, are too often willing to go along with "hearsay" evidence. Sorokin used the definition of marital happiness set forth by one sociologist as an illustration.

> Clifford Kirkpatrick operationally defines "marital maladjustment" as "that quality in marriage which causes one close friend to classify the couple as maladjusted." Thus, if a scholar wants to give an "operational" definition of happiness or "adjustment" in marriage, all he has to do is, first, to ask a friend of the married couple whether the marriage is "adjusted" or "maladjusted"; second, without any verification, to accept this opinion as valid and scientific; and, third, to build upon it a huge statistical superstructure of measurements and predictions of success or failure in marriage.[35]

Sorokin then went on,

> One can . . . sympathize with a physician who uses a thermometer to determine his patient's temperature or a cardiograph to diagnose his heart-activity, instead of adopting the much simpler and more infallible operation of just asking the patient or his friend whether the former's temperature and heart-activity are "normal" or "abnormal."[36]

These barbs, and others before them, did not endear Sorokin to members of the sociological community. Sociologists have been inclined to ignore Sorokin (which is roughly akin to trying to ignore the Eiffel Tower while visiting Paris) or to dismiss him with a casual shrug.[37] Yet Sorokin persisted, and his writings, in many places, remain viable while those of his critics have receded into obsolescence.

Sorokin's criticism of sociology is lengthy and negative, with only a brief and general suggested remedy. He recommended that integralist sociology replace the atomistic, analytic, pseudo-operationalistic, and empirical sociology of the present. As he developed his suggestion he also antagonized deeply those sociologists of today who are committed to "factual" sociology. The reason is apparent. Sorokin suggested that it

---

[34] For a very engaging discussion of the purely fictional qualities of a concept like *infinity*, read *Mathematics and the Imagination* by James Newman and Edward Kasner (New York: Simon & Schuster, 1940). Visualize, if you will, a quantity which, when divided by two, provides itself. That is infinity.

[35] Sorokin, *Fads and Foibles in Modern Sociology and Related Sciences*, p. 37.

[36] Ibid., p. 38.

[37] Cowell makes the following offhand comment concerning the response of the sociological community to Sorokin: "It has already been recorded that there was no discussion of Sorokin's views in the *Sociological Review*." *Pitirim A. Sorokin in Review*, p. 284.

146 was necessary to transcend the observable in order to understand the reality around us in a fuller sense.

> The integralist conception views psychosocial reality as a complex manifold in which we can distinguish at least three different aspects: sensory, rational, and supersensory-superrational. The sensory aspect is present in all psychosocial phenomena that can be perceived through our sense organs. The rational aspect is present in all the rational phenomena of the psychosocial universe: in logically and mathematically consistent systems of science, philosophy, religion, ethics, fine arts, up to the rationally motivated and executed activities of an individual or group. The supersensory-superrational aspect of psychosocial reality is manifested by the highest creative activities and created masterpieces of genius in all fields of cultural activity: by the great creative achievement of a genius-scientist, philosopher, founder of religion, great law-giver, great apostle of unselfish love, genius-writer, poet, painter, sculptor, composer, architect, and so on.[38]

What Sorokin is saying here (in terminology that lays him open to his own criticism of the sociologist's inclination for obtuse jargon) is that intuition and "spirit" are a part of the act of knowing. The present empirical psychosocial sciences have grown "tired" and "less creative." There is a need for a more daring integration of fact, reason, and intuition. Our awareness should not be subordinated to any single one of these three aspects of thought. In sum, Sorokin is saying that Sensate social science has exhausted itself as it passes into its "overripe" stage. The time has come to move back toward a more Ideational awareness of the nature of people.

Sorokin's criticism of the psychosocial sciences stands as a controversial statement, to say the least. It is written seriously, but not without humor. Sorokin indicated that he was shocked by what some of his colleagues were doing, but he was not so shocked as to divorce himself from the ranks of sociology. He depicted a situation which seemed nearly hopeless, but he never went to the extreme of claiming that it was. He grudgingly conceded that, when judged overall, the social sciences have provided people with important knowledge about themselves—but the time has come for reform. The wit and knowledge in Sorokin's critique, *Fads and Foibles in Modern Sociology*, make it useful reading for anyone about to enter the miasmic swampland of a career in the modern psychosocial sciences.

Altruistic Love

One phase of Sorokin's career must not be overlooked as we conclude this brief introduction to his work. At the end of World War II, Sorokin turned his attention toward a subject that other social scientists were inclined to ignore—the subject of altruistic love. One of the motivating

---

[38] Sorokin, *Fads and Foibles in Modern Sociology and Related Sciences*, p. 316.

factors behind Sorokin's interest in this subject was his growing awareness that democratic government, improved educational opportunities,
or increased religious dedication were not, in themselves, sufficient to
halt or even to slow down present levels and trends in intranational and
international violence. He wrote:

> Having completed my *Society, Culture and Personality* [first published in
> 1947], I began to orient myself in the vast and almost entirely unexplored
> field of the phenomena of altruistic, creative love. An "inventory" of the
> existing knowledge in this field showed that this gigantic problem had been
> largely neglected by modern science. While many a modern sociologist
> and psychologist viewed the phenomena of hatred, crime, war, and mental
> disorders as legitimate objects for scientific study, they quite illogically
> stigmatized as theological preaching or non-scientific speculation any in-
> vestigation of the phenomena of love, friendship, heroic deeds, and cre-
> ative genius. This patently unscientific position of many of my colleagues
> is merely a manifestation of the prevalent concentration on the negative,
> pathological, and subhuman phenomena typical of the disintegrating phase
> of our sensate culture.[39]

In 1948 he published *The Reconstruction of Humanity,* a book concerned with the topic of altruistic love. This, along with other works on
the same subject, reveals Sorokin's most serious intellectual involvement. The results, in terms of the extent to which they met support
within the greater public domain, were extremely disappointing to Sorokin—a disappointment which he covered with the statement, "the
results are more modest than I might have wished."[40] It might be worthwhile to conclude our discussion of Sorokin by outlining some of his
conclusions on the nature of altruistic love and creative genius, because,
we believe, young people today appear to be more overtly concerned
with the nature of love and the use of love than older generations seem
to have been.

The *Reconstruction of Humanity* is an unusual work. Certainly this
is true when it is viewed as the effort of a sociologist; it is also true even
if we disregard this fact. *The Reconstruction of Humanity,* like most of
Sorokin's efforts after 1937, contains reiterations of the main themes in
Social and Cultural Dynamics. Sorokin criticized Sensate values and saw
in them the cause of the decline of altruistic sentiments. He lashed out
at everything from decadent jazz music and demoralizing movies to the
loss of creative genius in the arts. Nothing, as Sorokin saw it, will bring
back altruistic morality short of a complete overhaul of the elemental
cultural premises upon which our society rests. To find altruism we shall
have to move away from Sensate values and toward Ideational values.
We shall have to return to universal moral precepts, and we shall have
to not only envision these precepts but establish a state in which people
live and act by them.

Sorokin made clear his position when he discussed what he con-

---

[39] Sorokin, *A Long Journey,* p. 277.
[40] Ibid., p. 292.

148 sidered to be the role of education in the improvement of society:

> As educational agencies the schools must establish a carefully elaborated system for developing altruism in their pupils. They must instill in them a set of universal values and norms, free from superstition and ignorance as well as from the degrading, cynical, nihilistic, and pseudoscientific theories of our time. This task should be deemed as important as intellectual training.[41]

But how is the foundation of the culture to be modified? How can we come to find the necessary "set of universal values and norms"? If it were found, how could people be made to endorse it and live by it? How could a self-indulgent, relativistic, and atomized society become unified in common expressions of the altruistic life? This question has probably concerned every person who has given serious thought to the nature of modern humanity. Each has tried, in various ways, to answer it, and each, possibly leaving some small mark, has generally failed. Nonetheless, Sorokin suggested, it is from the models offered us by the great altruists of history that we might find some solution. So it is that Sorokin's solution to modern world problems is essentially a religious one and is cast in the form of an ill-disguised sermon. In substance, Sorokin said we must turn to the model offered by the great Yogis, the Christian mystics, and the teachings of the great world religions—Buddhism, Hinduism, Christianity, Judaism.

It is surprising, as Sorokin developed his plea, to note the correspondence between his ideas and those endorsed by the recent "hippie" culture and, to a lesser extent, the "beat" culture that preceded it. Sorokin wrote:

> As a preliminary condition for obtaining control of the unconscious and conscious by the superconscious and for unlocking the forces of the superconscious, they unanimously demand the liberation of a person from all forms of egoism and the development of a love for the Absolute, for all living beings, for the whole universe, in its negative aspect of not causing pain to anybody by thought, word, or deed, and in its positive aspect of unselfish service, devotion, and help to and sacrifice for others.[42]

But the problem still remains: How do we achieve a general endorsement of such altruistic sentiments? How do we help precipitate the movement away from a Sensate system toward an Ideational one? Here Sorokin's platform falters on the steps of a series of "If only . . ." phrases. For example, he wrote at one point, "If most persons would even slightly improve themselves . . . the sum total of social life would be ameliorated."[43] It is difficult to disagree with this statement, and it is also difficult to do much with it.

Sorokin's program for social change and reform has grand aspira-

---

[41] Sorokin, *The Reconstruction of Humanity*, p. 153.
[42] Ibid., p. 224.
[43] Ibid., p. 233.

tions and a very naive and ill-developed sense of political strategy. Yet **149**
this may not be as bad or as common as it appears. Possibly Sorokin's is
one of the early voices calling for a return to more religious concerns
and understandings of ourselves and the mysteries in which we find
ourselves enmeshed. We need to look at science, at commerce, at education and the other orthodoxies of our time, and concern ourselves
with their excesses.

Our modern culture has produced a group of people, cryptic and
awkward, who are attempting to express in their own purposely inarticulate way, the same criticism that Sorokin stated academically and at
great length. Moreover, they are attempting to act according to the
precepts of what might be called modernized altruism. This group—the
new left—might not be exactly what Sorokin had in mind when he called
for a "well-planned modification of our culture and social institutions,"[44]
but they come closer to moving us in the direction Sorokin claimed is
necessary than do any other groups extant.

The Future

Like many of the other social observers considered in this book, Sorokin
was pessimistic about the future. He believed that unless humanity is
able to reverse its present egoistic and Sensate trend, we shall have to
resign ourselves to the inevitable end of creative culture. He saw hope,
but not much. He knew where we ought to direct our ambitions, but he
was, in the final analysis, unable to tell us how to acquire such direction.
Sorokin, like many other social scientists, reveals to us the frustration of
having knowledge and vision and, at the same time, knowing as fully as
it is possible to know, the frail capacity of a single person to act on the
basis of that knowledge.

The humanistic nature of Sorokin's writing and involvement is so
apparent we need only underscore it slightly to bring this chapter to a
close. He was a man of broad and critical knowledge. He was open in
his dislike and contempt for modern "Sensate" culture, and he was
strong in his enthusiasm for a return to more religious or "Ideational"
forms of culture. His endorsement of "superconscious" approaches to
the problems of life and the human social order endeared him to numerous churches. At the same time, we should recall Durkheim's admonition that even a society of saints will have its sinners. The history of
Ideational societies is also marked with grisly examples of inhumanity.

Problems and Issues

*Sorokin's thinking is based on
the belief that cultures must choose between two basic ways of viewing
the world: One of these is the Sensate view, in which one is expected to*

---

[44] Ibid., p. 234.

trust only one's senses. The other is the Ideational view, in which one seeks to "go behind" what is perceived by the senses. Sorokin, of course, believed that our times are dominated by a Sensate mentality. But is this so? Science, which is often thought of as being completely Sensate, is quite Ideational at times. Science teaches us about worlds that are far beyond our immediate senses. Much of our knowledge of "black holes," for example, does not come from direct observation but is, instead, "theoretical." Does science appear to be reaching a state of exhaustion of Sensate values?

Most controversial in Sorokin's thought is the idea of cyclical changes in culture throughout history. Sorokin is one of the last cyclical thinkers. At present there appears to be little likelihood that Western civilization will become less Sensate than it already is. What would have to happen to bring about Sorokin's belief that within the next century or two we will begin a turn toward a more Ideational form of culture?

Sorokin was concerned with the problem of altruism. Americans, generally, seem to be excessively interested in altruism and, in a more profound way, with the problem of love. What are the differences between a Sensate approach to love and an Ideational one? How have Sensate values influenced marriage, the family, and friendship? For example, this is a society in which friends are looked on as functional associates. When they no longer function to assist one in one's career, they should be dropped. Some corporations, today, are beginning to see that the executive who has to get a divorce may be more valuable to the company than one who insists on keeping his family intact. The former is probably getting a divorce because he works too much and gives his loyalty to the company rather than to his family.

Sensate values influence how we tend to evaluate people insofar as we attach much importance to "impressions." What evidence is there that Americans are nearly pathologically involved in the problem of their "looks"? Where did the idea of "beautiful" people come from? How beautiful are beautiful people? What constitutes an American's conception of "beautiful"?

The Science of Culture

The Views of

LESLIE WHITE

Science is not merely a collection of facts and formulas. It is pre-eminently a way of dealing with experience. The word may be appropriately used as a verb: one sciences, i.e. deals with experience according to certain techniques. Science is one of two basic ways of dealing with experience. The other is art. And this word, too, may appropriately be used as a verb; one may art as well as science. The purpose of science and art is one: to render experience intelligible.

The Science of Culture

BORN: 1900   DIED: 1975

In the movie *Fail Safe*, there is a scene in which two pilots for the Strategic Air Command talk about flying as they play billiards in the ready room. Both had flown in World War II and they nostalgically recall the pleasures of flying the old B-17 Fortresses and B-24 Liberators—they were great planes to fly. But modern planes are different, says one of the pilots; the thing about modern military aircraft is that you don't fly them—*they fly you!*

This is a fictional incident, but it points to a real and very serious problem—a problem that concerns the humanist and the social scientist of our time. In its simplest form, the problem can be stated as follows: To what extent are people becoming the agents rather than the masters of technology? Is technology a product of people's instinctive quest for improvement—a kind of epiphenomenon coming from some innate feeling expressed by the slogan *ad astra per aspera*? Is technology merely an extension of human nature? Or is our technology, our ambition, our desire, something external to us with a coercive force of its own which drags us in its wake? Do we run our machines or do our machines run us?

9

152   This is not a new issue. Humanists have responded to it for years with ideas varying from delight over our conquest of nature to brooding speculations about the triumph of matter over spirit.[1] Social scientists have also responded in varying ways. The most recent and faddish is to view complex and elaborate technological systems, along with their attendant demands on the social structure, as a sign of "modernization." Modernization is a goal that less fortunate countries should be encouraged to seek. Yet another way of looking at the rise of technology is to see it as something that has come into being despite intense resistance from humankind. It is, therefore, not an expression of human nature but a force that, in a sense, creates human nature.

It is in this latter fashion that the American anthropologist Leslie White examined the rise of technology and, more broadly, the entire evolution of human culture. We are wrong, says White, to think that human nature is the determinant of culture. It is quite the reverse; culture is the determinant of human nature. If we wish to understand people, we must understand their culture. To this reasonable—and not especially enlightening—statement he then appends another that seems less reasonable. We understand people by understanding their culture, but we cannot understand culture by studying people.

Culture, a Self-Generating Force

White's work[2] is not distinguished by the novelty of the issues he discusses, nor is it especially distinguished by the conclusions he reaches. But between the statement of the problem and the assertion of an answer are contained some of the liveliest and engaging and, for some, irritating arguments in the literature of social science. These arguments, radically extreme in the opinion of many scholars, nonetheless serve the purpose of providing the student of social behavior with a well-delineated statement of the distinction between our biological nature and our cultural nature. What, more specifically, is White's position?

The distinctive feature of White's thought is his constant reiteration of the importance of maintaining the distinction between what an individual is doing and what a culture is doing. We must, White asserts, be certain of our understanding of the difference between culturological and psychological interpretations of human behavior.[3] It has been pop-

---

[1] Compare, for example, Sandburg's eulogies to Chicago, "Hog Butcher for the World," with e. e. cummings's castigations of science.

[2] White published a large number of monographs and articles, most of which are very technical in character. This chapter leans heavily on his two best-known works, *The Science of Culture* (New York: Farrar, Straus, 1949), and *The Evolution of Culture* (New York: McGraw-Hill, 1959). Both books are attempts to reintroduce an evolutionary perspective into the thinking of the social scientist.

[3] Most, but unfortunately not all, social scientists are aware of the crucial nature of the distinction between social and psychological events. Developing this distinction is, for example, at the heart of Durkheim's thought (see Chapter 4). We have devoted this chapter to Leslie White because, in our estimation, no other writer is so single-mindedly concerned

ular in recent years to explain anything social or cultural in terms of the psychological make-up of individuals. War has been claimed to be a product of people's inner pugnacious character. It has been argued that submission to dictatorial regimes is a result of our deep inner craving for authority, certitude, and security. The institution of private property is merely an expression of natural acquisitive desires. Popular reliance on psychology for an explanation of social behavior has gone so far as to suggest that the prevalent use of blacks as slaves indicates an instinct for submission among black people.[4] This kind of thinking, says White, is wrong and misleading. It is, in fact, dangerously close to being in perfect opposition to what is actually going on. People do not have a competitive culture because they have a competitive psychological nature; we have a competitive psychological nature because we live in a competitive culture.[5]

This seems like a circular kind of situation because we can still raise the question: Where did the competitive culture come from? White has a ready reply: It came from itself. The historical process which gave rise to the culture is the source to which we must turn in order to understand why the culture places tremendous emphasis on competition. We cannot understand such competitive spirit merely by saying that it is the nature of people to enjoy competition.

As an illustration of what White is saying, we can refer to football—an institution generally in favor on American campuses and now highly popular as a national sport with professional teams. Once one acquires the spirit of the game, it seems almost instinctive to react with excitement and enthusiasm as the quarterback fades to pass the ball to a receiver

---

with making others aware of this distinction and its implications. After reading Leslie White, one finds it difficult to continue thinking that human behavior is subsumed by psychological theory and fact. This does not, incidentally, mean that psychology is in error or useless. It only means that psychology is, like any other field, limited in its application. Psychologists are not always easily convinced of this.

[4] White attributes this argument to the early twentieth-century psychologist William McDougall (1871–1938), who attempted to devise a theory of human behavior based on the idea of instincts. This theory has been generally considered to be inadequate. In its stead psychologists, social psychologists, and other social scientists have relied on the idea of more diffused biological drives that may be satisfied in a variety of ways and that provide the basis for rewarded or "reinforced" behavior of tremendous complexity and variety. White's reference to McDougall appears in *The Science of Culture*, p. 127.

[5] A stimulating antidote to this kind of cultural determinism can be found in the writings of Konrad Lorenz. Lorenz argues that the highly aggressive and predatory animals have biologically determined inhibiting mechanisms which prevent them from killing each other. Wolves, even when fighting for mates, do not struggle to the death. The defeated animal will bare its throat to the victor, who makes some menacing gestures and noises but then withdraws to enjoy his conquest. Gentler animals, on the other hand, do not have such built-in inhibitions. When they strike at each other it is usually sufficient protection simply to run away. But, if flight is not available, the results may be more bloody than a fight between predators. Lorenz cites the case of two doves who were left together in a cage overnight. When Lorenz returned in the morning, he found the female pecking and picking in the bloody skull of the male she had killed. See Konrad Lorenz, *King Solomon's Ring: New Light on Animal Ways* (New York: Crowell, 1952); also see *On Aggression* (New York: Harcourt, Brace, 1966).

154　downfield. Yet such behavior is quite obviously not instinctive. We have to learn enthusiasm—and it is a long and complicated learning process. Moreover, our enthusiasm is highly localized; we cheer our quarterback but groan with dismay when their quarterback shows signs of carrying the day. We turn out by the thousands to see a big championship play-off; while only a few hundred or so will sit and watch two freshmen teams play a hard-fought battle.

But most of all, the thing that is interesting about this game is the amount of publicity that must be given to it in order to get people excited about it. The game itself has many of the properties of a pagan rite.[6] Nubile young women dance before the crowds in the arena; batons are tossed high into the air; floats are paraded. Martial music is played. A very specialized group of performers attempts to solicit cheers from the fans in the stands.

Some people might suggest that all this is an expression of pent-up hostilities—a way of blowing off steam. But even a modest examination of what is going on raises the possibility that most of the steam being blown off is generated by the football game itself. This would be White's assertion. Football cannot be understood as a psychological event; it must be approached as a cultural event. There is no football instinct. There is, instead, only a socially and culturally supported pattern of behavior that retains its value and its meaning only so long as it has relevance within the greater cultural system.

The Process of Culture

Let us now look at how White expresses this in his own terms:

> If human behavior is to be explained in terms of culture, how are we to account for culture?
>
> Culture is an organization of phenomena—acts (patterns of behavior), objects (tools; things made with tools), ideas (belief, knowledge), and sentiments (attitudes, "values")—that is dependent upon the use of symbols. Culture began when man as an articulate, symbol-using primate, began. Because of its symbolic character, which has its most important expression in articulate speech, culture is easily and readily transmitted from one human organism to another. Since its elements are readily transmitted culture becomes a continuum; it flows down through the ages from one generation to another and laterally from one people to another. The culture process is also cumulative; new elements enter the stream from time to time and swell the total. The culture process is progressive in the sense that it moves toward greater control over the forces of nature, toward

---

[6] The young editors of an American high school newspaper had the temerity to suggest that there are close correspondences between the cheering at high school games and the slogans and chants once roared by Nazi youth groups.

greater security of life for man. Culture is, therefore, a symbolic, contin- **155**
uous, cumulative, and progressive process.[7]

The cultural elements that make up any given culture at a particular
point in time are not independent of each other. They exist within a
common culture and interact with one another. This suggests that culture
has properties unique to it—it is a system *sui generis.*[8] It is a force unto
itself.

Invention and Innovation

White develops this argument by concentrating on the nature of invention. An invention is, after all, the introduction of something novel into
the cultural system. We therefore have the problem of accounting for
novelty. As Berger has pointed out,[9] social and cultural systems tower
above the individual and they are essentially conservative—they are resistant to change. How, then, does change come about within the system? The most naive approach to this problem is to claim that invention
is a response to human need; to argue that necessity is the mother of
invention. This is not sufficient, for rather obvious reasons. In the first
place, people may long have had a need for certain inventions which
their limited cultural milieus prevented them from obtaining. People
could have used the farm tractor long before the twentieth century, but
their restricted cultural base prevented it from coming into being. More
significant, however, is the fact that time after time, people have proved
to be resistant to innovation, even when later events proved the invention to be generally beneficial, or at least not especially harmful. We are
told that necessity is the mother of invention. However, people have so
often been resistant to something new that it seems more appropriate to
claim that invention is the mother of necessity. That is, once the invention has come into being, people eventually make their peace with it.
This was certainly the case with Darwin's theory of the differentia-

---

[7] Reprinted with the permission of Farrar, Straus & Giroux, Inc., from *The Science of
Culture* by Leslie A. White. Copyright 1949 by Leslie A. White. Pp. 139–140. There may be
some inconsistency in this statement. White is not certain that current cultural developments are necessarily progressive. Culture has tended to make life more secure for people
but the future course of this tendency is open to speculation.

[8] The term *sui generis* (of its own kind) is often used by White. We saw this same term
being used in a slightly different setting in the works of Emile Durkheim. This is not an
accident. White was very strongly influenced by Durkheim and thought of him more as an
anthropologist than as a sociologist. Some idea of White's devotion to Durkheim can be
gleaned from the fact that he introduced three of the fourteen chapters in *The Science of
Culture* with lengthy quotations from Durkheim.

[9] It is interesting to contrast Berger's approach to social change with that of White. Berger
emphasizes a breakdown in the mythology which supports the *status quo,* while White
places emphasis on technology. The two points of view are not incompatible—they differ
essentially in emphasis. See Chapter 15 for a discussion of Berger.

156 tion of the species. The Victorian world did not immediately hail this as something wonderful that met the needs of the people.[10] There was a long and bitter fight culminating in the American comedy of the Scopes Trial.[11] What seemed to be happening in the case of evolutionary theory was that certain discoveries and the growth of knowledge led to the point where one or two men became the focal point for expressing a new concept. Once this concept was introduced into the culture, people had to take it into account and respond to it. But it did not come into being because there was a general demand for it. It came into being because the growth of culture had led to the point where it was a necessary consequence of a cultural system that had reached that particular level and form of development.

We can set forth two of White's most general principles at this point. The first is that an invention or innovation will not come into being until the culture base is sufficiently developed to permit its occurrence. This is a self-evident and not very interesting proposition. We can concede that early human beings were not able to invent the rifle because of cultural limitations, even though they were not lacking in intelligence. We can also presume they would have put such an invention to good use—that is to say, they had a need for it. Nonetheless, they did not get it because their culture was too limited in scope—the culture base itself did not permit the rifle to come into being.

The second proposition that White sets forth is much more interesting and contentious. This proposition asserts that when the culture base has reached the point where it is capable of supporting a particular invention, that invention will come into being whether people want it or not. If this is so, then culture is the force that generates culture. Before the invention of the gasoline engine, the possibility of powered, heavier-than-air flight was impossible. This is in keeping with the first principle mentioned above. However, once the gasoline engine was invented, the development of the airplane was assured. This is in keeping with the second principle.

Because the second principle is radical in its implications, White concentrates on developing it. The central historical fact that he utilizes as evidence in support of this principle is the phenomenon of multiple-simultaneous-independent inventions. History is loaded with many surprises when it comes to discovery and invention. We learn in our textbooks that Samuel Morse invented the telegraph.[12] A more serious study

---

[10] See William Irving's *Apes, Angels and Victorians: The Story of Darwin, Huxley and Evolution* (New York: McGraw-Hill, 1955) for an interesting account of how people reacted to Darwinian thought. They did not, in general, take kindly to it.

[11] See J. T. Scopes and James Presley, *The Scopes Trial: Center of the Storm* (New York: Holt, Rinehart and Winston, 1967).

[12] Morse was not unfamiliar with Henry's work on the telegraph. Henry seemed to be the more theoretical and basic inventor while Morse, who had also stumbled onto the same idea, moved in the direction of making it commercially feasible. See M. Blow, "Professor Henry and His Philosophical Toys," *American Heritage* (December 1963). The problem of independence of invention is a difficult one in listings of multiple-simultaneous-independent inventions, and the reader is cautioned to investigate in great detail the history of any invention before coming to some conclusions about who "really" invented it.

reveals that several men share the honors here. The telegraph was invented by Henry, 1831; Morse, 1837; Cooke-Wheatstone, 1837; and Steinheil, 1837. The feud that arose between Newton and Leibnitz over who developed the calculus is a well-worn example of the multiple-simultaneous-independent invention.[13]

History is replete with independent and simultaneous discoveries and inventions. The fact that priority of invention precludes the recurrence of the invention restricts the number of multiple-simultaneous-independent inventions that might have been recorded in history. That is to say, once the Wright brothers flew an airplane, the job was done. Something can be invented only once. Even in this case, however, it is still legitimate to wonder about who "really" invented the airplane. Langley's attempt, shortly before the successful efforts of the Wright Brothers, failed more from bad luck than bad design.

In any event, the multiple-simultaneous-independent invention is an historical fact. In case there is still some doubt remaining, the following list of such inventions and discoveries, prepared by William Fielding Ogburn, makes interesting reading.[14] The student is encouraged to scan this list and look for inventions like the phonograph and the steamboat—inventions often attributed to the inventive genius of a single person.

A LIST OF SOME INVENTIONS AND DISCOVERIES MADE
INDEPENDENTLY BY TWO OR MORE PERSONS

I

1. Solution of the problem of three bodies. By Clairaut (1747), Euler (1747), and D'Alembert (1747).

2. Theory of the figure of the earth. By Huygens (1690), and Newton (1680?).

5. Theory of planetary perturbations. By Lagrange (1808), and Laplace (1808).

8. Law of inverse squares. By Newton (1666), and Halley (1684).

---

[13] Discussing this same topic, Stuart Chase says, "Thus when physics reached a certain point of development in the seventeenth century, a dynamic mathematics was needed to carry on. Whereupon both Leibnitz and Newton invented the calculus independently. If neither had lived, calculus would have been invented by somebody else. History is filled with scores of simultaneous inventions of this kind." Stuart Chase, *The Proper Study of Mankind* (New York: Harper & Row, 1948), p. 119. Even so, Newton's name towers above that of Leibnitz. In one book on science Newton is mentioned eighteen times; Leibnitz is not mentioned at all. See Jacques Barzun, *Science: The Glorious Entertainment* (New York: Harper & Row, 1964).

[14] From *Social Change with Respect to Culture and Original Nature* by William Fielding Ogburn. Copyright 1922 by W. B. Huebsch, Inc., 1950 by William Fielding Ogburn. Reprinted by permission of The Viking Press. The list given here is an abridged version of the one given by Ogburn. However, his original numbering has been retained to indicate the extent to which other multiple inventions have been skipped over. A careful review of this list or, better yet, of the one by Ogburn, can be an educational experience. The student is encouraged to do more than read these pages in a desultory manner. Both the variety and the extent of inventions made by numerous individuals at the same time force upon the reader greater recognition of the degree to which invention is not a matter of personal idiosyncracy.

9. Nebular hypothesis. By Laplace (1796), and Kant (1755).

14. First measurement of the parallax of a star. By Bessel (1838), Struve (1838), and Henderson (1838).

16. Certain motions of the moon. By Clairaut (1752), Euler (1752), and D'Alembert (1752).

II

17. Decimal fractions. By Stevinus (1585), Bürgi (1592), Beyer? (1603), and Rüdolff? (1530).

18. Introduction of decimal point. By Bürgi (1592), Pitiscus (1608–12), Kepler (1616), and Napier (1616–17).

20. Logarithms. By Bürgi (1620), and Napier-Briggs (1614).

22. Calculus. By Newton (1671), and Leibnitz (1676).

25. The principle of least squares. By Gauss (1809), and Legendre (1806).

28. Geometry with an axiom contradictory to Euclid's parallel axiom. By Lobatchevsky (1836–40?), Boylais (1826–33), and Gauss? (1829).

30. Method of algebraic elimination by use of determinants and by dialectical method. By Hesse (1842), and Sylvester (1840).

33. Logarithmic criteria for convergence of series. By Abel, De Morgan, Bertrand, Raabe, Duhamel, Bonnet, Paucker (all between 1832 and 1851).

35. Circular slide rule. By Delamain (1630), and Oughtred (1632).

39. The law of quadratic reciprocity. By Gauss (1788–96), Euler (1737), and Legendre (1830).

III

45. Law of gases. By Boyle (1662), and Marriotte (1676).

46. Discovery of oxygen. By Scheele (1774), and Priestley (1774).

48. Method of liquefying gases. By Cailletet, Pictet, Wroblowski, and Olzewski (all 1877–84).

54. The Periodic Law. First arrangement of atoms in ascending series. By De Chancourtois (1864), Newlands (1864), and Lothar Meyer (1864). Law of periodicity. By Lothar Meyer (1869), and Mendeleeff (1869).

55. Hypothesis as to arrangement of atoms in space. By Van't Hoff (1874), and Le Bel (1874).

59. Discovery of elements of phosphorus. By Brand (1669), Kunckel (1678), and Boyle (1680).

62. Process for reduction of aluminum. By Hall (1886), Héroult (1887), and Cowles (1885).

IV

66. Air gun. By Boyle-Hooke (prior to 1659), and von Guericke (1650).

67. Telescope. Claimed by Lippershey (1608), Della Porta (1558), Digges (1571), Johannides, Metius (1608), Drebbel, Fontana, Janssen (1608), and Galileo (1609).

68. Microscope. Claimed by Johannides, Drebble, and Galileo (1610?).

69. Achromatic lens. By Hall (1729), and Dolland (1758).

71. Spectrum analysis. By Draper (1860), Angstrom (1854), Kirchoff- **159**
Bunsen (1859), Miller (1843), and Stokes (1849).

72. Photography. By Daguerre-Niepce (1839), and Talbot (1839).

73. Color photography. By Cros (1869), and Du Hauron (1869).

75. Thermometer. Claimed by Galileo (1592–97?), Drebbel? (1608), Sanctorious (1612), Paul (1617), Fludd (1617), von Guericke, Porta (1606), De Caus (1615).

76. Pendulum clock. Claimed by Bürgi (1575), Galileo (1582), and Huygens (1656).

78. Ice calorimeter. By Lavoisier-Laplace (1780), and Black-Wilke.

81. Kinetic theory of gases. By Clausius (1850), and Rankine (1850).

84. Principle of dissipation of energy. By Carnot? (1824), Clausius (1850), and Thomson (1852).

87. Apparent concentration of cold by concave mirror. By Porta (1780–91?), and Pictet (1780–91?).

89. Parallelogram of forces. By Newton (1687), and Varignon (1725?).

93. Law of inertia. By Galileo, Huygens, and Newton (1687).

V

96. Leyden jar. By von Kleist (1745), and Cuneus (1746).

97. Discovery of animal electricity. By Sultzer (1768), Cotuguo (1786), Galvani (1791).

98. Telegraph. Henry (1831), Morse (1837), Cooke-Wheatstone (1837), and Steinheil (1837).

99. Electric motors. Claimed by Dal Negro (1830), Henry (1831), Bourbonze and McGawley (1835).

100. Electric railroad. Claimed by Davidson, Jacobi, Lilly-Colton (1847), Davenport (1835), Page (1850), and Hall (1850–01).

104. Method of converting lines engraved on copper into relief. By Jacobi (1839), Spencer (1839), and Jordan (1839).

106. Microphone. Hughes (1878), Edison (1877–78), Berliner (1877), and Blake (1878?).

107. The phonograph. By Edison (1877), Scott? and Cros (1877).

108. Self-exciting dynamo. Claimed by Hjorth (1866–67), Varley (1866–67), Siemens (1866–67), Wheatstone (1866–67), Ladd (1866), and Wilde (1863–67).

109. Incandescent electric light. Claimed by Starr (1846), and Jobard-de Clangey (1838).

110. Telephone. By Bell (1876), and Gray (1876).

VI

114. Theory of infection of microörganisms. By Fracastoro (1546), and Kircher.

116. That the skull is made of modified vertebrae. By Goethe (1790), and Oken (1776).

121. Solution of the problem of respiration. By Priestley (1777), Scheele (1777), Lavoisier (1777), Spallanzani (1777), and Davy (1777).

160   123. Relation of microörganisms to fermentation and putrefaction. By Latour (1837), and Schwann (1837).

124. Pepsin as the active principle of gastric juice. By Latour (1834), and Schwann (1835).

125. Prevention of putrefaction of wounds by keeping germs from surface of wound. By Lister (1867), and Guerin (1871).

127. Invention of the laryngoscope. By Babington (1829), Liston (1837), and Garcia (1855).

128. Sulphuric ether as an anaesthetic. By Long (1842), Robinson (1846), Liston (1846), Morton (1846), and Jackson (1846).

129. That all appendages of a plant are modified leaves. By Goethe (1790), and Wolfe (1767).

VII

130. Theory of inheritance of acquired characteristics. By E. Darwin (1794), and Lamarck (1801).

131. Theory of natural selection and variation. By C. Darwin (1858), and Wallace (1858).

133. Theory of mutations. By Korschinsky (1899), and DeVries (1900).

135. Theory of color. By Young (1801), and Helmholz.

136. Sewing machine. By Thimmonier (1830), Howe (1846), and Hunt (1840).

137. Balloon. By Montgolfier (1783), Rittenhouse-Hopkins (1783).

138. Flying machine. Claimed by Wright (1895–1901), Langley (1893–97), and others.

139. Reapers. By Hussey (1833), and McCormick (1834).

140. Double-flanged rail. By Stephens and Vignolet.

141. Steamboat. Claimed by Fulton (1807), Jouffroy, Rumsey, Stevens, and Symmington (1802).

144. Typewriter. Claimed by Beach (1847–56), Sholes? (1875), and Wheatstone (1855–60).

146. Stereoscope. By Wheatstone (1839), and Elliott (1840).

147. Centrifugal pumps. By Appold (1850), Gwynne (1850), and Bessemer (1850).

148. Use of gasoline engines in automobiles. By Otto (1876), Daimler (1885), and Selden (1879?).

The Role of the "Great Mind"

White sees in this list the crucial documentation for his claim that culture is the cause of culture. We do not require great minds to lead us upward toward progress. We require, rather, an extensive cultural base to turn the trick. If we have that base, inventions and discoveries will take place with such force that they will appear at various points in the culture and at the same time. When culture is ready for an invention, that invention will come into being, even though there is no general desire for it within the greater society.[15] This observation forms the foundation for White's **161** position with respect to the role of the great mind in the progress of history.

> Briefly stated, the problem is this: are epoch-making social and historical events to be explained in terms of men of genius, or are great men explainable in terms of social process and historical trends? Or, do both, the great man and his social matrix, combine to produce the event or trend, and if so in what proportions?
> Most of those who have wrestled with this problem have championed either the great man or society as the motive force, as the cause, the other being regarded as the effect; few have been willing to give equal, or even approximately equal, weight to each factor. Let it be said at once that we have no intention of being "impartial" and of taking the latter course. We are convinced that the great man is best understood as an effect or manifestation rather than as a prime mover.[16]

White subordinates the person of genius to culture. In doing this he does not disparage the great minds of the past. He recognizes that they have made contributions to progress and he concedes that they have behaved intelligently. He is, however, concerned with pulling us away from the diffused inclination to worship heroes in any field of endeavor—a cultural innovation that probably has its origins in the rise of individualism in the late fourteenth and early fifteenth centuries[17]— and he concentrates on the cultural context within which great people were acting.[18]

[15] There is a problem here in determining what is meant when we say there is no desire or need for an invention or innovation. A vast majority of individuals probably had no desire for or even any conception of the possibility of Darwinian theories of evolution in the 1830s or 1840s. We are on rather firm ground, it would appear, when we claim in this case that there was no general need which brought the innovation into existence. On the other hand, the classic illustration of the atomic bomb is not so simple. No single individual had a need for such a device—and even its developers were appalled by the thought of it as they worked around the clock to bring it into being. But the bomb had an obvious utility for the waging of war; it was culturally necessary. Something can be needed by a culture and not be needed by most, or possibly all, of the people in that culture. This can extend to the point where the demands of a culture may prove lethal to the biological welfare of individuals. In reading White, at times one must pay close attention to the very specific and individualistic meaning he gives to the term *need*.

[16] *The Science of Culture*, p. 190.

[17] Hero worship has a long and general history, of course. We are referring here to the extension of such worship into fields such as art, intellectualism, etc.

[18] Herbert Muller has the following to say about Leslie White: "[The importance of the individual] was therefore most thoroughly discredited by anthropologists. He [the individual] served only to transmit the culture they studied, which was ready-made, intact, complete; they explicitly denied him any measure of independence, or of genuine individuality, by declaring that he was wholly a product of his culture. Even genius, according to Leslie White, is one 'in whose neuro-sensory-glandular-etc. system an important synthesis of cultural events has taken place'; culture somehow did all the work by itself (as one supposes it wrote the book to which White carelessly signed his own name)." Herbert J. Muller, *Freedom in the Modern World* (New York: Harper & Row, 1966), p. 222. This is a clever, but unfair indictment of White. White is thoroughly aware of the effects of individual eccentricity and accident in shaping the course of history and he discusses it at length.

162   The subordination of the genius to culture is achieved, in White's arguments, by his conception of invention. White defines an invention as a synthesis of existing cultural elements. For example, the invention of the steamboat was a matter of bringing together, or synthesizing, the boat and the steam engine. The invention of the airplane was a matter of synthesizing the glider and the gasoline engine. White is not always flattering in his comments on the inventive process. At one point he says:

> A consideration of many significant inventions and discoveries does not lead to the conclusion that great ability, native or acquired, is always necessary. On the contrary, many seem to need only mediocre talents at best. What intelligence was required to invent the steamboat? is great intelligence required to put one and one—a boat and an engine—together? An ape can do this.[19]

When we have two traits existing in a culture, the possibility of their synthesis exists. If the synthesis is realized and if it proves useful in some fashion, then it is incorporated into the cultural stream and becomes itself a trait which may be synthesized with something else. For this reason, cultural growth has an exponential or geometric character about it. By this we mean that culture growth reveals a kind of snowballing effect—it is ever more rapid. This exponential growth of culture has taken place while people have remained essentially the same in biological character and intelligence. We cannot explain cultural change, then, in terms of something which has remained constant. Therefore we must turn to something other than human nature. The only other thing left to turn to is culture itself.

The Exponential Character of Cultural Growth

There is a property of culture, however, that forces us to qualify the exponential growth idea. Such growth will take place until certain limits are reached. After all, the mathematical properties of exponential growth systems are such that one can reach infinite quantities within a finite period of time—and this is certainly impractical as well as impossible in the real world. What constitutes the constraining force in the exponential development of culture? White suggests that the constraining limits are imposed by a theme that operates as the unifying premise of a culture. Once the culture has exhausted the potentialities of the theme on which it is based, it either reaches a static level or it establishes a new theme.

> The development of geometry upon the basis of the axioms of Euclid had limits that were inherent in the system or pattern. A certain musical pattern

[19] *The Science of Culture*, p. 212. White, in his general works, writes with an unencumbered, blunt expressiveness. It makes for delightful reading, but it also calls for a willingness not to condemn him on minor points—after all, an ape could not invent a steamboat, despite White's claim to the contrary.

reached its culmination or fulfillment apparently in the works of Bach, Mozart, and Beethoven. Gothic art as a pattern was inherently limited. Ptolemy carried the development of a certain type of astronomic system about as far as was possible. All cultural development takes place within organized forms, or patterns . . . when a pattern has reached the limits of its potentialities no further development is possible. The alternatives then are slavish repetition of old patterns or the revolutionary overthrow of the old and the formation of new patterns.[20]

White sees an interaction between culture patterns or themes and the great individual. Greatness is, in White's thinking, dependent to a large extent on the accident of timing. If one is born after a pattern has reached its apex and is in a state of decline, one's chances of distinction are slight. But if fortune places one somewhere along a developing pattern, then the likelihood of achieving distinction is much greater. To be a genius requires more than brains and talent. As White puts it: "To become a genius it is necessary to be born at precisely the right time."[21]

Despite the limiting effects of patterns or themes in a culture, the development of culture when seen from a geological and world perspective has been essentially an exponential one. The reasoning here is relatively simple. Cultural accumulation is such that any item of absolute knowledge which comes into the culture becomes a factor promoting the further development of the culture. More significantly, it increases the possible permutations and combinations available for further innovation. Suppose, for the moment, we have a culture in which inventions consist simply of bringing two traits together to form a third. Thus, $A + B = C$. If we have only two traits to begin with, we can produce only one invention. But if we have three, we can produce three new inventions: $A + B$, $A + C$, and $B + C$. If we have four traits, we can produce six new inventions: $A + B$, $A + C$, $A + D$, $B + C$, $B + D$, and $C + D$. As the number of traits increases, the possible number of new inventions increases more rapidly. This is expressed in the following formula for combinations taken two at a time where N represents the number of existing traits or elements in the culture.

$$\text{Number of possible new inventions} = \frac{N(N - 1)}{2}$$

The graph in Figure 9-1 shows the possible number of inventions given an existing cultural base of N elements. This assumes, again, that the inventions consist of a simple combination of any two existing traits.

We have gone to the effort of developing this simple theme in

---

[20] *The Science of Culture*, pp. 215–216. The classical expression of this argument, in anthropological literature, is Ruth Benedict's *Patterns of Culture* (Boston: Houghton Mifflin Company, 1934). Benedict examined three primitive cultures and found that in each the various life-ways of the culture corresponded with a basic theme which permeated the culture. It should be mentioned here that there is considerable controversy among students of culture over the issue of whether or not cultures are "patterned."

[21] *The Science of Culture*, p. 218.

164 order to bring home a more basic point—a point that is at the heart of White's argument and is the motivating force behind it. A glance at the graph reveals a relationship between cultural innovation and the culture base *and excludes all other considerations.* Inventions or innovations are seen to be a function of the culture base. There is no need to include such biological or psychological concepts as drive, aspiration, genius, talent, ambition, altruism, greatness, or anything else. Culture is being used to explain or account for itself in terms that are extraindividualistic. White argues that we must not go down to the level of the individual to explain culture, but instead deal with culture in terms that are relevant to culture. This does not mean that culture exists without human beings; obviously it does not and cannot, at least at present. But we can understand culture without having to delve into psychology, just as we can understand the structure of language without having to take a course in cellular biology.

The formula and graph oversimplify the process, of course. They are merely devices for representing geometric progressions. In actual

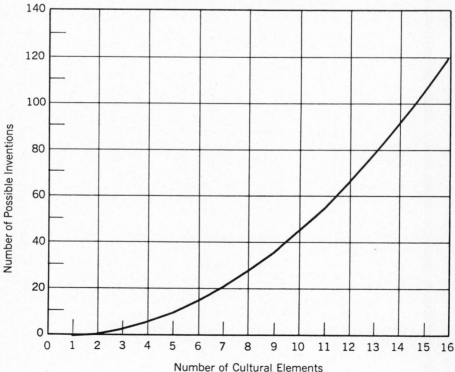

HYPOTHETICAL RELATIONSHIP OF POSSIBLE
INVENTIONS TO CULTURE BASE

cultural systems, we are confronted with the fact that many inventions are more than the synthesis or combination of two existing traits. We are also confronted with the fact that innumerable combinations of traits, while theoretically possible, are nonetheless meaningless or impractical. Only in our imagination will we combine a music stand with a mousetrap. Even so, some combinations, while seemingly silly, may nonetheless be given serious consideration. I am thinking, for example, of current serious efforts to combine the airplane with the submarine. Modern technology may permit a combination of elements which previously seemed out of the question.

The act of invention, once the mysterious realm of the quixotic genius, has been reduced more and more to a commonplace event. The story, possibly apocryphal, is told about David Sarnoff, who, on some occasion, brought his engineers together and informed them that television was an established fact—and so was the tape recorder. For his birthday he wanted to watch a tape-recorded television program. According to the story, Sarnoff watched a tape-recorded television program on his birthday. In this instance, the combination was apparent and was achieved in a more calculated fashion than has been the case in the past. Only since World War II have we very consciously and rationally invested heavy amounts of time and money in the act of promoting cultural progression. The question remains open, however, whether this investment will pay off. It might, as some intellectuals are beginning to fear, bring about a degree of cultural development that will outstrip our ability to adjust to our own creations.

So far we have concentrated on White's view that culture is a self-generating force that is evolutionary in character. White claims that culture should be understood in terms of its own dynamics—we must not resort to psychological explanations of cultural events.

"Come now," we can hear the humanist reply, "do you mean to say that the Great Person does not affect the course of history and political events? How can we hope to understand a happening like the Civil War without resorting to judgments concerning the psychological and even moral character of the people who occupied positions of importance and authority?" This is a vexing question and White is well aware of its existence. He replies by suggesting that many social scientists are incapable of making the distinction between temporal processes and temporal-formal processes.

> The temporal process, or "history," is a chronological series of events each of which is unique. We separate these events, by conceptual analysis, from their matrix of the totality of events. The temporal-formal, or evolutionist, process is a series of events in which both time and form are equally significant: one form grows out of another in time.[22]

[22] Ibid., p. 229.

This distinction, which White has some difficulty making and maintaining,[23] really centers on the way in which we define our mode of cultural analysis. If we define it in a narrow microhistorical or temporal fashion, the role of accident as an influential factor is increased. If we take a macrohistorical approach—or evolutionist, as White would put it—the influence of accident grows smaller and smaller.

At the temporal level, we must concede that Lee Harvey Oswald is a significant figure in history—even though he lacked the knowledge, power, and wealth of men who were far above him in social rank. Accidents and such unpredictable events as genius, power, eccentricity, talent, and the like are intermeshed at the temporal level; to try to ascertain which is important and which is not becomes impossible. White states it nicely:

> But in the succession of chance occurrences that is history, the individual may be enormously significant. But it does not follow at all that he is therefore a "genius" or a person of exceptional ability. The goose who saved Rome was more significant historically than many an emperor who ruled it.[24]

When culture is viewed more generally as an evolutionary process, however, accidents seem to have balanced out or been reduced in their effects. The argument is purely hypothetical, but White would evidently be inclined to assert that space-age culture would have been achieved regardless of the vicissitudes of specific history. Not only would we have had the airplane had the Wright brothers never lived; we would have passed through feudal into industrial and now welfare economies and societies if Europe had never existed.

It is in this sense that we must consider the formal properties of the cultural process without getting bogged down in the specific incidents that seem important but in fact prevent us from obtaining a broader conception of human evolution. When we are able to view culture as a self-generating force and, moreover, as an evolutionary formal process, we are freed from the problem of determining what specific incident and what individual was "important" or "great."

The last question we will raise here is to ask where this temporal-formal process is leading. White does not have much to say about this. Culture could destroy us or carry us to greater heights. Technology will become more complex, and great quantities of energy will be harnessed by the cultural process. Without making very specific predictions, White nonetheless argues that the study of culture, as he views it, is necessary for transcending the current limits of our ignorance about this force.

---

[23] It is worth noting that in illustrating the temporal process White resorts to an historical accident, Booth's assassination of Lincoln—an unpredictable event. But when he illustrates the temporal-formal process he turns to a physical example—the decomposition of a radioactive substance.

[24] *The Science of Culture*, p. 230.

If our ability to predict were greatly increased by the development and maturation of a science of culture the possibilities of a rational, effective, and humane adjustment between man and culture and between one cultural segment and another would be increased accordingly. If, for example, a science of culture could demonstrate that the trend of social evolution is toward larger political groupings, then the chances of making the futile attempt to restore or maintain the independence of small nations would be lessened. If the trend of cultural evolution is away from private property and free enterprise why strive to perpetuate them? If it could be shown that international wars will continue as long as independent, sovereign nations exist, then certain delusions now popular would find less nourishment and support. The fact is that culture has been evolving as an unconscious, blind, bloody, brutal, tropismatic process so far. It has not yet reached the point where intelligence, self-consciousness, and understanding are very conspicuous. Our ignorance is still deep-rooted and widespread. We do not understand even some of the most elementary things—the prohibition of polygamy for example. In short, we are so ignorant that we can still believe that it is we who make our culture and control its course.[25]

This is a strong plea for rationality in cultural affairs—a plea to recognize the importance and the true nature of cultural influences. It is a call to explore the implications of the fact that people are cultural beings. It is also a very "iffy" statement. After pointing the way, White seems to tell us to continue in that direction and, with a great deal of luck, we might get to wherever it is we want to go. White provides us with a widespread view of the past—history is transformed into units of geological scope and we begin to recognize culture as a very real element in the evolutionary process. In the beginning was matter; then came that mysterious step that led to the long and enchanting process of the evolution of living forms. Then came the equally magical step that brought into being the arduous, tangled, and continuous process that has culminated in modern forms of culture.

Although White, and the field of anthropology generally, offer us a grand vision of the past, they hedge when it comes to the future. Yet the problem of predicting the future is important. Unless the examination of culture can help us in this effort, says White, it is a very pure science indeed—without any application of significance.

Cultural Progression and the Future

What does White's thought suggest with respect to the future of humankind? Here we shall extrapolate beyond the writings of White and sketch a possibility his line of reasoning seems to suggest. White might disagree with the following paragraphs, but they are in keeping with the main themes of a radical cultural deterministic position.

The most extreme extension of White's thinking suggests a move-

---

[25] *The Science of Culture,* pp. 355–356.

168   ment toward a transference of the evolution of culture from people to machines. The cultural process, which consists mainly of the synthesizing of existing elements is even now gradually being removed from the minds and hands of people and transferred to modern thoughtful machines. Granted, these machines are not adept at the procedure as yet; and granted, we can still pull the plug on them if we are dissatisfied with their work. We can further grant that they work in a mechanical and unimaginative way—but then we have given them only a few years of practice and development.

There may yet come a time when we will look back on the past and reminisce about the days when people and their culture were organically related, and culture and people were only different sides of the same coin. The prospect for the future could be one in which we are mechanically related to culture and understand very little of it. The process of alienation, so significant in Marxist thought, may take a new form. People may not only find themselves removed from the product of their work and removed from much of what culture has to offer—simply because the content of that culture has become so massive; they may also find themselves removed from the containers of that culture. The time may be close at hand when the leading containers of culture will no longer be human intellectuals—narrowed by specialization and subject to the limitations of emotion and meager knowledge—but the thoughtful machine. The intellectual will be relegated to the status of a keeper of stored information whose nature and meaning will remain a mystery.

This, admittedly, is a far-out, though not especially novel, speculation. Moreover, it is based on a theoretical position in anthropology which is, itself, a very radical argument. But perhaps the important thing is not to be concerned with the accuracy of such prognostications, but to be concerned with the form and the sentiment of this consideration of the future.

White views people as the neurological locus of culture—as the lightning rod through which the forces of culture conduct themselves. If the cultural process stands at the apex of evolutionary development,[26] and if the cultural process can be transformed to nonhuman agents, then what does the future hold in store for us? We do not know. We can only speculate. Even if we had every reason to conclude that such speculation was perfectly accurate, would we be able to alter the course of cultural progression and regain our former place in nature—whatever it might have been? The answer is obvious and, at the same time, one which makes White's position appear more reasonable than we might, as humanists, wish it were.

---

[26] Any evolutionist will dodge when one starts engaging in teleological arguments about the "purpose" of evolution. Neither White nor we would claim that human culture is the goal toward which evolution has been working for millions of years. However, it does stand, at this moment, at the end of the evolutionary process on this planet. We can, therefore, act *as if* culture were at the apex of evolutionary development for the purpose of speculating a little about the future.

Problems and Issues **169**

Leslie White's writings stand as an antidote to the idea that cultural change and "progress" are dependent upon the particular mix of talent and genius that constitutes a "great man." Americans tend to rely on the cult of personality as a means of explaining the world around them. We have the light bulb because Edison just happened to come along. It is now evident, however, that social and cultural changes are progressing at such a rapid pace that we can no longer totally rely on the idea of the great man as an explanation of events. There is simply too much cultural change, while, at the same time, the general intelligence level of humankind has probably been fairly constant for at least the past 500,000 years. Why are things happening so rapidly today? For White, the answer is that culture is, itself, the major factor in the transformation of culture. The larger a cultural system becomes, the greater the possibilities for change. We do not need the works of Leslie White, however, to realize that the question before us is; Can we survive our own creations? If it were known, as an established scientific fact, that the continued use of fossil fuels would create a devastating greenhouse effect—and leading authorities and government officials are already deeply worried about this possibility—would we be able to stop what we are doing?

Virtually every significant aspect of living—love, warfare, inventiveness, art, science, religion, mental illness, and personality types—can be associated with culture. What are some of the problems involved in attempting to determine whether a given quality is genetic or cultural? What are some of the possible social consequences of concluding that a given human quality is one or the other?

White views the multiple, simultaneous but independent invention as incontrovertible evidence for the idea that culture determines culture. When a culture is ready for a particular invention, the invention appears, often regardless of whether the general membership of the culture want it or not. In other words, invention is the mother of necessity. Are there other ways of interpreting the multiple-simultaneous-independent invention? How does invention occur? Why did not the people of classical Greece and Rome invent machines? They did not, even though they had the technological base for it and did invent a few astonishing things—the differential gear, the mechanical reaper, and a rather sophisticated musical instrument that worked on the basis of an elaborate hydraulic system. Here is an instance where, it would seem, culture was "ready." However, growth of technology did not occur. How would White account for this?

The Unanticipated Consequences of Human Actions

The Views of

ROBERT KING MERTON

The concepts of manifest and latent functions are indispensable elements in the theoretical repertoire of the social engineer.

Social Theory and Social Structure

BORN: 1910

10 By the time America entered the 1960s, sociology had achieved enough notoriety to be of some interest to the general public. Popular writers were producing, here and there, magazine articles concerned with the problem of what sociology really is and what sociologists are like. The opinions expressed were not always flattering—and even when flattering, were sometimes backhanded.

In 1961 *The New Yorker* published a biographical profile of one of America's leading sociologists. The tone of the article leaves the reader with the feeling that its subject is a man regrettably squandering himself in a profession which, at best, is simple and gross.[1] The sociologist profiled in the magazine article was Robert King Merton—then, as now, one of America's foremost living sociologists.[2] The article describes Merton as a

---

[1] See M. M. Hunt, "Profile," *The New Yorker*, January 28, 1961, p. 39.
[2] The following selected listing of Robert K. Merton's works will provide an indication of the extent and variety of his contributions to sociological thought: *Contemporary Social Problems: An Introduction to the Sociology of Deviant Behavior and Social Disorganization*, edited by Merton and R. A. Nisbet (New York: Harcourt, Brace, 1961); *Continuities in*

tall, hollow chested man of fifty . . . thin lipped, rimless spectacles and earnestly talkative as the Hollywood stereotype of a minister, but with a quizzically twisted smile as a giveaway. . . . Socially . . . an agreeably convivial fellow, who, despite his somewhat austere appearance, steadily and tirelessly does away with Scotch . . .[3]

The author registers the same feeling toward sociologists that college students show toward their professors when they discover, in the course of growing up, that the professors have human as well as intellectual qualities.

Merton's career spans a crucial period in the development of American sociology—a period during which sociology in this country moved from rather simple factual conceptions of the social order to more abstract and sophisticated conceptions of human society. European sociology, typified in the works of Durkheim and Weber, was rooted in an examination of the moral order. American sociology, up to the time of World War II, was engaged in an indirect idealization of the American family farm and the small, semirural American community.[4] For many American sociologists the problem confronting humanity was how to regain a rural paradise lost. Sociological studies took the form of elaborate comparisons between rural and urban modes of living.[5] The rural mode, somehow, more often appeared as the better way of life.

But this naive and pastorally romantic sociology had to give way before more analytic forms of sociology—which attempted to identify and then relate the most fundamental, and therefore the most abstract, conditions of society. This approach to sociology is not especially concerned with such specific social problems as rural–urban contrasts in divorce rates. It turns, instead, to a consideration of what is meant by a

Social Research: Studies in the Scope and Method of "The American Soldier," edited by Merton and Paul F. Lazarsfeld (New York: Free Press, 1950); *The Focused Interview: A Manual of Problems and Procedures,* with Marjorie Fiske and Patricia L. Kendall (New York: Free Press, 1956); *Mass Persuasion: The Social Psychology of a War Bond Drive,* with the assistance of M. Fiske and Alberta Curtis (New York: Harper & Row, 1946); *On the Shoulders of Giants: A Shandean Postscript* (New York: Free Press, 1965); *Reader in Bureaucracy,* edited by Merton and others (New York: Free Press, 1952); *Social Theory and Social Structure,* rev. and enl. ed. (New York: Free Press, 1957); *The Student-Physician: Introductory Studies in the Sociology of Medical Education,* edited by Merton, George G. Reader, and Patricia Kendall (Cambridge, Mass.: Harvard University Press, 1957); *Sociology Today: Problems and Prospects,* edited by Merton, L. Broom, and L. S. Cottrell, Jr. (New York: Basic Books, 1959); *Sociological Ambivalence and Other Essays* (New York: Free Press, 1976).
[3] *The New Yorker,* p. 39.
[4] Much of the sociology of the 1930s consisted of elaborate distinctions between what were essentially rural and urban modes of living. To a surprising extent, even as late as the forties, American sociology classes could be found that ignored both Durkheim and Weber.
[5] A highly developed study of this type is Harald Swedner, *Ecological Differentiation of Habits and Attitudes* (Lund, Sweden: CWK Gleerup, 1960).

172 social system.[6] What are the properties of any social system? How are the elements within the system interrelated to form a structure? How do the parts, and the manner of their relationship, bear upon the performance of the entire system? What are the functions of the different parts? What are the consequences of a given structure for the people who move within it?

The Structural-Functional Approach

Sociologists taking this approach to the study of human social organization call themselves "structural-functional" sociologists. By the end of World War II, structural-functional analysis was an extremely active, if not dominant, school of thought within the sociological community of theorists and scholars. In 1949 the publication of *Social Theory and Social Structure* placed Robert Merton at the forefront of those who advocated structural-functional approaches to the study of society. To understand Merton's thought requires, then, that we turn to an examination of structural-functionalism.

The term *function* refers to the extent to which some part or process of a social system contributes to the maintenance of that system. It is necessary, if we are going to gain a clearer conception of Merton's use of this term, to note that *function* does not mean exactly the same thing as *purpose* or *motivation*. It means, instead, the extent to which a given activity does, in fact, promote or interfere with the maintenance of a system. As Merton puts it:

> Social function refers to observable objective consequences, and not to subjective dispositions (aims, motives, purposes.)[7]

It is one thing, for example, to speculate on the aims, motivations, and purposes underlying advertising in modern America and another to see it from a functional perspective. If we ask an advertising person to tell us the aims or purposes of the profession, he or she might mention several things.[8] Advertising exists to improve the level of living of Americans. Advertising seeks to make Americans aware of the wealth of goods and services that American industry has the capacity to provide. Advertisers are motivated to sell their clients' products. Advertising seeks to upgrade the consumer tastes of people. Advertising keeps alive the

---

[6] There is an important caveat to enter here. The structural-functionalist often presents the appearance of being a scientist analytically examining the parts of society in much the same manner as the biologist examines the functioning of the organs of a dog or monkey. Merton even relies on such an example in defining what he means by function. However, unlike biologists, sociologists *never* have an opportunity to observe the whole of society. They work, instead, with the idea or concept of a society.

[7] Merton, *Social Theory and Social Structure*, p. 24.

[8] For an extensive and engaging listing of the values of advertising see Kenneth M. Goode and Harford Powel, Jr., *What about Advertising?* (New York: Harper & Row, 1928), pp. 29–32.

American dream of happiness through possessions. We could go on and **173**
on.

A functional analysis promotes a different way of looking at advertising. What does advertising in fact *do?* Further, what are the consequences of what it does for the greater society? Compare the following functional evaluation of advertising with the above motivational evaluation.

It is well known that one of the things advertising does is to pretend to make significant differences out of what are known to be virtually identical products. It has been factually established, for example, that most consumers cannot tell one brand of cigarettes from another when blindfolded.[9] Most beer drinkers cannot distinguish between one brand and another. By creating differences where none in fact exists, advertising serves the function of enabling a variety of cigarette manufacturers, brewers, and other companies to survive where there is no utilitarian basis for their survival.[10] Thus, a functionalist would claim that one of the functions of advertising is to maintain a form of industrial pluralism. Along with this, advertising sustains the belief that such a pluralistic system does encourage true competition—that is, competition that leads toward improved products. The belief may or may not be true. The point is that one of the functions of advertising is to support this belief by encouraging industrial pluralism.

Manifest Functions and Latent Functions

Merton makes a distinction between two forms of social function. One of these he refers to as *manifest function* and the other as *latent function*. Manifest functions are objective consequences (for some person, subgroup, or social or cultural system) that contribute to its adjustment *and were so intended*. Latent functions are consequences that contribute to adjustment but were not so intended.[11] The distinction is a valuable one; it makes clear the nature of sociological investigation as perhaps few other distinctions do. Manifest functions are essentially the official explanations of a given action. Latent functions are the sociological explanations of a given action.

A variety of examples will help make the distinction and indicate its

---

[9] The irrationalities in consumer preferences are summarized in Vance Packard, *The Hidden Persuaders* (New York: McKay, 1957), pp. 13–23.

[10] This is very similar to the argument made by Emile Durkheim in *The Division of Labor in Society*, translated by George Simpson (New York: Free Press, 1964). The function of the division of labor, said Durkheim, is to provide conditions whereby a greater variety of life can be supported within the same ecological space. In a sense, then, advertising could be said to be a vital ecological process.

[11] It should be noted here that the basis for this distinction is a subjective one—that is, intention. Sociologists sooner or later find themselves having to rely on the subjective meaning of a given action in order to give the action wider value in their theoretical formulations. This is frustrating to thinkers who are seeking to produce an empirically oriented theory that is objective, not subjective.

174 sociologically heuristic value. An example used by Merton is the Hopi Indian rain ceremony. The manifest function—the intended use of the ceremony—is to bring rain. At the same time it is scientifically evident that these ceremonies do not bring rain. Even the Hopi who participated in such ceremonies over the long generations must have observed that there was little connection between annual levels of rainfall and the conduct of the rain ceremonies.[12] Yet the ceremony persists and there is sufficient reason for it to persist; so the Hopi have retained the ceremony regardless of its bearing on actual rainfall levels. The reason for such persistence, Merton claims, is that the ceremony performs other functions for Hopi society than merely bringing rain. To examine only the manifest functions of a ceremony, a tradition, a social group, or a particular role is to examine it at the most superficial level. The beginnings of sociological understanding often are found in a consideration of the latent functions. Referring to the Hopi rain ceremonies, Merton goes on to say,

> With the concept of latent function, we continue our inquiry, examining the consequences of the ceremony not for the rain gods or for meteorological phenomena, but for the groups which conduct the ceremony. And here it may be found, as many observers indicate, that the ceremonial does indeed have functions—but functions which are non-purposed or latent.
> Ceremonials may fulfill the latent function of reinforcing the group identity by providing a periodic occasion on which the scattered members of a group assemble to engage in a common activity. . . . Such ceremonials are a means by which collective expression is afforded the sentiments which . . . are found to be a basic source of group unity. Through the systematic application of the concept of latent function, therefore, *apparently* irrational behavior may *at times* be found to be positively functional for the group.[13] [Italics Merton's.]

One other example, drawn from more contemporary circumstances, may help further in revealing the usefulness of the manifest-latent function distinction. Consider the following statement from a newspaper article. It was made by Stokely Carmichael, the Black Power advocate who left the United States in 1967, vitriolically renouncing his native land to all the world: "It is time to let the whites know we are going to take over; if they don't like it, we will stamp them out, using violence and other means necessary."[14]

Recognizing that Carmichael's comments might have been taken

---

[12] When a latent function is important, even though the manifest function is not being met, there is a tendency to rationalize social action. Thus, when a rain ceremony does not produce rain, it is not considered the fault of the ceremony. Instead, the fault is likely to be found in the incompetent performance of one of the participants.

[13] Merton, *Social Theory and Social Structure*, pp. 64–65.

[14] From an article by Special Correspondent William L. Ryan, appearing in the December 2, 1967, issue of *The Rocky Mountain News*, p. 68.

out of context,[15] we can look at these statements first from the point of view of their manifest functions and then from the point of view of their latent functions. At the manifest level, Carmichael seems to be making highly irrational and ineffective threats. After all, even superb organization and armament could not enable the blacks of America—or of the world, for that matter—to stamp out the whites. In some ways, the scientific correspondence between Carmichael's ceremonial chants and the desired effects is about as remote as that of the Hopi rain dancer. But the concept of latent functions leads to further consideration of the matter. Carmichael's statements received widespread coverage in the press and were heard around the world by large numbers of people. There must be more to it than the irrational mouthings of an alienated American black man. The concept of latent functions asks for a thoughtful consideration of other possible social consequences coming from Carmichael's actions. Let us speculate on a few.

First of all, it is obvious that Carmichael was engaged in an extreme and vitriolic condemnation of the United States. Further, he is a black man. Moreover, he was being rewarded with publicity and worldwide attention for his audacity. One of the latent functions of Carmichael's behavior, then, is to provide a model for those people who have believed for generations that to insult a white man means immediate and personal catastrophe. Even nonwhites who might sincerely and thoroughly repudiate the radicalism of Carmichael's position cannot help being affected by the public performance they actually observe. Carmichael is a social fact and not a social aspiration. His actions have consequences, and a sociological examination of these requires that we distinguish between what Carmichael appears to be and what he is actually achieving.

Another possible latent function of Carmichael's actions might be to bring moderate nonwhite and white leaders together in attempts to forestall violence. If so, then the actual consequence of Carmichael's call for revolutionary violence would be a détente. Nonetheless, the consequence would serve the interests of the social system.

It becomes quickly apparent, from these illustrations, that the concept of latent function has some of the qualities of an after-the-fact rationalization or excuse for the way things are. The functionalist seems to be saying, "Well, if something exists in the social order, there must be a pretty good reason for it—otherwise it would not exist. Therefore, let us think long and hard on the matter, and sooner or later the reason for its existence will come to us."

Is a latent function an apology for the status quo? We found ourselves running into much the same problem when we considered Durkheim's discussion of crime (see Chapter 4). After all, when Durkheim said crime is necessary to any society, he was providing crime with a latent function. Now the structural-functionalist appears to be excusing

---

[15] It is enlightening to compare what newspapers had to say about Carmichael and what Carmichael has to say. See Stokely Carmichael and Charles V. Hamilton, *Black Power: The Politics of Liberation in America* (New York: Random House, 1967).

176 superstitious rain dances and radical revolutionaries as functional features of the social order. Merton was aware of this disturbing feature of structural-functionalist thought and tried to get around it by introducing yet another idea—the idea of dysfunctions.

The Dysfunctional Process

Dysfunctional events lessen the adjustment of a social system. Dysfunctional features of a society imply strain or stress or tension. Society tries to constrain dysfunctional elements somewhat the same way an organism would constrain a bacterial or viral infection. If the dysfunctional forces are too great, the social order is overwhelmed, disorganized, and possibly destroyed.[16]

One of the clearest examples we know of a dysfunctional feature in a social system was the Catharist heresy in Europe in the twelfth century. The Cathars were of the opinion that affairs of the flesh were damning to the spirit. As a consequence, they concluded that the ideal relationship between a man and a woman was that of brother and sister. They advocated brother-sister relationships in marriage. So extreme were their views that they would eat no food which they considered the product of a sexual union. They would not, therefore, eat eggs, milk, meat, or cheese. They married, but ideally they did not consummate their marriages sexually. Feudal leaders in provinces where such heretical views existed recognized fully the implications of such a point of view—it meant, if followed through, an attrition of population. Had the Cathars been completely successful, the consequence would have been the loss, in a generation or two, of the total society—a painless, perhaps, but certain loss. Despite their peaceful and gentle nature the Cathars were too threatening. They were destroyed. Their elimination from society was thorough; the only evidence we have of their existence is indirect, consisting for the most part of allusions to the Cathars in church records.

The next example, illustrating the possible dysfunctional use of prisoners as slaves in ancient Rome, is an engaging one.

> Lead poisoning, according to Dr. Gilfillan, killed off most of the Roman ruling class and damaged the brains of Commodus, Nero, and all those other mad emperors. Such poisoning became common, he points out, about 150 B.C., after the wealthy Romans began to use Greek prisoners of war as their household servants. These slaves brought with them the Greek custom of using lead-lined pots for cooking, especially for warming wine and for concentrating honey and grape syrup, the sweeteners most popular at that time. Nobody realized that food cooked in such utensils became highly toxic—although the Greek upper classes probably had been deci-

---

[16] It is worth noting in Merton's work that the idea of function is used more often than the idea of dysfunction. In *Social Theory and Social Structure,* for example, a book of over six hundred pages, the index mentions dysfunctions only three times.

mated by the same slow-acting poison a few generations earlier. Alexander the Great, for example, quite possibly died of it, rather than of alcoholism.

Writing in the *Journal of Occupational Medicine*, Dr. Gilfillan notes that fashionable Roman matrons began to drink wine at about the same time they acquired Greek cooks; and that they soon began to show the classic symptoms of lead poisoning—sterility, miscarriages, and heavy child mortality. Their surviving children often suffered permanent mental impairment. As a consequence, he estimates, the aristocracy lost about three-quarters of its members in each generation. As evidence he cites both census statistics and the heavy deposits of lead found in bones taken from the more splendid Roman tombs of the period.

The poor people, meanwhile, were spared—because they cooked in earthenware pots, and couldn't afford to drink much wine in any case. Moreover, they did not use the lead water pipes and lead-based cosmetics which the wealthier classes enjoyed. "The brightest and winsomest from the poorer class" did occasionally climb to positions of power and wealth—whereupon they too fell victim to the rich man's scourge. The result, Dr. Gilfillan argues, was a systematic extinction of the ablest people in the Roman world. He does not, however, draw any conclusions about later cultures which might have poisoned themselves—with tobacco, air pollution, radioactive fallout, or whatever—without realizing what they were doing.[17]

Let us suggest one more illustration of a dysfunctional process. Some demographers are of the opinion that medical technology may have dysfunctional effects for modern social systems if it succeeds in creating disproportionately greater numbers of old people than have existed in the past. A society that requires the flexibility and adaptability of youth and which, at the same time, is made up of relatively inflexible older people, might suffer as a consequence. That is, strain might be introduced into the system, leading to disorganizing conflicts, breakdowns in communication, and inflexible ways of thinking about national and international problems.

Values of Functional Analysis

The point of these illustrations is that functional analysis orients thought toward the social consequences—intended and unintended—of a particular action. Merton claims functional analysis has the following virtues.

First of all, it inhibits the tendency to dismiss a seemingly irrational social event with the casual observation that it is merely superstition, foolishness, or craziness. For example, a superficial response to a campus "panty raid" might be to dismiss it as "kids blowing off steam" or as "youthful foolishness and exuberance." Functionalists, on the other hand, are concerned with the form of the action: Why a panty raid and not some other form of foolishness? They are also interested in the

[17] John Fischer mentions this interesting theory in *Harper's Magazine*, December 1967, pp. 16 and 18.

178 functional nature of the raid: What is the relationship of the raid to other features of the campus social structure?

Second, the concepts of manifest and latent function provide sociologists with a means of probing into those features of social behavior that are more theoretically valuable. The sociologist can, for example, study the effects of a war bond propaganda campaign to determine its effectiveness. At the manifest level one can consider its avowed purpose[18] of stirring up patriotic fervor. Such an investigation is of primary value to administrators and others who are interested in producing an effective propaganda campaign. The latent consequences of the campaign can carry the sociologist further into the matter. Merton investigated the appeals used by Kate Smith during a war bond campaign in World War II. One of the latent consequences of the campaign was to stifle expressions of difference toward official policy.[19]

Third, a functional approach to social action has ethical and moral implications. Essentially, such an approach brings a more sophisticated awareness to the moral issues involved in a particular situation. Merton puts it this way:

> The introduction of the concept of latent function in social research leads to conclusions which show that "social life is not as simple as it first seems." For as long as people confine themselves to *certain* consequences (e.g., manifest consequences), it is comparatively simple for them to pass moral judgments upon the practice or belief in question. Moral evaluations, generally based on these manifest consequences, tend to be polarized in terms of black or white. But the perception of further (latent) consequences often complicates the picture. Problems of moral evaluation (which are not our immediate concern) and problems of social engineering (which are our concern) both take on the additional complexities usually involved in responsible social decisions.[20]

Thus, to return to an earlier illustration, at the manifest level the prolongation of life is an obvious moral good. At the latent level we need to consider the matter further. Could such a program lead to a society where a youthful minority might have to go to the extreme of considering ways of killing off their elders in order to avoid the repressive effects of their presence?[21]

A fourth value of structural-functional analysis, somewhat similar in nature to the last mentioned value, is that it replaces naive moral judgments with sociological analysis. Merton illustrates his meaning, in this instance, with a reference to political "machines." Traditionally the political machine in America has been viewed as an evil. It is a source of

---

[18] Merton uses the term *purpose* here. This is confusing because he has gone to considerable pains to make the distinction between function and purpose.

[19] See Merton, *Mass Persuasion.*

[20] Merton, *Social Theory and Social Structure*, p. 68.

[21] In a similar vein, Dick Gregory commented in the late sixties about the trend toward organ transplant surgery. Referring to the fact that the only living heart transplant patient at that time was relying on the heart of a black man, Gregory said he hoped white people were not thinking of using blacks as their general source for spare parts.

graft, it is corrupt, and it is a perversion of democratic processes. The **179** political boss buys votes instead of earning them through public service. The machine protects criminal elements rather than exorcising them. The machine gives public jobs and offices to loyal members of the organization rather than to people best fitted to the task. So the criticisms continue. A functionalist, however, argues that the extensive development of such machines and their continued existence over relatively long periods of time suggest that they are serving social ends that other, morally approved, organizations have abdicated. Merton says:

> Examined for a moment apart from any moral considerations, the political apparatus operated by the Boss is effectively designed to perform [various] functions with a minimum of inefficiency. Holding the strings of diverse governmental divisions, bureaus and agencies in his competent hands, the Boss rationalizes the relations between public and private business. He serves as the business community's ambassador in the otherwise alien (and sometimes unfriendly) realm of government. And, in strict business-like terms, he is well-paid for his economic services to his respectable business clients.[22]

This statement should not be read as an apology for bossism and the political machine system of municipal or local government. Merton hastily goes on:

> To adopt a functional outlook is to provide not an apologia for the political machine but a more solid basis for modifying or eliminating the machine, *providing* specific structural arrangements are introduced either for eliminating [certain] demands of the business community or, if that is the objective, of satisfying these demands through alternative means.[23]

If we wish, then, to operate either as relatively detached social analysts or as social and political activists, a structural-functional point of view is necessary.[24] It inhibits a tendency toward naive moralizing about social issues and it places any given social action within the greater context of the total social structure.

The Nature of Deviant Behavior

Of the various contributions to social thought by Merton, perhaps the best known and most generally applied has been his consideration of the nature of deviant social behavior. Rather than view such behavior as

---

[22] Merton, *Social Theory and Social Structure;* pp. 75–76. This point is nicely illustrated in the movie *The Last Hurrah*. In this film the political boss is sympathetically portrayed as a man to whom the people come for real help rather than bureaucratic pretenses at helping.
[23] Merton, *Social Theory and Social Structure*, p. 76.
[24] Kingsley Davis reacts to this argument in an interesting article. See "The Myth of Functional Analysis as a Special Method in Sociology and Anthropology," *American Sociological Review* 24 (1959) 757–772. Davis points out that structural-functional analysis is actually just another way of talking about sociological analysis. In other words, whether sociologists call themselves structural-functionalists or something else, they still use the same basic approach.

180   the product of abnormal personalities, Merton is concerned with the extent to which it might, at least in some considerable part, be a result of the structural nature of society itself. In this respect Merton knowingly endorses a position which by the middle of the twentieth century had become a labored cliché. However, Merton is concerned with more than merely stating a truism of the order that delinquents or social derelicts are the sorry products of the society that spawned them. He is, instead, interested in specifying the process whereby deviant action is generated within a social structure.

Deviant behavior presents a critical problem to those who accept a sociological perspective. The problem is this. On the one hand the sociologist is well aware that society and culture have an almost crushing capacity to induce conformity on the part of the individual. On the other hand, innovation does exist. The directives of the culture may be challenged or modified. How can deviation occur within a system which has so much power to prevent it? Merton deals with this problem in the following manner, using American culture as the basis for his observations.

To begin with, he has developed the reasonable argument that American culture places great emphasis on the value of individual attainment of success. At the same time, and this is quite significant, the means of achieving success are left pretty much up to the individual. Institutional means for attaining success—the legitimate pathways to money, fame, or power—are not given any special emphasis or consideration. Those who attain success by relying on quasi-criminal devices may be as admired as, or even more admired than, those who employ the legitimate structure. Having established this beginning point, Merton raises a more fundamental question:

> What . . . are the consequences for the behavior of people variously situated in a social structure of a culture in which the emphasis on dominant success-goals has become increasingly separated from an equivalent emphasis on institutionalized procedures for seeking these goals?[25]

Merton is concerned here with the problem of how people adapt to society and the ways in which the structural features of society affect the form such adaptations take. In his approach to this problem Merton has decided to strip social structure down to two elemental conditions that hold for any society. He does this by making a distinction between the goals of a culture and the means the culture provides for achieving those goals.[26]

---

[25] Merton, *Social Theory and Social Structure*, p. 139.

[26] On the surface, the distinction between goals and means seems simple and clear; in practice it is not. This is probably the major limitation to the utility of Merton's scheme or "social action" theories. To take a very homely example, grades may be viewed simultaneously as a means and an end to a college student. At one level they are a means of getting through school and getting into a profession. At the same time they may be a goal for which the student must prepare. In the final analysis, the extent to which something exists as a goal or as a means is subjective. In the realm of human conduct the external

If we grant the existence of these conditions—that society encourages an interest in certain goals and, at the same time, provides certain sanctioned means for attaining such goals—then the alternative forms of adaptation are limited to how the person responds to these goals and the means provided for their attainment. One may accept the goals and the means; one may accept the goals and reject the means; or one may accept the means while rejecting the goals. Merton summarized the five forms of adaptation possible (see Table 10-1).[27]

The nature of these alternative modes of adaptation can be illustrated by a brief examination of goals and means in institutions of higher learning. One of the legitimate goals of the system is the attainment of a high grade-point average.[28] The institutionalized means for achieving this is by study, hard work, and taking tests and examinations. If the student accepts both the goals and the means, then, according to Merton's scheme, he or she is a conformist—and this is one way of defining conformity.

Some students might, however, seek the goal of getting good grades but resent the means available for the attainment of such a goal. They could then respond by employing some kind of innovation. That is, they might use unacceptable means to attain an acceptable goal. They might cheat or have someone else take their examinations. Or, as has occurred in rare instances, they might attempt to gain access to the office of records and alter their grade report. If the pressure toward institutional goals is great enough, says Merton, while at the same time less emphasis is placed on the value of legitimate means, such innovative forms of adaptation will proliferate.

Table 10-1 *A Typology of Modes of Individual Adaptation*

Mode of adaptation	Culture goals	Institutionalized means
Conformity	+	+
Innovation	+	−
Ritualism	−	+
Retreatism	−	−
Rebellion	±	±

classification of an action as goal oriented is not possible. This, in part, was one of the main contributions of Freudian thought. A person who is ambitious and successful on the job would, from a Mertonian standpoint, be occupationally goal oriented. Freud would suggest, on the other hand, that maybe such an effort is really only a means of getting even with a spouse by asserting one's superiority. This example suggests the further possibility that the term *latent function* is actually a device to cope with the problems of determining human goals when using structural-functional theories.

[27] Merton, *Social Theory and Social Structure*, p. 140.

[28] For purposes of exemplification, we will simply assume that grades can be dealt with as a desired goal and ignore the possibility of looking on them as means.

182   A ritualistic form of adaptation is one in which the student rejects the idea of grades but latches onto the means employed to get grades as a way of life. Reading, study, and the taking of examinations become sufficient. Every campus has its "professional students" who make good enough grades to remain in college and who have little other aspiration than to hang around college, go to classes, and live a student's life. The professor who reads from yellowed notes the obsolescent ideas of another era is a ritualist. The students who come to class and then write letters during class time are ritualists. The school administrator who demands signatures on loyalty oaths—regardless of more concrete manifestations of loyalty—is a ritualist. In all these instances we have people placing emphasis on the means of attaining some end, often to the detriment of attaining the goal itself.

The fourth category of adaptive modes refers to the retreatist. Retreatists in college would be students who care nothing about grades and, furthermore, see little point in studying for or taking examinations. In effect, they withdraw from the system. They are dropouts.

Merton's discussion of rebellion is briefer than we would like it to be, and it is surprisingly vague. Yet rebellion is distinct from any of the other forms of adaptation. Rebels, unlike retreatists, are not apathetic about the situation in which they find themselves. Instead of passively withdrawing, they conclude that the system is sufficiently important to warrant being reformed. They are sufficiently caught up in the goals and the means of the culture to seek to change them. Rebels find the system frustrating enough to cause them to wish to change it but not so frustrating that they seek to withdraw from it. Most importantly, Merton suggests that the distinguishing characteristic of rebels is a belief that the source of social problems lies within the social order itself rather than within the individual. Their aspiration becomes one of changing the system. They are idealistic enough to believe in the higher aspirations of the culture but pragmatic enough to conclude that greater effort is necessary to move closer to those ideals. Examples of the rebellious mode of adaptation on the campus might be the minority student movements such as the Black Student Alliance and the Chicano Student Movement.

By making these distinctions, Merton is attempting to establish more than a simple typology of different forms of behavior. He is not only developing a distinction between the conformist and the innovator, for example; he is also attempting to locate the social conditions that increase the likelihood of getting one kind of behavior over the other. In effect, Merton claims that in those social circumstances where social goals are highly valued and the means for obtaining the goals are not as highly valued, the likelihood of innovation is increased. Criminal behavior, which is one kind of innovative action, is likely in a society that places great emphasis on individual success, wealth, and power, and which, at the same time, does not emphasize the value of the legitimate means for obtaining these goals. Merton argues that such a situation exists in the United States.

It is necessary, if we are to grasp the significance of Merton's thought, to recognize the extent to which he is giving culturally established, collectively held, value priorities a place in the interpretation of individual conduct. A culture that, for example, values cleverness over the dignity of work will be likely to find itself peopled with clever loafers. The source of the condition is, however, within the manner in which the culture establishes the balance between means and goals—not in the individual.

The Sociology of Science

At a less abstract level, one of Merton's strong interests has been a consideration of the sociology of knowledge and, more narrowly, what might be called the sociology of science. The emergence of science— the development of science as a massive and powerful institution—poses a great variety of sociologically valuable questions. Science is not, certainly, a simple response to the demands of a growing and expanding population. It is not a simple product of intelligence. It appears, rather, to be a way of viewing the world that has emerged from culturally established attitudes which were somehow conducive to its development. More specifically, Merton claims that science is an outgrowth of world views contained in early Protestantism. Weber saw capitalism coming from Protestantism; Merton sees science as yet another contribution of the Protestant Ethic.

Merton summarizes the character of his argument with the following statement:

> It is the thesis of this study that the Puritan ethic, as an ideal-typical expression of the value-attitudes basic to ascetic Protestantism generally, so canalized the interests of seventeenth-century Englishmen as to constitute one important *element* in the enhanced cultivation of science. The deep-rooted religious *interests* of the day demanded in their forceful implications the systematic, rational, and empirical study of Nature for the glorification of God in His works and for the control of the corrupt world.[29] [Italics Merton's.]

Merton isolated several facets of Puritan thought and practice and concluded that scientists of the seventeenth century were functioning as innovators. While they still held to the ethical, moral, and spiritual goals of Protestant-Christian doctrine, they were engaged in a modification of the means whereby such goals were to be attained. Specifically, they were in the process of turning to nature itself rather than to theological inspiration or speculation as a means of attaining Puritan goals.

Foremost among these goals was the endeavor to serve and glorify

---

[29] Merton, *Social Theory and Social Structure*, pp. 574–575. Pitirim Sorokin argues, more broadly, that both science and capitalism grew out of a movement toward "sensatism." This movement had an influence on all the institutions of Western European society. See Chapter 8 for more details.

184 God. If Puritanism instilled in people the desire to glorify God, and if Puritanism had some bearing on the development of early science, then seventeenth-century scientists would evaluate their work in terms of the extent to which it worked toward the greater glorification of God. This, claims Merton, is what did in fact happen. Seventeenth-century scientists not only prefaced their works as being dedicated to the greater glory of God but saw the true ends of science to be the glorification of the Creator.

> In his last will and testament, Boyle echoes the same attitude, petitioning the Fellows of the Society in this wise: "Wishing them also a happy success in their laudable attempts, to discover the true Nature of the Works of God; and praying that they and all other Searchers into Physical Truths, may cordially refer their Attainments to the Glory of the Great Author of Nature, and to the Comfort of Mankind." John Wilks proclaimed the experimental study of Nature to be a most effective means of begetting in men a veneration for God. Francis Willoughby was prevailed upon to publish his works—which he had deemed unworthy of publication—only when Ray insisted that it was a means of glorifying God. Ray's *Wisdom of God . . .* is a panegyric of those who Glorify Him by Studying His works.[30]

The Puritan Ethic was also strongly utilitarian—that is, it emphasized social welfare. Early scientists were as eager to indicate the social merit and worth of their work as they were to make it an effort dedicated to God's glory. Moreover, scientific studies promoted discipline, work, and serious rather than idle thoughts—all Puritan values. There is, then, a congruence between some of the basic tenets of Puritan thought and those of the early scientists. We are thereby brought before the irony, if this interpretation of the origins of science carries any validity, of observing a religious ethic bringing into being (or at least serving as the midwife of) an ideology which, in its extreme forms, has produced religion's most serious opposition and intellectual challenge.

Puritan values provided the sanction for science. Scientists could feel justified in the belief that their work was meaningful, not only to themselves but also in a much greater context—science was an entry into the works of God. There was a greater end to a scientific formulation than the mere statement of an empirical regularity.

The fact that Protestant thought emphasized individualism, rationality, utilitarianism, and empiricism might have had only a fortuitous relationship to the development of science. Merton has suggested that a significant test would be to determine whether or not Protestants, in the early days of scientific discovery, were more often found within the ranks of scientists than we would expect on the basis of their representation in the total population. To determine this, Merton investigated the membership of the Royal Society, an "invisible college" of scientists, in its early formative years. He comments:

> of the ten men who constituted the "invisible college," in 1645, only

---

[30] Merton, *Social Theory and Social Structure*, pp. 576–577.

one, Scarbough, was clearly non-Puritan. About two of the others there is some uncertainty, though Merret had a Puritan training. The others were all definitely Puritan. Moreover, among the original list of members of the Society of 1663, forty-two of the sixty-eight concerning whom information about their religious orientation is available were clearly Puritan. Considering that the Puritans constituted a relatively small minority in the English population, the fact that they constituted sixty-two per cent of the initial membership of the Society becomes even more striking.[31]

This disproportionate representation of Protestants within the ranks of science has occurred, as well, in present times. Merton cites the observations of Knapp and Goodrich to the effect that some Protestant denominations are proportionately several hundred times more strongly represented among lists of meritorious American scientists than we would expect on the basis of their representation within the general population. On the other hand, representation by Catholics is excessively low—although in other professional categories, such as law, the Catholics more than hold their own.[32]

One of the consequences, one of the latent functions of the Puritan form of Protestantism in the seventeenth century, then, was to set the stage for the development of rational and empirical science. Merton summarizes his argument by making four principal observations.

First, the relationships between emerging science and religion were indirect and certainly unintended.

Second, science, once the ideological orientation necessary for it was set, acquired a degree of functional autonomy—a character of its own, which eventually would lead to the point where science would appear to be completely removed from religious modes of thought.

Third, the process of institutional modification of thoughtways and the development of new institutional forms may be so subtle as to occur below the threshold of awareness of many of those involved in it.

Fourth, the dramatic conflict between science and religion—particularly in the nineteenth century—has possibly obscured the more significant relationship that exists between the two.[33]

Merton is explicitly aware that his study follows in the path of Max Weber. Weber was concerned with the influence of Protestant thought on the development of capitalism. Weber also suggested, in a very sketchy manner, that Protestantism had a similar influence on the development of science. However, Merton elaborates what Weber left implicit.

Merton increasingly became interested in the idea of the unanticipated consequences of social action until, eventually, it formed one of the most resonant underlying themes of his work. Out of Puritan religion, unexpectedly and without design, appears science. From propaganda campaigns designed to solicit money come unanticipated and subtle

[31] Ibid., pp. 584–585. (Merton cites Dean Stimson as the source of his data.)
[32] Ibid., p. 602.
[33] Ibid., pp. 605–606.

186 constraints on democratic political ideology. From fears of loss of freedom come repressive measures to assure that liberty will be preserved.
It is this feature of human social conduct which requires, if people are
to make the best social use of their reason, a constant and subtle examination of the functional aspects of any given social action. To evaluate
a policy only in terms of its apparent or official objectives is to see
considerably less than half of what is taking place.

There is a presumptuousness in Merton's writing. He makes much
of the fact that people are not always aware of the ways in which they
are shaping their own destinies. He then enjoins the sociologist to correct this situation by considering the latent functions of human endeavors. One wonders what the latent functions of a completely successful
sociological enterprise of this kind might be. Would an accurate manifest
and latent transcription of all human plans make the world a better place?
Is it better not to know?

The question is not purely academic. Sociology, like any other
scientific or humanistic effort, will never be perfectly successful. Yet,
through the efforts of men like Merton, it has achieved today a sufficient
level of success to make it an effective force in modern social life. It
therefore becomes a humanistic question to inquire into the latent functions of human beings who pursue the quest for latent functions. Do
they jeopardize the tenuous hold that official interpretations of reality
have and thereby dissolve the social bond? Or do they aid us in the
comprehension of our most serious irrationalities? It is a question for a
structural-functionalist to consider.[34]

Problems and Issues

*Merton views society as a sort
of "machine," with various elements that form a "structure." Each of the
elements has a "function" or "functions" and works to sustain the entire
structure. Whether we agree or not with this simile, it can be used to orient
us toward a variety of problems. In modern times sports have become an
entrenched element within the society. Merton leads us to consider the
manifest and latent functions of such activity. How do sports fit into modern
capitalistic and communistic societies? At the manifest level sports appear
to function as models of enterprise and equality of opportunity. At the
latent level sports may function to sustain inequality. Within what kind of
social structure are sports, as we know them today, most likely to develop?*

*Merton was interested in the extent to which discrepancies between
institutionalized goals and institutionalized means for achieving those goals
can produce deviant behavior. What are some of the "goals" that this
society promotes? Which people within the society appear to have greatest*

---

[34] Sociologists certainly have not ignored the question of the social functions of sociology.
For some interesting discussions of this matter see Maurice Stein and Arthur Vidich (eds.),
Sociology on Trial (Englewood Cliffs, N.J.: Prentice-Hall, 1963).

access to the requisite means for attaining those goals? When we begin talking about the structural features of a society we have moved away from a psychological approach to human behavior. Presuming, for the moment, that a psychological approach is more popular among Americans, why might this be so? What are the sociological functions of psychology in America today?

Among the social institutions which interested Merton is that of science. In many ways it is a unique social phenomenon—although any culture, no matter how primitive, must have some kind of working knowledge of nature in order to survive. But science does not claim to be simply an institution dedicated to the goal of obtaining working knowledge. Science claims to unravel the great mysteries of the universe. Science purports to explain and understand natural phenomena. Science also presumes to be toughminded insofar as it disavows mystical or mythical interpretations of the world. Yet Merton points out that many of the great early scientists, foremost among them Sir Isaac Newton, were profoundly involved in mysticism. How far can science go in its efforts to account for nature in nonreligious or nonmystical ways? What limits are imposed on scientific knowledge? By what devices do scientists seek social status within science? In what ways is the scientific enterprise influenced by the fact that people must create organizations in order to carry out scientific work? Are there myths about science itself that tend to promote a mystification of science? Even though science disavows religious involvement, it was deeply involved in religion in its formative period. To what extent can we see, even today, aspects of Christian doctrine in the belief system of agnostic scientists?

Most of us are all-too-familiar with the manifest functions of science; what are the latent functions of science? How many blacks have official access to atomic weaponry in American society today? What is the relationship between established wealth and the practice and development of higher science? Toward what ends do we expect people of high intelligence to dedicate themselves? How do we define intelligence? Are we coming to definitions of intelligence that permit us to think of eventually mechanizing such a quality? To what extent has science come to dominate our conceptions of consciousness, life, and social existence?

PART II

*Social Thought
After*
WORLD WAR II

Abundance, Leisure, and Loneliness

An Introduction to

DAVID RIESMAN

. . . typologies are scaffoldings, good for a single building only, and need to be scrapped when the movements of history and of thought present us with different problems and different ways of perceiving problems.

Abundance for What? And Other Essays

BORN: 1909

Every social scientist is confronted by the opposing demands of generalization and relevancy. On the one hand, social scientists are expected to produce abstract descriptions of the way things work in the social order. A slavish dedication to this horn of the dilemma results in formulations so general in character that they lose contact with the concerns of everyday living. When sociologists claim that a society must (1) control the environment, (2) gratify the system's goal, (3) maintain solidarity, and (4) reinforce the value system, they have formulated an abstraction so airy that its relevance to the ordinary affairs of people becomes difficult to demonstrate.

On the other hand, social scientists can, like journalists, get caught in some fad that defines the relevancies of the time and discover, after a few years have passed, that their research and ideas are no longer of any value. We are reminded, for example, of a colleague who was concerned with making advertisements in the yellow pages of the phone directory more effective. There is a relevancy to such research, but it can hardly, as this colleague tried to claim, be called "basic research."

Some social scientists are able to balance themselves between ab-

11

192 stract formulations that aid our understanding and practical aspects of modern living. In such cases we are offered ideas broad enough to provide general intellectual interest and yet specific enough to be relevant to events of the moment. These people produce books that endure. One such writer is David Riesman. Before taking up the central contributions of Riesman's thought, we would like to mention that it is necessary to be biased and selective in this brief review of his work. It is possible to offer little more than a fragmented sample of his ideas. The reader should browse through some of Riesman's better-known works. It will prove a rewarding experience.[1]

The work that brought Riesman more notoriety than he ever anticipated was a book entitled *The Lonely Crowd,* which he coauthored with Nathan Glazer and Reuel Denney.[2] We shall now examine the central ideas in this work—recognizing, again, that it is impossible to do justice to the variety and imagination of Riesman's thought.

The Relationship between the Individual and Society

One of the crucial concerns of the social scientist has been the nature of the relationship between the individual and society. Some, like Leslie White, find the individual so dominated by the society or culture that there is little reason for the social scientist to keep the individual in the picture. People are, as social beings, simply the biological expression of social forces. Others, like Peter Berger, see ways out for the individual, avenues of personal expression that are the creative act of the person and that offer the individual freedom from the constraints of social bondage. This view sees personality existing in the interstices of the social fabric.

The relationship between society and the individual is the fulcrum

---

[1] Much of Riesman's writing appears in the form of essays published in a great variety of journals. His major works are *Faces in the Crowd: Individual Studies in Character and Politics,* in collaboration with Nathan Glazer (New Haven: Yale University Press, 1952); *Individualism Reconsidered* (New York: Free Press, 1954); *Constraint and Variety in American Education* (Lincoln: University of Nebraska Press, 1958); *Thorstein Veblen: A Critical Interpretation* (New York: Scribner, 1960); *The Lonely Crowd: A Study in the Changing American Character,* with Nathan Glazer and Reuel Denney, abr. ed. with new foreword (New Haven: Yale University Press, 1961); *Abundance for What?* (Garden City, N.Y.: Doubleday, 1964); *The Academic Revolution,* with Christopher Jencks (Garden City, N.Y.: Doubleday, 1968); and *The Perpetual Dream: Reform and Experiment in American Colleges,* with Gerald Grant (Chicago: University of Chicago Press, 1976).

[2] Of the response to *The Lonely Crowd* Riesman says, "We did not anticipate such an audience, not only when the book was first published by a university press, but later when it was one of the first 'quality paperbacks,' for we and the publishers alike thought it might sell a few thousand copies as a reading in social science courses." *The Lonely Crowd,* p. xxix. Reaction to Riesman's work was so enthusiastically favorable that it led to the distinction of a cover story in *Time* magazine (see *Time,* September 27, 1954). As far as we know, Riesman is the only sociologist to have been so honored.

upon which Riesman's thought is balanced. But his approach is different. First of all, Riesman is not especially concerned with resolving the problem of the priority of society *or* the individual. He is not concerned with proving that society dominates the individual. Nor is he interested in proving that society is a collective manifestation of individual instincts—an elaborately spread-out form of human nature. Instead, he takes the problem of the relationship between the individual and society as a point of departure for an investigation into national character. All we need to do is to presume that if there is some kind of relationship between society and the individual—and this seems apologetically reasonable—then the historical experiences of our society may have a bearing on what we, as individuals, have become today.

This is the simple motif. In its abstract form it is not especially enlightening, nor is it subject to much in the way of critical comment. The premises with which he begins are modestly qualified; it is when Riesman gets down to the particulars of historical experience and their bearing on national character that he proves to be provocative. But what, specifically, does Riesman have to say about national social character?[3]

Three Types of Social Character

We can begin by assuming that the different demands placed on people by different kinds of societies produce unique "social" characters. Thus Riesman suggests that societies that are relatively primitive—folk-oriented, preindustrial, hunting, or agricultural societies—develop in their people a social character typified by a tendency to follow tradition. Riesman refers to such people as *tradition-directed* people and their

---

[3] In his evaluation of national social character Riesman is often critical. He exudes the indignant concern any sensitive observer of the American scene must feel when observing practices that fall beneath the potential of this culture. Perhaps the only difference between the writings of the objective professional sociologist and the free-swinging comments of Riesman is that Riesman is willing to let you know exactly where he stands with respect to the object of his observations. Consider, for example, the following comment on the typical American response to problems of foreign policy:

> Many Americans have no better utopia than a mad return to the epoch of Theodore Roosevelt, imitating both the bravado of our own past and that of the Soviet Union—as if it were possible to make a whole nation inner-directed again by internalizing the arms race under the label of "national purpose." If they win out, the fragile chance will be lost that America might offer the rest of the world some clues to the uses of literacy and abundance (*The Lonely Crowd*, p. xvii).

Such commentary, and the oversimplification that goes with it, is a sign of having fallen from the grace of objectivity. It cost Riesman considerable loss of respect from more scientifically oriented colleagues. At the same time, it won him a host of concerned readers who were wrestling with the problem of what it means to be an American today. Even so, Riesman should not be evaluated in terms of his occasional critical asides. What elevates him to a high intellectual status is his embracing interpretation of the development of American character and his ability to express this development with lucidity.

194 society as one which is dependent on tradition-direction.[4] The tradition-directed person possesses a social character uncritically accepting of tradition and resistant to innovation. The major problems of the society are resolved by the willingness of the individual to rely on tradition.

Tradition provides a place for the individual in society, and the individual responds by tenaciously endorsing tradition. In contrast to other societies, traditional societies incorporate all their members. No one is "surplus."

> Indeed, the individual in some primitive societies is far more appreciated and respected than in some sectors of modern society. For the individual in a society dependent on tradition-direction has a well-defined functional relationship to other members of the group. If he is not killed off, he "belongs"—he is not "surplus," as the modern unemployed are surplus, nor is he expendable as the unskilled are expendable in modern society. But by very virtue of his "belonging," life goals that are *his* in terms of conscious choice appear to shape his destiny only to a very limited extent, just as only to a limited extent is there any concept of progress for the group.[5]

A small and relatively stable society may be able to maintain itself almost exclusively in terms of traditional definitions of roles and interpersonal behavior. Then, for reasons not well understood today, such societies may undergo a number of small but cumulative changes that tend to destroy the effectiveness of tradition as a basis of organization. With a decline in the effectiveness of tradition, the society enters a transitional stage of development and, during this stage, relies on a different form of social character—that of "inner-direction." Riesman puts it this way:

> In western history the society that emerged with the Renaissance and Reformation and that is only now vanishing serves to illustrate the type of society in which inner-direction is the principal mode of securing conformity. Such a society is characterized by increased personal mobility, by a rapid accumulation of capital (teamed with devastating technological shifts), and by an almost constant *expansion:* intensive expansion in exploration, colonization, and imperialism. The greater choices this society gives—and the greater initiatives it demands in order to cope with its novel problems— are handled by character types who can manage to live socially without

---

[4] The extent to which tradition is not only losing its utility in modern society but becoming downright dangerous—a luxury only more primitive social systems can afford—is hinted at by Norbert Wiener. Speaking of war games, he says, "It has been said that in every war, the good generals fight the last war, the bad ones the war before the last. That is, the rules of the war game never catch up with the facts of the real situation." In the context here, Wiener is pointing out that the traditionalist in war is the one who stands the greatest chance of losing. Ominously enough, he adds, "Moreover, remember that in the game of atomic warfare, there are no experts." The course of social movement today is one which provides less and less traditional basis for decision making. These statements by Wiener appear in *God and Golem, Inc.* (Cambridge, Mass.: MIT Press, 1964), pp. 60, 85.

[5] Riesman, *The Lonely Crowd,* pp. 11–12.

strict and self-evident tradition-direction. These are the inner-directed **195** types.[6]

The inner-directed person is provided with the ambition to seek out generalized social goals. This may require novel solutions to problems that a traditionalistic approach would not have been able to resolve, or that, more likely, would not even have occurred. Inner-directed individuals are not completely lacking in a tradition-directed society; but—and this is Riesman's point—they will be more typical of a society that has need of them. They are more likely to be aberrant or unique in other forms of society. Inner-directed people appear when a society is in process of expansion.

After the expansive movements of a society have been completed, a new problem arises. During the expansive phase, the problem is to cope with novel situations and to pursue doggedly the task of exploiting a hostile environment; once this has been achieved, the problem then becomes one of making peace with success. A period of entrenchment ensues. The land, the resources, the markets, the colonies have been successfully exploited. But the process of exploitation, of developing these resources, brings into being powerful agents of control; the most significant of these is the large-scale organizational system. Whereas people previously found themselves locked in dubious battle with nature, now they find themselves confronted with bureaucracies. The problem is to adjust to others around them. Social adaptability rather than inner moral strength becomes a leading characteristic of the successful type in this new stage of social development.[7]

Because relations with other people become crucial and because the individual is sensitive to the demands of others, Riesman calls a person having this form of social character "other-directed." He defines the other-directed person and society in the following way:

> Under these newer [other-directed] patterns the peer group (the group of one's associates of the same age and class) becomes much more important to the child, while the parents make him feel guilty not so much about violation of inner standards as about failure to be popular or otherwise to manage his relations with these other children. . . . What is com-

---

[6] Ibid., p. 14.
[7] Some people fear that Riesman is opposed to inner moral strength and that he is justifying more callow forms of opportunistic conformity. This would be unfair. Riesman is trying, as realistically as possible, to evaluate the impact of modern forms of social organization on character, and he concludes that, for the most part, a common character of the hardheaded inner-directed type would prove extremely disruptive. Ayn Rand's plea for a return to older individualistic values is not so much right or wrong as it is unrealistic. A few people of the character of the hero of *The Fountainhead* can be absorbed by this society. But such willfulness would prove intolerable in great numbers. Riesman, incidentally, views Rand's work as a caricature of inner-directed values. In any event, we cannot avow the rightness or wrongness of strong moral character. We can, however, consider the possibility of its disruptive effects if practiced on a large scale in a society where the central problem confronting people is that of making their peace with other people.

196

mon to all the other-directed people is that their contemporaries are the source of direction for the individual—either those known to him or those with whom he is indirectly acquainted, through friends and through the mass media. . . . This mode of keeping in touch with others permits a close behavior conformity, not through drill in behavior itself, as in the tradition-directed character, but rather through an exceptional sensitivity to the actions and wishes of others.[8]

This tripartite typification of societies and social character, relatively simple and straightforward, proves to have astonishing success in making sense out of a tremendous variety of social events, ranging from changes in child-rearing practices to the problems of personnel management in modern industry. As we shall see, practices taking place in one sector of society are not always as removed from those taking place in another as it might first appear. Indeed, the hallmark of an outstanding social scientist is the capacity to reveal commonalities in events that have, in the past, seemed perfectly disparate.[9]

If vast changes in the social structure can be summarized in terms of pervasive effects on social character, then we should be able to find these effects at work in almost any setting. We should be able to see shifts from tradition- to inner- to other-direction at work in the army, the school, the practice of medicine, the practice of law, the treatment of criminals, the practice of business, leisure pursuits, literature, government, religion, and any other part of the social order. One social activity that occupies much of Riesman's thinking is education, and he turns toward a consideration of the tradition-, inner-, and other-directed school.

Schooling in Different Societies

In the tradition-directed society, children are likely to have little encounter with schooling. The traditions they come to rely on are acquired through intimate observation and involvement with adults and peers. For example, Navaho children whose parents belong to the Native American Church, a peyote-using religion, are taken to all-night peyote sessions and allowed to watch and participate to whatever extent they can. When they become sleepy, they are allowed to fall asleep. The children are

---

[8] Riesman, *The Lonely Crowd*, pp. 21–22.
[9] John Kenneth Galbraith expresses this point better in his description of Marx as a social scientist. He refers to

> the breath-taking grandeur of Marx's achievement as an exercise in social theory. No one before, or for that matter since, had taken so many strands of human behavior and woven them together—social classes, economic behavior, the nature of the state, imperalism, and war were all here and on a great fresco which ran from deep in the past to far into the future (*The Affluent Society* [New York: New American Library, Mentor Books, 1958], p. 63. Originally published by Houghton Mifflin; Boston, 1958).

allowed to experiment with peyote at any time they wish—regardless of **197** age.[10]

In the inner-directed society, the problems of education are more complicated. Children must be infused with general goals that they are willing to pursue even though it may exact a cost in terms of indifference and hostility on the part of others. The governess in Victorian England helped promote such a character. The relationship of the governess to the head of the household was such as to provide the child with a very realistic training in the disparities of power. A child reared under such conditions was less likely to be awed by the authority of his or her teachers. As Riesman puts it:

> When he goes off to boarding school or college he is likely to remain unimpressed by his teachers—like the upper class mother who told the school headmaster: "I don't see why the masters can't get along with Johnny; all the other servants do." Such a child is not going to be interested in allowing his teachers to counsel him in his peer-group relations or emotional life.[11]

The character of schooling in the inner-directed society can be summed up as follows: The task of the teacher is to train children in matters of decorum and intellectual subjects. The approach is impersonal. The sexes are segregated. The emphasis is on learning a curriculum, and whether or not one enjoys it is really beside the point. Standards are unequivocal—they are immutable. They cannot be challenged nor can they be seen in a relative manner—they apply to all. They are not held to be more appropriate for some students than for others. Thus, children are ranked in terms of their ability to conform to the standards, and the security they achieve from knowing where they stand in terms of these standards is balanced by the fact that little mercy is shown them by taking into account any psychological or social handicaps under which they might be straining.

George Orwell, describing his experiences at Crossgates, nicely underscores Riesman's main point:

> That was the pattern of school life—a continuous triumph of the strong over the weak. Virtue consisted in winning: it consisted in being bigger, stronger, handsomer, richer, more popular, more elegant, more unscrupulous than other people—in dominating them, bullying them, making

---

[10] We are indebted to Professor Omer C. Stewart of the University of Colorado for this illustration. Reliance on tradition does not necessarily mean a stultified life-form for the tradition-oriented person. Part of the peyote ritual consists of singing hymns. These hymns are traditional, but they can be varied to a considerable degree within this limitation. Professor Stewart illustrates this nicely by singing a peyote hymn he learned from a Navaho Indian. The Navaho learned the hymn, in turn, from the generator of his automobile as he was driving home one evening.

[11] Riesman, *The Lonely Crowd*, p. 56.

them suffer pain, making them look foolish, getting the better of them in every way. Life was hierarchical and whatever happened was right. There were the strong, who deserved to win and always did win, and there were the weak, who deserved to lose and always did lose, everlastingly.

I did not question the prevailing standards, because so far as I could see there were no others. How could the rich, the strong, the elegant, the fashionable, the powerful, be in the wrong? It was their world, and the rules they made for it must be the right ones.[12]

But times and social character have changed—and these changes can be seen dramatically within the context of the school. Riesman describes schooling in an age of other-direction: Children go to school at earlier ages, and the two- to five-year-old school children come to associate school more with playing and with games than with forbidding adults and dreary subjects. Physical arrangements are altered. The sexes may be mixed, and alphabetic placement of students may give way to sociometric forms of seating—children sit not where they are told to sit but where they find their friends. Concern is focused increasingly on problems of group relations and decreasingly on problems of production. The teacher

conveys to the children that what matters is not their industry or learning as such but their adjustment to the group, their (carefully stylized and limited) initiative and leadership.[13]

In the other-directed school there is a deemphasis on the content of learning and an emphasis on democratization of social relationships. What a child learns is not too important—so long as he or she learns it in a way that shows a capacity to get along with others. Children are readied for their place in a society that is moving increasingly from a dedication to morality to a promotion of morale.

The value of Riesman's inner- and other-directed classification of social character is, as we mentioned before, that it has the capacity to bring together a great variety of social threads and show them to be part of a common cloth. We have, at this point, briefly examined differences between schooling in the inner-directed and other-directed society. Now let us examine Riesman's treatment of sexual relations in the inner- and other-directed systems.

---

[12] Few reading experiences more dramatically reveal how education practices have changed than reading Orwell's description of his experiences as a boy in attendance at Crossgates. See George Orwell, "Such, Such Were the Joys," in *A Collection of Essays by George Orwell* (Garden City, N.Y.: Doubleday Anchor Books, 1954), pp. 9–55. The quotation cited here appears on pages 43–44.

[13] Riesman, *The Lonely Crowd*, p. 63.

Sex in Different Societies

Sex for the inner-directed person had[14] a character different from what it has for the other-directed person. For example, it played a less predominant role in the life of the inner-directed man. Sex was an integral element in the daily round of coping with problems of production—and sex, though enjoyed for its own sake, was never removed from the fact of its consequences. For the inner-directed man, preoccupation with the more serious concerns of struggle and control gave sex a smaller role to play in the scheme of life. Life and business could be and was, in many instances, a grim and gloomy confrontation with conflicting ambitions. Sex could be treated as gloomily. In inner-directed ideology, at least, masturbation was a peril to be avoided at any cost. The modest pleasures of onanism could not be permitted to appear to compete with the serious moral dedication necessary for bringing the material resources of nature to heel.

Relationships between the sexes verged on the morbid. The wife of the inner-directed man was not to allow herself expressions of pleasure in sex. The emancipated woman with whom the inner-directed man might allow himself relations was socially inferior. The sexual conduct of the inner-directed man was supposed to be restrained and subordinated to the higher directives of social and economic exploitation of the frontier.

If in private practice sex was constrained and even dismal by modern standards, its presentation in literature and drama was often humorous. Sex was something you could poke fun at, but a serious scientific treatise on the subject was less tolerable. Sex, in an age of inner-direction, could also be used as a means for self-advancement. Women, especially, could and did use sex as a means to status in spheres controlled by men. Even so, such practices were conducted in private, and the ideal was to respect the secret nature of the relationship by maintaining confidences.

Sex apparently has a different meaning today. Furthermore, the difference is not simply attributable to greater knowledge about sex. Rather, it is a reflection of changes that have been taking place in various sectors of society, which in turn have had a bearing on sexual attitudes and conduct. Riesman argues that sex takes on greater importance for other-directed persons because they lack the grand moral imperatives that give meaning and a sense of being to life. Sex is something that lies within, and its imperatives still remain alive even when social imperatives have been reduced to the level of "Mickey-Mouse" playacting. Women are no longer objects in a gloomy exercise of power but emancipated

---

[14] It is problematic whether one should use the past or present tense here. Riesman tends to use the past tense when talking about inner-direction. However, Riesman is well aware that inner-directed people are still with us and that inner-directed characteristics are to be found even in highly developed other-directed types. So, we can also correctly say that sex *has* a different quality for inner-directed people.

200   members of the peer group—sensitive and knowing consumers in the realm of sex. As Riesman notes:

> While the inner-directed man, who could still patronize women, complained to his mistress that his wife did not understand him, the other-directed man in effect complains that his women understand him all too well.[15]

Sex, in an age of other-direction, has become a competitive and continuous quest for experience or, more properly, a development of talent, which previously was encountered, if at all, in a visit to a brothel. Because sex remains an inner-compulsion in an age of other-direction, its demands must be met. At the same time, the private nature of sex[16] leaves the other-directed male consumer in something of a quandary about how he matches up with others in this now significant realm of social action. Inner-directed man did not especially care how he compared with others and, even if he did, he could count on women to remain discreet about his talent or lack of talent—they could at least be counted on not to tell him if he was incompetent. But in an age of other-direction, as Riesman notes, men—and women as well—have to contend with the fact they may be understood all too well. Being told where one ranks in sexual consumership is not the problem.[17] The problem comes from being ranked while, at the same time, being denied access to a direct observation of the performance of one's peers.

---

[15] Riesman, *The Lonely Crowd*, p. 280.

[16] Riesman, a perceptive but tasteful observer of social events, would not have mentioned in his writing the possibility that sex might move in the direction of losing its privacy. It has become increasingly realistically portrayed in the movies—losing some of its mystery there and granting the other-directed observer the opportunity to match his experiences and capacities with those heroically depicted on the screen. For an interesting discussion of sex and the movies see Arthur Knight and Hollis Alpert, "The History of Sex in Cinema" *Playboy*, April 1967, pp. 136–143 and 196–212. This is one of a series of articles on the subject.

More importantly, some young intellectuals are convinced that parties should be held in the nude with participants indulging privately or openly and without shame in whatever forms of conduct they feel moved to indulge in. (See also "The Sexual Freedom League" by Jack Lind in *Playboy*, November 1966.) Riesman would suggest that this is not only a revolt against the presumed prudery of Victorian times, it is an attempt to provide other-directed young people with the opportunity to see for themselves the levels of talent against which they are to measure themselves. This might appear, to a liberal person, like a healthy return to the direct observational learning of the tradition-directed child who observes his parents in coitus or indulges in direct sexual play with his friends. It differs, however, in the amount of importance that is given to sex and in the competitive attitudes that develop—attitudes directed by social responsiveness.

[17] In the movie *Georgy Girl*, the heroine is told by her lover that her problem is not so much that she is ugly and heavy but that she tries too hard to save people. In an age of inner-direction, the relation between the sexes was such that chivalrous attitudes toward the female were supposed to protect her from such blunt evaluations of her character. The women reciprocated by not telling men what they thought of them.

Literature and Entertainment in Different Societies

Let us turn from education and the relation between the sexes to Riesman's comments on literature and entertainment and their relation to ideals of success. As we go from a period of inner-direction to one of other-direction:

> We can trace an edifying sequence that runs from the success biography of the Samuel Smiles or the Horatio Alger sort to the contemporary books and periodicals that deal with peace of mind. The earlier books were directly concerned with social and economic advance, dealt with as achievable by the virtues of thrift, hard work, and so on. . . .
>
> From then on, inspiration literature becomes less and less exclusively concerned with social and economic mobility. Dale Carnegie's *How to Win Friends and Influence People,* written in 1937, recommends self-manipulative exercises for the sake not only of business success but of such vaguer, non-work goals as popularity.[18]

This reference to Carnegie is pertinent because *How to Win Friends and Influence People,* perhaps more than any other written work, illustrates what Riesman is saying. It is worth spending a few moments to look further at this extraordinary book.

What Carnegie does, in effect, is lay down a set of rules or suggestions for transforming the individual into an other-directed person. Carnegie boasts:

> The rules we have set down here are not mere theories or guess work. They work like magic. . . .
>
> To illustrate: Last season a man with 314 employees [applied these rules]. For years he had driven and criticized and condemned his employees without stint or discretion. Kindness, words of appreciation, and encouragement were alien to his lips. After studying the principles discussed in this book, this employer sharply altered his philosophy of life. . . . Three hundred and fourteen enemies have been turned into three hundred and fourteen friends. As he proudly said . . . "When I used to walk through my establishment, no one greeted me. My employees actually looked the other way when they saw me approaching. But now they are all my friends and even the janitor calls me by my first name."[19]

It is difficult to imagine an earlier, inner-directed employer being concerned with getting someone to call him by his first name. He might,

---

[18] Riesman, *The Lonely Crowd,* pp. 149–150.
[19] Dale Carnegie, *How to Win Friends and Influence People* (New York: Simon and Schuster, 1937), p. 22. This book, published in 1937, is still selling. Few books provide a more blunt and open insight into the American ideal. Here is Willie Loman's bible, leading him to happiness on a shoeshine and a smile.

202 to the contrary, have found the whole idea worse than an affront; it would have made things messy.[20]

It is possible that the other-directed person, at least as that individual appears in Carnegie's writing, loses a great deal of individuality in the attempt to be delicately and sensitively responsive to the needs of others. Consider the implications, for example, of the following observation by Carnegie:

> I go fishing up in Maine every summer. Personally I am very fond of strawberries and cream; but I find that for some strange reason fish prefer worms. So when I go fishing, I don't think about what I want. I think about what they want. I don't bait the hook with strawberries and cream. Rather, I dangle a worm or a grasshopper in front of the fish and say: "Wouldn't you like to have that?"[21]

One sacrifices one's taste for "strawberries and cream" in order to gain access to the other person's preference for worms. Such a procedure, it seems, would strip both individuals of the vigor of their own characters and identities. Evidently, in this scheme of things, the extent to which this would greatly facilitate social exchanges would make it worth the cost.

It is instructive to note further, in Carnegie's bible for the other-directed person, that he often dehumanizes his subject by making use of figures of speech that reduce humans to animals. He does it in the above quotation by talking about dangling "worms" in front of "fish." He does it again in the following suggestion:

> Many of the sweetest memories of my childhood cluster around a little yellow-haired dog with a stub tail. "Tippy" never read a book on psychology. He didn't need to. . . . He had a perfect technique for making people like him. . . .
> Do you want to make friends? Then take a tip from Tippy. Be friendly. Forget yourself. Think of others.[22]

Or consider the following:

> That is why dogs make such a hit. They are so glad to see us that they almost jump out of their skins. So, naturally, we are glad to see them.[23]

---

[20] We encounter a similar thing happening in Dickens's *A Christmas Carol*, but the effect is achieved through the power of Christmas. We are not as inclined to see the victory over the inner-directed person in *A Christmas Carol* in the same way we see the victory over the inner-directed person in a work like Carnegie's. Yet Scrooge, before his transformation into a "nice guy," was a man who drove himself as hard as he drove his employees. If he was grim toward them, he was equally, if not more, grim toward himself. We tend to react negatively toward the Scrooge-like character that makes up a greater portion of the inner-directed person. For this reason it is enigmatic that students seem to romanticize the inner-directed person—finding in that kind of individual a moral quality they believe is lacking in the other-directed person.

[21] Carnegie, *How to Win Friends and Influence People*, p. 56.

[22] Ibid., p. 83.

[23] Ibid., p. 97.

Finally, we should consider one last quotation from Carnegie. Here we come to possibly the ultimate reduction of the worth of the individual. While reading this quotation keep in mind that the individual is being subordinated to the greater goal of making him or her socially viable. It is supremely ironic that this book, which in our estimation is perhaps the most deviously anti-individualistic work ever written, has been magnanimously endorsed by the more conservative business elements in American culture—a group which likes to believe it stands behind the cause of individualism. Carnegie says:

> We ought to be modest, for neither you nor I amount to much. Both of us will pass on and be completely forgotten a century from now. Life is too short to bore other people with talk of our petty accomplishments. Let's encourage them to talk instead. Come to think about it, you haven't much to brag about anyhow. Do you know what keeps you from becoming an idiot? Not much. Only a nickel's worth of iodine in your thyroid glands. If a physician were to open the thyroid gland in your neck and take out a little iodine, you would become an idiot. A little iodine that can be bought at a corner drugstore for five cents is all that stands between you and an institution for the mentally ill. A nickel's worth of iodine! That isn't much to be boasting about, is it?[24]

What an astounding assertion! A human being is worth a nickel . . . one must be modest . . . one's accomplishments are petty . . . encourage the other person to talk . . . be responsive . . . avoid argument . . . watch what the other is doing so you will know how to match his or her performance . . . do not assert yourself.

In Carnegie's book we have a direct, if crude, delineation of the personal qualities of the other-directed person. Though Carnegie unwittingly makes the other-directed type of character look bad, it is not necessarily true that such a character is bad. The friendly, sociable, other-directed kind of person can be and is socially valuable. Carnegie was only gauche enough to make the social and individual costs of other-directed morality glaringly apparent.[25]

The literature of the other-directed society achieves an extreme form in the works of Dale Carnegie. But the other-directed theme appears diffusely throughout a great variety of novels, stories, movies, and dramas. The gangster, for example, is mentioned by Riesman as a case in point. The gangster is a tragic hero despite, rather than because of, his violation of the rules of the law-abiding community. If he is successful, he isolates himself not only from society at large but from his own

---

[24] Ibid., p. 205. This is one of the most peculiar pieces of humanistic reasoning in Western literature. The individual is evaluated in terms of chemical makeup and its current price on the market. After being reduced to physical nature, one is then, not surprisingly, found to be worth nothing! In his eagerness to create a friendly, outgoing, socially sensitive, other-directed kind of person, Carnegie loses sight almost completely of the broader implications of his arguments and his imagery.

[25] Riesman is aware of the problem. At the beginning of the revised version of *The Lonely Crowd,* he comments on the preferences of students for the inner-directed type. He goes on to point to the sensitivity and adaptiveness of the other-directed person—qualities that can be and are virtues. Each social type has virtues as well as vices.

204 gang as well. Success forces him into a cul-de-sac where he must wait, alone and frightened, for the miserable finish to his career.[26]

But there is more to other-directed and inner-directed literature and entertainment than its content. There is the way one is supposed to respond to it.

> Though popular culture on one level "fills in" between people so as to avoid any demand for conversational or sexual gambits, on another level the popular-culture performance is not simply a way of killing time: in the peer-group situation, it makes a demand that it be appraised. The other-directed girl who goes in company to the movies need not talk to the others during the picture but is sometimes faced with the problem: should she cry at the sad places or not? What is the proper reaction, the sophisticated line about what is going on? Observing movie audiences coming out of "little" or "art" theaters, it is sometimes apparent that people feel they ought to react, but how?
>
> In contrast to this, the inner-directed person, reading a book alone, is less aware of the others looking on; moreover, he has time to return at his own pace from being transported by his reading—to return and put on whatever mask he cares to.[27]

Riesman's approach to individuals, society, history, human character, and action is thematic. Like a composer from the Romantic period, he takes a simple but expressive theme and then proceeds to create a series of variations. Eventually we are overwhelmed by the potential contained within what, at first, seemed to be no more than a minor melody. This, incidentally, seems to be characteristic of many of the works on individuals and society that have gained great popularity in recent years.[28]

[26] Riesman, *The Lonely Crowd*, p. 155. Riesman refers here to Robert Warshow's article, "The Gangster as Tragic Hero," which appeared in *The Partisan Review* XV (February 1948), 240–244.

[27] Riesman, *The Lonely Crowd*, p. 158.

[28] Any number of examples come to mind. Arnold Toynbee's "challenge and response" theme was applied to the historical development of all of civilization. Pitirim Sorokin utilized the theme that cultures go through cycles of intense religious experience and then degenerate into "sensate" forms of experience, from which they return to the religious state. Ruth Benedict used a simple dichotomous theme of Dionysian and Apollonian ways of living to bring together a variety of behaviors. Freud took the elementary theme of conflict between human animal nature and the demands of society and worked it into one of the most fully orchestrated and developed variations on a theme in the literature of psychology. Marshall McCluhan hit upon a responsive theme with the simple idea that the medium of a message is of as much importance as the message itself. A similar theme, developed in a slightly different way, is Goffman's elementary observation that how one says something is as important as what one says. In each case, the simplicity of the theme is shocking. The theme often boils down to a cliché or bit of folk wisdom that everyone has known for centuries. After all, the men in Caesar's armies probably joked about the relationship between sexual deprivation and nervous conditions several thousand years before Freud came along. The difference, of course, between the soldiers' superficial grasp of a truth and that of a perceptive intellectual is in the capacity to see that truth in thousands of different settings and applications—recognizing those where it has a validity and those where it does not. In this respect, when someone says that psychology or, more often, sociology, is an elaboration of the obvious, they are many times quite correct. The point is, the process of elaboration is often worth the effort. Proper elaboration of the obvious can lead—and almost invariably does lead—to the not so obvious. If this is disputed, look to the humble origins of modern mathematics and physical science.

Riesman takes the rather simple theme, then, of three types of people: tradition-directed, inner-directed, and other-directed. This theme is applied to various settings, ranging from sexual behavior to the realm of political action, and, seemingly, it brings together what otherwise would remain greatly disparate areas of social behavior. But what is the final movement? Where do the variations lead? In music, despite pretensions to the contrary, it is not proper to ask such a question. A string quartet, after all, is a string quartet. It really is not supposed to lead us anywhere—it begins and ends with itself. However, people can and do ask more of the social scientist. It is not sufficient for science or the humanities to begin and end with themselves—though some scientists and humanists would insist that this is exactly what they should do. There is always some pressure to bring thought around to application— to orient science, whether physical or social, to some kind of utility. Does Riesman have utility? Or is his work like a symphony by Mahler, something that induces a mood, something that depends on the artistic or humanistic sensitivity of the person responding to his work?

The Adjusted, the Anomic, and the Autonomous

In the final passages of *The Lonely Crowd,* Riesman provides his readers with what amounts to a set of program notes on how to interpret and respond to what he has had to say in the earlier segments of his work. The notes lean, interestingly enough, on another tripartite classification of people—the adjusted, the anomic, and the autonomous. The adjusted are those who conform to, and at the same time make their peace with, the demands of their culture—whether it is tradition-, inner-, or other-directed. The anomic are those who are, in some serious way, shattered or broken by the culture; they are those who cannot, for whatever reason, meet the demands of the culture; they are lost in their culture. The autonomous are those who neither become lost to the demands of the culture nor are broken by them. They live within the culture, but they retain a strong and assertive sense of self. It is the autonomous type, the most difficult and yet the most engaging of the three, that receives most of Riesman's attention.

The attainment of autonomy for the tradition-directed person is extremely difficult, if not impossible. Riesman tells the story of the Lebanese farmers who for centuries suffered from invasions by Arab horsemen; it never occurred to the farmers to become horsemen, and it never occurred to the horsemen to become farmers. Through the centuries they remained locked in a pattern which had an almost animalistic inevitability about it. Then Riesman makes his point:

> If Arabs could imagine becoming cultivators, and vice versa, it would not necessarily follow that the symbiotic ecology of the two main groups would change. These tradition-directed types might still go on doing what they realized they need not do. Nevertheless, once people become aware, with the rise of inner-direction, that they as individuals with a private destiny are not tied to any given ecological pattern, something radically new hap-

pens in personal and social history. Then people can envisage adapting themselves not only within the narrow confines of the animal kingdom but within the wide range of alternative possibilities illustrated—but no more than illustrated—by human experience to date. *Perhaps this is the most important meaning of the ever renewed discovery of the oneness of mankind as a species: that all human experience becomes relevant.*[29]

Relevant to what? Relevant to our own autonomy would be the reply. The practical consequence of social knowledge is that it provides the individual with the capacity to empathize with others and thereby gain two very broad but powerful extensions of choice. One can, for example, empathize to the point where one becomes the other in actuality. A person might gain sufficient understanding of the life of an executive to enable him or her to rise to that status—or decide not to take on that role. The second consequence of empathetic knowledge is the extent to which it can promote manipulation. If one does not elect to become an executive on the basis of this knowledge, one may, nonetheless, find such knowledge helpful when it comes to managing those whose task it is to manage.

The fate of autonomy is different in inner- and other-directed societies. Riesman speculates that the attainment of autonomy—the maintenance of individuality in the midst of social control—is probably easier to achieve in an inner-directed society than in modern other-directed forms of society, though it is not easy to attain in any society. Society has a way of either inducing one to adjust to its demands or breaking one, leaving the person in an anomic condition in the process.

In the inner-directed society a person's place in the social order was relatively definite, and the boundaries of custom were sufficiently clear to enable the autonomous person to define the enemies, to define the causes, to assert the self as a unique force. It is no longer so simple. In an age of other-direction, individuals seeking autonomy are confronted not only with the problem of determining who is, in fact, the enemy to serve as the background for the portrayal of self; they are also confronted with the problem of their own motivations. There always exists the possibility, in an age of social and psychological enlightenment, that the other person is not really the enemy after all but only a projection of some despised element of one's self.

In an age of inner-direction, autonomous people could assert themselves against the tastes and insensitivities of the middle class. Today such an enemy is both difficult to find and, at the same time, too much on the defensive when discovered. In part, this is why the quest for autonomy within Bohemia is probably more deceptive today than in the past. Bohemian conduct is simply too matter-of-fact to allow us to view it as a manifestation of autonomy. There are exceptions. Allen Ginsberg qualifies, but for many others it may be a different matter. As Riesman

---

[29] Riesman, *The Lonely Crowd*, p. 246 (emphasis added).

expresses it:

> Young people today can find, in the wide variety of people and places of metropolitan life, a peer-group, conformity to which costs little in the way of search for principle.[30]

The only road to autonomy, if this is a valued goal—and Riesman makes it apparent that it ought to be—is, paradoxically enough, through further self-consciousness. It is paradoxical because it has been self-consciousness that has made the acquisition of autonomy more difficult.

> This heightened self-consciousness, above all else, constitutes the insignia of the autonomous in an era dependent on other-direction. For, as the inner-directed man is more self-conscious than his tradition-directed predecessor and as the other-directed man is more self-conscious still, the autonomous man growing up under conditions that encourage self-consciousness can disentangle himself from the adjusted others only by a further move toward even greater self-consciousness. His autonomy depends not upon the ease with which he may deny or disguise his emotions but, on the contrary, upon the success of his effort to recognize and respect his own feelings, his own potentialities, his own limitations. This is . . . the problem of self-consciousness itself, an achievement of a higher order of abstraction.[31]

The consciousness of self, the ability to provide an identity for one's self in the midst of pressures to dissolve into the tastes and sensitivities (or insensitivities) of the other-directed society, is the only way, as Riesman sees it, one can achieve autonomy.

Riesman's contribution, in the final pages of this still powerful and relevant book,[32] is not only to bring together in a meaningful way the many practices of society—probing them with the concepts of inner- and other-direction. More importantly, Riesman tries to retain a sense of social values and relate his thought to such values. He is not radical in the selection of new values. He is quite conservative when he chooses freedom and autonomy and the dignity of the individual as his primary values. But he is radical in his comprehension of what is involved in the quest for such values and in his analysis of the relationship between the individual and society and the bearing of that relationship on the development of individual worth.

Small wonder, then, that Riesman has proved popular among many

---

[30] Ibid., p. 258.
[31] Ibid., p. 259.
[32] *The Lonely Crowd* stimulated considerable discussion and criticism. The interested reader is encouraged to examine Seymour M. Lipset and Leo Lowenthal, *Culture and Social Character* (New York: Free Press, 1961). In the last chapter of this work Riesman replies to his critics. See also Walter Williams, "Inner-Directedness and Other-Directedness in New Perspective," *Sociological Quarterly* 5 (Summer 1964), 193–220; Carl N. Degler, "The Sociologist as Historian: Riesman's *The Lonely Crowd*," *American Quarterly* 5 (Winter 1963), 483–497; and Cushing Strout, "A Note on Degler, Riesman and Tocqueville," *American Quarterly* 16 (Spring 1964), 100–102.

208 humanists and social scientists. He has shown, perhaps better than any other writer living today, the promise that modern social science holds for deepening further our comprehension of age-old humanistic concerns.

Problems and Issues

Whether we are trying to understand physical nature or the social systems of human beings we run into a common problem. Nature and society manifest themselves in numerous and complex ways. If we are to have any kind of understanding, we must select from the complex reality before us features that appear to be especially significant and that manifest themselves within the greater complexity. Any society is nearly infinitely complex in the variety of possibilities it offers for interpretation. How do we go about selecting what we are going to focus on as key features of the society? This is no small issue. Many of our modern social controversies derive from precisely this problem. Should we concentrate on the activities of the wealthy? the intellectuals? the workers? the young? the old? Where do we turn to bring together the myriad goings-on of human communal life? What are the implications of selecting any particular theme over any other?

David Riesman attempted to account for major historical changes in American character by the concepts of inner-directed and other-directed people. Is other-directedness a reasonable interpretation of modern character and institutions? What are some other ways in which one might explain changes that have taken place in the institutions of American society? For example, would it be more correct to argue that America has gone from an agricultural-rural society to a technological-urban one?

Riesman's well-known book, The Lonely Crowd, *caused a considerable stir when it was published in 1961. What does the great public interest in works such as this indicate about society?*

Readers of Riesman often find themselves sympathizing with the older, inner-directed type as characterizing a person of strength and fortitude. The other-directed type is less attractive, appearing to be a weaker character. How do you account for this—presuming that it is true? Is the inner-directed type essentially "masculine"—people often cite John Wayne as an ideal inner-directed character—and is the other-directed type "feminine"? Do Riesman's concepts offer some clues for further understanding and interpretation of the feminist movement in America today?

At one point Riesman notes that the individual has a worth in traditional societies that he does not necessarily have in modern societies. That is, concepts such as surplus labor (surplus people) are not as prominent in primitive societies. This suggests a change in the value assigned to the individual in modern societies. We claim to value the individual while, at the same time, calling large numbers of individuals "surplus." What is the

American attitude toward the individual? How do you think such attitudes developed? Are we as interested in the welfare of the individual as we claim to be? In what ways can an individualistic social morality work against the individual?

The Sociologist in Anger

The Views of

C. WRIGHT MILLS

The idea of a mass society suggests the idea of an elite of power.

The Power Elite

BORN: 1916   DIED: 1962

12 Sociologists usually follow either of two separate paths during their professional lives. The first path moves toward a sense of detachment from social affairs; greater sophistication of social knowledge, and the comfortable jobs that can be obtained with such sophisticated knowledge, elevate people until they are looking down on the world, at which point they seem to lose any strong sense of involvement with it. In this instance, the acquisition of social sophistication produces the feeling that this is the best of all possible worlds. Or, if it is not, then certainly it is a world so big and so massively organized that there is not much anyone can do about it.

The second path—one which many a sociologist has traveled—leads to a personal anger and sense of frustration. The more one becomes aware of human irrationality and self-deception, and the more one becomes aware of the extent to which people could spare themselves much of the suffering they have had to endure, the more it seems necessary to lash out at human folly. This second pathway is, in some respects, professionally unbecoming. It means, to use nonacademic terms, that one has blown one's professional cool. But for the sociologist who cannot help being personally dismayed by what he or she learns about people, it may only mean a greater emotional commitment to all of humanity than to the small segment of it that forms the professional community of sociologists.

To elect one path or the other establishes how one will express whatever power one possesses as an intellectual. For Mills, the first path meant an abdication of responsibility. It led to either the cult of alienation or the fetish of objectivity. It led to the sentiment that the social scientist has the right to analyze but not the power to criticize.

C. Wright Mills went down the second pathway. His work began with several relatively objective and empirical studies. Gradually, toward the end of his career,[1] his writing became more vehement and took on the character of moral sermonizing. He became famous as a young man with a rather "cool" examination of the white-collar worker. He closed his career with violent denunciations of the clergy,[2] American culture, and the historical drift toward war. The more heated his accusations became, the less he was tolerated by some of his colleagues. Even so, he earned the attention of students and humanistic intellectuals who were looking for people with sociological sophistication to give them new critical perspectives. C. Wright Mills did just that.

Mills's career was brief. His first essay was published when he was twenty-five.[3] His work ended twenty years later when he died from a coronary condition. During the last years a friend visiting Mills told him candidly that he looked terrible. Mills replied, "Yes, I know. But God, how I have lived."[4] Perhaps it was this zest for living as well as his social criticism that made Mills the idol of young liberal intellectuals of the fifties.

The Question of Power

Though social change is so rapid today that social commentary becomes dated as quickly as the news, Mills's observations have retained much of their original relevance. There is a good reason for this. Mills was con-

---

[1] A comprehensive listing of the works of C. Wright Mills appears in *Power, Politics and People: The Collected Essays of C. Wright Mills,* edited by Irving Louis Horowitz (New York: Oxford University Press, 1963), pp. 614–641. This list also includes various reviews and essays that have taken the work of Mills as their subject. It will suffice to mention here some of the more important or well-known of Mills's works: *The New Men of Power: America's Labor Leaders,* with the assistance of Helen Schneider (New York: Harcourt, 1948); *White Collar: The American Middle Classes* (New York: Oxford University Press, 1951); *The Power Elite* (New York: Oxford University Press, 1956); *The Causes of World War III* (New York: Simon & Schuster, 1958); *The Sociological Imagination* (New York: Oxford University Press, 1959); *Listen Yankee: The Revolution in Cuba* (New York: McGraw-Hill, 1960).

[2] Both *The Causes of World III* and *Listen Yankee* illustrate the "preachiness" of Mills. Mills himself referred to his work as "preachings." See Horowitz (ed.), *Power, Politics and People,* p. 2.

[3] C. Wright Mills, "Language, Logic, and Culture," *American Sociological Review* IV (October 1939), 670–680.

[4] This anecdote comes from a conversation with William Bruce Cameron, Professor of Sociology and Dean, Liberal Arts College, University of South Florida.

212 cerned with one aspect of society that never loses its significance—the question of power. His work remained centered on power—the nature of power, the distribution of power, the uses and abuses of power, the person of power, the power of organizations, the myths of power, the evolution of power, the irrationality of power, and the means of observing and comprehending power in the vastness of modern society.

In his writings Mills concentrated particularly on power elites within business. He was concerned with both the business executive and the labor leader. He was interested in the political influence of business and labor, and he examined the extent to which business elites were tied in with military and governmental elites. The observation that the leaders of various sectors of the society are rubbing elbows with each other is not, as one British review of Mills's work put it, very shocking. It has been going on for years in all civilized countries. But this criticism misses the point. It was not the relationship between the elites per se that was the motivation behind Mills's effort. He was interested in the relationship because of its historical and political significance in a nation that subscribes to an ideology of democracy and to the separation of administration among the various parts of the system. The most notable of these "separations," of course, is the constitutionally authorized guarantee of separation of church and state—a separation that Americans have never been able to achieve with complete comfort and satisfaction.[5] But the American system, in its ideal form, also seeks to hold military authority in a position subordinate to and somewhat independent of civilian governmental authority. A similar position is supposed to exist between government and business.[6]

Mills was vehement in his argument that American military, industrial, and political leadership was integrated. It worked together to form what he referred to as a *power elite*. The merging of powers at the highest level was cause for concern, according to Mills, because it could lead to a disengagement of leadership from the problems of the people whom that leadership was supposed to represent. In other words, the growth of a power elite in America was contradictory to the democratic principles upon which the nation is supposed to conduct its affairs. What concerned Mills most of all was that an emerging power elite would, in protecting its interests, lose sight of the greater interests of the people. The "realities" that confronted the elite would be those that dominate the industrial-military mentality. The result would be a continuing drift toward war. Long before the Nixon administration became caught up in such a drift, Mills was labeling the attitude of American leadership as

---

[5] Despite a Supreme Court ruling to the contrary, many schools throughout the country, with the tacit support of state and local authorities, still have prayers in class. The same authorities reveal a certain hypocrisy in wondering at times why "other" people are lawless.
[6] The conservative idea, of course, is to keep government out of business. The position with respect to keeping business out of government is less clear. As Galbraith has observed, however, existing tax structures, transportation regulations, antitrust laws, the need for governmentally supervised inspection procedures, and the like have led to a situation where the distinction between private and public industry is becoming increasingly hard to establish.

one approaching catastrophic madness—he referred to it as *crackpot* **213** *realism*.

American leadership was drifting, Mills claimed, from a democratic separation of powers toward concentration of power in the hands of a strong, but informally related, elite. This elite is inclined to accept simple notions of what constitute the economic and military realities of the present world. Mills became increasingly critical as he searched for more and more evidence to support his beliefs. We wish to point to three features of his writing at this point. First, Mills was rhetorical as well as scholarly. His writing was engaging to large numbers of people because he was not afraid to lean on common language. Instead of using some elaborate psychiatric or academic term, he used such terms as *crackpot realism*. Second, Mills believed he had evidence that American leadership was becoming more and more an ingrown elite. This claim led to a lot of discussion and research among American social scientists. The present attitude toward Mills's argument is that power in America is not as centralized and concentrated as Mills claimed. Still, Mills raised the issue in a sufficiently demanding manner to lead to a careful reconsideration of what was, in fact, taking place in American halls of power. Third, Mills was a social critic who lived through the period when America had revealed, most fully, its military power—culminating in the staggering display of weaponry that heralded the close of World War II. America's military and economic power was great, and it was all the more imperative that such power not be allowed to come into the hands of people who lacked the sense and sensibility to employ it properly. At the same time, Mills felt that even the most reasonable people, when placed in positions of power, are subject to the corruptions of power. This makes it vital, then, that those checks which have been placed on the unhampered centralization of power in America be sustained. Mills—and this is important—was not concerned with attacking the personalities of people in power—a simplistic approach to power that remains popular in America down to the present moment. He was, instead, concerned with the structural systems that sustained and also limited power. If those features of the American political structure which restrained the concentration of power were weakened, the result would be a growing centralization of power. Centralization of power would, in itself, produce the blindness and madness that would result in a drift toward the ultimate catastrophe.

It is important then, in grasping Mills's conception of power, to know that he located power, much as Weber did, within an institutional context. In order to have power, one must, as it were, be able to tap the power of something greater than oneself. The "something greater" consists of the collective power of an institution. This is practically tautological; yet, in a society that goes so far to celebrate the individuality of the person of power, it is a necessary corrective. Mills said:

> If we took the one hundred most powerful men in America, the one hundred wealthiest, and the one hundred most celebrated away from the institutional positions they now occupy, away from their resources of men

and women and money, away from the media of mass communication that are now focused upon them—then they would be powerless and poor and uncelebrated. For power is not of a man. Wealth does not center in the person of the wealthy. Celebrity is not inherent in any personality. To be celebrated, to be wealthy, to have power requires access to major institutions, for the institutional positions men occupy determine in large part their chances to have and to hold these valued experiences.[7]

People of power must be understood, then, to derive their power from an institutional base. This means, very broadly, that the exercise of power cannot be simply the exercise of individual eccentricity but must, to a considerable extent, run parallel with the "grain" of power that characterizes the institutional source. This is obvious in the case of political and church leaders, where adherence to the policies of the system is a *sine qua non* of an individual's ascendancy in the hierarchy. The study of power, then, becomes the study of institutions, the power relations between institutions, and the people who represent the expressions of those institutions.

Although Mills claimed that power has its locus within supporting institutions, he still was concerned with the fact that it is individuals who make decisions and are responsible for the consequences. Mills was torn on the one hand by an analytic perspective that properly locates the individual within the broader system and on the other by a humanistic sensitivity that made him critical of any apparent inability on the part of powerful individuals to assert their autonomy.

The Power Elite

In *The Power Elite*, Mills made explicit his belief that the American doctrine of balances of power or "checks and balances" is an ideal showing less vigor today than it did in the past. Particularly significant in this respect has been the very recent and very noticeable ascendancy to power of the military in American life. In the nineteenth century, the American military establishment was relatively weak, subordinate to civilian authority, and even respectful of civilian values and ways of life. Today, primarily because of the growth of military technology—a truly devastating technology with implications that cause civilian politicians to shy away from decisions involving its use—the military elite is acquiring greater authority in nonmilitary contexts. If the military has acquired a greater voice in American affairs than has previously been the case, it has not been because the military man has aggressively sought political power. It has been, instead, because of civilian political default.[8] Mills viewed this state of affairs with open dismay.

Once war was considered the business of soldiers, international relations

---

[7] Mills, *The Power Elite*, pp. 10–11.
[8] Ibid., p. 205.

the concern of diplomats. But now that war has become seemingly total and seemingly permanent, the free sport of kings has become the forced and internecine business of people, and diplomatic codes of honor between nations have collapsed. Peace is no longer serious; only war is serious. Every man and every nation is either friend or foe, and the idea of enmity becomes mechanical, massive and without genuine passion. When virtually all negotiation aimed at peaceful agreement is likely to be seen as "appeasement," if not treason, the active role of the diplomat becomes meaningless; for diplomacy becomes merely a prelude to war or an interlude between wars, and in such a context the diplomat is replaced by the warlord.[9]

Although Mills viewed the ascendancy of the military in modern America with a sense of dismay, he did not limit his concern to the military man. If there is a military ascendancy—and Mills openly and vehemently believed this to be the case—then it extends beyond the confines of our military institutions. It is more than simply the rising power of a military clique. The various institutions of our society have, through the rise of modern technology, the practices of big business, and the irresponsibilities of American politics, found a military posture socially expedient. It is expedient with regard to our international image; it is expedient with regard to internal control and management.[10]

Internal control or management means, essentially, handling a large and amorphous mass of people who take on the character of a market. The mass market exists not only with respect to the sale of Mustangs and motorcycles but also with respect to the "sale" of opinions. Thus the people became a *media market*.[11] This "media market," this mass of people, stands passively at the bottom of American society. Just above it is an increasingly ineffective and fragmented middle level of professional people, politicians, educators, and intellectuals who are alienated from the lower levels and not a part of the power elite. At the top stands an increasingly unified and coordinated elite of power. This, as Mills saw it, is the trend in American social structure. It is a trend which, as he put it, is moving

> a considerable distance along the road to the mass society. At the end of that road there is totalitarianism, as in Nazi Germany or in Communist Russia. We are not yet at that end. But surely we can see that many aspects of the public life of our times are more the features of a mass society than of a community of publics.[12]

The impact of *The Power Elite*, then, comes not from the observation that the "high and mighty" share clubs and secrets, profits and

[9] Ibid., p. 206.
[10] An exclusive concentration on this point is made in Fred J. Cooke's *The Warfare State* (New York: Macmillan, 1962). A better treatment of the economic factors involved in the ascendancy of the military in America can be found in Seymour Melman, *Our Depleted Society* (New York: Dell, 1965).
[11] Mills, *The Power Elite*, p. 304.
[12] Ibid., p. 304.

216 power. The impact comes from Mills's insistence that the extent to which this is so is increasing in America. Moreover, this is a trend that violates the liberal democratic traditions of the society.

White Collar

The Power Elite, when viewed from the vantage point of the present, seems like a very natural development in Mills's thinking. Five years earlier Mills published *White Collar: The American Middle Classes* and gave Americans a not very flattering look at themselves. Most significantly, Mills saw the middle stratum of American society as people who had gained economic security and material advantages and had lost just about everything else. Above all, they had lost any sense of personal power or the sensible use of power. If *The Power Elite* is a discussion of the locus of power in America, *White Collar* is a discussion of those Americans who, like Sinclair Lewis's Babbitt, are losers and really never know it—they are the unwittingly passive voice in American politics. They suffer from the illusion of having power while, in fact, they have none. Mills made this very explicit from the beginning:

> The white-collar people slipped quietly into modern society. Whatever common interests they have do not lead to unity; whatever future they have will not be of their own making. If they aspire at all, it is to a middle course, at a time when no middle course is available, and hence to an illusory course in an imaginary society. Internally, they are split, fragmented; externally, they are dependent on larger forces. Even if they gained the will to act, their actions, being unorganized, would be less a movement than a tangle of unconnected contests. As a group, they do not threaten anyone; as individuals, they do not practice an independent way of life.[13]

It is extremely difficult, indeed impossible, to ascribe a unitary character to that segment of American society that refers to itself as white collar. The training of such people can vary from a few days to twenty or more years. Income of white-collar workers can vary from minimal wage levels to high six-figure salaries. White-collar workers can be occupied with work that is physically exhausting—as is much sales work in department stores—or work that places modest demands on mind and body. White-collar workers can be aggressive sales people or retiring laboratory technicians. They can operate within a system that nearly guarantees the opportunity to rise to higher levels or they can be caught in a cul-de-sac. Their work can be clean or it can involve an element of dirtiness—as is the case with technicians who must examine specimens of excrement.

Yet, despite this tremendous variety of social character, the term

---

[13] C. Wright Mills, *White Collar*, p. ix. Political leaders we have talked with are well aware that today the masses no longer consist of the disgruntled poor. They consist of the more or less disgruntled middle-income elements.

white collar has a special significance for American culture. Migrants to this country saw white-collar employment as a hope for their children if not for themselves. It was an ambition worthy of self-deprivation and suffering toil. The most vulgar form of the American dream has been to strike it rich—to stumble on an oil well or to inherit an astounding fortune from a distant relative. The realistic American dream has been to find a good white-collar job—to work, if necessary, but to work "respectably." It was the aspiration of people who sought to disengage themselves from their peasant status—it was the collective impetus of people who were being subjected to the pressures of urbanization. City life was better than country life, and, within the city, white-collar status was better than blue-collar status. To understand the white-collar class, then, requires a comprehension of the quest for prestige in America. It requires, as Mills put it, an examination of the "status panic."

In traditionalistic societies, prestige claims are relatively easily recognized and persons making the claims are likely to have them honored. In our society the situation is more anomic. People cannot be certain that their claims for prestige will be honored and, if they are, they cannot always be certain that the claims are being honored for the proper reason. Although not all the way there yet, America is moving in the direction of becoming a society where

> all the controlling devices by which the volume and type of deference might be directed are out of joint or simply do not exist. So the prestige system is no system, but a maze of misunderstanding, of sudden frustration and sudden indulgence, and the individual, as his self-esteem fluctuates, is under strain and full of anxiety.[14]

The status panic, the drive for prestige, is a central, though not all-encompassing, characteristic of the white-collar worker. Some white-collar workers experience less panic than others. Even so, concern with status is probably more characteristic of white-collar workers than blue-collar workers. Mills observed that the blue-collar workers' greater concern with the immediate necessities of living—a fair day's pay for a fair day's work—made them easier to organize in the labor movement. White-collar workers have had a tendency to feel that such organization is degrading—it results in an association with the tactics of blue-collar workers.[15]

It is this feature of the prestige quest among white-collar elements that Mills found especially intriguing. Prestige, or lack thereof, does not particularly come from the value or lack of value of the work performed. Instead, to a great extent, it comes from the real or imagined associations of white-collar workers. They obtain their prestige from the capacity to identify with some source that does, in fact, have recognition. The me-

---

[14] Ibid., p. 240.
[15] College professors, until recently at least, have been very sympathetic with the labor movement in the United States. This sympathy, however, has been restricted pretty much to intellectual support. The academic world has been resistant to unionization for itself.

218 chanic in the shop might be making a good income and performing miracles in the way of taking apart and putting together complex machinery. The minimal wage, forty-words-a-minute, fresh-out-of-high-school typist in the front office may, however, feel hers is the more prestigious work. The reason is apparent—it is easier to associate oneself with the management when working in the front office. The prestige of the white-collar worker is often a borrowed prestige.

In surveying the status panic Mills looked to the future and reached a grim conclusion. One of the features offering greater status to white-collar workers has been the fact that often their work identifies them as people of superior education. By virtue of being a bank clerk one can be more readily associated with people of some education than would be the case if one were a filling station attendant. At the same time, in the driving surge for better positions, national educational levels have been rising; and as they have been rising, the educational demands of most white-collar positions have, according to Mills, been falling.

> As the general educational level rises, the level of education required or advisable for many white-collar jobs falls. In the early 'twenties, personnel men said: "I think it has become a principle with the majority of our progressive offices that they will not take into the office any person or candidate who has not had the benefit of at least a high-school education." But soon they began to say that too much education was not advisable for many white-collar jobs.[16]

If this is so, then the disparity between the reality and the ideal—the hope education offers and the actuality it brings—may produce profound disillusionment. At best, said Mills, it opens the white-collar worker to a precarious psychological life.

The white-collar mentality—combined with the vastness of the white-collar element in American society—makes it a key to the understanding of American character. For this reason Mills devoted much effort to an attempt to fathom the nature of this class of Americans. His conclusions seem to be as valid today as they were when he wrote them in 1956. In sum, Mills said, (1) white-collar workers are being squeezed economically and in terms of real power by the unionized blue-collar, wage-earning workers; (2) white-collar status claims are becoming more precarious and unrealistic; (3) the threat of growing discontent and frustration among white-collar workers is enhanced by the flood of educated young people coming into the labor market and the increasing simplification of routinized clerical work; (4) the lack of political identity among white-collar workers makes them a politically malleable group for the power elite; and (5) the traditional signs of success will be increasingly evaluated in an ambivalent or confused fashion—is it worth it to fight one's way to the top? Of these possibilities, the political malleability of the white-collar class and the psychological strains of what Mills termed the status panic could produce a strain toward authoritarianism—the

---

[16] Mills, *White Collar*, p. 247.

quest for clearly delineated status in a nation-state geared to attain goals of simplistic and readily determined worth.

If there is a strain toward authoritarianism in America today, then one form it might be readily expected to take would be an acceptance of military regimentation. Thus, Mills's concern with *The Power Elite* was a logical extension of observations made during the preparation of *White Collar*. His interest in the power elite increased further his concern that America was indeed moving in the direction of a capitulation to the simplicity and formality of military regulation and military thought. This capitulation, he felt, was thrusting the world ever closer to World War III.

The Causes of World War III

In *The Causes of World War III* Mills repeated the central ideas of his earlier works. He noted again the ineffectiveness of the white-collar element and he commented on the solidarity of the power elite. But in this work he was more concerned with the historical implications of these observations. What are the possibilities for the future? The possibilities that seemed clearest to Mills were those leading toward war. Moreover, the historical possibilities were leading us toward war of a new kind—war that promoted efficiency and impersonality in much the same manner that a large industry promotes impersonal and efficient production. Long before the Vietnam War forced greater consideration of moral issues and split the nation into "doves" and "hawks," Mills was saying:

> In the expanded world of mechanically vivified communication the individual becomes the spectator of everything but the human witness of nothing. Having no plain targets of revolt, men feel no moral springs of revolt. The cold manner enters their souls and they are made private and blasé. In virtually all realms of life, facts now outrun sensibility. Emptied of their human meanings, these facts are readily got used to. In official man there is no more human shock; in his unofficial follower there is little sense of moral issue. Within the unopposed supremacy of impersonal calculated technique, there is no human place to draw the line and give the emphatic no.
>
> This lack of response I am trying to sum up by the phrase "moral insensibility," and I am suggesting that the level of moral sensibility, as part of public and of private life, has sunk out of sight. It is not the number of victims or the degree of cruelty that is distinctive; it is the fact that the acts committed and the acts that nobody protests are split from the consciousness of men in an uncanny, even a schizophrenic, manner. The atrocities of our time are done by men as "functions" of social machinery—men possessed by an abstracted view that hides from them the human beings who are their victims and, as well, their own humanity. They are inhuman acts because they are impersonal. They are not sadistic but merely businesslike; they are not aggressive but merely efficient; they are not emotional at all but technically clean-cut.[17]

17 C. Wright Mills, *The Causes of World War III*, pp. 78–79.

220   The driving energy that employs moral insensibility and uses it in the working out of our fate comes primarily from our conceptions of the realities of our circumstances. If, for example, we are walking past a graveyard on a dark and eerie evening and we begin to walk faster and faster and then break into a run, the driving energy that impels us comes from our conception of the "reality" of the situation. If we believe we are in a dangerous setting then we react accordingly—regardless of the "realities" surrounding us. Those in power, like umpires at a baseball game, must give their conceptions of the complex interplay between nations the imprimatur of realism. They must refer to themselves as realists and as leaders who see the situation realistically. A seat of power is no place for idealistic indulgences. And so it comes to pass that from the offices of the high and mighty come supposedly hardheaded and realistic appraisals of world tensions. But just as an individual walking past a graveyard can be unrealistic in his or her appraisal, so can those in power collectively become deceived while, at the same time, patting each other on the back for their "realism." This, says Mills, might better be termed crackpot realism.

Crackpot Realism

Among the features of crackpot realism that define world realities today are the following salient elements:[18]

1. The belief that war, rather than peace, is the natural character of people and nations; it is only realistic to assume as belligerent and as potentially destructive a posture as it is possible to assume.
2. It is only realistic to assume that the "other side" is as anxious to see us fail as we are to see them fail. National paranoia, suspicion, and ill-will are universal, permanent, and part of the primitive and unalterable nature of humanity.
3. It is simpler and more realistic to prepare for war than to prepare for peace. The problems of preparing for peace are more complicated and abstract than those involved in the preparation for war. It is therefore more realistic to solve human problems by resorting to military coercion.
4. Since war is natural, suspicion and ill-will universal, and a military posture the simplest solution, then it follows that our military leaders are the most qualified to cope with the complexities of the modern world situation. It is only realistic to give over to the warlord the control of enlarged and centralized means of violence. To be realistic is to give the generals free rein in the conduct of war.
5. It is, if the preceding "realities" are reasonable, only a matter of being realistic for politicians to encourage the growth of a military bureaucracy rather than the building of a civilian civil service of real integrity.

[18] This list of the features of crackpot realism is a highly modified version of one appearing in Chapter 13, pp. 81–89, of *The Causes of World War III*.

6. For businesses, given the preceding set of realities, it is only **221** hardheaded business realism to take advantage of the situation. This means the exploitation of circumstances in which there is profit in the manufacture of the means of violence and profit in the use of government-supported research that comes from the quest for ever greater sources of destructive power.

7. It is also realistic and simple, indeed it is a cliché, to recognize that the economy is supported by the war effort—whether the effort is sustained in a shooting war or a "cold war."

8. The very simplicity and "reality" of the situation has led to a circumstance whereby the different political parties have accepted a common definition of the world situation. The consequence is a political climate in which there is no real choice. It is realistic to have a political directorate composed of former generals and former corporation men— whose world appraisals share so much in common.

9. The massive hold of this "reality" has been overwhelming for both the general public and for members of the leading intellectual, scientific, and religious circles. For the general public the "realistic" response is that of moral insensibility. For the intellectuals and scientists, the "realistic" response has been to echo and endorse the confused reality of officialdom. The intellectual's greatest moral failure has been an incapacity to propose alternatives and to retain tenacity in the support of alternatives.

10. Crackpot realism replaces the goal of an anxiously held and frustratingly established state of peace and balance of power with the idea of "winning." One is never told what is won. It is sufficient simply to seek to win. To desire to win, even without knowing what it is that one is to win, is more "realistic" and sensible than to abdicate the concept of winning.

11. The general product of crackpot realism is a slow movement toward World War III. The individual consequences of such "realism" are, generally speaking, beneficial. People are rewarded for endorsing these conceptions of the world situation—they benefit individually. But the collective and historical thrust of these opportunistic views of world reality will be toward total military engagement.

And so, in the name of realism, people behave unrealistically. It was a view that Mills could see only as absurd.

If the view of world realities as seen by men of power today (whether in Peking, Washington, or the Kremlin) is appropriately termed crackpot realism, then what does it mean, given present world conditions, to think in a manner that can be called hardheaded realism? We must recognize, perhaps above all else, that war and war alone is the greatest enemy confronting humanity today. We must come to see world reality in terms other than those imposed by a military metaphysic. Industry must be used as a means of coping with world problems rather than as a means of buoying further the consumptive egos of those countries that have achieved industrialization. Finally, using Mills's phrasing,

The world encounter of coexisting political economies must be conducted in cultural, political, and economic terms.[19]

We must, as individuals, never lose our commitment to humanity. We must not allow ourselves, individually, to represent the broader trend of moral insensibility. Mills expressed this preachment eloquently:

> What scientist can claim to be part of the legacy of science and yet remain a hired technician of the military machine?
> What man of God can claim to partake of the Holy Spirit, to know the life of Jesus, to grasp the meaning of that Sunday phrase "the brotherhood of man"—and yet sanction the insensibility, the immorality, the spiritual irresponsibility of the Caesars of our time?
> What Western scholar can claim to be part of the big discourse of reason and yet retreat to formal trivialities and exact nonsense, in a world in which reason and freedom are being held in contempt, being smashed, being allowed to fade out of the human condition.[20]

An academic sociologist might shake a finger at Mills and chastize him not for his eloquence but for his presumption—and eloquence often flows from presumption. After all, can we reasonably conclude that reason and freedom are being held in contempt? How can we be sure? How does one measure reason and freedom? How rapidly are they fading out? Are things really as bad as Mills said they are? Was Mills crying out against injustices and human circumstances that came more from his own fears and anxieties than from the world itself? Certainly the strong possibility of this would seem to be sufficient to incline us to ignore Mills when we settle down to the task of creating a serious sociology.

Mills would reply, we believe, somewhat as a meteorologist might: In predicting storms it is better to say that one is coming when, in fact, it might not be. The other kind of error is more disastrous. We leave ourselves defenseless when we conclude that a storm is not on the way—even as it bears down on us.

If Mills erred, he erred on the side he believed to be morally more defensible. Sociologists are involved in the system they are writing about and attempting to fathom. Mills saw the sociologist as a person morally obligated to provide social knowledge that is significant. Because society is essentially a moral order, as Durkheim had already noted, this means that significant social knowledge must be morally significant. The sociologist must attempt by writing as well as by observation to prevent people from falling into patterns of belief and action that appear catastrophic from a sociological perspective.

Mills functioned as a critic of the greater society and, as a critic, expressed great concern over the role of the intellectual. More specifically, he was concerned with the duties and character of the social scientist. He was quite unappreciative of the sociologist who teased at trivialities in a pseudoscientific mumbo-jumbo jargon. His irritation with

[19] Ibid., p. 98.
[20] Ibid., p. 125.

the work of some of his colleagues appears in nearly all his works. However, it is elaborated and expressed most fully in *The Sociological Imagination*.

The Sociological Imagination

Like Mills's other works, *The Sociological Imagination* reveals a man exasperated by the discrepancy between the potential value of a human effort and its actual value or attainment. If Mills lambasted some features of sociology, it was because he felt they deserved criticism. Sociology is too important to be ignored and it is not beyond the need for some reforms. It is the intellectuals who stand as one of the constraints against the abuse of power—but only for so long as they retain their sense and sensibility.

The importance of sociological thought comes out of the fact that it is not something limited to professors of sociology or courses in modern society on the campuses of American colleges. Instead, it is an exercise that all people today must attempt with more or less success. For Mills the difference between effective sociological thought and that which fails rests upon the use of imagination. This would not seem especially radical were it not for the fact that Mills's assertion appears as a reaction against the sociology of the thirties and forties, which argued, in effect, that worthwhile sociological thinking comes mostly from facts. Theory is supportive, but its main function is to lead to further facts. The product of this kind of sociology, said Mills, is factual, in a sense, but lacking imagination. More importantly, it often, in the quest for factual information, bypasses problems that are more centrally significant. Speaking of studies of voting behavior—an area of interest that lends itself to empirical or factual examinations of opinion—Mills said:

> It must be interesting to political scientists to examine a full-scale study of voting which contains no reference to the party machinery for "getting out the vote," or indeed to any political institutions. Yet that is what happens in *The Peoples' Choice*, a duly accredited and celebrated study of the 1940 election in Erie County, Ohio. From this book we learn that rich, rural, and Protestant persons tend to vote Republican; people of opposite type incline toward the Democrats; and so on. But we learn little about the dynamics of American politics.[21]

There is the suggestion in Mills's criticism of what he refers to as abstracted empiricism that sociological research is guided more by the requirements of administrative concerns than by intellectual concerns. The "scientific method" followed by the contemporary empirical sociologist is actually more an administrative method than a scientific one.

---

[21] Mills, *The Sociological Imagination*, pp. 52–30. Mills was critical of both narrow factual scientism and grand theory. The former gets lost in trivialities and the latter gets lost in its word play. Because of space limitations we have emphasized Mills's critique of empiricism.

224   Certainly, Mills suggested, it is more an administrative method than an intellectual one. The results of an opinion survey or a political preference poll can be of inestimable value to an official running for office. At the same time, it has relatively restricted scientific value. Because administrative concerns are virtually infinite and can penetrate into the most trivial aspects of organization, the kinds of research that can come out of an administrative interest will be infinitely varied and range from that which has some possible promise as an intellectual interest to that which will have none whatsoever.

The narrow concern with "factual science" that attracts many sociologists today, said Mills, has produced a very constrained view of humanity. It is a view which, incidentally, would be in keeping with an "administrative view" of humanity. That is, abstracted empiricism fits nicely into a research program geared toward the more effective control of human beings. Indeed, sociologists such as Lundberg have specifically stated that the goal of science—and they include sociology here—is to achieve prediction and control. With respect to human behavior, this means controlling the lives and actions of people—and this concern is the paramount concern of the administrator.

The field of demography offers us an example of research that has great administrative value. No administrator can function very well without reliable census information concerning his organization and the community and state within which it operates. At the same time, the scientific character of demography suffers from a peculiar constraint—there is only so much one can do with census data. Usually academic or scientific considerations of census data prove to be elaborate exercises in the use of statistical devices. So severe is the problem with respect to population studies that some of the finest demographers and human ecologists in the country have seriously dealt with the issue of whether or not there is such a thing as population theory and what theory means in the field of population studies. Demography is preponderantly the accumulation of facts for the purpose of facilitating administrative or political decisions.[22]

It is elementary but necessary to remember that sociological writing, like any other, is concerned with convincing others. Convincing others involves at least two rudimentary and important considerations. First of all, we need to convince others that what we have to say is significant and worth the effort of their review. Secondly, we must convince others that what we are saying is valid. The empiricist has concluded that the only form of validity is that established through fact and, moreover, that validity provided through fact is more important than any other consideration in the communication process. The result, Mills wryly observed, is thin.

But there is more to it than that. It is not so much that the empirical sociologist has become bogged down with statistics; this in itself is not

---

[22] Population studies received their initial impetus from political and military concerns. The development of census data in the United States came originally from the need for population data to determine the distribution of representation in Congress.

a completely hopeless situation. A person living under a haystack of facts and figures might reasonably be expected to dig out to a point where he or she could see clearly the outlines of what previously had only been a dark and suffocating pressure. The serious problem, as Mills viewed it, is that empiricists, even as they suffocate, think that building haystacks is the best of all possible lives. But perhaps this figure of speech goes too far. Mills put it this way:

> What has happened in the methodological inhibition is that men have become stuck, not so much in the empirical intake, as in what are essentially epistemological problems of method. Since many of these men, especially the young, do not know very much about epistemology, they tend to be quite dogmatic about the one set of canons that dominate them.[23]

But if facts are not enough—if the empiricism of modern sociological research is producing inconsequential and "thin" results—then what is one to do? Mills set forth his own conception of how a social scientist should undertake the work. He endeavored to convey a sense of what it means to be an intellectual who concentrates on the social nature of man and who seeks that which is significant. (It is worth a parenthetical comment here to observe that Mills recognized that one can make a significant statement that is not necessarily factually valid. For example, the philosopher Karl Jaspers, in an essay on the nature of totalitarianism, comments that totalitarianism cannot be destroyed from within; it must be destroyed from without.[24] It is difficult to assess whether historical records will back up such a statement. The statement is nonetheless significant when we wish to consider the nature of the completely autocratic state. Jaspers is correct in a logical or definitional sense, though he might be subjected to criticism from an empiricist.)

Mills was critical of textbooks used in sociological courses. In his criticism he indicated the direction he thought contemporary sociology should take. Sociological texts suffer from being overly concerned with settled conceptions and they tend to ignore new ideas. The textbook provides the student with old ideas supported by new facts. New ideas might endanger the number of adaptions of the text.

Mills illustrated his point with a consideration of the concept of *cultural lag*. This concept, popular in sociological thought down to the present time, has achieved an almost venerable position in the lexicon of sociological terms. The concept of cultural lag claims, essentially, that there are two aspects of culture. One aspect is the immaterial—consisting of ideas, sentiments, beliefs, values, interests, meanings, and other facets of a subjective or mental character. The other aspect consists of the material features of the culture—such as tools, artifacts, equipment, hardware, produce, chemicals, and other directly observable and "touchable" features. The concept of cultural lag then goes on to suggest that the immaterial aspects of culture "lag" behind the development of the

---

[23] Mills, *The Sociological Imagination*, p. 74.
[24] Karl Jaspers, "The Fight against Totalitarianism," in *The Dilemma of Organizational Society*, edited by Hendrik M. Ruitenbeek (New York: Dutton, 1963), p. 6.

226 material aspects of culture. We have a twentieth-century technology, for example, embedded in a moral, religious, and legal system that has its roots in a Mediterranean pastoral society that existed three thousand years ago. We have the atomic bomb and, at the same time, a conception of warfare and conduct between nations more in keeping with the ideas held by Napoleon.

It is not so much that the concept of cultural lag is "bad" as that the sociologist tends to use it in an uncritical, unexamined, and unimaginative way. All too commonly the notion of cultural lag is used as a simpleminded "scientific" justification for a progressive ideology which holds that the problems of the present lie in the moral inadequacies of the past. The concept of cultural lag enables us to make value judgments about where we ought to go and what ought to lead our movement—namely technological advancement and physical science—while at the same time disguising the fact we have been making value judgments.

But it is not the naive hypocrisy of the sociologist who thinks in this fashion that bothered Mills the most. Certainly it is inconsistent to claim to be making objective statements about the social order that are, by their very nature, moral judgments. However, as Mills viewed it, this is not the most serious fault of sociology. The most serious fault is the lack of imagination and the dullness of thought that characterizes much sociological work. There is, said Mills, quite a difference between the way the sociologist uses an idea like cultural lag and the way a thinker of the magnitude of Thorstein Veblen uses the same idea.

> In contrast to many sociologists' use of "lag," Thorstein Veblen's phrase "lag, lead and friction" led him to a structural analysis of "industry versus business." He asked: where does "the lag" pinch? And he attempted to reveal how the trained incapacity of businessmen acting in accordance with entrepreneurial canons resulted in an efficient sabotage of production and productivity. He was also somewhat aware of the role of profit-making within a system of private ownership, and he did not especially care for the "unworkman-like results." But the great point is that he revealed the structural mechanics of "the lag." Many social scientists, however, use the politically washed-out notion of "cultural lag," which has lost any such specific and structural anchorage: they have generalized the idea in order to apply it to everything, always in a fragmenting manner.[25]

But what, in more specific terms, did Mills have to suggest? How, if it is so, is the sociologist to break away from the "washed-out" usage of social concepts and ideas? In answer, Mills provided some guidelines which he believed led toward a greater sense of intellectual craftsmanship.[26]

---

[25] Mills, *The Sociological Imagination*, pp. 89–90.
[26] Ibid., pp. 195–226. In a lengthy appendix, Mills set forth a number of very sensible suggestions concerning intellectual craftsmanship. The list presented here is a highly modified summary of Mills's comments.

Guidelines for Intellectual Craftsmanship   **227**

First of all, a good scholar or intellectual does not split work from life. Both are part of a seriously accepted unity. Life experience can be used in one's work, and the fruits of one's work can be used to enrich life. The sociologist must not bureaucratize work and conclude that it is a nine-to-five business, to be abandoned with a sense of relief when the whistle blows in the late afternoon.[27]

Second, a good scholar must keep a file. This file is a compendium of personal, professional, and intellectual experiences. Such a file promotes organization, the preservation of experience, and the discipline of writing.

Third, a good intellectual engages in continual review of thoughts and experiences. One does not write for the moment—one does not wait until the pressures of professional advancement call for writing up a request for governmental or foundation funds and then sit down and think up a "project."

Fourth, a good intellectual may find a truly bad book as intellectually stimulating and conducive to thinking and effort as a good book. Reading, whether it is a good book or a bad one, must be an intense experience and one that has relevance for the file. But, at the same time, reading is a matter of balance—one should know when to read and when not to. To soak up too much literature is to risk being drowned by it.

Fifth, in the development of a system of notes, it is a good idea to lay out, at least in a sketchy manner, designs for research that would be relevant to interests stimulated by reading or by other experiences. In the course of this there is a constant rearranging of ideas and approaches. It is in the exercise of rearrangements that imagination is stimulated.

Sixth, there must be an attitude of playfulness toward phrases, words, and ideas. Along with this attitude must go a fierce drive to make sense out of the world.

Seventh, the imagination is stimulated by assuming a willingness to view the world from the perspective of others. It is stimulating to the imagination of the sociologist to wonder how, for example, a political scientist, a historian, or a biologist might think about the topic under investigation.

Eighth, one should not be afraid, in the preliminary stages of a speculation, to think in terms of imaginative extremes.

Ninth, one should not hesitate to express ideas in language as simple and as direct as one can make it. Ideas are affected by the manner of their expression. An imagination encased in deadening language will be a deadened imagination.

In this manner C. Wright Mills left behind a statement of his concerns and his mode of living with those concerns. His attempt to delineate the way to a brighter sociological "imagination" was, in a more

---

[27] The imagery employed here is not immoderate. The University of Kansas actually uses a factory whistle to call students to class. The same whistle tells professors when to go home in the evening.

228 serious sense than perhaps some of his colleagues would accept, an attempt to correct the excesses of an unimaginative empirical methodology.

Yet Mills was excessive in the other extreme. He seemed too involved. He was too much a part of the times. He was too clever in his writing. He showed too much interest in the well-turned phrase and possibly too little in the well-turned fact.[28]

If so, Mills was aware that this was his personal choice. Social thought, to Mills, was a matter of individual commitment—and it involved a sense of responsibility. The greater the commitment, the greater the responsibility. To Mills, social thought was the stuff of life. To live intensely was to think and to work intensely. Life, work, and thought were inseparable. This was what Mills meant when he said, a year or so before his death, "God, how I have lived." It was a fitting commentary on his work.

Problems and Issues

Americans have a certain reputation for being idealists. People from other countries thought it was strange that we should be so upset over the discovery of criminal activity in the Nixon administration. The question of idealism is a part of Mills's concerns. Mills believed that as a nation is progressively freed from the pressing demands of hunger, privation, and vulnerability, it is increasingly called upon to put into effect the higher ideals of a civilized society. Mills argued that as we are freed from the harsh realities of existence, it becomes more possible to be idealistic. At the same time, there is a strong pragmatic streak in American culture that distrusts idealism. What constitutes "realistic" thinking today? Is Mills correct in suggesting that we must either become more idealistic or die?

Mills, like many other intellectuals of the 1950s, was deeply concerned with the issue of authoritarian rule. Mills feared, above all, that there might be a tendency toward authoritarianism in America. People in a "panic" to establish status might seek some system in which worth would be well defined and delineated. Mills warned of the possibility that the white-collar element might accept a more repressive social structure to resolve the stresses of uncertainty. What evidence is there for such a development in modern America? What argument can be made that American society is suffering, not from an increasing authoritarianism, but from a crisis of the weakening of authority?

It is an old maxim in social philosophy that power corrupts and

---

[28] Mills was candid. At one point he said, "Now I do not like to do empirical work if I can possibly avoid it. . . . It is a great deal of trouble." *The Sociological Imagination*, p. 205. Mills was suggesting, however, that all other avenues of exploration should be exhausted before taking up the empirical one.

absolute power corrupts absolutely. Mills elaborated on this observation. He argued that the person who is in an office which represents power must appear positive or "realistic," even though the problems of making decisions require that such decisions often be highly arbitrary or even capricious. Mills recognized that the consequences of holding a powerful office flow more from the demands of the office than from any "irrational" quality of the individual. What does it mean to have "power"? What constraints are placed on the person who is in a position of power? Is it possible for a person to reconcile the conflicting demands of idealistic conceptions of social order and the realistic demands of power? What are some examples?

Cultural Dreams and Nightmares

Observations by

JULES HENRY

Social scientists consider protection a requisite for society, but it is also essential that society make men vulnerable. If a man is invulnerable society cannot reach him, and if society produces men who cannot be reached it cannot endure.

Essays on Education

BORN:1904   DIED: 1969

13

It is one thing to define a term and quite something else to use it in a way that furthers understanding. *Human being* can be defined, for example, as a bipedal animal without feathers, but this does not greatly enhance our understanding of people or of ourselves. We encounter much the same problem with many of the concepts used by social scientists. A case in point is the concept of *culture*—one of the most profound concepts to come out of modern social science. This term is simple to define, yet it is difficult to comprehend. Textbook definitions of culture are numerous,[1] and students, after going to the trouble of

[1] Brace and Montagu define culture quite simply as "the part of the environment that is learned, shared, and transmitted in society. The man-made part of the environment." C. L. Brace and M. F. Ashley Montagu, *Man's Evolution: An Introduction to Physical Anthropology* (New York: Macmillan, 1965). Wissler, much earlier, defined it as "the aggregate of standardized beliefs and procedures followed by the tribe." Clark Wissler, *An Introduction to Social Anthropology* (New York: Holt, 1929). A number of slightly varied definitions of culture appear on pages 46 and 47 of M. F. Ashley Montagu's *Anthropology and Human Nature* (Boston: Sargent, 1957).

memorizing one of these definitions, believe they have a sturdy grasp on the meaning of culture. However, if they remain in anthropology or sociology, they begin to recognize—after several years of study have passed—that they are only on the threshold of comprehending what anthropologists are talking about when they use the word *culture*.

What Culture Is

At the simplest level, culture is *everything* learned and shared by people. Culture is not simply a knowledge of the arts or the social graces; it is much more. It includes the profane as well as the sublime, the secular as well as the sacred. What we learn from others and what we share with them is the basis of our humanity. We learn and we share the language we use for communication—language is a part of culture. We learn and we share the attitudes that affect our behavior toward others—these attitudes are a part of culture. We learn and we share certain conceptions about how we should behave as a boy or a girl—sex roles are a part of culture. We learn and we share various ideas about the nature of God— religious beliefs are a part of culture. And so we could continue. But this is prosaic stuff. All we have said so far is that we learn many things, and much of what we learn we hold in common with others who share and transmit their cultural background. What is so profound about this?

The profundity of the concept comes from the extent to which it can be applied to innumerable realms of human conduct. To the extent we can do this, we are able to ascertain that people are ruled not so much by biological or physiological demands as by different ways of perceiving the world; and these modes of viewing the world are shaped by cultural background. For example, we recall once hearing a physiologist refer to love as nothing more than deoxyribonucleic acid calling out to itself. A student of culture is aware, by contrast, that for culture-bound creatures like ourselves love is considerably more. Culture can prescribe whether or not a woman is more likely to fall in love with a fat man than with a thin man. It can determine whether people will fall in love at all. It can determine whether husbands will respond jealously or happily to the attentions that other men give their wives. It can affect the extent to which people are aggressive or passive in making love. It can influence the extent to which people are aware or unaware of their sexual natures.[2] In a word, a comprehension of the nature of culture

---

[2] Morton M. Hunt refers to the case of a man who lived for ten years with a woman who accused him of being sexually inadequate because he could delay himself no more than half an hour during coitus. The husband had to be informed by a psychiatrist that he was extremely unusual and was, contrary to his wife's opinion, quite a man. (See The *New York Times Magazine*, January 1, 1967, p. 16.) The point is that the sexual conduct of this man and his response to it was a function of his understanding of sex and of the meanings given it by others around him. Since, in our culture, we are generally kept ignorant of sexual functions and norms, it is not unusual to encounter people who are either confused, unhappy, or morbidly fascinated by this aspect of their lives.

extends our understanding of the degree to which we are more than chemistry or physiology or a set of biological drives or animal instincts.

The concept of culture is similar, in at least one respect, to a physical concept like gravity. Both culture and gravity gain their value from the degree to which they are found to operate in the universes they deal with. Neither culture nor gravity is especially useful or valuable as an explanatory concept in individual cases. If, for example, we say that a ball fell to the floor because of gravity, we have not really said much. After all, how do we know gravity exists? We know it exists because the ball fell to the floor. So when we say that something fell because of gravity, we are only saying that it fell because it fell.[3] The significance of the concept of gravity, first grasped by the genius of Newton, comes from the fact that gravity is seen to reach out beyond the trees from which apples fall, above the mountain heights, and farther yet—continuing forever into the outermost reaches of the physical universe.

The significance of the concept of culture is similar. As we begin to comprehend people's cultural nature, we begin to see—in ever more subtle extensions—the intrusion of cultural influences. Emotions that may have their chemical origins in deoxyribonucleic acid will have the style and form of their expression dictated by culture.

How an Anthropologist Views Culture

In modern times we have acquired so much cultural baggage that the problem of determining what is significant and what is not has become a central task of the intellectual. One kind of intellectual especially qualified to perform this service is the anthropologist; after all, an examination of culture, either primitive or modern, is this person's professional concern. What do anthropologists see when they examine a complex modern culture such as the one existing today in the United States? Numerous examinations of American character and culture can be found in anthropological and sociological libraries. However, we shall concentrate on one of the better examples of this kind of effort and examine what the anthropologist Jules Henry has to say about the American way of life.[4]

---

[3] This is called a tautologous or circular form of reasoning. It is surprisingly common and even more surprisingly satisfying—revealing the possibility that we are more willing to have our curiosity satisfied than aroused. In any event, this kind of thinking goes on in all fields.

[4] Henry should be compared with C. Wright Mills, David Riesman, and Pitirim Sorokin, among the writers discussed in this book. All these authors are concerned, ultimately, with the application of various social concepts to the American scene. They are interpreters of modern America. Riesman begins with an examination of social character. Mills was concerned with the distribution of power. Sorokin dealt with America as a form of Sensate society. Henry begins with America as a complex cultural system and then selects three critical aspects of this culture—advertising, xenophobia, and child-rearing practices. That each of these authors despairs in his observations probably reflects more the critical nature of any intellectual than it does the possibility that all four are employing observational techniques that have high scientific reliability.

Henry's concerns are personal and therefore arbitrary. He is willing to indicate at times that there are things he does not like. Yet his point of view is never divorced from what might be called an anthropological perspective, which can be summarized as follows. Very early in their development, perhaps as long as one million years ago, human beings gained the capacity to transmit to others, and then to preserve, the lessons they had learned through hard experience. The capacity to preserve experience set in motion the development of culture. In its earliest stages this "preserved experience" served the purpose of enhancing people's possibilities for survival. Also, in its earliest stages culture was probably closely identified with human needs and survival demands. But the growth and development of preserved experience brought about a force which, in some ways, was unique to itself and which occasionally became alienated from primary human needs. Henry suggests that possibly we have today a situation in which culture is served as much by people as people are served by culture. Indeed, we may have reached the point where culture has turned against us.

Ours is a culture, says Henry, that imposes unessential and possibly degrading needs on us. We respond. But to the extent this is so, we become the servants of culture rather than having culture serve us.

> It is the deliberate creation of needs that permits [American] culture to continue. This is the first phase of the psychic revolution of contemporary life.[5]

Henry is concerned with the extent to which culture imposes rather than disposes itself. He asks, in effect: What are the *particular* consequences for us as members of a *particular* culture? And he draws a gloomy picture for us.

The anthropologist has found mythology, folklore, stories, or culturally transmitted fantasy one vital way of entering into a comprehension of primitive culture. Henry, following his anthropological inclinations, does much the same thing with American culture. But what is the mythological locus of the American dream? What literature spells out most clearly the irrational nature of our cultural commitments? Henry searches and finds in advertising the American analogue to the mythology of the primitive.

---

[5] Jules Henry, *Culture against Man* (New York: Random House, 1963). This chapter is based almost exclusively on *Culture against Man*, Henry's most widely known work. (His other works are primarily articles and monographs of a technical nature.) Another work that might be of interest to the new student is *Jungle People* (New York: Vintage Books, 1964). Two more of Henry's works were published posthumously: *Pathways to Madness* (New York: Random House, 1971) and *Jules Henry on Education* (New York: Random House, 1972).

234   *The Place of Advertising in American Culture*

Henry claims that the American dream is lodged within the para-poetic[6] exaggerations and claims of American advertising. It is here we glimpse the sex dreams of the American woman, the virility models of the American man. The pecuniary aspirations and urges of every American are reflected in and shaped by advertising. So Henry begins with an examination of the advertising industry and the endless dream it manufactures. The essential character of the dream is infinite indulgence in a world capable of producing an infinite supply. Yet, for all of its indulgence, it is a troubled dream.

Dreams are violations of reality. We may, in the course of our individual dreams, violate physical reality, as when we dream we are able to step from a high tower and sail out over the earth. Or our dreams may violate social taboos or norms, as when we dream we are naked before a large assembly. Just as our personal dreams usurp the traditional controls of society, so does advertising circumvent the higher values of the system—and it is this feature of advertising that is of greatest concern to Henry. Like the inner personal dream that steals upon us while we sleep, advertising bypasses the more rigorous established values of our culture. A dream may lead us to indulge in fantasies that violate our individual sense of decency, modesty, and shame. So does advertising. A dream may circumvent rationality and logic. So does advertising. Degradation of our sense of decency and reason is the result, and we become objects of contempt.

Advertising is forced to bypass the sternest values of our culture. It cannot, for example, rely on traditional logic and scientific modes of establishing truth about consumer goods. Advertising operates on the basis of a different logic—pecuniary logic. It is a logic never meant to be taken seriously, and yet it is a logic which works, that is, it sells things. It is a logic that operates alongside the formal and demanding logic of science and is competitive with it for dominance within the culture. Henry explains:

> In order for our economy to continue in its present form people must learn to be fuzzy-minded and impulsive, for if they were clear-headed and deliberate they would rarely put their hands in their pockets; or, if they did, they would leave them there. If we were all logicians the economy could not survive, and herein lies a terrifying paradox, for in order to exist economically as we are we must try by might and main to remain stupid.[7]

Examples of what Henry means by pecuniary logic are easy to find. Consider the following advertisement.

"BLACK & WHITE"
SCOTCH FOR PEOPLE WHO KNOW THE DIFFERENCE

[6] Henry never tells us quite what he means by this term. It could mean a disordered or abnormal kind of poetic expression or a form of poetry which only resembles true poetry.
[7] Henry, *Culture against Man*, p. 48.

The logic is elementary, though slightly ambiguous, and the threat and insult are only slightly more subtle. The pecuniary logical implication is that if you are sophisticated enough to know the difference, you will first buy and then drink the Scotch whiskey pictured in the advertisement. If you are not drinking the Scotch shown in the advertisement, you presumably are gauche enough to drink pretty much anything. There is a logic here, but the important thing Henry points to is that it is a logic not meant to be taken seriously. At the same time it is a logic that flows from a serious and highly competitive industry—the advertising industry. Though we are not supposed to take this logic seriously, it is nonetheless valid enough to warrant the expenditure, at the present time, of over ten billion dollars each year.

The producers of the dream, the advertisers, must live with the fact that they are the agents of mass-produced hallucination and delusion. Their response is, on the one hand, an attempt to legitimize their work by referring to it as a profession and, on the other hand, the acquisition of a cynical contempt for the public. Henry mentions a sign hanging over the desk of a Hollywood press agent: "The only thing we have to fear is the truth."[8]

The form of the dream is installed early in life. Children, like adults, are exploited by the dream. Through the dream they acquire the motivation and the capacity to consume almost unthinkingly. Consumption becomes a way of life and the measure of what is good. Children are exploited by the dream and parents are exploited by children. The consequences are sometimes comic and sometimes pathetic. Henry cites the following instance:

> [A father is quoted as saying:] "My youngster is only 5. He cannot read. It's a helluva thing to spend $15 on a toy and then see my kid sit down and cry because it doesn't fly like the one he saw on television."[9]

Indulgence and Permissiveness

Coming of age in America, as Henry views the process, involves learning the dream as it appears in advertising. There is more, of course, but the dream is central and shapes many other facets of the child's life. For example, one of the most critical features of the relationship of parent and child in America is the indulgence pattern that exists between them. Henry comes to this conclusion after examining the responses of several hundred children and teenagers in St. Louis to a questionnaire that asked them to list what they liked most and least about their mothers and fathers. An example of the kind of response he received is the following from a twelve-year-old girl:

> I like my father because he is kind, good and funny, when he is with my brothers and sisters and I. When I bring my friends home with me, he is

[8] Ibid., p. 91.
[9] Ibid., p. 75.

very nice to them and shows us a good time. He also lets me go to Plankville to see my grandparents, aunt and uncle and my two cousins every summer. This summer he talked Mother into letting me go to Bigtown, with my aunt, uncle, and cousins.

I don't like my father because he doesn't believe in letting me go to the show at night, and he won't let me wear lipstick. Even if he knows that he is wrong, he won't admit it to anybody. He insists on wearing his hair in a crewcut, even though he is losing most of it.

I like my mother because she lets me go to visit my friends often. She lets me invite them over whenever I please. If it was up to her, I would get a lot more allowance than I do. She lets me help her fix supper when I want to, and is very nice about it, when I make a mess (even though I have to clean it up). She also lets me do almost anything I want.

I dislike my mother because she gets mad so easily. On Saturday morning she makes me clean the house, while she goes shopping. She won't let me wear lipstick, or go to the show at night. She makes me take care of my brothers and sisters (ugh).[10]

It is obvious that what the child likes about her parents is their permissiveness. Note the number of times she refers to whether a parent "lets me" do something. The parents are not admired or respected or liked for what they are or for qualities they might possess. They are judged instead on the extent to which they permit self-indulgence. Rarely, Henry observes, do children say they like their parents because they are thoughtful or proud or dignified or intelligent or ambitious. To come of age in America is to become attuned, early in life, to a way of living that concentrates on permissiveness and self-indulgence.[11]

Adults express the mature and full pattern of self-indulgence, and children are expected to wait somewhat impatiently on the sidelines until they possess the right to full expression of self-indulgence. Henry observes that our culture, probably more than any other, attempts a total division between impulse release patterns in children and adults. This is not so elsewhere. Henry comments:

> Among my friends the Pilagá Indians of Argentina, children of all ages attempted or had intercourse with one another, played sexual games, listened to and told sexual stories, and smoked if the adults would let them have tobacco (which was very rarely, because there was so little). Older children did not go near the beer fiestas because this was for older men, not because it was "immoral." Thus, since the Pilagá have no impulse logic according to which children are excluded from the impulse release patterns of adults, when children engage in them they need not do it surreptitiously and are not made to feel immoral.[12]

---

[10] Ibid., pp. 133–134.
[11] The theme of the indulgent parent is exploited by the movies. The strong character of the father in the film *Mary Poppins* is undermined by a magical nanny whose special magic is her capacity to play the role of imp in the mental world of the child. In the end it is the father's character that is finally forced to meet that of the child, and we leave daddy in the last scene out in a field flying a kite.
[12] Henry, *Culture against Man*, p. 237.

Of course, our culture cannot, willy-nilly, adopt the ways of the Pilagá. The point is, however, that the given forms of impulse release in our culture virtually force the child into subterfuge, sham, and guilt.

The relationship between children and parents is complicated and tense. The self-indulgence of the child must be catered to and yet not allowed to go too far. The child must be readied for life in a society that subscribes to a metaphysic of fun and subordinates everything to the attainment of a "high standard of living." Parents must provide a covert model of the awaiting pleasures and at the same time deny their children the overt practice of those activities that will specifically define their maturity for them. The parental model flowing out of this complicated system of impulse control is the parent who conducts himself or herself as an "imp of fun."

The role of "Puck" or "fun-imp" is especially noticeable in the father. Because his work is often abstract in nature and removed from the direct view of his children, because he seeks their approval and recognition, and because he competes for this approval with the mother, whose value to the children is direct and obvious—the father compensates by entering the child's world as a fun figure. He becomes the Mary Poppins of the family. Henry suggests that the mother may be sufficiently challenged by this response on the part of the father to feel impelled to take on some of the qualities of the "fun-imp" herself.

During adolescence the conflict between adult law that constrains impulse release and informal cultural pressure to engage in impulse release produces further complications. For girls, Henry expresses the problem simply:

> Girls fear they will not attract boys, and paradoxically, they fear the boys they attract too well. It is a difficult life to lead.[13]

Girls indicate the conflict by wearing padded bras and provocative slacks and blouses while, at the same time, confessing that the boys in their high school do not know they are so falsifying themselves. The implication is apparent. The girls do not permit the boys to uncover the deception. Moreover, the girls interviewed by Henry expressed contempt for boys who went out for "what they could get." Part of the contempt stems from the fact that such boys are unwilling to accept the conventions of legitimate ambiguity and misrepresentation which the other adolescents consider binding.[14] That is, they are not willing to accept being misled.

Henry suggests that maturity in Western culture is found in the capacity to misrepresent while being able, at the same time, to avoid being misled by the misrepresentations of others. Adolescence is a period during which the child begins to grasp the techniques of skilled misrepresentation. To be direct is to run the risk of being labeled a delinquent. The girl who, for example, is a real lover rather than a

---

[13] Ibid., p. 211.
[14] Ibid., p. 211.

238 misrepresentation of a lover, is apt to find her status in jeopardy. The boy who is unwilling to accept the pseudo-nature of the pseudo-nymph has no "cool." Maturity, says Henry, is the capacity not to care if you are misled.[15]

The Nightmare of Failure

If unfettered consumption is the glowing dream of American culture, failure is its darkest nightmare. Without appearing to do so, American schools teach children how to hate. Very important here is the possibility that they teach children how to hate themselves when they fail. That is, the culturally induced response to failure is self-hatred. The schools also teach children to hate the successful person. Henry refers to the following observational notes to develop his point:

> Boris [a fifth grader] had trouble reducing "12/16" to the lowest terms, and could only get as far as "6/8". The teacher asked him quietly if that was as far as he could reduce it. She suggested he "think." Much heaving up and down and waving of hands by the other children, all frantic to correct him. Boris pretty unhappy, probably mentally paralyzed. The teacher, quiet, patient, ignores the others and concentrates with look and voice on Boris. She says, "Is there a bigger number than two you can divide into the two parts of the fraction?" After a minute or two, she becomes more urgent, but there is no response from Boris. She then turns to the class and says, "Well, who can tell Boris what the number is?" A forest of hands appears and the teacher calls Peggy. Peggy says that four may be divided into the numerator and the denominator.[16]

This is such a common incident in our culture that one untrained in anthropology or sociology might find in it little cause for comment. To Henry, however, it is a small drama revealing a startling amount of unconscious cruelty. Henry goes on:

> To a Zuñi, Hopi, or Dakota Indian, Peggy's performance would seem cruel beyond belief, for competition, the wringing of success from somebody's failure, is a form of torture foreign to those noncompetitive redskins.[17]

The school is teaching this fifth-grader, but it is teaching him much more than exercises in the reduction of fractions. It is teaching him a lesson in self-control. Boris is expected to remain at the blackboard and live with the nightmare of his own public confrontation with self-inadequacy. It is putting it too mildly to say that Boris is being taught. Henry suggests culture goes further. It invades the mind. Its lessons become obsessions that dictate how the world is to be seen. Boris is learning the

---

[15] Ibid., p. 274.
[16] Ibid., p. 296.
[17] Ibid., p. 296.

nightmare of failure and he is learning his vulnerability before a yapping and critical public. One consequence of this lesson is that Boris is very likely to become willing to believe anything that will spare him further painful confrontations, regardless of whether it is true or false, useful or useless. Paradoxically, then, only by remaining willing to be absurd can Boris feel free from the fear of being absurd.

The Nightmare Fear of the Enemy

At the individual level the nightmare is the dream of failure. At the national level it is the recurring pathogenic fear of communism embodied in the form of the Soviet Union and Red China. We believe, regardless of whether the situation calls for it, tthat others should have and employ a democratic government operating hand-in-hand with a market economy based on private profit. Like Boris, we are threatened if someone else does something differently and, at the same time, successfully. So it is that our newspapers have dwelt at great length on every failure experienced by Castro, Mao, Brezhnev, or any other threatening international figure. The best we can manage is to wish them the worst and then relish every setback. This culturally induced malice is another side of American culture—the nightmare side of the American dream.[18]

Very broadly, the American nightmare of the Soviet Union has produced (1) an economic reliance on the fear of war, (2) the commitment of our cultural elite to an attitude of "fun-and-games" in war, (3) total immersion in the struggle—with civilians included as warlike agents along with military people, (4) simple dichotomization of the world into friend and foe, (5) fear of trade and the extension of economic ties, (6) a reliance on the internal domestic economy to maintain production control, (7) an atmosphere of security and secrecy, (8) the development of a powerful and potentially uncontrollable military-industrial complex, (9) irrational negativism toward domestic public programs, and (10) obsessive concern with obtaining immediate relief from the problems of international struggle. Each of these points will be elaborated slightly.

1. An economic reliance on the fear of war by American industry is significant insofar as it narcotizes our sense of the consequences of conflict.[19] Henry puts it this way:

> The fact that the Soviets are in the opposite situation has helped to save us, for since their way of life is threatened by war, they lack the temptations

---

[18] Henry is aware, of course, that Russia is not exactly inclined to cheer American successes either. The point is not that Russia or the United States is "evil" in its malice but that the source of the malice is found within cultural rather than biological factors.

[19] Henry, in a different way, is talking about the same thing Bronowski discusses in his treatment of science and human values (*Science and Human Values,* rev. ed., 1965). To put this in Bronowski's terms, Henry is concerned with the extent to which we are encapsulated from the consequences of our decisions by the immediate comforts of our economy.

we have. The reader need only imagine what his own attitude toward war would be if mere *preparation* for it meant that his clothes would become tattered, he would taste meat only once a week, he would have no butter or coffee, gasoline would be available only once a week and in two-gallon allotments and he would have to wait in line for it; that if his car needed repairs he would have to make them himself or wait weeks to get the job done, etc. In such a case even the most warlike statesmen would think a thousand times before announcing the possibility of war.[20]

2. The commitment, the degree of interest and reward that our cultural maximizers (scientists, intellectuals, industrial administrators, and politicians) now have invested in war, is, to Henry, more than alarming; it is morbid. It is an investment in death. Our cultural elite have become an elite of death. Moreover, death, once the final test of courage in individuals, is now the loser's trophy waiting for the elite and the nation whose computers and sense of strategy in gamesmanship are lacking. Death has become a game.[21] Henry quotes from an advertisement by the RAND Corporation to make his point.

> War *games* play an important part in RAND formulations. *Game* theories frequently evolve into doctrines of military strategy. *Playing games* simulating attack conditions provides answers to such problems as how to supply threatened fighter bases around the globe, and how to defend cities against bomber or missile strikes or even satellite bombings. . . .[22]

3. Modern commitments to war as a form of conflict resolution have meant an increasing involvement of civilians. Civilians have become involved not only as casualties in the devastating air raids of World War II; they have, more importantly, become active participants in the war effort. The current personification of the culture hero in the folk-art media is not the soldier-killer-fighter but the civilian-killer-fighter. A number of such civilian heroes come to mind; James Bond is the outstanding one. These heroes are often spoofed and often two-dimensional. However, this does not make them any less significant. Whether we are confronted by an obviously bungling comic hero or more "realistic" members of some saboteur team, the interesting thing about the hero is his civilian attire and his military mentality. Meanwhile, in the more down-to-earth activities of the Pentagon, there is concern over whether the military or the civilian strategist and tactician is going to have the final say about the disposal and utilization of today's instruments of war.

[20] Henry, *Culture against Man,* p. 102.
[21] More broadly, in a society that faces the problem of how to cope with leisure time on a scale never before confronted by a large cultural system, games become a way of dealing with many facets of life. Thus, love is a game, business is a game, social relations are a game, marriage is a game; indeed, life in general is an extended playing of a game. RAND theorists justify their actions on the ground that we should try to know as much about war as it is possible to know, so we might be able to control it. This is a most reasonable argument. The interesting thing is that RAND theorists seem to think they can know all there is to know about war by playing games.
[22] Henry, *Culture against Man,* p. 108. Italics are Henry's.

4. In a time that calls for an evaluation of world problems on the basis of extremely complex social and economic concerns, we have remained with the simpler position of evaluating people on the basis of whether we believe they are friends or foes. The archaic and irrational posture this forces us to assume can be seen if we draw an analogy at the individual level. Suppose you were to go to a psychiatrist for help and he told you he would not be willing to treat your case unless he knew how friendly you were toward his religious and personal beliefs. Such an attitude would probably be surprising and you would begin thinking of trying somewhere else. Yet such attitudes prevailed in our culture until recently; a person might be refused aid unless his religious and moral beliefs were in conformity with those offering it. Such attitudes still operate at international levels, even though our arsenal of atomic weapons makes us capable of destroying as much of this planet as we desire. Despite such military security—to attack us would be to commit suicide—we still think in terms of threat from the foe and we respond in terms of fear and retaliation. Henry finds this somewhat enigmatic. How can we account for it unless we concede that the culture, though not necessarily the individual, has something to gain in terms of solidarity and economic benefits from fear of the foe?

5. Our fear of the enemy has produced an obvious warlike posture. One element of this posture is the constraint of trade we have indulged in (and forced our allies to indulge in) with the hope that it would hurt the enemy. Henry has the following to say with regard to the consequences of the economic battle.

> High tariffs, economic isolation from the Communist countries, and the fact that much of the non-Communist world is too poor to buy from us, have made it necessary to consume at home most of what we produce. This is *relative consumption autarchy*. The growth of advertising is the institutional response to this, and the era of self-indulgence and fun is the emotional one.
>
> But consumption autarchy is not a viable form in an industrial nation, and billions of dollars have gone abroad looking for quicker and higher profits in countries where markets are expanding more rapidly than ours. The resulting loss of gold has become a constant headache because of the threat to the value of the dollar. When we cut ourselves off from Communist trade we open our own veins.
>
> Thus we come to one more delusion created by The Great Fear—the delusion of the effectiveness of economic warfare. It is delusive on two counts: first, it is not hurting the Russians; second, we are the only ones who think it important.[23]

6. Economic warfare has meant that the internal economy must be relied on to attend to national needs and an internal market must be relied on to consume what is being produced by national industry. The economic consequences cannot be traced out in any detail here. But two central consequences of concern to Henry are the load placed on ad-

[23] Ibid., p. 114.

242 vertising to promote consumption and the role that war fear acquires as a means of stimulating a relatively self-contained economic system.

7. The atmosphere of insecurity and secrecy that war fear breeds is so apparent that it almost seems unnecessary to comment on it. We cannot give our precious secrets to the enemy. But Henry observes that the fear and the secrecy go further than this. Obviously we cannot give precious secrets to the enemy, but in our state of fear we eventually find ourselves unwilling to declassify even mundane and useless information.

> To the fear of leakage was now added the underlings' fear of releasing any information at all that might conceivably be interpreted as "embarass-ing" to the Department [of Defense] or as giving aid and comfort to the enemy. In these circumstances every employee ran the risk of a surprise reprimand for releasing even the most innocuous information, and it there-fore became a regular practice for Department workers in all echelons to stamp as "secret" or "confidential" documents that could have no imagi-nable value to the enemy. It was repeatedly brought out in the hearings that any employee who had his head screwed on right would sooner withhold a document than release it to the public . . .[24]

It is not secrecy that gives away our fear; it is the extent to which secrecy is carried.

8. The alliance of industry and the military[25] has had the conse-quence of consolidating further the economic base from which this nation is thrust more solidly toward a warlike posture. Henry mentions the following result as only one of several:

> Since fear (i.e., defense) contracts are sound investments, banks lend more eagerly to companies having them than to others. The situation is made even more trying by the fact that domestic loans are more readily collectable than foreign ones; banks more easily lend to companies work-ing for defense than to exporters shipping to troubled Latin America, Asia, and the Near East. Domestic fear is a better investment than foreign un-certainty. If anyone should ask me how to invest his money, I would say, "Invest in domestic fear. Fear and dollars grow together like root and branch."[26]

9. Although sociologists tend to emphasize the rational character-istics of administrative decisions in bureaucratically organized govern-ments, Henry concentrates on the irrational. Fear produces more action than rational decision making. America, confronted by the nightmare of Russia, is more inclined to give in to this fear than it is to promote

---

[24] Ibid., p. 119.
[25] This subject is covered in greater detail, though not without considerable bias and distortion, in Fred J. Cook's *The Warfare State* (New York: Macmillan, 1962). Despite the bias in this work, it is worthwhile reading. It at least provides one with some idea of the vastness of the military-industrial complex in America. When one considers the matching complexes found among our allies and enemies, it becomes difficult to face the future with much optimism.
[26] Henry, *Culture against Man*, p. 104.

domestic programs. Domestic programs advanced under the country's aspiration to achieve the "Great Society" were given their impetus by the fear of internal rioting and the fear that America would appear tyrannical toward her minority groups unless something was done to alleviate their condition.

Is fear a proper foundation for government? Henry, if he were a more cautious social scientist, would hesitate even to ask such a question, and he certainly would not try to answer it. Yet Henry does give his opinion:

> A nation that will respond only to fear cannot govern itself wisely, for it has no destiny but fear, while its overshadowing goal is to defend itself.[27]

10. A last consequence of the nightmare is the desire for immediate relief from the problems imposed upon us and which we feel we—a good and just nation—do not deserve. Henry is suggesting that a realistic understanding of international tensions is one that comprehends them in their full complexity and recognizes, at the same time, that they cannot be resolved through any simple and immediate means. We cannot, for example, resolve our problems by going all out and winning the war with the Communists by total conquest and total military commitment. The reason, simple to an anthropologist, is that the problems that brought on, let us say, the Vietnam War, were not essentially military problems and could not be resolved by military means.

We want an end to the nightmare, and we want it now. We can have an end to it, perhaps, suggests Henry, by responding not with fear but with comprehension. We must not allow our vision to become narrowed by terror.

> The Great Fear resembles a true obsession: like all obsessions its perceptions and anxiety-reducing measures transgress the bounds of reality; fly in the face of the fact; have widely ramifying, unanticipated consequences; and, most important, are self-destructive over the long run. A person with an obsession takes steps that give him *immediate* relief from his anxiety, seizing upon what seems at the moment to be the element that immediately threatens his survival, only to discover later that he has chosen wrongly. A person in such a state is driven also to bizarre ways of protecting himself. . . .
> The American public has been so thoroughly educated to fear that statesmen think they would risk their political future by coming to an accommodation with the Russians on the only firm basis possible—the resumption of trade. But without it disarmament is only a dream, for we cannot continue economic *warfare* and expect that disarmament will bring military *peace*.[28]

So our culture contains within it two opposed and yet reciprocal

---

[27] Ibid., p. 113.
[28] Ibid., pp. 117–118. Italics are Henry's.

244 forces. There is the dream of indulgence on the one hand and, on the other, the nightmare of "those" who would take from us our freedom to indulge. The nightmare encourages us to engage in ever more exotic and full-blown forms of self-indulgence. The more we indulge, the more frightening the nightmare becomes and the more we have to fear those who might interrupt our "Midsummer Night's Dream." We remain, for all our technological and material development, still driven by fear.

The Transmission of Culture

Thus Henry provides us with an overall delineation of what he considers to be some of the major features of our culture. He is concerned, on the one hand, with the content of our culture—the ideas, beliefs, fears, aspirations, tools, and sustenance it provides. On the other hand, he is concerned with the process whereby, in daily human interactions, the content of culture is transferred to those who become transformed by it. As we mentioned earlier, culture does more than teach. As Henry put it, culture "invades" the mind. The lessons acquired from culture become obsessions. One finds oneself welded to certain beliefs and attitudes and finds them as difficult to change as it is difficult to change one's language.

Despite elaborate public systems designed to pass on cultural traditions, there is some possibility that we get less consistent transmission of culture from generation to generation than is the case in simpler cultures. Part of this is because it is impossible to pass on a cultural heritage so vast to each member of the culture. Another reason rests on the fact that one of our cultural traditions grants adults the right to bring their children up however they wish—so long as the children are not physically injured or so seriously damaged in character as to constitute a social menace. This means there has been a reduction in the extent to which others may correct faults implanted by the parents. Children, instead of acquiring culturally stable beliefs and ways of relating to others, may acquire distorted and lethal ideas and be launched down a pathway to madness. Henry observes:

> In our culture babies are a private enterprise—everybody is in the baby business as soon as he gets married. He produces his own babies; they are his; only he has the right to a say-so in their management; they cannot be taken from him without due process of law; he has the sole responsibility for their maintenance and protection. He has the right to expand his production of babies indefinitely and curtail it whenever he wishes. As long as he takes care of his young children the outside world has no right to cross his threshold, to say "No" or "Yes" about anything he does with his children. Pinched off alone in one's own house, shielded from critical eyes, one can be as irrational as one pleases with one's children as long as severe damage does not attract the attention of the police.
>
> In other words, there is minimal *social regulation* of parent-child relations in our culture; this is, above all, what makes lethal child-care practices possible. In a primitive culture, where many relatives are around to take an

active interest in one's baby, where life is open, or in large households, where many people can see what a mother is doing and where deviations from traditional practice quickly offend the eye and loosen critical, interested tongues, it is impossible for a parent to do as he or she pleases with his children. In a literal sense, a baby is often not even one's own in such societies, but belongs to a lineage, clan, or household—a community—having a real investment in the baby. It is not private enterprise. The almost total absence of the *social regulation* of parent-child relations in our private enterprise culture is a pivotal environmental factor. . . .[29]

Within the home, then, removed from the eyes of neighbors, children receive an educational treatment from their parents long before they enter school—when social regulation begins to put in an appearance in the parent-child relationship. This treatment can be socially damaging to children. It can impress upon them the more self-destructive features of our economy. Most importantly, and what Henry is getting at here, this treatment is not—despite its sometimes bizarre and possibly lethal nature—removed from our culture. It comes out of it and appears in the form of exaggerated and distorted elements that already exist within the culture.

Henry came to these conclusions after spending a number of weeks living in the homes of children considered sufficiently disturbed to require psychiatric care. Henry concerned himself especially with the relationship between the parents and the children in these homes. More significantly, he was concerned with the extent to which the parents misused culturally sanctioned values and, as a consequence, damaged their children. A case in point is the relationship existing between Mr. Portman and his son Pete. The Portman home was one observed by Henry for some time. He says of the father–son relationship:

> Mr. Portman expresses his love for his son through throwing him around, punching him in the belly, and imitating a devouring animal. Pete cannot fail, therefore, to associate love with physical violence: to love a person is to throw him around, wallop him, and symbolically chew him up—in other words, to have fun. Pete tries a baby version of this on Elaine, his little playmate next door. Thus the toughness-love-violence combination, so common in our movies, is here built into the child's flesh and bone through the basic biological mammalian function of play.[30]

In a final summary of his observations of the Portman family, Henry makes the following statement:

> Coming together in *lethal* form in Mr. and Mrs. Portman, widespread

[29] Ibid., pp. 331–332. Unfortunately, examples of what Henry is talking about are common. A graduate student we know of was shaken up by a recent experience. He had been working with a little girl who seemed to be unusually anally compulsive in her behavior. Then he learned that she is one of five children in her family, each of whom gets a daily enema from mama. The mother is not malicious. She simply has taken too much to heart the adage that cleanliness is next to godliness. And, within the privacy of her home, she is determined to have clean kids—inside as well as outside. Italics are Henry's.
[30] Ibid., p. 347.

American personality characteristics such as shallowness of involvement, confusion and vagueness, a tendency to read life off in terms of a dominance-submission struggle, a tendency to sacrifice tenderness to strength, and a tendency to humiliate others, have produced a dreadful, unplanned and unintended but nevertheless pathogenic entanglement of parents and children that has the quality of destiny and tragedy. In this state, isolated from public view, husband, wife, and children live out their secret misery. Babies are private enterprise in Western culture and so are misery and dissolution.[31]

So, from the perspective of the anthropologist, culture worms its way into our innermost beings. It is there when we are rationally calculating the orbital pattern of an artificial satellite. It is also there when we march down some seemingly lonely road to madness. It elaborates our fears and provides a platform for our vanities. It is the source of our knowledge and, at the same time, it determines those things of which we must remain ignorant. It can provide us with our most courageously human qualities and, paradoxically, it can be the source of our most wretched absurdities. It can dominate us to the point where we find it difficult to tell where a culturally instilled desire begins and animal nature leaves off. Culture can extend our vision in one direction and completely blind us in another.

The concept of culture is quite abstract, and cultural forces themselves are extremely vast, powerful, and subtle. Yet, despite this, the anthropologist does not lose sight of the fact that the matter of culture is essentially a matter of what we do to ourselves. For after all, culture is simply what generations of people have passed on to those who follow. Culture is the hand of the dead on the shoulder of the living. It may be a very powerful hand, but it is still human and still fallible.

We can gain some idea of the extent to which the hand of the dead is still operative in American culture when we observe the extent to which we are motivated, in the midst of opulence, to pursue the ideal of a rising standard of living. How far must we go in this pursuit—the foundation of the older American dream—before we have exhausted it and ourselves? Perhaps, as Eric Hoffer suggests (and Henry, we think, would have agreed), it is time to aspire to rising standards of intellect rather than rising standards of living. If this is a reasonable ideal, it makes Henry's observations all the more poignant; for one of the most effective ways in which culture stands mobilized against humanity today is the extent to which it frustrates the pursuit of this ideal.

Though Henry's commentaries are depressing, they are not lacking in hope. Unlike primitives or members of societies ruled by tradition, modern men and women do not have to accept uncritically the dictates of a tyrannical culture. They have the opportunity to stand back and evaluate what the culture is doing to them. They can ask questions concerning their nature. Henry is not so presumptuous as to claim that he has answered these basic humanistic questions. However, he does

---

[31] Ibid., p. 349.

tell those who are involved with them that many of the answers do not lie within a searching of the individual soul. Instead, we must consider the extent to which we, as cultural beings, have been helped or hindered by our culture. We must look around us as well as within ourselves. We must learn to recognize the lethal as well as the life-giving elements in our culture—for these appear ultimately within each of us.

Problems and Issues

Despite the nearly universal condemnation of advertising in the American press and other media, advertising is as much a part of the national scene today as it has ever been. Jules Henry emphasized the fact that few things more completely reveal the banality of the commercial mentality than advertising. But, Henry asks, what does advertising reveal, in the profoundest sense, about our culture? How can we begin to comprehend the extent to which it shapes our views of the world and the ways in which we should develop our lives? Advertising, in effect, tells us to eat, drink, and drive. Later, if we are to get a good night's sleep, we should take an antacid before retiring. What would life be without advertising? What are the moral effects of advertising? Is Henry being too severe when he suggests that this is a nation in which we must exert every effort to remain stupid if we are to continue to exist economically?

Along with advertising, perhaps the American school system has received more than its fair share of criticism and condemnation. Henry examined the American school system and concluded that its major effect was to instill a lifelong distaste for the life of the mind. How does education in a complex society differ from the education in simpler social systems? Americans tend to think of education as a process in which one acquires mastery over traditional, basic skills—reading, writing, literature, mathematics, and science. However, schooling is a process in which much more than formal or informational learning takes place. Learning about social behavior is also acquired. Boys learn about girls, girls about boys. One's popularity and the basis for it is revealed. What sorts of "reform" of the American high school system are implicit in Henry's critical commentaries? Would such "reforms" lead to a more effective educational program? Why are Americans so critical of schools?

Henry also deals with the child in the confines of the family. As an anthropologist he was concerned with the extent to which it was possible to gain further understanding of American culture by keeping in mind how our culture compares with other cultures. How do young people in other cultures achieve maturity? How do young people in this culture deal with the problem of maturity? We have people in their forties and fifties who wonder if they ever "really" found maturity. Presuming the problem of maturity to be one that does bother people in this culture, we must ask why they do so. Henry says that we define maturity in terms of our capacity to misrepresent while avoiding being misled. Maturity is a matter of "staying cool." But is this really so? How can such an assertion be proved? Even if Henry is too severe, what kinds of questions does his writing stimulate concerning the problems of growing up and maturing in the United States?

We note there is a tendency on Henry's part to romanticize simpler cultural systems. He does this when he describes the embarrassment of a fourth grade boy at the blackboard, struggling to reduce a fraction, which would not have happened had he been a youngster among the Zuñi, Hopi, or Dakota Indians. What can we learn from studying other cultures? What kinds of problems might arise from attempting to inculcate the lifeways of another culture into our own? What features of other cultures seem to be most readily absorbed into our culture—and which are more difficult to incorporate?

Theory and Practice

The Views of

HOWARD S. BECKER

. . . we can never have a "balanced picture" until we have studied all of society simultaneously. I do not propose to hold my breath until that happy day.
Sociological Work
BORN: 1928

Theory Versus Practice

14

Theory, in and of itself, without any consideration for practical applications, can be an intellectually engaging activity. Indeed, it is intellectual activity par excellence. Theory is always an endeavor to press beyond the present appearances of reality. It is an effort to examine the masks that might lie behind the masks we see. Great theorists, regardless of the fields within which they work, represent a synthesis of thought and observation that is the greatest offering of their field. Even so, there are differences from field to field in the way theorists are regarded by their colleagues.

This is most clearly seen in mathematics, where we can make two general observations of interest. First, mathematical theoreticians occupy a lofty status vis-à-vis their colleagues. Practical mathematicians are not as likely to share the same prestige as that offered to theoretical mathematicians. Second, theoretical mathematicians do not vindicate them-

249

250 selves by attempting to develop practical justifications for their work.[1] Like the pure artist (whatever we might mean by that term), the pure mathematician works in a realm that is beyond immediate practical applications.

The situation is not greatly different in the social sciences. Some of the most prestigious figures in the field are generally thought of as social theorists—Marx, Weber, Durkheim, Parsons, Merton, Sorokin, and Simmel, to name only a few. However, unlike the theories of the natural scientist or the mathematician, the theories of the social scientist come close to the heart of our most profound concerns. The social theorist probes into the character of our institutions, our values, our folkways and mores, our ideals, and our beliefs concerning which people we think we should look up to and which we should look down upon. The distinction between what a mathematical theorist does and what a social theorist does is so great that we are inclined to believe separate terms should be used to describe the nature of their accomplishments. However, tradition has granted these diverse activities the title of theorizing, and we shall continue in this tradition. We suspect, however, that it is a bit of misleading terminology. After all, there is a difference between what is done in the theory of numbers and the theory of, let us say, social stratification. But this topic is beyond the present limits of our discussion.

Although the theoretician is sometimes an object of disdain to those who think of themselves as practical individuals, we would like to suggest that, at least with social theory, there are almost always practical implications in any theory. We do not wish to spend a lot of time trying to support this contention. The argument, essentially, is based on the observation that most social behavior is motivated or given form by some kind of theory people have about how they ought to behave. Racist theory, for example, has very practical implications for blacks in America who are trying to get a job. Evolutionary theory has practical implications for fundamentalists who are pondering the question of where to send their children to school. Theories concerning the relationship between mental illness and criminal action have practical implications for the design of systems of incarceration. And so on. While we do not care to spend much time in the justification of theory by pointing to its practical consequences, we nonetheless feel that the student should not casually dismiss anything that is labeled theory as being, by virtue of that fact, without consequence in the real world. Social theories can be as beneficial as a gentle rain during a drought and as lethal as an arrow. They merit respect.

---

[1] The real situation is more complicated, perhaps, than some of the mathematical theorists might like to believe. After all, mathematics has its origins in rather ordinary and practical concerns, such as keeping track of the seasons, problems of the marketplace, and geometries of construction. Furthermore, theoreticians are not bashful about pointing out that some of their more esoteric imaginings ultimately have led to startling applications (for example, the application of Boolean algebra to some forms of telephone circuitry).

Theory and Novelty

This chapter will briefly consider several features of the work of a man who has combined some overtly practical interests with a theoretical sophistication that has resulted in an unusual interpretation of human action. The work of Howard S. Becker reveals the close working relationship between theory and practice. Before moving into a consideration of Becker's work, we will comment on one further feature of theory (whether it is theoretical physics or social theory) that should be discussed. We are thinking, now, of the element of novelty or surprise that often adds to the significance or importance of theory and, of course, to related research. Theory might impress us simply by its novel features. In the realm of physical theory this is easy enough to illustrate. A number of people, for example, are currently interested in the peculiar properties of black holes in space. The practical applications of such speculation are not immediately evident. This, however, does not deter us from seeking further understanding of the nature of such phenomena. Even in our sophisticated, technological, and possibly jaded and exhausted society, the sciences are able to continue to stun and provoke us with the novelty of their views. In a most real sense we are, even today, still struggling to adjust ourselves to the wide-ranging implications of these modern scientific interpretations of the world around us.

Within social theory, however, we encounter some problems with regard to the attainment of novelty or intellectual astonishment. Studying human society from the stance taken by sociologists poses particular difficulties when it comes to exciting or delighting the mind or senses. Unlike artists, sociologists are not supposed to embellish their work with hyperbole or imaginative invention.[2] They are not supposed to make use of literary or rhetorical devices that might make their case appear more persuasive. They are called on, instead, to use an academic prose style, which can remove much of the joy from a presentation of even the most novel findings and arguments. Sociology is commonly offered with a sonorous heaviness, a Germanic ponderousness that we usually reserve for higher theological debate.[3]

There are further constraints on the ability of the social sciences to offer a sense of novelty. Foremost among these constraints is the simple

---

[2] Sociology promotes the sentiment that it is composed of people who do not indulge themselves in hyperbole or imaginative invention. They simply compile facts and generate scientific theory. This, of course, just is not so. Sociologists do engage in hyperbole and they do make use of quite imaginative inventions in the description of social reality. However, they are required, by the rules of the game, to stay within the constraints imposed by metaphors acceptable to those who take a scientific, intellectual stance toward the world. This imposes relatively severe limitations when contrasted with the license given to artists for undertaking the same job.

[3] Few critics of sociology have ignored this feature of the discipline. Even critics from within the field have commented on it. Most devastating in this regard have been the comments of Mills and Sorokin. See C. Wright Mills, *The Sociological Imagination* (New York: Oxford University Press, 1959) and Pitirim Sorokin, *Fads and Foibles in Modern Sociology and Related Sciences* (Chicago: Regnery, 1956).

252   fact that all people receive an intensive social training as they mature. It really makes little difference whether this training is correct or not. By the time people reach adulthood, they are already generally informed, one way or another, about the society of which they are a part. It is not especially exciting to many people to encounter descriptions of a social world they believe they already know. Moreover, in modern society the mass media are always ready to offer social understanding and stories of human conflict and anguish in a manner designed to attract large audiences. The ingenious understandings and interpretations of a Durkheim or Weber, a Mead or Duncan, have to compete with the more bizarre and novel off-the-cuff commentaries of guests on the Johnny Carson Show.

So, if we make the assumption that one of the charms of either the arts or the sciences is the generation of novel understandings, we are brought to the problem of how this is to be achieved in a discipline that prosaically investigates matters that most people believe they already understand as well as anyone does.

There are two ways of dealing with this problem. The first is to generate theories and observations that appear to be totally contradictory to the basic beliefs of a majority of the people. This is an adventurous road to follow. If taken too far, it leads, of course, to a rejection of the argument. The theorist may be imaginative, but he or she will also be considered insane or, at the very least, foolish. If not carried far enough, one risks presenting just another banal and obvious finding. The second, and safer, approach is to provide information about the behavior of people who are in some way or other outside the social knowledge of most people. The sociologist who takes this avenue in quest of novelty allows us vicariously to be a kind of peeping Tom. This approach exploits existing esoteric and exotic subcultures. We are told the secrets of lives carried on outside the realms of conventional morality. A middle-class college student, for example, is given a glimpse of what it is like to be a ghetto black.

This is commonly done in the social sciences as a whole and is not necessarily a bad thing. Whatever might be wrong with it is a consequence of bias in the types of groups selected. We have thousands of research monographs and reports on the slums and the ghettos, the indigent and the crippled, but only a few on the inside lives of the extremely powerful and wealthy. One of the most astounding revelations of recent times has been the information contained in the taped conversations between President Nixon and his aides that were made public as a result of the Watergate investigations. The social sciences are not to be faulted for studying esoteric practices, but they can be criticized for the bias displayed in who is to be studied. A truly democratic sociology would mean that any group's likelihood of being selected for study would be some kind of random function of its size or significance. At present this is not the case.

The quest for novelty through the study of esoteric behaviors, we have suggested, is common in the social sciences as a whole. Consider how anthropology handles the problem of novelty. Cultural anthropology, for example, caters to our interest in the unusual by studying and reporting the behavior of people who live in cultures remote from our own. Descriptions of the cannibal dances of the Kwakiutl tell us something different about human possibilities. Within the behavioral sciences cultural anthropology serves much the same purpose that the reflecting telescope serves in the study of physical reality. It enables us to begin to comprehend the great distances, as it were, that are involved in the range of actions and feelings of which people are capable. It serves to make us more aware of the extent to which each of us, as an individual, is subject to the caprices of the various times and places into which we are born.

Unlike cultural anthropology, sociology restricts itself largely to modern and technologically advanced societies. Much of it deals with Western culture. In sum, sociology deals with the most familiar realms of social conduct for the American student—modern Western society. Sociology is thereby handicapped at the outset. It is plagued with the problem of the extent to which it is, in a sense, bringing coals to Newcastle. That is, it has to run the risk, always, of telling people much that they already know. This handicap can be reduced, however, if the sociologist takes a leaf from the notebook of the cultural anthropologist and concentrates on subcultures that are relatively distant from the typical experiences of the people who are likely to constitute the sociologist's audience.

The "Outsiders"

The dual problems of practicality and novelty in social theory can achieve a kind of simultaneous resolution through making that which is novel in human social actions also that which should be of practical concern. So it is that we have concentrated on the insane, the criminal, the destitute, and the dissolute people of our society—the so-called "social problems." In studying the lifeways of such people we feel that we have both engaged ourselves in a study of the exotic or novel elements within our society and concerned ourselves with work of a practical nature. It is possibly a misguided notion.

So it is, then, that sociologists have moved within the wide limits set by their interests and have established as part of their subject matter the study of people who are considered to be "deviants" or "problems" for the greater society. From this perspective we have some sociologists writing descriptions of the activities of people who engage in homosexual relations in public places, and others who engage in studies of striptease artists. Much can be made of the behavior of those who are outside the ordinary routines of ordinary people—the criminal, the mentally ill, the divorced, the suicidal, the drug user, and the bitterly impoverished. Sociology is not above relying on a little sensationalism to maintain interest.

At the same time, there is more to the examination of exotic life styles than simply the pursuit of sensational information. We come to

254 the exotic life style thinking, at first, that our interest is provoked by the difference that seems to exist between "them" and "us." Further examination brings us to an understanding even more revealing. We find there is much "we" share in common with "them."

Becker[4] is part of a group of influential modern sociologists who did their advanced studies at the University of Chicago in the late forties and early fifties. These people were especially influenced by the teachings of Everett Cherrington Hughes.[5] One of the directions that Hughes gave to the study of social behavior involved the investigation of various careers. Where the cultural anthropologist examined remote and not-so-remote cultures, Hughes had his students investigate remote and not-so-remote careers—the career of the professional boxer, the career of the mortician, the career of the urban schoolteacher, and so on.

Some of the novelty of these studies came from the exotic nature of the careers being studied. However, a number of the careers, such as that of the urban elementary schoolteacher, have to be seen as prosaic. After all, virtually everyone of us, at some time or other, has had extended encounters with elementary schoolteachers. Nonetheless, it was among the contributions of Hughes and his students to reveal novel possibilities inherent in the examination of the most ordinary daily routines of ordinary people. As we shall see later, a more extreme extension of this sort of effort is being carried out today by Harold Garfinkel, who has uncovered some interesting possibilities in the most commonplace kinds of human social moments.

As we mentioned earlier, Becker did his graduate work under Hughes; for his dissertation he undertook an examination of the career of the public school teacher in Chicago.[6] The methods of research developed then, and the conception of lives as passing through "careers," were to be interwoven into the greater part of the work Becker undertook after leaving Chicago. His interests have proved to be diverse. He achieved some notoriety following the publication in 1953 of a paper based on his studies of marijuana smokers.[7] He then became involved in the activities of the Society for the Study of Social Problems. He wrote a book based on research done in a medical school[8] and another based

---

[4] The major works of Howard S. Becker include: *The Outsiders* (New York: Free Press, 1963); *Making the Grade: The Academic Side of College Life,* with Blanche Geer and Everett Hughes (New York: Wiley, 1968); *Sociological Work: Methods and Substance* (Chicago: Aldine, 1970); H. S. Becker et al., *Boys in White: Student Culture in a Medical School* (Chicago: University of Chicago Press, 1970); *Campus Power Struggle,* 2d ed. (New York: Transaction-Society Books, 1973).

[5] Hughes has been the mentor and guide of a surprisingly large number of influential modern social scientists. Becker is strong in his acknowledgement of the influence of Hughes.

[6] H. S. Becker, "Social Class Variation in the Teacher-Pupil Relationship" *Journal of Educational Sociology* 25 (1952), 451–465.

[7] H. S. Becker, "Becoming a Marihuana User," *American Journal of Sociology* 59 (1953), 235–242.

[8] Becker et al., *Boys in White.*

on research (carried out at the University of Kansas) into the careers of **255**
undergraduates as they progress through an academic setting.[9]

He has been more prolific, however, as a writer for professional
journals and as an editor. Whether it is the secretive and cultish behavior
of drug users or the mundane activities of students hustling for a grade
in an English "lit" course, there is one pervasive quality that characterizes
Becker's work—it is grounded in the constant application of intelligent
and theoretically sophisticated observation.

Becker's work offers us an opportunity to consider at some length
the difficulties we come up against when we undertake the study of what
we commonly refer to as "social problems" or of people who are looked
on as social "deviants." Like many modern sociologists, Becker's approach to deviance is sufficiently general for us to improve our understanding of both deviant and nondeviant forms of behavior. That is, what
Becker has to say about deviants applies to nondeviants as well. The
processes that generate classes of people who acquire the label "deviant" are much the same processes that generate classes of people who
are labeled "normal."

Our emphasis is on the idea of *process* or, to use another term, the
career of the normal or the nonnormal person. Becker is interested in
the ways in which people who are probably biologically or "mentally"
typical can be led into behaviors that cause them to be given the label
of deviant. The central thrust of such theorizing is to assert the claim
that deviant behavior is not the product of a deviant personality. Or, at
the very least, this perspective argues that if the personality is a product
of some kind of social relationship with others, then the entire process
must be examined.

Statistical and Medical Definitions of Deviance

To gain some idea of the extent to which Becker's thinking is different,
it is necessary to review, briefly, a few of the more common ways we are
inclined to think about deviant behavior. One of the simplest is the idea
that deviant behavior is any behavior that is unusual. This, basically, is
a statistical definition of deviant behavior. It presumes that we can arrange people according to how far they stand from some average level
of performance or character. If they are significantly above or below the
average, then they are deviant. Such an approach has the advantage of
being simple and the quite marked disadvantage of being too inclusive.
If we go by this definition, then everyone is deviant in some way. We
are either "too" tall or "too" short, "too" fat or "too" thin, "too" bright
or "too" stupid.

This, of course, produces the logical impasse of making abnormality

---

[9] H. S. Becker, Blanche Geer, and Everett Hughes, *Making the Grade: The Academic Side
of College Life* (New York: Wiley, 1968).

256 a normal condition. More seriously, it bypasses what is usually a central concern with the problem of deviance—that is, it ignores the relationship that exists between social norms or rules and the violation of those rules. When we view social deviations as problems, we generally do so because such deviations threaten the social order in some way. A man who is seven feet tall is a statistical deviant. Unless his height threatens some existing socially relevant norm, however, we are not especially concerned with his deviance. We might add the obvious observation that the relevance of context to any consideration of deviance is quickly made apparent by considering what it means to be seven feet tall when you want to join a submarine crew or a basketball team.

Another approach to deviance is to view it as something harmful or dangerous or pathological insofar as the smooth operation of the community is concerned. This is an attempt to apply a medical analogy to the social body. The deviant individual or group is something potentially or actually injurious. The deviant is somewhat akin to a cancer cell in the healthy body; if deviance is allowed to proliferate, organized maintenance of the body will eventually become impossible.

There are several serious limitations to this argument. It presumes to know what constitutes a healthy social body. Such "healthiness" is generally defined in terms of the existing or prevailing power structure. That is, the "healthy" society always manages to look very much like the status quo. Therefore, from the perspective of those who define deviance as pathology, anything that sustains the status quo is "healthy" and anything which does not is "pathological."[10] This form of defining deviant behavior obviously has social control implications. Anyone who is rocking the boat is deviant. To be deviant is to be pathological. By this procedure it is possible to confuse those who are engaged in serious political and social reform or change with those who are suffering from some real illness and are, in fact, pathological cases. As Maslow has observed, a person who did not go along with the Nazis was considered pathological by them. Obviously, if "pathological" people are in charge, then being labeled pathological by them suggests something to the contrary.

Labeling a deviant person or group pathological can generate some problems. First, it disguises the possibility that a person is being labeled pathological simply for not going along with the existing system.[11] Second, and more importantly, it tends to locate the "pathological" char-

[10] Any number of social theorists have found themselves stumbling as they attempted to provide "scientific" justifications for condemning particular kinds of social actions. Structural-functional theorists, for example, have employed the term *dysfunctional* to refer to collective actions disruptive to the maintenance of the greater social order. This presumes, of course, that one can tell when the greater social order is worth maintaining. Merton's efforts to develop such an approach are particularly interesting. See R. K. Merton, *Social Theory and Social Structure* (New York: Free Press, 1957).

[11] Psychiatry has been condemned by a number of critics on just this ground. There has been a good deal of criticism of psychiatric practice in the Soviet Union. It seems, according to the criticism, that the Russians have found it expedient to label intellectual critics of the government as people who are psychotic or pathological. It is an old game.

acter of the deviant person within himself or herself. By doing this, the person labeled pathological is made the source of culpability for his or her deviant actions.[12] There is some trickery here insofar as attention may be shifted away from the possibly pathological character of the situation in which the person was involved and turned, instead, toward the person.

A general illustration of the tricky nature of the medical analogy lies in current problems revolving around understanding the nature of paranoia. Much psychiatric thinking about paranoia has tended to focus on the individual and his or her aberrant fantasy life. Paranoia, according to this point of view, is something which comes about when individuals, for some reason unique to each, take off on a path where their imagination leads them to believe that people are out to destroy them. One writer, for example, has referred to the "pseudo-community" the paranoid person constructs in imagination and to an overwrought fantasy life. More recently, however, psychologists have found that there is a good possibility that people who are paranoid may have some reason for it. Others really may be out to get them. Or at least the paranoids' delusions of persecution may not be totally unreasonable interpretations of the situations in which they find themselves. People cannot be understood independently of the circumstances in which they are enmeshed.

A third and final (for purposes of this discussion) reason for being careful with the concept of social pathology comes out of its implicit endorsement of the "healthy" parts of the system. That is, there is always the possibility that pathological developments within a society arise out of weaknesses or deficiencies that have their origins in the apparently "nonpathological" parts of the society. The simplest illustration is to be found in the so-called "race" problem. Some of the older approaches to this "pathology" concentrated on the nature and character of black life in America. But by the close of World War II most of the attention being given to the problem had turned toward the nature of racial bigotry. The bigot was thought to be a semipathological type, and many books and articles explored the unfortunate consequences of having an "authoritarian" personality. Today neither of these approaches is adequate. The race problem is certainly not just a black problem but a white problem as well. White bigots, moreover, are not simply accidents. They are not merely occasionally pathological people. They are people who serve the interests of others who may or may not, in themselves, possess negative racial attitudes. In brief, it is just too simple to attribute the racial issue to some pathological element. In so doing we may be shifting the blame from hidden and subtle characteristics of the morally substantial elements in the community and loading it onto the backs of those who have

---

[12] It is difficult to track down collective sources of individual actions. They are lost in a complex past. Yet when things go wrong, some explanation is sought. It is not easy to make large groups or organizations culpable. Culpability must be concretized, and this is done by selecting some individual or some relatively small number of people who are to be held personally accountable for an event that cannot reasonably be accounted for in terms of the actions of any single individual or small number of individuals.

258 achieved a kind of visibility. When we do this we engage in a double irony. The victims of inhuman practices are the ones blamed for the inhumanities they must suffer. It is a galling experience.

Let us add one further comment. The medical analogy is more than misleading. It is an attempt to add to the moral stigmatization of the poor and indigent, the crazed and degenerate, the rebels and dropouts, a stigmatization that carries its authority not from the church but from the sterile—and prestigious—laboratories of medical science. Because the stigmatization of people is difficult to avoid in even the most carefully constructed descriptions of human social action, this would not be an especially damning indictment of the medical analogy as an approach to the study of human affairs. However, the more serious aspect of this form of stigmatization is that it removes from consideration the possible complicity of those who do not see themselves as pathological. It is, in brief, an arrogant perspective that hides its arrogance behind the benign appearance of medical altruism.

The Social Nature of Deviant Behavior

Neither the statistical approach nor the medical approach, then, is adequate even for defining the nature of deviant behavior. Becker turns to another point of view for dealing with so-called "social problems" or "deviant behavior." This point of view sounds disarmingly simple and reasonable at first glance. Its implications, however, lead us far afield from the directions we might take with either the statistical or medical approach to deviance. Becker opens his arguments with the following statement:

> The central fact about deviance [is that it is] created by society. I do not mean this in the way it is ordinarily understood, in which the causes of deviance are located in the social situation of the deviant or in "social factors" which prompt his action. I mean, rather, that *social groups create deviance by making the rules whose infraction constitutes deviance*, and by applying those rules to particular people and labeling them as outsiders. From this point of view, deviance is *not* a quality of the act the person commits, but rather a consequence of the application by others of rules and sanctions to an "offender." The deviant is one to whom that label has successfully been applied; deviant behavior is behavior that people so label.[13]

As we said before, there is a disarming simplicity in this. It is easy, for example, to agree with Becker that no matter what we mean by deviance, we are talking about something that violates the existing rules of the society—whatever those rules may be. When women were not "permitted" to smoke, those who engaged in such behavior risked ac-

---

[13] Becker, *The Outsiders*, pp. 8–9. Italics are Becker's.

quiring the status of deviant. This, of course, parallels present times, when anyone who participates in the use of marijuana risks acquiring the status of deviant. It makes little difference whether he or she is otherwise a good and proper citizen of the community. Participation in such action, because it is illegal, always means there is the possibility that one will be apprehended and informed that one is no longer a good and proper citizen. People can be labeled as deviants even if they are engaging in activities that are relatively common or ordinary. Those who are so labeled may constitute a small proportion of the total population engaging in the behavior that is illegal or negatively sanctioned. The large numbers of those who do not receive the label of deviant suggest that trying to see deviance exclusively in terms of personality characteristics is a misguided effort. This contention will be developed further.

So far the argument is simple. Part of understanding the nature of deviant behavior must include a consideration of those rules that are, in themselves, the defining mechanism of deviance. Understanding deviant behavior, then, calls for more than giving attention to the person who has been labeled deviant. It means that attention must also be given to an analysis and understanding of the rules that define the behavior as deviant. To do this adds complications to the examination of social problems. At the same time, it avoids the ultrasimplistic formulations of either the statistical or medical approaches. Deviant behavior, from this perspective, is seen in part as a symbolic process that always involves at least two parties—the person who is labeled and the person who has the authority or the right to invoke the label.

Even a brief consideration of the implications of Becker's arguments brings several new complications into the study of social behavior in general and the problem of deviant behavior more specifically. We cannot consider deviance simply a manifestation of some particular configuration of personality traits; it is not exclusively a psychological problem. The reason is simple. The process of labeling people deviant is not infallible. Some who have not engaged in deviance of a particular kind might be given the label,[14] while some who have engaged in such deviance might not be so labeled. In other words, the group classed as deviant is not homogeneous; this is because there are extremely difficult problems involved in the accurate and certain identification and labeling of deviants. The greatest difficulty, and the most obvious one, results from the fact that many, many people are able to disguise or hide their deviant characters. Homosexuals pass as straight. Drug users learn that they can get high and still go shopping at the supermarket, and no one notices. An unknown number of men, but probably a surprisingly large one, practices transvestism and, while dressed as women, make use of

---

[14] It recently has been shown that "normals" will be accepted as mentally ill by the members of the staff of hospitals that deal with psychological problems of this sort. Once a person is labeled with some kind of mental malfunction, it is extremely difficult to convince the staff that he or she is actually normal and should be released. See D. L. Rosenhan, "On Being Sane in Insane Places," *Science* 179 (1973), 250–258.

260 women's public restroom facilities.[15] The ability of people to disguise deviant behavior provides, at one and the same time, a part of our interest in such behavior and the nearly impossible likelihood of ever having a truly solid body of empirical knowledge that deals with the issue.

The point of the discussion, so far, is to reorient thinking about deviant behavior. Becker would like to have us change from a psychologistic view, where we are inclined to see deviance as something *within* the deviant, to a more sociological point of view, where we see deviance as something residing in a rather complex relationship between the person who is labeled deviant and the person who is doing the labeling.

If we want to control deviance, we might be able to deal with it in part by raising the question: To what extent is it necessary to label any particular pattern of behavior as deviant? That is, one way of reducing so-called "social problems" is by dismissing them as problems. From this perspective, one of the sources of social problems is the group that somehow acquires the capacity to define a situation or happening as a problem.[16]

Control Agencies

As we mentioned before, deviant behavior, considered at its most abstract and elementary level, involves *at least two components:* (1) an agency or authority that has acquired the power to define some action or condition as improper and to act in terms of that definition and (2) some event or occurrence that enables those in authority to label an individual as a deviant person.

This treatment of deviance forces us to consider some of the qualities of the agency that takes upon itself the task of defining which behaviors constitute deviance. When we do this, some otherwise inexplicable aspects of the way we deal with deviants become understandable.[17] For example, the Catholic Church, during the medieval period, took upon itself the task of defining behaviors considered "sinful." Masturbation was among those behaviors. At the same time, masturbation was (and still is) a common pastime, and today it is looked upon as something almost any healthy person enjoys on occasion. It is apparent,

---

[15] It is difficult to ascertain just how much of this behavior is carried out. Columnists who give advice on domestic problems, such as Ann Landers and Abigail Van Buren ("Dear Abby"), receive a number of letters each year in which this is mentioned. Where the husband is a transvestite, the couple often view the practice as a bit of harmless practical joking or as something almost cutely humorous.

[16] There is more here than simply a discussion of social problems. Becker is moving toward the central issue of what constitutes a social structure. One way of defining such a structure is to see it as consisting of ways of defining people so that some of us have the right to define others as "problems." We are then permitted to act in terms of that definition.

[17] Ken Kesey's novel, *One Flew over the Cuckoo's Nest*, concerns itself with correcting the common fault of seeing neurosis and insanity as being lodged in a hospital's patients, while the staff is sane and good. Kesey's depiction of "Big Nurse" suggests that the staff might be at least as mad as the people over whom it holds power.

261

without belaboring the issue too much, that such impossible ideals of virtue and proper conduct produced as much sin as they curbed. The church, being in a position to absolve sinners of their sins, found it expedient (perhaps unconsciously) to create sinners. The church then had a supply of sin with which it could concern itself. The modern analogy is the tendency in psychiatry to set up situations where it is nearly impossible for a person not to express some kind of neurotic behavior. Once the neurosis is apparent, psychiatry can step in with its services.[18] *Deviant behavior, then, can be created to maintain the agencies that exist to control the deviant behavior.*

The relationship between the defining agency and the deviant is more subtle than this, however. For example, once a pattern of deviant behavior has been defined by a controlling agency, the very existence of the behavior, now defined as deviant or bad, is threatening to that agency. On the other hand, if the deviance does not exist, that also is threatening. Or, as Becker phrases it: "Enforcement organizations . . . typically oscillate between two kinds of claims. First, they say that . . . the problem they deal with is approaching a solution. But, in the same breath, they say the problem is perhaps worse than ever . . . and requires renewed and increased effort to keep it under control."[19]

This might help account for why enforcement agencies often make much of those whom they are able to apprehend and label as deviant. The existence of the problem must be made apparent to all. The public must be kept aware that deviants are around and that enforcement agencies are on the job. Thus it comes about that the label of deviant is given considerable precedence over many others. For example, individuals who have been arrested for a crime soon find that the criminal status preempts most other considerations. They have a "record." They are criminal first and anything else second. Their status as criminal becomes a "master" status, and other statuses are subordinated to it.[20] Job applicants learn that having had psychiatric therapy in the past can give them a master status as an "unbalanced" person.[21]

---

[18] This is a fairly common pattern of behavior. We do not want psychiatrists to think we have singled them out for special abuse. Teachers, for example, sometimes operate on the principle of making students feel stupid or ignorant. The teachers are then able to provide the commodity for which they have created, as it were, a demand. During the 1972 presidential campaign, there were efforts to make certain radical groups look unusually violent by infiltrating them with agents who provoked such violence. The official establishment then could justify its existence by suppressing a condition for which it was, in part, responsible. This process is a lot like what Fritz Redl has referred to as "protective provocation." You provoke a response that will permit you to do what you intend to do.

[19] Becker, *The Outsiders*, p. 157.

[20] Becker acknowledges an indebtedness to Everett C. Hughes for the concept of "master status." See E. C. Hughes, "Dilemmas and Contradictions of Status," *American Journal of Sociology*, March 1945, pp. 353–359.

[21] Application forms for civil service jobs at the University of Colorado, for example, ask the applicant to indicate *any* psychiatric treatment received during the past *three* years. It is difficult to believe that anyone who had to indicate such treatment would not be under some handicap in getting a position.

262

We are suggesting, then, in keeping with Becker's arguments, that deviant behavior is not something that exists independently of enforcing agencies and for which such agencies came into being. Social deviation is intricately related to more general problems that elites have with regard to maintaining social order. There is more to deviant behavior than simply some kind of failure of character or some flaw in personality. Becker expresses his argument in the following way:

> When the deviant is caught, he is treated in accordance with the popular diagnosis of why he is that way, and the treatment itself may likewise produce increasing deviance. The drug addict, popularly considered to be a weak-willed individual who cannot forego the indecent pleasures afforded him by opiates, is treated repressively. He is forbidden to use drugs. Since he cannot get drugs legally, he must get them illegally. . . . Hence the treatment of the addict's deviance places him in a position where it will probably be necessary to resort to deceit and crime in order to support his habit. The behavior is a consequence of the public reaction to the deviance rather than a consequence of the inherent qualities of the deviant act.
> Put more generally, the point is that the treatment of deviants denies them the ordinary means of carrying on the routines of everyday life open to most people. Because of this denial, the deviant must of necessity develop illegitimate routines.[22]

The claim made here is not especially new. Particularly since marijuana smoking has become so common, people have been aware that the attempt to curb a social problem can possibly be more damaging than the problem itself.[23] Indeed, marijuana smoking, in and of itself, may not be a socially serious problem at all.

Deviant Behavior as a "Career"

To make some of his general ideas more specific and give them substance, we can turn to one of Becker's early studies. The publication of "Becoming a Marijuana User" helped establish Becker as a leading advocate of a more sociological approach to such behavior. The study, originally published in 1953, is now dated. However, this gives it, we believe, an added interest. Because there is much argument at present over the pros and cons of marijuana and its effects on both individuals and the community, it is informative to look at some earlier studies. To appreciate Becker's effort, we should keep in mind some awareness of the extent to which public sentiment toward marijuana smoking was less liberal at that time than it is today.

---

[22] Becker, *The Outsiders*, pp. 34–35.

[23] Timothy Leary's sentence of thirty years in prison and a $30,000 fine for possession of a half ounce of marijuana is a case in point. Of course, in Leary's trial there was more than a half ounce of marijuana involved. Leary's notoriety transcended the delinquency of possessing a small amount of marijuana. At the same time, the ability of the court to impose a sentence as severe as this for such a crime is revealing. If too much control of a social problem can become a social problem in its own right, then we are confronted with the difficult issue of what constitutes optimal control.

The value of Becker's study lies in the twist he gave to older approaches to the understanding of deviant behavior. He attacked the idea that deviant behavior of this variety is caused by some kind of personality trait or motivation. The older concern was with the question: Why would anyone do something like smoking marijuana? Popular forms of speculation in response to this question have relied heavily on the idea that people must do it because they have some kind of personality trait—for example, a need to escape or live in fantasy—which predisposes them to such forms of behavior. Becker turned this conception around.

> To put a complex argument in a few words: instead of the deviant motives leading to the deviant behavior, it is the other way around; the deviant behavior in time produces the deviant motivation. Vague impulses and desires—in this case, probably most frequently a curiosity about the kind of experience the drug will produce—are transformed into definite patterns of action through the social interpretation of a physical experience which is in itself ambiguous. Marijuana use is a function of the individual's conception of marijuana and of the uses to which it can be put, and this conception develops as the individual's experience with the drug increases.[24]

As we review this examination of marijuana smoking, we should keep in mind that Becker's paper was published in 1953. The ideas behind the paper were formulated more than a quarter of a century ago—during a time when marijuana smoking was looked on by most people, including college students, as a degenerate activity. Perhaps it is an easy matter to conclude that people who indulge in degenerate activities have degenerate characters or personalities. Becker argued, to the contrary, that personality is not an appropriate concept for the examination and understanding of marijuana smoking. Instead, what you have is something akin to the development of a "career progression" in which the individual, once he or she forms an association with others who smoke marijuana, comes to learn the techniques of smoking and otherwise ingesting marijuana. More significantly, however, the new user acquires a set of "understandings" about the drug and those who smoke it.[25] The progression of this *career*, rather than motivations or personalities, is the proper focus of concern.

As Becker found in the early fifties, marijuana smokers go through a career which, in brief outline, appears to develop in the following way:

1. They learn about the existence of the drug and have a generally interested attitude toward it—wondering how it would affect them,

---

[24] Becker, *The Outsiders*, p. 42.

[25] While this career progression is probably still typical for most persons who take up marijuana smoking, it is probably not as necessary today as it was in the fifties and earlier. Today it is possible to purchase manuals in bookstores that will provide detailed information on how to find, hide, prepare, smoke, cook, and eat marijuana. See, for example, Jack S. Margolis and Richard Clorfene, *A Child's Garden of Grass: The Official Handbook for Marijuana Users* (New York: Simon & Schuster, 1969). Current movies are also showing their audiences what it is like to use marijuana. An individual can, then, get an education in the use of marijuana without relying on close associates.

264 whether they could take it without "cracking up," and otherwise showing a general and vague interest in it.

2. Then, by happenstance, they gain access to the drug and have an opportunity to try it. This is generally done in the presence of associates and friends, who are encouraging and who are already experienced in marijuana usage.

3. They are introduced to the techniques of smoking and the differences between smoking tobacco and smoking marijuana. (If an initiate does not learn the procedures for acquiring sufficient amounts of the drug to obtain some kind of effect, he or she discontinues use.)

4. They begin to recognize the relationship between the ingestion of the drug and the effects that are a consequence of its ingestion. This is an important step in the "career" of smokers. Even if effects are produced, unless the initiates are able to associate them with smoking, they will not continue using the drug. *The initiates turn to the more experienced users and seek information concerning how they might reasonably expect to feel.* Here is an excerpt from an interview with a person who recounts his early experiences with the drug:

> I didn't get high the first time . . . I don't think I held it in long enough. I probably let it out, you know, you're a little afraid. The second time I wasn't sure, and he (smoking companion to me), like I asked him for some of the symptoms or something, how would I know, you know . . . So he told me to sit on a stool. I sat on—I think I sat on a bar stool—and he said, "Let your feet hang," and then when I got down my feet were real cold, you know.
>
> And I started feeling it, you know. That was the first time. And then about a week after that, sometime pretty close to it, I really got on. That was the first time I got on a big laughing kick, you know. Then I really knew I was on.[26]

5. With a recognition of the relationship between ingestion of the drug and physical responses, users come to interpret their reactions, finding in them something interesting to talk about—both to themselves and to others. They reach a point where they probe the nature of the effects they have experienced and become sophisticated about the character of these effects. They learn that they can appear in public when high and not be detected. They think they can drive a car safely while experiencing effects that previously seemed incapacitating.

6. In the final stages of the career, the users become connoisseurs. They are able to detect differences between lower and higher grades of marijuana. They also probably have friends who are sophisticated in the use of marijuana, and they themselves are active in introducing others to the drug and helping them become sophisticated in its use.

In this career development, the most significant feature of the process is the manner in which newcomers to the scene are given information by the more experienced practitioners of the art. They must not only

26 Becker, *The Outsiders,* p. 50.

ingest the drug but must also come to define its effects as pleasant. *They do not do this alone.*

One of the central concerns of this point of view is to develop the argument that the circumstances which lead to deviant behavior are, in their general form, much like the circumstances which lead to normal behavior. If this sort of argument can be sustained, then it tends to weaken the position that deviant people are the products of deviant motivations or deviant personality structures. Instead, it generates the idea that deviant people are much like nondeviant people in their personality and psychological characteristics. The primary difference between deviants and nondeviants lies in the career path they take, and this can be a matter of chance. Once the path is taken, deviant behavior will produce deviant motivations; it is not the other way around.

One other aspect of deviant behavior leads Becker to the conclusion that it should not be viewed from the perspective that it is the exclusive product of "warped" or abnormal personalities. He presumes, first of all, that there is a great deal of so-called deviant behavior being expressed continuously within the greater society. Whether one must go through the process of being labeled deviant and dealt with as such depends upon whether one is singled out as such a person and presented before others in this light. This is a highly capricious matter.[27] It is extremely difficult to ascertain the proportion of various offenders of conventional morality who get caught relative to all of those who engage in the offense. In the case of marijuana usage, for example, perhaps twenty million or so persons in the United States have violated the conventions. The number who are brought to public attention for this practice, however, is much smaller. Becker wryly comments, at one point, that being caught is about like being hit by lightning.[28]

This being the case, the position taken by those who seek to label the marijuana user as some kind of abnormal person possessed of a predisposing deviant nature have their argument weakened. They must, if they are to establish their point, be able to impose such qualities on relatively large and hidden populations.

Rather than turn to deviant or abnormal personalities, Becker suggests that we add a couple of new considerations to the problem of deviant behavior. We must, as was suggested earlier, consider how the rules defining deviant behavior are established. If, for example, a ruling power comes to the conclusion that being Jewish is wicked and that anyone possessed of Jewish qualities should be exterminated, we can quickly comprehend the unreasonable nature of the rule. It is unreasonable because the rule, in and of itself, condemns people most of us would be willing to accept as "normal" or "good." But the establishment

[27] Being arrested for using marijuana is often incidental to some other event. For example, newspapers commonly report happenings like this one: "Three persons were arrested . . . when . . . detectives found suspected marijuana. . . . A detective reported going to the residence to investigate a theft complaint and when the door was opened he smelled what he believed to be marijuana. He said he also saw a suspected hashish pipe in the room which was then searched." *Boulder Daily Camera*, April 11, 1972.

[28] Becker, *Sociological Work*, p. 333.

266 of rules that might actually possess abnormal or deviant qualities within themselves is not always so evident. Indeed, somehow the imposition and execution of rules generally seems reasonable.

The entire machinery of lawmaking institutions and the police agencies that enforce the laws are given a rationality or reasonability by the very fact that this machinery is supported by the state. The majority of Germans felt that the "Jewish Problem" was being handled properly in the late thirties. At the same time, the institution of rules defining deviant behavior may, in and of itself, be the source of the problems that the rules seek to curb. Or, to put it more simply, one way of reducing crime, deviance, and other such social ills is to reduce the number of rules that define such problems. One way to solve the "social problem" of homosexuality is simply to redefine it as not being a social problem.

Becker suggests, then, that an examination of the process by which various agencies come to define certain behaviors as deviant should be an integral part of the study of deviant behavior. Another feature of Becker's approach is his concern with deviance as a kind of "career," which can, like any other career, bring about changes in motivations, perceptions, attitudes, tastes, values, and other qualities of the person. Rather than conclude that one has deviant motives which lead to deviant behavior, Becker argues that the existence of the career pattern is the most significant objective fact about a given deviant action. Deviance is a sociological as well as a psychological condition. This is, perhaps, a cliché in its straightforward form; if so, it is a cliché that can lead to some subtle forms of understanding.

Conclusion

This brief essay on Becker and his work has tried to present some idea of the possibilities that exist for combining practical interests—such as deviance, social problems, and the control of such problems—with theoretical perspectives that are generally congenial to a symbolic interactionist point of view. While Becker is certainly not the only writer to carry off such a venture, his work reveals that it is possible to make good use of theories that are often viewed as being irrelevant to the concerns of those who have to deal with "real" problems.

Problems and Issues

Galileo found that people would sometimes refuse to look through his telescope to see what he had seen. They thought it was a "trick" of some kind. If Galileo had difficulties showing people the planets, what kinds of problems do sociologists encounter when they try to tell people about what they know? What right does a sociologist have, anyway, to presume to know more than anyone else about human social affairs? On a more basic level, there is the issue of how we get social information that we regard as valid. In simpler social systems such information was provided primarily through the family and one's associates. In complex societies we have moved more toward the expert and people who specialize in informing us about the social world— journalists, entertainers, teachers, psychologists, sociologists, philosophers, ministers, counselors, novelists, and a variety of other people. How do we evaluate the merits of what we are being told? Who, in other words, can we trust? How do we know we can trust them?

One social issue that concerns most people is deviant behavior. What is deviant behavior? What should we do about it when we encounter it? Why do Americans tend to associate deviant action with a deviant personality? For example, if a person steals a car for a lark, he or she is likely to be labeled a "thief." This is viewed as a quality of the self. Is such labeling explanatory or is it, rather, directed more toward problems of social control? A person once labeled as a thief is vulnerable to continued identification as such. Moreover, other people, presuming they view such a label negatively, will be influenced against behaving in a similar manner.

Becker notes that in order to have deviance, you have to have at least two people—one to engage in an action and another to label that action as deviant. This suggests that so-called "social problems" have at least two possible sources. One might lie in the activities of the group labeled deviant; the other in the activities of those doing the labeling. What are some examples from contemporary society of this observation by Becker?

We noted, in our discussion of Becker's work, that people who are "normal" or "sane" find themselves having considerable difficulty in trying to get the doctors and staff of mental institutions to release them after they had been falsely admitted as mentally ill. There was some evidence which suggests that the patients of such hospitals were more perceptive of the real condition of the "planted" fake patients than were the doctors. What are the implications of this with respect to the use of rational approaches to dealing with deviant behavior? Is it possible to establish purely rational means for dealing with deviance?

The Use of Sociology as Bad Faith

The Views Of

PETER L. BERGER

. . . one must keep a kosher kitchen if one's intellectual nourishment is not to become hopelessly polluted—that is, one must not pour the milk of subjective insight over the meat of scientific interpretation.

Invitation to Sociology

BORN: 1929

15 One of the most expressive writers in modern sociological literature was, at one time, a professor at a seminary in Connecticut. Perhaps his research and writings in the field of religious institutions made him more receptive to humanistic issues than is common among sociologists. Possibly the fact that he came here from Europe in his late teens led him to acquire a humanistic bent before going into sociology. Whatever the reason, Peter L. Berger has produced several books graced by style and dramatic quality.[1] In the work to be discussed here, Berger achieves this

---

[1] Peter Berger's major works include *Invitation to Sociology: A Humanistic Perspective* (Garden City, N.Y.: Doubleday, 1963); *The Human Shape of Work,* edited by Berger (New York: Macmillan, 1964); *The Noise of Solemn Assemblies: Christian Commitment and the Religious Establishment in America* (Garden City, N.Y.: Doubleday, 1961); *The Precarious Vision: A Sociologist Looks at Social Fictions and the Christian Faith* (Garden City, N.Y.: Doubleday, 1961); *The Sacred Canopy: Elements of a Sociological Theory of Religion* (Garden City, N.Y.: Doubleday, 1967); *The Social Construction of Reality* (Garden City, N.Y.: Doubleday, 1966); *Sociology: A Biographical Approach,* with Brigitte Berger (New York: Basic Books, 1972); and *The Homeless Mind,* with Brigitte Berger and Hansfried Kellner (New York: Random House, 1972); *Facing Up to Modernity: Excursions in Society, Politics, and Religion* (New York: Basic Books, 1977).

dramatic effect by bringing several incompatible ideas together. The **269** result is like that arising from the meeting of a cold weather front with a warm front—there is a stormy period before the air is cleared again. In his most general work, *Invitation to Sociology*, two sets of incompatible ideas are brought together. First, Berger presents us with a heavily lined sketch of what might be called classical sociological thought. He pares away most of the academic issues that float about sociology and lets us take a look at its essence; thus we have sociology stripped of those qualifications which often hide its fundamental character. Then Berger confronts us with existentialist thought—the warm front that clashes with the colder views of sociology. Both positions have legitimacy and both certainly have a large number of followers; yet the two seem to be in opposition. Sociology, for example, is analytic and deterministic; existentialism is personal and volitional. Sociology is reliant on a scientific approach to people; existentialism is more subjective and humanistic. Let us see how Berger describes the conflict between these ways of thinking by beginning with his consideration of sociology.

Traditional Sociological Thought

The traditional sociological view comes close to reducing people to the level of being victims of their society.[2] A person is simply born into society and then is controlled by it. In a sense, as Berger nicely puts it, a person is a prisoner of society. Society is the walls of our imprisonment in history.[3] And it guards us closely; even seemingly harmless acts, like growing a beard or mispronouncing a word, are apt to bring ridicule or some other form of social constraint.

Society is an external force, as coercive and constraining as the physical and biological environments with which we have to cope. Moreover, society is internal as well as external. Not only are people within society; society is within people. The very ways one comes to see oneself, the daydreams one has, the aspirations and longings that come to dominate one's thoughts, are not random or independent of society. They are subjective social actions that parallel the larger society. Thus one might daydream of military exploits as a jet pilot, or of intellectual attainments as a writer, or of business successes as an industrialist—or one might dream of murder.[4] Even so, the form of the daydream—distorted by the individual's ignorance and desires—will conform generally to the model provided by the society. It is in this sense, then, that Berger makes his first point. The sociological view of people reveals

[2] An academic and well-developed criticism of this point of view can be found in the article "The Oversocialized Conception of Man in Modern Sociology" by Dennis H. Wrong, which appeared in *American Sociological Review* 26 (April 1961), 183–193.

[3] Berger, *Invitation to Sociology*, p. 92. This is Berger's expression.

[4] It might seem, from one point of view, that dreams of murder are antisocial. Yet, in a sense, they follow a model provided by society. Though we disagree with many of his particulars, Dr. Frederic Wertham is correct in general as he develops this theme in both *Seduction of the Innocent* (New York: Holt, Rinehart and Winston, 1954) and *A Sign for Cain* (New York: Macmillan, 1966).

270　them as victims of their society. They are controlled by it from without and from within.

Let us examine this matter of social control in a little more detail. We have to get a better sense of the extent to which the sociological "cold front" is in fact "cold."

A person is born into a social system and eventually is coerced, in various ways, into meeting its demands. Some idea of what is taking place might be obtained by imagining human bodies as a form of money that must be distributed and allocated throughout a banking system. Some money must go into certain kinds of activities and other money must go into yet other kinds of activities. But it is the banking system which does the allocation. In the case of actual money and banking systems, we are dealing with an inanimate element, money, which goes wherever it is directed; the problems of allocation are not disturbed by any presumptions that might exist within the money itself.

But in society the problem is different. When we are allocating human beings to different activities, we find ourselves working with a more truculent and complex agent in the process of distribution. Yet the problem of allocation is there, and if society is to retain its integrity as a system, the means of allocation must be efficient enough to protect the system from disruption by the irritable qualities of human beings themselves. The problem, in brief, is to make certain, within limits, that people do what they are told.

Social Control

In order to achieve reasonable certainty that people will, in fact, do what they are told, society has a variety of devices at hand. The range and character of these devices impress upon us the extent to which we are subject to control from others. Furthermore, as Berger notes, the control that comes from others has at the same time an effectiveness and yet a remoteness that can induce a feeling of helplessness on the part of an individual. For example, lower-class people talk about having to do things the way an impersonal "they" want them done. Blacks refer to being exploited by "the man." One's history on this planet is not only narrowly circumscribed by the social milieu into which one is born, but most of that milieu is composed of strangers—people one has never met and never will. Even though the demands may come from distant (and usually long dead) strangers, the devices society uses for controlling people are sufficient to see that the demands are met. What are these devices?

The most common and most fundamental device is a reliance on violence. People are kept in their place by either a threat of injury to their physical beings or an actual act of violence. No matter how sophisticated a society may be, it nonetheless shares with the most primitive a reliance on this form of social control. The police officials of a modern state are unique within the general population insofar as they have the legitimate right to engage in violence—to use physical force to bring order and stability into the community. The resort to violence to ensure control is simple and generally effective. But it is not, of itself, sufficient; it is not the only device upon which a society must rely.

The threat of violence is the demand that the individual conform or suffer. But there are times when the individual would rather suffer any form of physical injury than conform. For example, Sir Thomas More elected to have his head cut off before he would concede to the authority of his king. The Romans fed many a Christian to the lion, but they could not kill Christianity. Men and women have gone to the stake and the scaffold. They have stood smiling in front of firing squads. They have taken themselves and their families into confrontations with spitting mobs. They have been tortured with the thin edge of the razor. Yet, despite these physical horrors, they have kept their integrity. They have not conceded to the demand. They have not sold out when the ultimate pressure was brought to bear.

For this reason, violence is insufficient as a control device. There is yet another reason. Violence, for all its dramatic simplicity, does not control the individual other than by the most outward manifestations. People who are forced to do something or else suffer a bash in the nose may do it, but their attitude toward the whole procedure will likely be one of scheming to find ways to escape. When the Union, through military power, defeated the Confederate states, it was able to dictate its terms. But a military defeat does not always mean a defeat of spirit. The South, even today, still manages to retain many of the sentiments and culturally prescribed ways of behaving that existed long before the Civil War.

Violence may be necessary, but it is extremely limited as a social control device. It produces a minimal outward conformity, but at the price of generating hatred toward the conformity-inducing agent. It would be better to achieve conformity and, at the same time, have the conforming individual love the coercion to which he or she is being subjected. If necessary, one can always physically threaten a potential nonconformist. However, it is better to win that person's loyalty. Then he or she conforms and, at the same time, brags about it.

Society can win a person's loyalty by means of a second device it has to achieve control. This device consists of controlling an individual's beliefs. At birth a person is perfectly vulnerable with respect to what he or she can believe. This fact provides the community with an opportunity to use belief as a means of controlling individuals and seeing to it that they fit into their place. Most significantly they will fit into their place because they believe it is a true and proper place.

A good example of the relationship between belief systems and social control appears in Malcom X's autobiography.[5] Malcolm X was a leading spokesman for black pride in the 1960s. He was assassinated in 1965. In his autobiography Malcolm X describes his experience when he received his first "conk." Conking is a process whereby a black person's kinky hair is straightened to look more like the hair of a white person.

[5] Malcolm X, with the assistance of Alex Haley, *The Autobiography of Malcolm X* (New York: Grove, 1964), p. 55.

272   What is important to note here is that black persons who conk their hair believe straight hair is better. Conking is, then, just one way of acknowledging the natural superiority of whites. Malcolm X describes his experience:

> My first view in the mirror blotted out the hurting. I'd seen some pretty conks, but when it's the first time, on your *own* head, the transformation, after the lifetime of kinks, is staggering.
> The mirror reflected Shorty behind me. We both were grinning and sweating. And on top of my head was this thick, smooth sheen of shining red hair—real red—as straight as any white man's.
> How ridiculous I was! Stupid enough to stand there simply lost in admiration of my hair now looking "white," reflected in the mirror in Shorty's room. I vowed that I'd never again be without a conk, and I never was for many years.
> This was my first really big step toward self-degradation: when I endured all of that pain, literally burning my flesh to have it look like a white man's hair. I had joined that multitude of Negro men and women in America who are brainwashed into believing that the black people are "inferior"—and white people "superior"—that they will even violate and mutilate their God-created bodies to try to look "pretty" by white standards.[6]

Malcolm X was influenced by belief. He later came to believe differently, and at that point he became more truculent toward white domination. His description of conking reveals how far the white belief system was able, at one time in his life, to induce conformity to its ideals.

To the threat of violence and control by belief we can add a third device available to society—ridicule. Ridicule is essentially a veiled threat to withdraw affection. For example, one teenager might say to another, "If you don't take that turn at eighty-five, you're chicken." The threat of ridicule exists, then, if the taunted person does not respond. This is a common enough way to control the behavior of another person. The surprising thing is that such a taunt works. Logically, ridicule of this sort is saying, "If you don't take the turn at eighty-five, we will place you in the class 'chicken.' We do not like people who fall in the class 'chicken.' Therefore, if you don't take the turn, we won't like you any more." Ridicule is, therefore, an indirect assertion of possible dislike or disaffection—but the indirection of the statement seems to make it more effective. In any event, ridicule is an effective means for controlling behavior. We might add here that Japanese parents use it as a means of curbing their children by cautioning them with the admonition, "People will laugh at you."

A fourth, and very common, device is the use of fraud. If you cannot force or persuade or ridicule people into conforming, you can sometimes trick them.[7] The following illustration of the effectiveness of fraud took place during World War II in North Africa. Allied interrogation officers wanted to determine the identity of some new German divisions

---

[6] Ibid., p. 54.
[7] The pervasive use of fraud in everyday life as a means of gaining control over others is the basis of much of Erving Goffman's approach to human social conduct.

that had just entered the North African campaign. The use of force against captured German soldiers had not been effective. Finally, one interrogation officer suggested that the German prisoners be taken outside into a compound. He then had a variety of numbers put up on stands in an assembly building. After setting up the situation, he told the guards to march the prisoners into the building on the double—with the order the prisoners were to line up by their division numbers. The prisoners were then rushed rapidly into the assembly hall, and, as the interrogation officers watched, some prisoners ran over to and stood beside some new division numbers. What force had been unable to extract, cunning had.[8] Again, the point is that fraud exists as a device enabling control to be maintained over others. The German prisoners had tried to avoid giving information to the enemy; nonetheless they were coerced into behavior that went contrary to their individual preference or choice.

A fifth device used by society to achieve compliance is the threat of ostracism. Ostracism includes elements of physical violence or injury and elements of ridicule. Yet it is sufficiently different to warrant separate consideration. Ostracism says, in effect, that if you do not "shape up" and do what you are told, you will be asked to remove yourself from the group.[9] This social control device is very popular at universities. A student is not subjected to physical violence nor is he or she especially ridiculed or tricked into doing what is required by the school. The primary social control mechanism is ostracism; if you do not study and do what your teachers ask of you, you will be asked to leave the organization. As a matter of fact, you will be *required* to leave it. This threat is usually sufficient to maintain at least a semblance of order.

A sixth device for promoting conformity is occupational control. If one does not behave as one should, there are ways of seeing to it that the better jobs are somehow made unavailable. An interesting manifestation of this appears in the following quotation from the *Congressional Record*. In this quotation we witness an attempt to control religious belief by using occupational controls.

> Mr. Ashbrook (R.-Ohio): Mr. Chairman, I offer an amendment [to the Civil Rights Bill]: " . . . it shall not be an unlawful employment practice for

[8] We cannot vouch for the particulars of this illustrative anecdote. It came from a naval intelligence officer several years ago. We like the story because it illustrates, as well as any we know, the place fraud can have in controlling behavior.

[9] In earlier times, ostracism could be an occasion for a ceremonious pronunciamento. An example is the excommunication order of Spinoza, which read, in part: "We order that nobody should communicate with him orally, or show him any favor, or stay with him under the same roof, or within four ells of him, or read anything composed or written by him." This statement also demanded that Spinoza "should be cursed by day and night, lying down and rising up, going out and coming in."

The above accounting of the excommunication statement appears in *Heroes and Heretics* by Barrows Dunham (New York: Knopf, 1964), p. 335. Spinoza was excommunicated for suggesting in the seventeenth century that the origins of religious doctrine were located in human historical processes rather than in divine miracles. When we ostracize people today we make less show of it, perhaps, but it is still an effective social control device.

an employer to refuse to hire and employ any person because of said person's atheistic practices and beliefs."

Mr. Elliot (D.-Ala.): We leave the right of an atheist to believe, or not to believe, as may be his choice. All this amendment does is preserve for the American employer a freedom to insist that his employees be under God.

Mr. Jones (D.-Mo.): It would be interesting to see how many people are going to stand up here and be counted, and say they feel an employer is compelled to give consideration to the hiring of an atheist, when he is trying to run a business that is based on good moral grounds.

Mr. Wickersham (D.-Okla.): You might even require the churches and lodges, clubs and businessmen and Congressmen to hire atheists unless this amendment is accepted.

The question was taken, and on a division demanded by Mr. Celler, there were—ayes 137, noes 98.[10]

It seems, from the above discussion, that religious freedom extends only so far as the right to believe in some religion or other—it does not extend all the way to having the freedom to believe atheistically. The amendment considered in this debate is interesting because it permits the discussants to feel they are permitting freedom ("the right to believe . . . as may be his choice") while, at the same time, invoking a possible penalty if the individual is so naive as to tell a Christian or Jewish employer that he or she is an atheist. So occupational control is another device available for inducing conformity and compliance from people who might otherwise behave "badly."

A seventh device referred to by Berger in his discussion of the force that society can bring to bear on the individual is control coming from the "sphere-of-intimates." This is a subtle but effective form of control. Studies of soldiers in combat have revealed that the ordinary soldier is not motivated to fight by lofty political ideals and moral philosophy. He fights because his buddies are fighting. Another illustration of what Berger means by influence coming from the "sphere-of-intimates" is suggested in the following passage from Vance Packard's *The Hidden Persuaders*:

> A young New York ad man taking a marketing class . . . made the casual statement that, thanks to TV, most children were learning to sing beer and other commercials before they learned to sing the Star-Spangled Banner. Youth Research Institute, according to *The Nation*, boasted that even five-year-olds sing beer commercials "over and over again with gusto." It pointed out that moppets not only sing the merits of advertised products but do it with the vigor displayed by the most raptly enthusiastic announcers, and do it all day long "at no extra cost to the advertiser."[11]

[10] A fuller treatment of this debate appears in the February 8, 1964, issue of the *Congressional Record*. Although much of the *Congressional Record* is not exciting reading, there are more than occasional passages which surpass *Alice in Wonderland* when it comes to whimsy and fantasy. We are indebted to *The Realist*, a somewhat obscure but free-swinging paper, for bringing this debate to our attention.

[11] Vance Packard, *The Hidden Persuaders* (New York: David McKay, 1957), p. 159.

Finally, there is an eighth way in which the behavior of the individual is directed and controlled by others—through systems of mutual obligation. This is essentially a contractual variety of relationship that states, either explicitly or implicitly, "If you do such and such, then I shall do so and so." The point here is that once the contract is entered, the behavior of the individual becomes controlled by it. Even when a person may prefer a different course of action, he or she can still be coerced into conforming through the stipulations of reciprocal contractual agreements. For example, many of the letters addressed to Ann Landers and Dear Abby have to do with some problem arising from a reciprocal obligation that has gone sour. The following example is possibly too obvious a case in point,

> Dear Abby: Please help me. I'm in terrible trouble and I'm just sick about it. Yesterday a salesman came to my door, showed me his product and, before I knew it, I had signed a contract to buy it. I have two years to pay, but now I'm afraid to tell my husband about the monthly installments.
>
> I don't know what got into me, Abby. I really don't need that product and we certainly can't afford it at this time.
>
> Is there any way I can get out of it now? I would appreciate any help you can give me.

> SIGNED WITHOUT THINKING[12]

Society has, then, at least these eight devices for assuring itself that any given individual will not step very far out of line. So when Berger says a person is the prisoner of society, he identifies the bars of the prison: threats of violence, belief systems, ridicule, fraud and deception, threat of ostracism, occupational controls, the influence of intimates, and reciprocal obligations. These are effective constraints and most people are kept in line by them. But they still do not exhaust the extent to which a person is "held" by society. We must not only see the person in society; we must become aware of the extent to which society is in the person.

Social Identity

Society enters a person by providing him or her with an identity. Identity is related to the social class into which one is born; more specifically, it is related to the social roles one is required to play as a member of the social system. Berger phrases it succinctly:

> This significance of role theory could be summarized by saying that, in a sociological perspective, identity is socially bestowed, socially sustained and socially transformed. The example of [a] man in process of becoming an officer may suffice to illustrate the way in which identities are bestowed in adult life. However, even roles that are much more fundamentally part

---

[12] The quotation was taken from a recent column of "Dear Abby."

276

of what psychologists would call our personality than those associated with a particular adult activity are bestowed in very similar manner through a social process. This has been demonstrated over and over again in studies of so-called socialization—the process by which a child learns to be a participant member of society.[13]

The belief system into which children are born has, in addition to providing them with ideas about the world around them, the special capacity of providing them with certain notions about themselves. It is in this sense that society can enter a person's character and thereby "victimize" that person. Certain conceptions that people acquire about themselves are relatively enduring. Beliefs related to major organizational elements of a society are especially connected to concepts of self. For example, in India caste has been a central organizational feature of Indian society. It is essential that people born into the different subcaste levels acquire beliefs about themselves that permit the caste system to operate relatively smoothly. In order that a member of a depressed caste will in fact feel inferior and unworthy, the caste system has imposed the following restraints on lower-caste persons, requiring that they—

1. cannot be served by clean Brahmins;
2. cannot be served by barbers, tailors, and the like who serve caste Hindus;
3. may pollute those with whom they come in contact;
4. cannot serve water to caste Hindus;
5. cannot use public conveniences such as ferries, wells, or schools;
6. may not enter Hindu temples;
7. must engage in a despised occupation.[14]

After being worked over in this fashion, it is not surprising that individuals, as they mature, take on an identity that fits them into the caste system. They accept the allocated slot—no matter how wretched that slot might be.

It is, however, an oversimplification to see society as a static structure with various positions to be filled and people placed in these slots to remain there throughout their lives. Two complicating factors have to be taken into account. In the first place, positions that once were functional in a society may lose their meaning or value. Thus, with the advent of the automobile, a person trained as a blacksmith had to change his character. In the second place, it is generally necessary for a person growing up to make some modifications in social position. After all, one cannot be treated like a child all one's life. These two simple qualifications require consideration of the problem of identity changes. Berger

[13] From Berger, *Invitation to Sociology*, pp. 98–99.
[14] Kingsley Davis, *Human Society* (New York: Macmillan, 1949), p. 380. We are aware, of course, that India is at present concerned with doing away with such caste constraints. But India, like the United States, finds the process of removing the inequities and inhumanities of caste a slow and troublesome one.

refers to more pervasive and durable forms of identity change as *alternation*. Thus, a student who comes to college with strong religious faith as an integral part of his or her identity and then becomes an atheist in the senior year has undergone alternation.

Alternation and Lack of Character

Alternation can be a relatively gentle process or an extremely violent one—depending on the extent to which the individual must be protected from further alternations. For example, if it is necessary to create a definite cleavage between a boy and his mother when the boy reaches adulthood, a society is likely to achieve this through rigorous and painful tests of manliness. Any future alternation away from a manly identity is made less probable by such tests. Where alternation is not as much of a problem, initiation rites are less severe. Alternation suggests that social identity is subject to change. A person can be one thing at one time and something else at another. Berger is more descriptive—he uses the term "lack of character" to refer to this feature of human behavior.

People lack character insofar as they are able to undergo changes in identity. The pacifistic civilian can be transformed into a bayonet-wielding marine. In an example used by Berger:

> The Nazi concentration-camp commander who writes sentimental letters to his children is but an extreme case of something that occurs in society all the time.[15]

Or, for a further example, consider the subtle lack of character described by W. B. Cameron, who observed jazz musicians engaging in jam sessions that had the purpose of purifying the musicians after they had contaminated themselves by playing "good" music before a square audience.[16]

For the sociologist, lack of character is not a cause for a diatribe on hypocrisy. It is, rather, a cause for emphasizing more fully the social character of self. If lack of character is typical, and observation seems to support this view, then to whatever extent character exists, it is implanted there by the social performance required of the person. Identity, self, and character are sustained by social demands and cannot exist independently of such demands. Thus, jazz musicians who play before "square" audiences feel themselves possessed of a corrupt character which later must be washed away by a ritualistic musical performance. Or we find the sadistic Nazi storm trooper being brutal in one context and gentle in another.

These are not insincere or hypocritical performances. When Berger says people suffer from a lack of character he does not mean they are

---

[15] Berger, *Invitation to Sociology*, pp. 108–109.
[16] William Bruce Cameron, "Sociological Notes on the Jam Session" *Social Forces* 33 (December 1954), 178.

278 entirely without character of any kind. He means, instead, that the characters people possess are highly responsive to the social situation in which they find themselves. It can vary considerably from setting to setting, and yet the individuals can retain a sense of sincerity in their actions.

> That is why insincerity is rather a rare phenomenon. Most people are sincere, because this is the easiest course to take psychologically. That is, they believe in their own act, conveniently forget the act that preceded it, and happily go through life in the conviction of being responsible in all its demands. Sincerity is the consciousness of the man who is taken in by his own act. Or as it has been put by David Riesman, the sincere man is the one who believes in his own propaganda.[17]

The individual responds, then, to group opinions and can, within certain latitudes, adhere to contradictory identities and behave accordingly. What an individual "really is" amounts, in the final accounting, to an enumeration of the situations in which he is one thing and those in which he is another.[18]

The fact that people lack character means they are susceptible to identities imposed on them by others. The illustrations just given are concerned with making the point that social identities do in fact have a social locus because they are subject to change. If, for example, the Nazi were cruel in all circumstances, we would have some reason to suspect that his character reflects a genetic or inborn quality. However, because he is gentle toward some and cruel toward others, submissive to his superiors and belligerently domineering toward his inferiors, we can conclude his character is actually quite variable—responding to the demands made by particular social occasions and relationships. We lack the ability to give meaning to ourselves in isolation from others. Others provide us with an identity, and we have little recourse but to respond accordingly. This identity, furthermore, has a "real" quality. A woman who, as a result of an indiscreet love affair, finds others referring to her as a "slut" and a "tramp" might find the alternation being demanded of her impossible. She might react by becoming depressed or perhaps even going so far as to attempt suicide. Thus, the identity problem is sufficiently intense or real to produce behavior that can run contrary to the naturally grounded demands of biological survival.

The Mechanical Conception of People

Let us now pause for a moment and pull a few ideas together. Berger first attempts to overwhelm us with an extreme statement of what sociological determinism means. It means, in a metaphorical way, that we are the prisoners of society. Society has and uses a variety of devices to

---

[17] Berger, *Invitation to Sociology*, p. 109.
[18] The phrasing here is Berger's.

make certain we remain in line. The devices are generally successful because, by and large, people do conform. Look around you. In their public appearances, at least, people show a surprising "standardization." They talk alike, they dress much alike, and they generally keep out of trouble. Berger indicates why. Nonconformity is socially disruptive and will invoke controls over the individual. If one becomes too recalcitrant, one will be removed from the picture—sent either to an asylum or to eternity.

So, people are prisoners of their society. But this is not all—they are willing prisoners. They come to want what society wants them to want. They are not only controlled by external forms of coercion; they are controlled by internal coercion that takes the form of social identity. A person is granted a certain identity and comes to view the self accordingly. Eventually the person attempts to respond as he or she believes someone who has such a character ought to respond.

We now have some idea of the extent to which sociology presents a cold and mechanical conception of people. Whatever we are, we are by virtue of the fact that we exist within a greater social structure. Our character and our fate are determined by where we happen to be born within that structure. All else is irrelevant to the sociological quest.

A Discussion of Freedom

Overdrawn as this picture is, there is much truth in it. Still, it is a disturbing kind of truth, and we find ourselves longing for alternatives that might yet allow us to view ourselves as creatures with heroic qualities. We want to think of ourselves as more than pawns or agents of social force. Berger examines a possible alternative by entering into a discussion of freedom. To what extent can people break free from the constraints of society and still survive as individuals? What means are available to a person for finding freedom and individuality?

We can begin by considering a characteristic of the mechanical conception of sociology outlined in the previous pages; in at least one respect it bears a striking resemblance to instinct theory. Behavior in an ant is channeled by instincts; in a person it is channeled by institutional directives. Both the ant and the person behave because of coercion. The only difference, it would seem, is that the coercion to which the ant is subjected comes from "inside"; that to which a person is subjected comes from "outside." The ant responds to instinct; the person responds according to social character.

So, both the ant and the person, when asked why they behave as they do, might respond, "Because I must." However, such a reply is perfectly correct only in the ant's case. People more often deceive themselves when they say, "Because I must." We employ the phrase, "I must!" to hide from ourselves the fearful thought that it might be otherwise—the thought that we have elected to behave the way we are behaving. We may be only pretending something is necessary when, in fact, it is not. Jean-Paul Sartre refers to this as "bad faith." Berger de-

280 scribes it in the following way:

> To put it very simply, "bad faith" is to pretend something is necessary that in fact is voluntary. "Bad faith" is thus a flight from freedom, a dishonest evasion of the "agony of choice." "Bad faith" expresses itself in innumerable human situations from the most commonplace to the most catastrophic. The waiter shuffling through his appointed rounds in a café is in "bad faith" insofar as he pretends to himself that the waiter role constitutes his real existence, that, if only for the hours he is hired, he *is* the waiter. . . . The terrorist who kills and excuses himself by saying that he had no choice because the party ordered him to kill is in "bad faith," because he pretends that his existence is necessarily linked with the party, while in fact this linkage is the consequence of his own choice. It can easily be seen that "bad faith" covers society like a film of lies. The very possibility of "bad faith," however, shows us the reality of freedom. Man can be in "bad faith" only because he is free and does not wish to face his freedom. "Bad faith" is the shadow of human liberty. Its attempt to escape that liberty is doomed to defeat. For as Sartre has famously put it, we are "condemned to freedom."[19]

With this statement Berger has seemingly reversed himself and, by doing so, has thrown everything into a state of confusion. Until now Berger has spent a great deal of effort confronting us with a sociological conception of humanity that finds people "locked" in society. Now he turns around and tells us that Sartre is correct when he says that we are "condemned to freedom." What is going on? If we stay with Berger a little longer, we will find he is not expressing ideas that conflict with each other as much as it may seem at first. The existentialist position of Sartre can, if we think about it more carefully, mesh with the arguments and perspectives of the sociologist. For the moment, let us return to a further consideration of the existentialist position.

> Sartre has given us a masterful vista of the operation of "bad faith" at its most malevolent in his portrayal of the anti-Semite as a human type. The anti-Semite is the man who frantically identifies himself with mythological entities ("nation," "race," "*Volk*") and in doing so seeks to divest himself of the knowledge of his own freedom. Anti-Semitism (or, we might add, any other form of racism or fanatical nationalism) is "bad faith" *par excellence* because it identifies men in their human totality with their social character. Humanity itself becomes a facticity devoid of freedom. One then loves, hates and kills within a mythological world in which all men *are* their social designation, as the SS man *is* what his insignia say and the Jew *is* the symbol of despicability sewn on his concentration camp uniform.[20]

Society has imprisoned people. But it has been able to do this only when people have permitted the deceptions foisted on them by society to have the status of reality. What Berger is suggesting, as a sociologist, is that people are kept prisoner by society only to the extent to which

---

[19] Berger, *Invitation to Sociology*, p. 143.
[20] Ibid., p. 144.

they permit themselves to remain ignorant of its influence. With knowledge and understanding of the way society operates, people can begin to free themselves of its controls. They can begin to comprehend the extent to which choice is available. We can play various social roles knowingly or blindly. When we play them blindly, we are the victims of society. When we play them knowingly, society becomes the medium through which we express our volition.[21]

This conception of freedom suggests that social knowledgeability is a means toward attaining personal freedom. Social awareness prevents us from being "duped" or overwhelmed by the social fictions surrounding us. It would then seem reasonable to conclude that sociology—one way of obtaining a more sophisticated understanding of social reality—would be a certain route to the attainment of greater freedom. Unfortunately, it is not possible to make such claims for sociology. Sociology can be used as an academic justification for existing inhumanities or it can be an approach to a morally critical understanding of our injuries to each other. There is nothing within sociology itself that dictates the use to which it might be put. Berger states the problem:

> Sociological understanding itself can become a vehicle of "bad faith." This occurs when such understanding becomes an alibi for responsibility. . . . For example, a sociologist located in the South may start out with strong, personal values that repudiate the Southern racial system and he may seek to express these values by some form of social or political action. But then, after a while, he becomes an expert, *qua* sociologist, in racial matters. He now really feels that he understands the system. At this point, it may be observed in some cases, a different stance is adopted *vis-à-vis* the moral problems—that of the coolly scientific commentator. The sociologist now regards his act of understanding as constituting the sum total of his relationship to the phenomenon and as releasing him from any of those acts that would engage him personally.[22]

Berger is aware that the socially responsible use of sociology is not easy to describe. The cool and dispassionate scientist, described in the above paragraph, can be exemplifying bad faith or he can be acting on very sound moral principles. Whether it is bad faith or morally responsible action must rest, in the final analysis, on the sociologist's careful evaluation of whether, by maintaining a coolly analytical point of view, he is working toward the attainment of humanistic ends. There is always the possibility that the detached objectivity of the sociologist has become a way of appearing to be interested, when in fact, objectivity and sociology have been allowed to operate in lieu of personal commitment.

---

[21] This idea appears in Richard Kim's taut novel *The Martyred*. Kim contrasts two Christian ministers. One believes in the validity of his God and, in the final moments before he is executed by a Communist firing squad, abandons his faith and his God. The second does not believe, but finds in his role as a minister a way of bringing aid and assistance to a suffering humanity. See Richard Kim, *The Martyred* (New York: Braziller, 1964).

[22] Berger, *Invitation to Sociology*, pp. 153–154.

282   *Sociology as a Humanizing Endeavor*

In his final evaluation of sociology, Berger finds it to be a humanizing endeavor, although, of course, it is not necessarily such—sociologists can promote inhuman or dehumanizing efforts as well as humanizing ones. It depends, totally, on the manner in which sociology is to be used. As Berger puts it, it is not easy to find a humanistic dimension in research that is trying to find the optimum crew composition of a bomber or seeking ways to entice a somnambulant consumer into buying a particular breakfast cereal.[23] Even so, the typical or general effect of sociological sophistication is to bring about a more humanistic sense. The kinds of understanding that sociologists have brought to matters like the social meaning of race, sexual conduct, and capital punishment have had liberating moral implications. Studies by criminologists, for example, that have shown there is no relationship between capital punishment and indulgence in crime have torn at the fiction that stipulates that capital punishment is necessary. If we retain capital punishment, we do so now more from choice than from necessity.

The important thing Berger gets at, however, is a recognition of the fact that sociology is not *necessarily* morally liberating. A sociological understanding of the race problem can result in profound comprehension of why, for example, the American black has been held in bondage for centuries. Berger is well aware, as we have already seen, that such comprehensive understanding can produce a feeling of acceptance—it is simply the way things are. The powerful and grinding interplay of vested interests, ingrained social beliefs and fictions, the processes of intergroup conflict and struggle, social differentiation, role demands, and the needs of a greater social system can, as one begins to comprehend them, generate the attitude that it is only *natural* some people must suffer in any social system.

If a sociologist or a student of human behavior gets no further than this, then he or she is likely, in a very real sense, to employ sociology as a form of bad faith. Existing inhumanities are justified in scientific terms and there is nothing we can do to correct them. We can lecture about them, or we can research them, or we can write books about them; but when it comes to improving someone's lot, there is nothing to do but stand aside and assume the cool and quite patronizing attitude of the dispassionate observer. Berger, of course, does not endorse this attitude, and he is willing to go considerably outside the limits of formal sociological scholarship to find a way of avoiding sociology as bad faith. It is for this reason he touches on existentialist philosophy. The sociologist must not become the apologist for the existing system. He or she must not be the Western equivalent of the articulate and educated Indian who says that the caste system is good because it permits the maximum amount of social differentiation with the minimum amount of friction.

Sociology and existentialism seem so fundamentally different in character that we need to attempt some kind of resolution of these

---

[23] Ibid., p. 169.

differences before bringing this chapter to a close. A partial resolution, at least, can be achieved by comprehending the differences in what each approach seeks to achieve. Sociology is analytical. Essentially it takes events after they have occurred and asks the question, "Why?" Once an event has occurred it is really quite foolish to rely on concepts like *choice* or *freedom* or *volition* as ways of bringing understanding to the matter. If a race riot has torn apart a Los Angeles black ghetto, then it gets us nowhere to say, "They did it because they chose to." After Adolph Eichmann had sent hundreds of thousands of people to their deaths in gas chambers, it would have been quite ridiculous to say he was expressing his volition. We now know that. He did what he decided to do, and we know he decided to do it because he did it. This gets us nowhere at all. We still want to know why he chose this particular course of action over alternative courses of action that confronted him.

In response, historians and sociologists might point to such conditions or influences as the cultural reaction of Germany as a nation to the insulting demands of the Versailles Treaty, the charismatic qualities of Hitler, or the ability of the Nazis to dominate the military—but less brutal—Junker class. Psychologists might concentrate on the personal life of Eichmann, his relationship toward his Jewish friends, and his own fears and anxieties. So it continues, and out of the past comes at least a partial understanding of people's inhumanity to other people.

If concepts like *choice* and *freedom* are useless within a sociological context, how do they acquire validity within an existentialist context? Existentialism is able to maintain a validity of its own when it uses terms like *choice* and *freedom* because it is concerned with getting people to recognize that before an event occurs one does have choice. There is a place in the mental realm of human beings which cannot be touched by science or analysis—and this place is the subjective anticipation that occurs prior to taking a course of action.

The point is that, prior to acting, the individual is free to behave in a contrary fashion. There is still available the possibility of conducting oneself in a fashion that a psychologist or sociologist would not have anticipated. Existentialist thought tries to make the individual face up to the possibility of choice in life. Existentialism attempts to turn the individual toward the coming moment rather than the past determinant. Existentialism attempts to reconstruct a philosophy of individual responsibility. Above all, existentialism, as Berger is concerned with it, attempts to bring us to an awareness that inhumanity cannot be rationalized. When we impose suffering and misery on others, we do so through choice—not through necessity. After the fact, perhaps, we can explain away what has been done. But before the fact, we have chosen our course of action.

A trivial, but common enough, example may help clarify some aspects of this discussion. Teachers who isolate themselves from students, who curtly dismiss those in trouble as "stupid" and "worthless," and who take pride in the high percentage of failures in their classes are behaving in an inhuman fashion. They may rationalize their behavior by pointing to the necessity to do research. The point is, however, that they

284 have chosen from several alternatives the one which they find self-gratifying. There was no necessity. The dehumanizing use of epithets like *stupid* and *worthless* may be a device protecting the teacher from the moral sense of conscience this decision implies. "They" are stupid; "I" am wise. "They" are wrong; "I" am right. It is this kind of attitude that the existentialist fights, forcing the individual to see such conceptions of others as a matter of choice and personal responsibility. Sociology also fights such an attitude, but from another vantage point. The analysis of the past reveals, time after time, the social fictions that caught people up and led them into frightfully inhuman acts. And so sociology and existentialism may have a meeting place after all.

Sociology, by emphasizing the "fictional" nature of much social behavior, provides the basis for seeing human behavior as a "construction." It is not something immutably determined by "human nature" or our genes. The hope exists that, with greater knowledge, human beings can create social systems that offer greater opportunity for the full expression of human life and consciousness. We can modify the set of fictions that surround us and bind us. But to do so, we must sense the possibility of escape. It is this sense of possibility that existentialist thought offers. Sociology provides the blueprints and plans that show the structure of the prison that contain us. Existentialism presents the possibility, indeed the moral necessity, of an escape into something better.

Sociologists like Peter Berger add a further dimension to sociology. In their hands it becomes not only an instrument for analysis; it takes its place between science and the humanities. It becomes a further means of developing a humanistic perspective. Peter Berger is not willing to let the sociologist say, "Sociology for the sake of sociology." Unless sociology is used for humanity's sake, it is worse than an empty effort. Its use becomes an institutionalized and legitimized form of bad faith.

Problems and Issues

Berger offers us an opportunity to consider some of the observations and general arguments of sociology together with some of the observations and general arguments of modern philosophy—particularly existentialist philosophy. He begins with a consideration of the extent to which we are virtually prisoners of the historical epoch into which we are born—we are the children of our cultures. We grow up and we acquire language, attitudes, ideas, knowledge, understandings, and rather solid perceptions of the world around us that are derived from the culture. Given the forces of social control, it is surprising, not that people conform but that they manage to display whatever eccentricities they do. Why are Americans so concerned with the problem of conformity? Why do high school and college students idealize nonconformity and, at the same time, show a high degree of conformism in dress, speech, inter-

ests, and tastes? Is this a form of hypocrisy or is it evidence of the extent to which people conform unconsciously?

Is violence, or the treatment of violence, the most effective means for achieving conformity? Why do Americans subscribe to violence in movies and television as a device for resolving problems, and, at the same time, condemn it? Are Americans, much like the German people of recent times, supportive of violent systems of control so long as they do not have to be a direct part of them? Are minority group reports of police and criminal violence exaggerated? To what extent are Americans concerned with controlling the life of the individual? The American system subscribes to "freedom" and, at the same time, has created the most massive legal code in the world directed toward controlling the affairs of the individual. The problem of control cannot be avoided in any social system. Young people, for example, who do not wish to be controlled by their parents must in turn exercise some kind of control over them if they are themselves to avoid control. Is it possible to have a conception of freedom that does not involve, at the same time, an implicit form of control over someone? If I am seeking to drive my motorcycle down city streets at one hundred miles per hour, then my action will control the efforts of those who are attempting to negotiate traffic in a less sensational manner. Does this imply that the quest for freedom is actually only another way of phrasing the question of who is to control whom?

Berger makes a surprising statement for a sociologist: he argues that any attempt to identify people in their totality with their social character is an act of bad faith. Yet the foundation stone of sociological thought is to locate the nature of people in those values derived from the fact of their social existence. Is this contradictory? Does sociology, in itself, imply that people are not being understood in a "human" way? If so, then how do we achieve a more "human" understanding of human behavior?

Humanity as the Big Con

The Human Views of

ERVING GOFFMAN

To stay in one's room away from the place where the party is given . . . is to stay away from where reality is being performed. The world, in truth, is a wedding.

Presentation of Self in Everyday Life

BORN: 1913

16 In the course of growing up, we learn the language of the culture in which we live. It is a thorough and exact form of learning. We learn a language so precisely that phonetics experts, like the fabled Professor Higgins in Shaw's *Pygmalion*, can identify a person's birthplace merely by listening to idiosyncracies of the person's dialect. The learning is not only precise, so that we are instantly attuned to a slightly mispronounced word, but it is extensive. By this we simply mean that we learn a complex and vast amount of material. The typical child entering school between the ages of five and six already has a vocabulary of some two thousand words at his or her command.[1] Moreover, mastery of the art of language

[1] Fred J. Schonell, *The Psychology of Teaching and Reading*, 4th ed. (New York: Philosophical Library, 1961), p. 36. The total vocabulary of twelfth-grade high school students ranges from 36,700 to 136,500 words. D. McCarthy, "Language Development in Children," in L. Carmichael (ed.), *Manual of Child Psychology* (New York: Wiley, 1946), p. 59. Cited in the student manual, *Stereotypes*, prepared by Sociological Resources for Secondary Schools, 1966, p. 7. Figures such as these are not very reliable. Even if they were, they would not give a good indication of the full complexity of speech and language. For example, the sentence *"You know what I mean,"* has five different words; but it can be given many different meanings by changing intonation or word order. Thus, we might say, "What *I mean*, you know." Or, "You mean I know *what?*" For a graciously written exposition of such complexities of language, see J. R. Firth, *The Tongues of Men* (London: Oxford University Press, 1964), p. 34.

is virtually universal within a culture; even persons with low intellectual endowments may acquire at least a working knowledge of the language of their culture. Though this mastery is an astonishing feat of memory and learning, it is so common we take it for granted. Only when we try to learn a foreign language do we begin to discover how much we learned of our mother tongue. And only when we cease taking language for granted do we become aware of its deep influence in our lives.

Learning language is obviously important in becoming "human," and it is also obviously necessary for maintaining the elaborate social and cultural systems within which we operate today. But just what is it we learn when we learn a language? Certainly we learn more than spoken or written words. What symbols, words, or meanings are involved in human social exchanges? How does language work? What are the effects of language? We shall explore these questions throughout this chapter and arrive at some engaging conclusions and observations. The most general and most significant conclusion we shall come to might be stated in the following manner.

Humans and Symbols

Suppose we begin by accepting the fact that human beings are symbol-using creatures. (Walt Kelly, creator of the comic strip *Pogo*, once said people are "symbol minded.") If we recognize at the same time that symbols are, in a sense, "false" because they are never the same as the reality they represent, then people are, in a sense, "false." Unlike the nonsymbolic animals around them, people cannot merge with nature. We are, by benefit of language, separated.² This separation is a product of the deceptive and imperfect nature of language. To begin to dwell on the implications of people as symbol-using creatures leads us to view people as deceived by their own words. We deceive ourselves and deceive others. There is no way out of this situation. To be human is to use and to be used by language.

It is this feature of the human condition that receives the attention of Erving Goffman. Essentially, all that Goffman does is make evident the fact that in the course of social action, people influence each other by means of elaborate symbolic devices. In itself this is nothing new. It certainly does not seem, at least at first sight, to be especially shocking or penetrating. Nonetheless, Goffman's works³ form the foundation for

---

² We are again indebted to Professor Warriner of the University of Kansas for warning us against giving the impression of a false dichotomy. One can, for example, view symbols as enabling people to merge more consciously with nature. A debate on whether symbols enable us to merge with nature can quickly turn into a profitless metaphysical dispute. We are only trying to suggest, through this phrasing, that labeling an object or event has the capacity to separate us from other qualities which that object or event might possess.

³ Possibly the most significant of Goffman's books is *The Presentation of Self in Everyday Life*, which was first published as a monograph at the Social Sciences Research Centre at the University of Edinburgh in 1956. This chapter is based on materials appearing in the Anchor Books version (Garden City, N.Y.: Doubleday, 1959). Goffman's other major works include *Encounters* (Indianapolis: Bobbs-Merrill, 1961); *Asylums* (Garden City, N.Y.: Doubleday, 1961); *Behavior in Public Places* (New York: Free Press, 1963); *Stigma: Notes on*

a view of humankind even more disenchanting than that emanating from Darwin's theory of evolution or from Freud's conception of human beings as impulsive animals held in an uneasy state of control by society.

Darwin leaves open the possibility that if people are animals of low heritage, at least they are intelligent ones. If humans are animals, they are, nonetheless, animals capable of building vast cultures. Above all, Darwin permits us to view people as creatures standing at the apex of an evolutionary process whose origins are lost in time. Darwin allows us to keep intact our view of people as something special and privileged in nature's realm. Freud, on the other hand, disenchantingly leaves us at the mercy of unconscious and devious impulses. Even so, the Freudian picture is a dramatic and thoroughly romantic one. Though Freudian man or woman may be crushed by a repressive morality, he or she never admits defeat without a fight. The fight may take place within the unconscious, but it is always a fight. Freud sees people embroiled in combat with society throughout the entirety of life; it is an invigorating if not flattering conception.

But Goffman leaves us, at first glance anyway, with practically nothing. Goffman appears to divest us of our sanctity by suggesting that we are all incorrigible con artists—and that we have no choice. Moreover, the same tricks that make a con game work are basically the devices used in the act of being "human."

Goffman sees a person as a manager of impressions. These impressions, grounded in the meanings we give to appearances, gestures, costumes, settings, and words, are all that a person *is* as a social being. Strip these away and we have dehumanization. Conversely, cloak people with those fragile devices that permit them to maintain an impression before others and we have given them the shaky essence of humanity. This perspective reduces humanity to an act or performance; moreover, it is a performance based on dreadfully flimsy devices. At the same time, to become aware of the devices being used to sustain a performance causes us to respond to the performance with a different—and generally more negative—attitude than before. A child who discovers an uncle hiding behind Santa's false whiskers might continue to play the game, but more from choice than from a belief that he really is playing with Santa Claus.

It is in this sense, then, that Goffman appears to leave people more naked and alone than did Darwin or Freud. The distinctive feature of human activity resides ultimately in something little more than a Santa Claus outfit. To be human is to perform, like an actor, before audiences whom we con into accepting us as being what we are trying to appear to be. And our humanity is the costume we wear, the stage on which we perform, and the way we read whatever script we are handed.

---

the Management of Spoiled Identity (Englewood Cliffs, N.J.: Prentice-Hall, 1963); *Interaction Ritual: Essays on Face-to-Face Behavior* (Chicago: Aldine, 1967); *Frame Analysis* (New York: Colophon Books, 1974); *Gender Advertisements* (Cambridge, Mass.: Harvard University Press, 1979).

Two Aspects of Language: Content and Style

When we try to impress others, two somewhat separate kinds of language are involved. We impress others by *what* we say; and, of course, we impress others by *how* we say it. Usually we do not think of *how* we say something as a form of language. We reserve the idea of language for the content of what we wish to express. *How* we express ourselves we generally think of as "style" or "technique." Goffman suggests that what we commonly consider to be style is, in actuality, another manifestation of language. In fact, it is a form of language that serves the significant purpose of validating whatever it is we wish to express as content.

A simple illustration will quickly make clear what Goffman means when he refers to the validating properties of style of expression. The difference between a performance of Hamlet by Laurence Olivier and one by a not particularly talented high school student is certainly not a difference of content. Both are expressing the same words or lines from identical scripts. However, the performance of Olivier is believable. It impresses us as authentic. It appears to be a valid characterization. That of the high school student may appear lifeless, dull, artificial, stilted, or unreal. We know the high school student is not "really" Hamlet, but Olivier can "con" us into accepting that he is Hamlet. The difference, of course, rests in the style of the performance. But if style can communicate a sense of validity, then it must be seen in itself as a form of language. Moreover, its importance must not be overlooked; lack of control of the language of style may mean the difference between having one's message or performance accepted by others or having it rejected.

Symptomatic Behavior

Goffman uses the term *symptomatic behavior* to refer to what we are calling the language of style.[4] By this he means certain actions are symptomatic of a valid performance. For example, an erudite and competent professor who comes to class the first day with trembling hands may lose his audience because students will see this as symptomatic of fear or nervousness; if he is confident in his knowledge, then his hands should not reveal a nervous tremor. The fact that the professor suffers from an incurable nervous disorder does not prevent his trembling from symbolizing something quite different to the class. In this illustration, the nervous disorder is seen as symptomatic of a person who does not have completely valid claims to the performance he is about to stage. Conversely, a calm, poised, and steady bearing is symptomatic of a valid claim to the performance.

We have identified two classes of symbolic behavior so far. One of

---

[4] *The Presentation of Self in Everyday Life,* p. 2. Goffman's emphasis on the symbolic nature of social interaction places him among those sociologists who refer to themselves as "symbolic interactionists." The foundations of symbolic interactionist thought were laid by George Herbert Mead and Charles Horton Cooley.

Table
16-1   *Relationship between Content and Symptomatic Behavior*

Content	Symptomatic behavior	Audience reaction
1. Positive	Positive	A person possessing control over both levels of expression will be highly effective.
2. Positive	Negative	Despite content mastery, such a person may lose the audience because of incongruities in performance.
3. Negative	Positive	This person may prove acceptable so long as the existing incongruity is concealed.
4. Negative	Negative	This person will be highly ineffective.

these is the content of the performance and the other is the symptomatic behavior that validates or lends reality to the performance. The relationship between these two classes of symbols can be summarized (see Table 16-1). The first and fourth cases in this scheme are self-evident. The second and third cases are the interesting ones. Consider the second case, where a person may have content but lack mastery over symptomatic behavior. Such a person, despite control over content, may not be able to disguise ineptness with regard to symptomatic behavior. The lecturer whose hands shake illustrates this condition. A specific and actual case in point was the platform conduct of Thorstein Veblen, the great American economist and social analyst. Although his brilliance was widely recognized, and although hundreds of students flocked to his classes, the end of the semester would find the classroom nearly empty.[5] Students would abandon his courses by the hundreds. Veblen's lack of concern for classroom oratorical devices eventually proved more than his audience could bear.

[5] A student of Veblen's is quoted as having said, "Why it was creepy. It might have been a dead man's voice slowly speaking on, and if the light had gone out behind those dropped eyelids, would it have made any difference? But we who listened day after day found the unusual manner nicely fitted to convey the detached and slightly sardonic intellect that was moving over the face of things." Even so, Veblen's classes dwindled, and one ended with only a single student. See Robert L. Heilbroner, *The Worldly Philosophers* (New York: Simon & Schuster, 1953), p. 214.

"Phony" Behavior

The third case represents a type we usually refer to as a "phony." The person is capable of manipulating appearances to make the performance look like the real McCoy. However, the performance is invalid because the performer does not possess content. We witnessed a case in point during an amateur performance of *The Merchant of Venice*, when an actor momentarily forgot his lines. His stage presence was impressive, however, and he continued talking and gesturing as though nothing were wrong—all the while spouting a phony form of Shakespearean dialogue which he invented as he went along. Eventually he recalled his lines and continued with his part. The attention of the audience was retained, and it appeared to us that very few people were ever the wiser. In this instance, the performer was able to disguise the fact that he had momentarily lost mastery over the content of his performance. So long as the disguise was effective, the incongruity between loss of content and retention of symptomatic behavior never became apparent.

We cannot, of course, presume that the phony is superior to the person who lacks control over symptomatic behavior. Loss of either aspect of a performance is threatening to the maintenance of the performance. The phony is more likely to be effective simply because it is often easier to disguise lack of content. Students, for example, have been known to prefer a teacher who is a kindly-appearing old phony over an ominous-appearing recognized authority simply because they could not distinguish between the two on a professional basis.

It is apparent that a phony performance will be successful only to the extent to which the performer is capable of concealing from the audience the fact that he or she does not possess control over the legitimate content of the performance. But concealment in other forms is involved in situations where the performer is not a phony and not careless or incompetent.

> Some of these matters for concealment may be suggested here.
>
> First . . . the performer may be engaged in a profitable form of activity that is concealed from his audience and that is incompatible with the view of his activity which he hopes they will obtain. . . .
>
> Secondly, we find that errors and mistakes are often corrected before the performance takes place, while telltale signs that errors have been made and corrected are themselves concealed. In this way an impression of infallibility, so important in many presentations, is maintained. . . .
>
> Thirdly, in those interactions where the individual presents a product to others, he will tend to show them only the end product, and they will be led into judging him on the basis of something that has been finished, polished, and packaged. In some cases, if very little effort was actually required to complete the object, this fact will be concealed. . . .
>
> A fourth discrepancy between appearances and over-all reality may be cited. We find that there are many performances which could not have been given had not tasks been done which were physically unclean, semi-illegal, cruel, and degrading in other ways; but these disturbing facts are

seldom expressed during a performance. . . . We tend to conceal from our audience all evidence of "dirty work," whether we do this work in private or allocate it to a servant. . . .[6]

Concealment is a necessary element in practically all social performances, and it poses a rather trying dilemma for the actor. If one is honest and open, that is, if one refuses to engage in concealment, then one risks losing the audience. If one engages in concealment, then one is practicing deceit. All human social performances, from Goffman's perspective, involve a constant weighing of the costs of losing one's audience against the cost of losing one's integrity by behaving in a deceptive manner. Doctors may have to convince the patient that they are more certain of the effects of a given therapy than they may be in fact. Teachers may have to conceal from their students the doubt that plagues them as they present a lecture. Salesmen may have to conceal their contempt for the customer. So it is, then, that all social performances have a "phony" element about them. Not only does the fraudulent performer conceal his or her ignorance, but also the legitimate performer conceals items of information that would, if they became known, cause rejection by the audience.

This human dilemma can be seen in an overly cynical manner. Such a view is depicted, for example, in J. D. Salinger's novel *The Catcher in the Rye,* when Holden Caulfield discovers that people all around him are engaging in a variety of deceits. He concludes that people, especially adults, are phony. Caulfield's rejection of these "phonies" is based on his feeling that phony behavior betrays a great weakness in the character of the person. Goffman would suggest something different. "Phony" behavior is a product of the relationship existing between the performer and those who observe him or her. If retention of the audience is important, then deceit may be necessary. Thus, the teacher who is committed to the ideal of educating youth can do so only by retaining the attention and the acceptance of the students who are of immediate concern. This can be achieved only through performances that convince the audience of the worth of the performer. Such performances will necessarily conceal errors, hidden pleasures, "dirty work," and tedium. On these occasions the performer often cannot escape the sense of deception that he or she is practicing.

Goffman locates phony behavior not within the actor but within the complex of social relationships containing the actor. Consider the following situation. If an organization in which a person is located demands adherence to several conflicting standards or ideals, the individual will probably hide unavoidable violations of one of the ideals. A person will usually hide those violations that are easiest to hide. The act of hiding violations of the ideal, however, serves the purpose of keeping the ideal intact. Goffman gives the example of an attendant in an asylum for the mentally ill who must maintain order and must, at the same time, con-

---

[6] Goffman, *The Presentation of Self in Everyday Life,* pp. 43–44.

form to the ideal of not physically injuring patients. Violations of the latter ideal are more easily disguised than those of the former. Therefore, the attendant may indulge in such practices as "necking" a patient, forcing the person to behave by the act of throttling with a wet towel—an act which leaves no mark.

We are inclined to criticize the behavior of the attendant. Goffman suggests, however, that such behavior is an attempt to maintain the ideals of the social organization. If keeping order and not physically injuring the patient are both legitimate ideals and, at the same time, difficult to achieve simultaneously, then the only way they can be kept intact is to hide the fact that one of them must be violated. The behavior of the attendant, when viewed in terms of conflicting legitimate ideals of the organization and the endeavor to preserve these ideals, becomes less susceptible to criticism. The point that Goffman makes is that critical response to the *individual* in a situation such as this is misdirected. Attention should be given instead to the ideals of the organization and the means made available to the individual for supporting those ideals.

A similar situation can be found in the typical grade school. Among its varied concerns the school must deal with imparting knowledge, and it must also maintain a semblance of social control or order. Of these two concerns, the loss of order in the classroom is more readily apparent than are problems with respect to imparting knowledge. If one or the other ideal must be sacrificed, it will be the ideal of imparting knowledge. The teacher, then, who insists on order, regardless of whether teaching is taking place, is responding to structural features of the situation in which he or she has been placed. It is important to note, in all of this, that Goffman does not locate phoniness or deception or inclinations toward concealment as qualities of personality. They are, instead, qualities that arise out of the demands of performance. People cannot be understood apart from the greater social situations in which they have been placed.

Cynical and Sincere Behavior

Goffman shows us, perhaps more sympathetically than any other observer of human behavior, that there is a large element of phoniness in all human interaction. We pose, as it were, behind a variety of masks used to frighten, intimidate, implore, awe, beg, or otherwise elicit from others the kinds of reaction we seek. Sometimes we do this self-consciously; at other times we may be unaware of the extent to which we use these devices.

Goffman calls consciously manipulative behavior "cynical" behavior, while an unconscious use of manipulative devices produces behavior that is "sincere." It is worth noting that this places sincerity and cynicism within the subjective understanding of the actor. It is impossible to detect it from outside. For example, a cynical man may consciously and knowingly behave ineptly in order to convince the woman he is trying to seduce that he is sincere. A sincere lover, unknowingly, may behave

294 in a similar manner. The performances might be virtually identical; the difference is subjective. Goffman makes the difference subjective to highlight the significance of the performance itself. The cynical performer or the phony is a threat not because he or she performs less effectively; to the contrary, the threat or concern exists because the performance is so good! The effective cynic or phony demonstrates that it is not necessary to be friendly in order to act as a friend; it is not necessary to be in love in order to be a lover; it is not necessary to be respectable in order to appear respectable.

There is a real problem, then, in everyday behavior when it comes to evaluating the sincerity or value of a performance. If two performers are equal in skill, the only difference being that one is legitimate or sincere and the other not, then how is legitimacy to be established?

This problem is solved by the institutionalization of "labels" that give the performer a legitimate claim to the performance he or she is conducting. We establish licensing agencies to perform the service of providing documentary evidence that an individual has the right to engage in certain types of performances. In effect, this is one of the major services provided by educational systems. It is well known that many people come out of such systems with little more knowledge and enthusiasm than when they went in. It is known, also, that people can acquire an education of considerable merit without attending school. Nonetheless, all college graduates get a certificate that legitimizes their level of learning; the self-made person does not. It is especially important to see that an effective fraudulent or phony performance conducted by an "illegitimate" performer threatens the legitimizing agency.

Consider, for example, the following instance:

> A victim of his latest ruse calls "Dr." Arthur Osborne Phillips "one of the most remarkable medical phonies of all time."
> And from his jail cell, "Dr." Phillips replies: "I'm a genius. I had to be a genius to do all that I did with no formal medical education."
> "All" he did was hoodwink the federal government and authorities in 10 states during a 40-year career as a phony doctor.
> The 70-year-old man's latest caper was working on delicate research into the surgical use of the laser light at the University of Colorado medical center in Denver. His associates there said he "did competent work."
> According to prison records, Phillips' career began when he worked as an orderly during World War I for a Dr. James Herman Phillips of Doro, Ala. The real Phillips died in 1920 and the phony Phillips, according to the records, took over his name, medical shingle and license.
> While working as a "surgeon" with the Civilian Conservation Corps in Wyoming, Montana and Idaho in the 1940's, Phillips performed 32 successful appendectomies.[7]

In this case we are confronted by a person who, according to his colleagues, does "competent work." But if his performance is compe-

---

[7] A United Press International news item that appeared in the Urbana, Illinois, *News-Gazette*, January 20, 1966, p. 12.

tent, even though he did not attend medical school, then what is the point of medical school? It is in this sense that the phony performance is threatening. Let us make explicit once again that the legitimacy of the performance is not determined by the adequacy of the performance. Legitimacy is external and is bestowed on an actor by an established legitimizing agency such as a school, military system, church, political party, or family heritage.

The phony or illegitimate performer is threatening only to the extent to which the performance is competent. After all, if the phony is incapable of performing competently, then the problem of identifying the illegitimate performer is simple, and the need for legitimizing agencies is reduced. This appears to be pretty much the case with professional athletics. In the athletic contest the claims of the performer are expressed in the performance, and the criteria for evaluating the performance are clear-cut. The only problem here is to assure that a performer is not lying when he or she claims a lack of skill. In situations where the performance is the criterion of adequacy, the phony may be a person who is pretending to be less skilled or experienced than he or she is in fact. An example of this is the "hustler" in golf or pool who makes a living by leading an unsuspecting "pigeon" into a wager that the pigeon cannot hope to win. Some kind of legitimizing device must exist, therefore, to assure that a person who claims to have a certain lower level of skill does not, in fact, possess a higher level. For this reason performances such as those given by the athlete are divided into amateur and professional categories, and elaborate means are taken to ensure that professionals do not pose as amateurs.

There is one other area where legitimizing a performance introduces some interesting problems. Where no professional legitimizing agency exists, and where the criteria of competency are not clear, other lines may be drawn for distinguishing between the "true" performer and the performer whose actions are suspect. This occurs in the theater, where people who live by acting will make much of the distinction between themselves and actors who do not make a living by performing. Presumably the claims of the person who does not make any money by acting are suspect, and this may be the case regardless of the quality of the performances given by the amateur.

The scheme we now have is sufficiently developed to let us see, along with Goffman, that social performances are rather fragile. The problem of making your audience believe you *really* are what you are trying to be involves several layers of symbol—the content and symptomatic actions—and it may involve legitimacy as well. To the extent a person has control over these elements, the performance is affected accordingly. But some social roles make it easier to control these elements than others. This is especially important to note because it forces us to recognize that human behavior is not a simple manifestation of personality or "inner" character. Rather, it is a very complex exchange of symbols and meanings between at least two people. Sometimes, in this exchange, a person is required to perform a routine that lacks dramatic quality. To recognize that such a performance is required im-

296 plies that it is not a simple product of personality. At the same time, the fact that the performance is lacking in dramatic quality produces an interesting problem for the individual. Let us see how Goffman describes this problem.

Dramatic Realization

Some performances are developed in such a manner as to convince audiences easily and quickly of the "reality" of the performance. That is, the person is seen as being what he or she is trying to appear to be. Moreover, the person is able to do this easily. Other kinds of performances do not easily dramatize themselves. In such situations a person may, even though doing the work, have some difficulty impressing others that this is so. We can, therefore, talk about the extent to which a role permits "dramatic realization."

Goffman relies on the example of the medical nurse and the surgical nurse to illustrate what he means by this. The duties of the surgical nurse are such that the performance is quickly accepted. As the nurse stands beside the surgeon, masked and attentive, no one is doubtful about the work performance. The case of the medical nurse is different. In this instance, the nurse may come to the door of a patient's room and casually converse with the patient. While conversing the nurse may be observing changes in the patient's skin color, breathing, voice, and so on. Each of these observations may provide pertinent information about the progress of the patient's condition. Even so, the nondramatic character of these actions may cause the patient to conclude that the nurse is simply "messing around" or "goofing off."

The medical nurse, to avoid this, may invent or develop routines that lend dramatic quality to the performance. But some of these actions, because they are added merely for this reason, may interfere with the task that has been assigned. Therefore, a "dilemma of expression" develops. The dilemma rests on the following horns: (1) if the nondramatic task is adhered to exactly, it may result in the actor being rejected by the audience; however, (2) if dramatic elements are added to the task in order to retain the audience, they may interfere with the proper conduct of the task. The performer is required to create a balance between impressing people and getting the job done. Goffman puts it this way:

> A *Vogue* model, by her clothing, stance, and facial expression, is able expressively to portray a cultivated understanding of the book she poses in her hand; but those who trouble to express themselves so appropriately will have very little time left over for reading. . . . And so individuals often find themselves with the dilemma of expression *versus* action. Those who have the time and talent to perform a task well may not, because of this, have the time or talent to make it apparent that they are performing well. It may be said that some organizations resolve this dilemma by officially delegating the dramatic function to a specialist who will spend his time expressing the meaning of the task and spend no time actually doing it.[8]

[8] Goffman, *The Presentation of Self in Everyday Life*, pp. 32–33.

Role Expectation

Any performance, whether on a theatrical stage or in everyday life, requires some conception of what is expected of the performer. Sociologists refer to this as "role expectation." Goffman suggests that role expectations may be realistic or idealized. The difference between a realistic and an idealized conception of a role seems to hinge on whether or not the conception derives from the experience of an "insider" or the credulity of an "outsider." Goffman gives the following examples of what he means by "idealization," and this characterization probably still holds for much of American society.

> American college girls did, and no doubt do, play down their intelligence, skills, and determinativeness when in the presence of datable boys, thereby manifesting a profound psychic discipline in spite of their international reputation for flightiness. These performers are reported to allow their boy friends to explain things to them tediously that they already know; they conceal proficiency in mathematics from their less able consorts; they lose ping-pong games just before the ending . . .[9]

Goffman quotes a girl who is concerned with how she impresses her boyfriend:

> "One of the nicest techniques is to spell long words incorrectly once in a while. My boy friend seems to get a great kick out of it and writes back, 'Honey, you certainly don't know how to spell.'"[10]

The realities of a woman's role are known best by women. In the instance cited above, however, the woman is not "being herself." She is putting on a performance. Moreover, it is a performance that fits the myths and stereotyped roles of American society. It is in this sense, then, that the woman is behaving in terms of an idealized conception of her role.

Girls who misspell words, blacks who put on a dumb show for the benefit of whites, and morally proper college boys who pretend to be rogues are all engaging in performances that involve idealization. In such instances the form that the idealization takes may be to play down certain attributes the actor possesses. The girl plays down her knowledge, the black plays down his abilities, and the college boy plays down his secret commitment to old-fashioned morality.

Idealization may work in the other direction. College students who complicate their prose because they think intellectuals write in an incomprehensible manner are doing this. The housewife who usually prepares common meals for her family but presents guests with an elaborate feast is indulging in a form of role idealization. In such cases the performer expects to lead a credulous audience into an acceptance of the performer

---

[9] Ibid., p. 39.
[10] Here Goffman quotes Mirra Komarovsky, "Cultural Contradictions and Sex Roles," *American Journal of Sociology* 52, 186–188, in *The Presentation of Self in Everyday Life*, p. 39.

on the basis of the performer's conception of how the audience feels the role should be played. Moreover, the performer is playing up certain abilities that, in actuality, he or she may either lack or be less inclined to exercise.

Idealization and its relationship to performances is significant because it forces us to recognize that human social behavior involves (1) our own understanding of how our role should be played; (2) the conceptions others have of how the role should be played; and (3) the possibility of discrepancies between these conceptions. Severe discrepancies will result in performances that are bizarre and ineffective. Lower-class people who think upper-class people are arrogant and who try to emulate this pattern as they strive to be upwardly mobile will in all likelihood simply lose their friends.

There is an important difference between roles played on the stage and those played in everyday life. The former are well defined. A script is provided the actor and the performance is directed in a manner that reduces errors of which that person may not be aware. In some instances everyday roles are also very well defined. Take, for example, the role expected of us when we are called upon to participate in certain rituals. A priest conducting a high mass goes through a set of role behaviors virtually as well defined as those in a play. On the other hand, the behavior expected of us when we have been introduced at a party is, within considerable limits, subject to a variety of possibilities. Actors are on their own. They may feel they are supposed to be congenial and amusing; but how they elect to do this must come from their own background, abilities, and conceptions of the responses others will make to their actions.

In such circumstances a person has an opportunity to "ad lib" and to play the role creatively in terms of his or her interpretation of that role. This allows the performer to engage in role "idealization." One may attempt to upgrade or downgrade oneself, but in doing so one conforms to a conception of how such downgrading or upgrading should take place. One has, in other words, a model of performance that one follows in order to achieve the particular effect one seeks. In this respect the person is never, in performances before others, completely independent of social roles and the definitions that society has given to these roles.

This view of people as performers before audiences they are trying to impress seems cynical. It suggests, as we said before, that much of what is human is really a kind of show. Humanity is a matter of putting people on. There is a deceptiveness and a phoniness about much of human conduct. Goffman gives us a picture of human beings that emphasizes this "artificial" quality in our behavior. However, it is necessary to be careful in this evaluation of Goffman. In the first place, although in much of his writing he views people as "phony," he does not judge this as "bad." To the contrary, Goffman forces us to see much of this behavior as an unavoidable consequence of our attempts to please others; such behavior usually facilitates those affairs of daily life necessary for survival and comfort.

A cynic is defined as a person who thinks any action is motivated by the worst of motives. Goffman is cynical insofar as the motivation he gives to human action is often that of the "con." But Goffman, unlike a thoroughgoing cynic, does not consider this the worst of motives; the con more often than not is altruistic. Con behavior or phoniness is certainly universal, and we are on dangerous ground when we begin to criticize others for *their* phony conduct.

Above all, Goffman probes deeply enough to make us see that what we consider a "real" performance has elements identical to those involved in the phony performance. This requires us to think in new ways about the essential nature of humanity. When we see the larger conception of human nature that Goffman reveals, we find it will not permit us to define humanity simply in terms of the trappings people use to frighten and awe each other. In this sense Goffman is the most humanistic of the authors discussed in this book. He views sardonically the shows people put on before each other, and he views them as an outsider would. But throughout his work there can never be any doubt that his basic conception of humanity cuts through to the inner experiences and understanding of the world which any individual human being has. He is concerned with how one's relation to others and to society affects the understanding of oneself and the world. In other words, Goffman relates society and the person; but of the two, the person is always the more important.

The Problems of Stigma

Goffman's humanism is brought out by the unique treatment he gives to the problems experienced by people suffering from stigmata of different kinds.[11] Goffman defines *stigma* in the following way:

> While the stranger is present before us, evidence can arise of his possessing an attribute that makes him different from others in the category of persons available for him to be, and of a less desirable kind—in the extreme, a person who is quite thoroughly bad, or dangerous, or weak. He is thus reduced in our mind from a whole and usual person to a tainted, discounted one. Such an attribute is a stigma . . . [12]

It is important at this point to see that stigmata are *not* purely physical defects, even when the manifestation of the stigma is, let us say, a scar that runs from a man's ear to his mouth—giving him a twisted, leering expression. Stigma must be viewed always in terms of a language of relationships. What the scar, in this case, is defined as being (much as what a word is defined as being) determines whether or not the rela-

[11] *Stigma* traces some of the problems and involvements that arise when an individual is forced to play the social game while, at the same time, wearing a mask that is marred or reading a script that is flawed.
[12] From *Stigma: Notes on the Management of Spoiled Identity* (Englewood Cliffs, N.J.: Prentice-Hall, 1963), pp. 2–3.

300   tionship between the person with the scar and those without it will take a certain form. If, for example, the scar is obtained by a German university student while a member of a *Schlagende Verbindung*, or dueling society, he may define it in terms of virility, courage, and military values, and wear it as a badge authorizing him to assume an arrogant stance toward those without it. If, on the other hand, the scar is obtained in an automobile collision in the United States, and the victim is a woman, the whole thing will be interpreted quite differently.

Our reactions to people possessing a stigma of some kind are influenced by the common theories we have regarding the nature of that stigma. Goffman points out:

> By definition, of course, we believe the person with a stigma is not quite human. On this assumption we exercise varieties of discrimination, through which we effectively, if often unthinkingly, reduce his life chances. We construct a stigma-theory, an ideology to explain his inferiority and account for the danger he represents, sometimes rationalizing an animosity based on other differences, such as those of social class. We use specific stigma terms such as cripple, bastard, moron in our daily discourse as a source of metaphor and imagery, typically without giving thought to the original meaning. We tend to impute a wide range of imperfections on the basis of the original one, and at the same time to impute some desirable but undesired attributes, often of a supernatural cast, such as "sixth sense," or "understanding."[13]

Stigmata fall into three broad classes: gross physical defects, defects in character, and membership in a social class or group that is not acceptable. Stigmata may be acquired at birth or at any time during the life of the individual. Although there are some variations caused by the kind of stigma or the time of its acquisition, most stigmatized persons share a number of common problems and common strategies by which they meet these problems. Goffman sees stigmatized persons generally as humans who employ strategies designed to meet a particular difficulty—that of managing the "spoiled" identities they have acquired. But that identity is not inherent in the manifest form of the stigma. A stigma is, in Goffman's terms, a "perspective":

> May I repeat that stigma involves not so much a set of concrete individuals who can be separated into two piles, the stigmatized and the normal, as a pervasive two-role social process in which every individual participates in both roles, at least in some connections and in some phases of life. The normal and the stigmatized are not persons but rather perspectives.[14]

A stigma does not determine the type of performance required of the person having it, but it does help determine the extent to which a person will have to accept whatever role is given. Goffman is saying that a stigma such as epilepsy, for example, does not in itself produce a

---

[13] Ibid., p. 5.
[14] Ibid., pp. 137–138.

particular way of life for the person having epilepsy. Nor, on the other hand, does it, in itself, establish the manner in which the epileptic is to be viewed by persons who do not have this condition. However, once a set of norms are generated that define how an epileptic is to relate to others, then the epileptic will have a greater likelihood of encountering these requirements. Thus, in cultures where an epileptic is believed to have divine powers, the likelihood of encountering this expectation is increased for the epileptic to the point that he or she is likely to conform and accept the role of shaman. On the other hand, in a society where epilepsy is degrading, the person having this condition is more likely to encounter perspectives that lead to a self-derogating view.

Goffman's treatment of stigmatized people is concerned with the extent to which certain signs or manifestations of character increase the likelihood that they will be coerced into a social performance that sets them at a disadvantage. The social relevance of the stigma is that it moves individuals into playing the social game with the cards stacked against them. The problem for stigmatized people is to attempt to minimize the extent to which they will be injured or suffer loss by such circumstances. There are several things they can do. They can attempt to withdraw and not play the game. They can try to withhold information and thereby avoid getting themselves into a position where they have to play against the stacked deck. Or they can develop ways of meeting the situation directly. It might be possible, for example, to take advantage of the fact that the other players feel a sense of guilt because they know the deck is stacked.

Withdrawal as a means of coping with the situation does not mean that the stigmatized person is completely isolated. One might withdraw by encapsulating oneself within a group who know about the condition and will not use it against the person. One such group may be those persons who share the stigma; another may be those who are normal but sympathetic.

Normal and sympathetic people know about the condition of the stigmatized person and, at the same time, behave in a manner indicating that the stigma does not matter. In the company of such people, the person with a fault need feel no shame nor exert any special form of self-control. Goffman cites an example from the world of prostitutes:

> Although she sneers at respectability, the prostitute, particularly the call girl, is super-sensitive in polite society, taking refuge in her off hours with Bohemian artists, writers, actors and would-be intellectuals. There she may be accepted as an off-beat personality, without being a curiosity.[15]

There are differences between groups sharing the stigma and those composed of the sympathetic. Perhaps the most significant is that the stigmatic group dramatizes the stigma through formalized organizations or journals devoted to a treatment of how to live with the stigma; stories

---

[15] Goffman quotes J. Stearn, *Sisters of the Night* (New York: Popular Library, 1961), p. 181, in *Stigma*, p. 28.

302 are told of individuals who have achieved outstanding success despite possession of the stigma. Contrary to this, groups made up of the sympathetic are more inclined to reinterpret the stigma in a way that minimizes its existence; for example, the call girl is seen as an "off-beat personality."

A second way in which stigmatized persons can avoid playing against the stacked deck is to attempt to control their identity so that the stigma will not be perceived by others. Thus, illiterates may wear the trappings of the literate. Goffman cites the following illustration:

> When goal orientation is pronounced or imperative and there exists a high probability that definition as illiterate is a bar to the achievement of the goal, the illiterate is likely to try to "pass" as literate. . . . The popularity in the group studied of window-pane lenses with heavy horn frames ("bop glasses") may be viewed as an attempt to emulate the stereotype of the businessman-teacher-young intellectual and especially the high status jazz musician.[16]

Identity control may or may not be effective, of course. If it is effective, the stigmatized person is able to "pass" for a while as a nonstigmatized person. But the matter is more complex than merely a successful disguise of a stigma. Between people who can completely cover their stigma and pass without fear of discovery and those who can never cover their stigma lies a great range of cases.

> First, there are important stigmas, such as the ones that prostitutes, thieves, homosexuals, beggars, and drug addicts have, which require the individual to be carefully secret about his failing to one class of persons, the police, while systematically exposing himself to other classes of persons, namely clients, fellow-members, connections, fences, and the like. . . . Secondly, even where an individual could keep an unapparent stigma secret, he will find that intimate relations with others, ratified in our society by mutual confession of invisible failings, cause him either to admit his situation to the intimate or to feel guilty for not doing so. In any case, nearly all matters which are very secret are still known to someone, and hence cast a shadow.[17]

Within this range stigmatized people have several alternative modes of information control. They may pass, as has been suggested, or they may attempt to convert the stigma into some lesser form. Some blind persons wear dark glasses which immediately identify them as blind, but which may simultaneously disguise or hide facial disfigurements that accompanied being blinded.

Finally, the stigmatized person is confronted with unique problems in the realm of audience management. In these cases the stigmatized person has to play the game but he or she attempts to minimize the handicap by playing on the meanings that others give the condition.

[16] Goffman takes this example from H. Freeman and G. Kasenbaum, "The Illiterate in America," *Social Forces* 34 (May 1956), 374. See *Stigma*, p. 44.
[17] *Stigma*, pp. 73–74.

"Breaking the ice" exemplifies what is meant here. Initial contacts are important in determining how an interaction between two or more persons will continue. The stigmatized person can be either an object of pity—and thereby subject to those subtle forms of discrimination reserved for objects of pity—or the person can establish individuality and rights as a human, by how he or she handles initial meetings with others. For example, a man who has lost both hands and is served by artificial limbs may, on a first encounter with others, take out a cigarette and light it regardless of whether or not he feels like smoking. This ostentatious display of skills within a stigmatic context is sufficient to warn the audience that there is no need to go beyond the normal set of social understandings.

Goffman as Scientist and Humanist

Whether it is a person with a stigma or a normal individual coping with a common problem in everyday life, Goffman concentrates on how people manage the impressions they try to convey to others. Goffman is not, in the usual meaning of the term, a "scientist." His work does not rely on elaborate measurements. His major works are not based on questionnaires or even structured interviews. He is not at all hesitant to make use of literary examples if they help illustrate a concept or an idea.

Yet it would be a mistake to discount Goffman as a scientist. There is in his writing a more dispassionate and unbiased reporting of human events than is to be found in many studies more heavily armored with quantitative data and statistical analysis. Goffman's methods, which consist largely of careful observation combined with extensive scholarship, flow from his general conception of human conduct. Human behavior, for Goffman, is not a series of discrete actions that result from biologically derived urges or drives. Nor is it a manifestation of some inner condition like "personality." Instead, human behavior is distinctively complex and consists for the most part of an elaborate progression of symbolic performances. This conception of humanity forces us to see our conduct as though it were a work of art. We are artists—con artists, Goffman might suggest, but nonetheless artists. If this is so, then the important thing is to see the total impression created by our behavior. But this cannot be done unless we try to evaluate or understand the complete performance. We would have a very limited understanding of a painting by Picasso if we were informed only of the percentage of the painting that is blue.

Goffman stands back and observes, through the perspectives of science, the artful behavior of people. The effect is powerful. The large following Goffman enjoys today in both sociological and psychological circles is a result of the fact that he brings together the synthetic powers of the humanistic artist with the analytic and objective powers of the contemporary social scientist.

To read Goffman is to be brought directly and cleverly to a perception of people as role players and manipulators, of props, costumes,

304 gestures, and words, Goffman is able to suggest, indirectly, the injustices that such role playing can produce, as when, for example, we deny a woman status as a warm and intelligent human being because she is deformed and dwarflike. But if Goffman is able to penetrate into the most subtle irrationalities of human conduct, he simultaneously is generous in the extent to which his conception of humanity embraces all. Goffman's writing asserts that no person is more human than another, but that one person might be able to give a certain kind of performance better than another. If so, then in human terms a beggar is the equal of a king. Goffman finds people caught up in myriad con games; at the same time the objective and cold vision of this social scientist upholds in a devious way one of the most sympathetic of human values—the fundamental equality of all human beings.

Problems and Issues

Few writers offer a better opportunity for questioning the peculiar properties of human social behavior than Goffman. His works provide a basis for entering into a discussion of such matter as "phoniness," hypocrisy, sincerity, and the "reality" of social action. How do we, in fact, determine whether a person is phony, and why are we so worried about phony actions? How do we determine whether or not a person has the "right" to do whatever he or she is doing? Is our intense interest in such things as movies and popular magazine literature associated with our desire to be able to identify and deal with social performances?

While we tend to condemn "phoniness," we also seem to want it. That is to say, we like to be conned or "smooth talked." We are also aware of the extent to which we feel impelled, at times, to "put on an act." Goffman raises the question of the place of phoniness in social relations and refuses to permit us to dismiss it as an easy issue by saying that phoniness is bad and we do not want anything to do with it. How do you differentiate the phony from the sincere act? More importantly, to what extent has "phoniness" become an important part of modern American society? What kind of culture or society would produce a book such as Goffman's Presentation of Self in Everyday Life?

Perhaps phoniness is an essential part of human conduct, and Americans are simply too idealistic. For example, it is probably necessary to "pose" for a while in a social role before coming to the point at which one is competent in the role. A student has to pose as an intellectual for a while before really becoming one. The interval of posing may be relatively short in the case of a brilliant student or quite long in the case of someone less competent, but, for a while, the "pose" is necessary. This raises the possibility that some of the anxieties of youth in our culture—and young people seem to be the ones most concerned with phoniness—are products of the

fact that young people must pretend to occupy roles which are not fully **305**
legitimated.

Goffman is sometimes referred to as a "dramaturgic" sociologist. That
is to say, he relies on the metaphor of drama and dramatic action to interpret
the world around us. To what extent do people "build" drama into their
lives? How important is drama to us? Does drama incline us toward irrational
action? What does it mean to be "dramatic"? How is drama transformed
into reality—that is to say, how do we realize drama? How does stigmatization influence dramatic performance? Football players engage in high
drama on Saturday and Sunday afternoons. They also have a high probability
of injuring themselves. What does this suggest with respect to the question
of whether or not people prefer drama over physical welfare?

Accounts, Works, and Ethnomethodology

HAROLD GARFINKEL

Indeed, the more important the rule, the greater is the likelihood that knowledge is based on avoided tests.

Studies in Ethnomethodology

BORN: 1920

17 Studying the Commonplace

Most of the social actions in which we engage from day to day are commonplace events. These are the ordinary, the usual, the routine, the obvious patterns of behavior that we have little cause to question. If we do question them, we tend to come up with commonplace observations. The significance of the commonplace and ordinary actions of day-to-day existence is that we do *not* question them. They acquire a taken-for-granted quality that removes them from our examination and consideration. This gives them a hold over us that most other events, those which fall outside the commonplace, do not have.

But how can we approach the commonplace without coming up with observations so banal and commonplace in their own way that we are prevented from achieving intellectually interesting results? It is not difficult to imagine writing something interesting about events taking place in the White House on some particular occasion. To gain access to such an unusual arena of human activity virtually assures a reporter of a

good story. But what about reporting on how people walk down the
sidewalk, or how they pass through the check-out counter at the supermarket, or what happens when two people greet each other in the halls
of a building on campus?

Our experience has been that students believe that writing a paper
about commonplace experiences is an easy assignment. After all, the
material is available and "human." They feel they can rely on immediate
and direct observations. When the completed papers are turned in,
however, they usually consist of extremely ordinary and uninteresting
observations—they lack intellectual interest. Now it is possible to study
the commonplace in an uncommon way, but it takes an unusually well
trained mind to move beyond the obvious and apparent features of such
activity. It requires being able to question that which few people ever
question during their lifetimes. It requires, in a way, an ability to become
a stranger in an unstrange land.

Granting these difficulties, there are still several reasons why common, ordinary, day-to-day events are particularly significant for advancing our understanding of human social behavior. In the first place, most
human behavior is of the ordinary variety. Even people who acquire the
label *extraordinary* spend most of their time in commonplace activities.
If we ignore the commonplace, we bypass most of what is going on
among human beings. In the second place (and this is by far the more
important and interesting consideration), the fact that a social relationship is commonplace tends, as we have said, to make it impervious to
deeper examination. After all, it is not worthy of analysis or examination;
it is something that can and should be taken for granted.

Yet, it is this very taken-for-granted quality of the commonplace
event that gives it a special power over us. It is significant because it is
not examined. It has a hold over us because we accept the demands of
the taken-for-granted moment without question, without conscious consideration.

But do commonplace events really have to be beyond intellectual
question, or is there something to the mundane events of day-to-day
living that is a key to the "higher" moments of our lives? Is there perhaps
a special way to approach the commonplace so that more is revealed
than the taken-for-granted matters of the moment?

This, in part, is the question Harold Garfinkel turns his attention
to. It is a profound matter, in the final analysis, because it has to do with
how we come to accept as "real" various features of our social and
physical world. How does one penetrate a reality so "obvious" to those
who are caught up in it that they cannot even begin to question it? One
way Garfinkel attempts to delve into the structure and character of the
commonplace is by the simple device of disrupting it. The disruption
does not have to be especially profound to achieve its effect. Garfinkel
has obtained some revealing responses merely by interrupting an ordinary conversation with an innocuous question. What Garfinkel does is
have his students ask a person with whom they are talking to elaborate
on something the person just said. Students are instructed, however, to
make this request at a point in the conversation where everyone involved

308 will have reason to think that what has just been said is perfectly clear and obvious.

For example, the student could be talking with someone in the hall just outside the classroom before a lecture begins. The conversation might go something like this:

Friend: That sure was a great party at your place last night. Everybody had a really great time. You know what I mean?

Student: No, I'm not certain I do know what you mean.

Friend: Come on. You know.

Student: No, when you say that everybody had a great time, just what are you talking about?

Friend: You know. They really had a good time.

Student: Yes, you said that before; but I want to know what you *mean* by a good time.

Friend: Jesus! What's gotten into you? You know what I mean. They had a good time!

This might sound like a bit of minor sadism on the part of Garfinkel's student, but the response of the friend is revealing. He is puzzled. The normal expectations around which ordinary day-to-day forms of expression take place have been challenged.[1] Still, it is not *unreasonable* to ask for an elaboration of a statement—or is it?

When do we have the right to question, and when does the act of questioning interfere with a process that is not supposed to be questioned? A number of people who were questioned like the student above became distressed, upset, or otherwise flustered over the disruption of what appeared to them to be a perfectly normal sequence of events. If you tell someone that you recently had a flat tire, and that person asks you what you mean by *having a flat tire*, it is likely that you will respond the way one person did when questioned by a student of Garfinkel. That is, you will wonder aloud why anyone would ever question what you meant. Everyone should "know" about such things. You can behave in a predictable, ordinary way with others only if you can presume they share a common background with you. If something takes place that disrupts your trust of that common background, then suddenly your interaction is forced into new and uncertain pathways. You may begin to wonder about the other person's sanity, perhaps; and in some instances you may begin to wonder about your own.

Another way in which Garfinkel attempts to move behind the ordinary conventions that buttress our day-to-day social affairs is to have his students report on some social scene or event as though they were

[1] Details of such conversations will be found in Harold Garfinkel, *Studies in Ethnomethodology* (Englewood Cliffs, N.J.: Prentice-Hall, 1967), pp. 42–44. This book, the major work by Garfinkel currently in print, consists in large part of material originally published in other sources, including: Harold Garfinkel, "Studies of the Routine Grounds of Everyday Activity," *Social Problems*, Winter 1964; and Garfinkel, "Common Sense Knowledge of Social Structures," in J. Scher (ed.), *Theories of the Mind* (New York: Free Press, 1962).

not really an integral part of it. For example, students were asked to write up a description of a holiday visit home as if they were outsiders rather than members of the family. How would they view their parents, for example, if they were only boarders in the house instead of being related as son or daughter? Some of the papers that Garfinkel received from this assignment have an almost bizarre quality to them. There is a detachment and objectivity to the observations, and the identities of the people involved get shifted around in strange ways. It is one thing to see your mother as your mother; it is something else to see her at any one time simply as a woman who is serving a meal.[2] Garfinkel literally asks his students to become strangers in unstrange places.

Finally, though it is a bit removed from the commonplace events we have been discussing, we will present an ingenious demonstration by Garfinkel that reveals some unusual aspects of the generation of social values. Notice particularly how people elaborate their experiences until, eventually, the experiences make "sense" to them.

Elaborative Experiences

In this particular demonstration, students volunteered for psychiatric counseling about their personal problems. Each student provided the "counselor" with background information on some problem and then asked a question that could be answered yes or no by the counselor. The student and counselor were separated by an opaque screen. After the student heard the counselor's reply to his or her question, he or she recorded reactions to the counselor's reply into a tape recorder. The counselor could not hear the reactions. When the student was ready with the next question, he or she addressed the counselor, asked the question, and then continued with an evaluation of the counselor's next Yes or No response. Here are some excerpts from one such counseling session.[3]

> *Subject:* I happen to be of the Jewish faith and I have been dating a Gentile girl. . . . My dad is not directly opposed . . . but at the same time he will come up with digs and sayings that make me feel very ill at ease. . . . My question is . . . Do you feel that I should continue dating this girl?
>
> *Counselor:* My answer is no.
>
> *Subject:* No. Well, that is kind of interesting . . . I suppose or maybe it is easier for an outsider to see certain things that I am blind to at this moment. . . . I would like to ask my second question . . . Should I have further discussion with Dad over this subject about dating the Gentile girl?

[2] Again see Garfinkel, *Studies in Ethnomethodology.*
[3] Selectively quoted from Garfinkel, "Common Sense Knowledge of Social Structures." Garfinkel refers to the "counselor" as an "experimenter" for reasons which will become apparent.

Counselor: My answer is yes.

Subject: Well, I feel that is reasonable . . . I guess we should have a discussion based on what the future possibilities might be and how he would feel about that. He may not be too strongly opposed now because we are only dating, but perhaps he sees future complications that he would really like to get off his chest at the moment. I am ready for my third question now.

If . . . Dad . . . says to continue dating her, but . . . he really does not want me to date her, but he is only doing it because he wants to be a good Dad, should . . . I still date the girl?

Counselor: My answer is yes.

Subject: Well I am actually surprised at the answer. . . . Even though he might have said go ahead and date her I perhaps would feel guilty in knowing that he really did not want me to continue to date her. Though I don't know that it would actually help the situation any . . . I am ready for the fourth question now . . . do you think it would be proper for me to have my mother have a serious talk with him and therefore try and get a truer reaction to Dad's opinion on the situation?

Counselor: My answer is yes.

Subject: Well this seems fair to me. I feel perhaps that he would be honester with Mother about the situation. . . . she would be a little more liberal about things like this . . . at least I feel that we are moving along some way. I am ready for my fifth question now. . . . Do you feel that I should tell the girl that I am dating the problems that I am having at home over her religion?

Counselor: My answer is no.

Subject: . . . I am surprised. Of course, that might depend on how much you care for the girl . . . I . . . feel . . . that it is only right to tell her . . . if she feels that this will be a block then I feel perhaps that would end the situation right there . . . I am ready for my sixth question.

[If we planned to marry] . . . do you feel . . . I should ask her to change her religion . . . ?

Counselor: My answer is no.

Subject: . . . Well, this has me stymied. No . . . unfortunately I have never seen a family with a split in religion that really has been able to make a success out of it . . . I think that perhaps I would be tempted to ask her to change. I don't think that I would be able to really. I am ready for number seven.

> Do you feel that it would be a better situation if . . . we bring our children up in a neutral religion other than the two that we believe in?
>
> Counselor: My answer is yes.
>
> Subject: Well, perhaps this would be a solution. If we could find a religion that would incorporate our two beliefs to a certain extent . . . I guess I should follow this along a little bit further and see exactly what happens. I am ready for number eight.
>
> If we were to get married would it be best for us to live in a new community where we will not be in contact with our parents if we were getting a lot of family pressure over religious differences?
>
> Counselor: My answer is no.
>
> Subject: Well I kinda tend to agree with this answer. I feel that you wouldn't be accomplishing too much by running away from the issue. . . . So we best remain there and try to work it out. I am ready for number nine.
>
> If we did get married . . . would we just bring them [the children] up in this new religion . . . that we talked about and let them believe that that is what we originally believed in?
>
> Counselor: My answer is no.
>
> Subject: . . . if they did find out that there was this difference that we once had they would feel that we were sneaking . . . this would not be the best situation either . . . I am ready for number ten.
>
> Do you feel that our children . . . would have any religious problems . . . because of . . . our difficulties?
>
> Counselor: My answer is no.
>
> Subject: Well I really don't know if I agree with that or not . . . I kinda feel that if their religion was a wholesome one which supplied the needs of a religion that there would not be any problems with them . . . I am finished with my comments now.

The session was then closed, but the subject was asked to make some comments about the counseling he had received. Among his comments were some of the following statements:

> The answers that I received were for the most part aware of the situation as we moved along . . . they had a lot of meaning to me. . . . his answers as a whole were helpful . . . he [the counselor] was completely aware of the situation at hand . . . I feel that it had a lot of sense to me and made a lot of sense.

As you may have guessed by now, the interesting feature of this study is that the counselor's advice consisted of random yes or no responses. The counselor, actually an "experimenter," was replying to each

312 question, in effect, by tossing a coin and saying "Yes" if it turned up heads and "No" if it turned up tails. This did not make any difference, however, for the subjects. They felt that the answers were "aware of the situation . . . helpful . . . had a lot of sense."

But what is the point of all this? Garfinkel gets people to tease their friends by asking them to elaborate on the meaning of commonplace utterances. Students describe what it is like to see their own household from the perspective of a boarder. People make sense out of counseling that is random and unrelated to the questions they ask. At first, Garfinkel's work seems playful and prankish—like something Allen Funt might have pulled on people for "Candid Camera." But the tricks played on people for the television program were simply pranks, putting people in situations that were amusing. The idea behind Funt's work, of course, was to entertain people. Garfinkel, on the other hand, is singularly humorless in his writing. His style is cumbersome and tortured—a virtual necessity to prevent the reader from concluding that he is simply messing around. When Garfinkel plays a "joke" on people, it is for the sake of trying to uncover the "devices" that enable them to carry off complex and abstract actions.[4] Moreover, these actions are so taken for granted that challenging them can be a disturbing experience. So Garfinkel disturbs people slightly in their ordinary routines and then looks for what is revealed by these disruptions.

Interpreting the Commonplace

As we argued before, the problem with the commonplace is that it is commonplace. When people are questioned about their commonplace activities, they (curiously enough) are not as well able to describe what they are doing as when they are engaged in not-so-commonplace activities. The paradox of the commonplace moment is that the actors feel their behavior is unproblematic despite the fact that they can be extremely vague in describing what they are doing. We cannot come to grips with familiar and ordinary behavior by asking the persons involved in it to tell us about it. They are too immersed in the familiar to be able to recognize it or articulate it. Somehow, the imagination of the actors and the events within which they find themselves become a single, reasonable happening. They are able to take whatever is there and transform it into something that "makes sense." But, more significantly, it can make so much sense that there is little point in discussing the matter. It simply takes place.[5]

[4] Garfinkel's "pranks" become the loci of a profound interpretive effort, well worth studying despite the ponderous prose.

[5] One theory of religious practice is that it came out of people's awed response to their world. We begin discussions of this theory by asking students in our classes how they feel about the classroom and the moment they are in. They usually reply by asking, "What do you mean, 'How do I feel'? What is there to feel anything about?" The casual, matter-of-fact response of students to the peculiar circumstances in which they move—their striking lack of awe—illustrates not only a weakness of the religion-as-a-response-to-the-awesome theory but also Garfinkel's concern with "matter-of-factness." The surprising thing about people is not that they are awed but that they are so little awed—that they take so much for granted, that they accept their accounts of events as reasonable.

What is the influence behind the "reasonableness" of the ordinary **313** event? What gives it its "hold" over people? How is it possible to investigate and understand what happens at the point where imagination and reality join together to create the acceptable social act? Because the acceptable social act is so acceptable, the persons caught up in it cannot articulate readily what it is they are caught up in. They may, however, give some clues about the forces which contain them if the smooth operation of those forces is interrupted.[6]

Garfinkel is explicit about his method of approach. He argues that we should subject commonplace, everyday, familiar interchanges between individuals to intense examination. What is "really" going on when people sit down together for breakfast, or walk across the campus, or talk together in the halls? Some would argue that we do not need to know about such matters. After all, they pretty much take care of themselves, and it is silly to analyze something that is not a problem or a source of trouble. Garfinkel, however, insists that the commonplace *is* important and that the way to study it is by disrupting it and then observing carefully how people deal with the disruption. It is in dealing with the disorganizing moment that the structure which holds the interaction together is revealed.[7]

Garfinkel is interested, then, in producing moments of small madness. To the extent that we can understand such madness and produce it at will, we may be able to understand greater madnesses also. However, Garfinkel is little concerned with whether his work will have such beneficial effects. The task, as he sees it, is to observe and to struggle to understand regardless of whether such efforts promote humanistic values or a "better" society.[8]

Another way of looking at Garfinkel's work is to see it as an attempt to separate individuals momentarily from the social supports that hold them up and give a "natural" quality to the commonplace action. When individuals begin to behave truly as individuals, we might be able to compare their behavior with the way they behave when sustained by their ordinary social backgrounds. Garfinkel suggests that much can be gained from observing those moments when individuals are pulled free and then have to behave relatively independently of whatever constitutes their social nature. In the contrast we can uncover the difference be-

---

[6] Garfinkel's approach to the study of human social events is similar to that used by the physicist trying to fathom the nature of matter. The "building blocks" of social reality are examined by a process of subjecting them to collisions that reveal their nature—much as the collisions between particles in a cloud chamber give clues to the nature of matter.

[7] It is possible, after all, that the commonplace has implications for the not-so-commonplace. The behavior that leads us to accept the reasonability of an ordinary encounter might offer clues as to why we think it is "reasonable" to engage in war or ravage the resources of our planet or send a condemned person to the gas chamber. Garfinkel's work is a relatively pure form of social research. It will take some time before we can judge its full implications for the promotion of our understanding of human social behavior.

[8] Garfinkel explains: "Ethnomethodological studies are not directed to . . . arguing correctives. . . . They do not formulate a remedy for practical actions, as if it was being found about practical actions that they were better or worse than they are usually cracked up to be. Nor are they in search of humanistic arguments . . ." (*Studies in Ethnomethodology*, p. viii.)

314   tween the social actor and the individual. As a uniquely sociological procedure for investigation, Garfinkel suggests that people be placed in circumstances where they are denied their normal reliance on social understandings and must struggle with the situation on their own.

This kind of observation of the individual as individual can be achieved through a variety of devices. One device is to engage in an apparent breach of convention during a social happening. This is what went on when Garfinkel had students press someone with the question: "What do you mean by that?" Another device is to have the observer attempt to divest himself or herself, through an act of imagination or by changing identity, of the social background normal to the usual circumstances of his or her life. This was the effort in the case of the students who were asked to view their personal households as if they were boarders. Still another device is to have the individual unwittingly engage in a relationship which he or she has interpreted one way but which is moving along some other avenue of development—somewhat independently of anything the person is doing. This was the case with the students who were being "counseled" by random yes and no replies from the "counselor." In each of these situations people have been placed in circumstances where they continue to behave socially. But the form of the social behavior is revealing in what it does *not* offer them. More significantly, it is revealing in how they respond to that lack.

These observational devices are designed to allow the researcher to "observe" the ways in which people attempt to reconstruct a relationship that looks as though it is going "sour." Relationships are based on commonly understood rules that enable the participants to make sense out of the relationship and the world around them. This is what "common sense" is all about. If you are enjoying a conversation with someone and your common sense is thrown into doubt, it is a disturbing experience. Not only is the relationship threatened, but there is the potential for a threat to one's total understanding of the way the world is supposed to be ordered.

What Is Ethnomethodology?

Garfinkel refers to his work as ethnomethodology. *Ethno-* refers to people. *Method-* refers to method. *-Ology* refers to study. *Ethnomethodology*, then, is an examination of the methods people commonly use to sustain some kind of consensus about the world and to solve problems that often have highly irrational features. Garfinkel, for example, was, at one point in his career, interested in how people came to conclusions about the motives and events that led up to certain deaths by suspected suicide. Garfinkel was caught up in the observation that no matter how vague the clues might be, people assigned the task of commenting on a suicide were invariably able to say something about it. One of the fascinating features of social behavior is that it operates on the basis of uncertain knowledge. To present as simple an example as possible, students and instructors in a typical college classroom do not know much about each other's lives. Students do not have any truly good awareness of the past experiences and understandings of the instructor, and it is much the same for the instructor's understanding of the students' lives. This does not, however, prevent both the students and the instructor from constructing understandings of each other and then acting on the basis of those understandings. It is this process that interests Garfinkel.

Implications of the Counseling Study

We can gain further insight into what Garfinkel is trying to do by returning to the "counseling" study. The experiment with the "counselor" offers an explicitly developed set of findings. These findings offer us a way of entering into the vision of human social activity generated by an ethnomethodological approach. We would like to suggest that these findings also offer some insights into the nondeterminant or "artful"[9] and complex nature of human social behavior in even its most simple and commonplace forms.

There is a bit of paradox in the fact that Garfinkel's investigations of commonsense understandings of the world are probably not especially commonsensical. Some sophistication is required to follow Garfinkel's interpretation. In the material that follows we have listed the findings from the Garfinkel study separately in much the same way as they were presented by the author. We have somewhat modified the order of presentation and we have deleted comments outside the range of a book of this kind.[10] We have also taken the liberty of suggesting concepts that, we think, might help the student comprehend a little better the thrust of what is being talked about. These concepts—"loading," "patterning," and so on—do not appear in the original and are intended, again, only as devices to help the student. We have added some commentary to underscore how an ethnomethodologist looks at what is going on when people seek to construct meaning in their social affairs. While the findings are drawn specifically from the "counseling" demonstration, they apply more broadly to the general interpretations of social behavior subscribed to by ethnomethodologists.

FINDING 1 "Typically the subjects heard the experimenter's answers as answers-to-the-questions. Perceptually, the experimenter's answers were motivated by the questions [p. 89]."

This sounds like a peculiar "finding." One's first reaction, we should think, would be to say, "Of course they did, you fool." But such a quick reply would miss the point—and it is a basic point from an

[9] Garfinkel uses the term *artful* several times to describe social behavior. He begins his preface, for example, with a reference to the ordinary artful ways of social accomplishment. See *Studies in Ethnomethodology*, p. vii.
[10] Our discussion follows the general character of Garfinkel's "Common Sense Knowledge of Social Structures"—reprinted in *Studies in Ethnomethodology*, pp. 89–94. *Studies in Ethnomethodology* combines many of Garfinkel's works, and the student will probably find it easier to use for that reason.

316 ethnomethodological viewpoint. First of all, it is necessary to keep in mind the simple fact that *the answers were not answers to the questions.* If this is kept constantly in mind, then what Garfinkel is saying becomes a reasonable foundation for much of what follows.

We shall refer to this aspect of human social behavior as *naive perception.* That is to say, people tend to respond to symbolic definitions of events as "reality," unless there is good reason to suspect otherwise. In other words, symbolic realities are "real." The students saw their "counseling" as "real" counseling despite the fact that it was not. The value of the counseling did not come from the stimulus event, per se, but rather from what the student subjectively perceived and manipulated as a stimulus event.

So we have on the one hand "counselors" who are essentially commenting at random at the request of other people. The people making the requests have been "set up"[11] to deal artfully with those random comments—and they do so! They begin to create a set of "meanings" around the random commentaries of the "counselor." These meanings acquire their value not from anything intrinsic within the counselor's comments but from something more complex. For the moment we shall call the source of the comments "background." This background involves not only the various recalled experiences and knowledge of the person but also the sets of rules that determine how information will be used in encounters with others. While experiences vary considerably from individual to individual, it is possible that the rules that are part of the *common* sense of experience are similar. If so, then we might be able to describe the normative regularities that underlie complex social relationships. In this sense, then, despite the apparently eccentric nature of Garfinkel's work, it falls definitely within the conventions of scientific investigation. That is, it is empirical and it is concerned with uncovering regularities in its object of study.

FINDING 2 "All [subjects] reported 'the advice that they had been given' and addressed their appreciation to that 'advice' [p. 89]."

This observation underlines Finding #1, with the perspective changed only slightly. Garfinkel is particularly interested in the extent to which a social exchange involves what, for want of a better term, might be called *loading* or *overloading.*[12] The Yes and No responses are just

---

[11] We have used the term *set up* to attempt to convey some sense of what Garfinkel is talking about, even though he does not use this term.

[12] Once more we must emphasize that we are using terms which are not used by Garfinkel but which we hope convey the spirit of his interpretations. It is extremely significant to note here that Garfinkel is adding a dimension to a problem raised by Emile Durkheim. Durkheim was concerned with the intensity of human punishment, which usually far transcends the often banal qualities of the crime for which it is imposed. He believed that the extreme nature of much human punishment came from the augmenting of human motivations by the powerful "collective conscience." The collective is bigger than the individual not only in size but also in its capacity to generate and sustain emotion. Durkheim, however, was not able to say how this process worked. It seemed reasonable to conclude that the intensification of emotion came, somehow, from involvement with and within the "collective conscience." But how? Garfinkel suggests the answer in a simple demonstration in which students give much "deeper" meanings to an event than the event contains within itself.

that—Yes and No statements coming from a predetermined random process. But they are invested with particular meanings by the subjects, who
"load" them with an understanding that is not within the statements
themselves. The subjects have been "set up" to deal with the responses
in a manner that overlays them with meanings that the subjects are able
to elaborate in terms of their own conceptions. The important thing to
remember is that the subjects are creating a social relationship—even
against a random event. They are loading the responses of the counselor
with meanings they can then respond to.[13] This is common in all human
social communications.

In ordinary and not-so-ordinary social moments, the constant operation of this inclination to overload messages sustains social behavior
and, at least in part, provides it with continuity. Terms such as *Black
power, freedom, love,* and almost any other socially significant concept
far transcend the simple meaning of Yes or No. They are invitations to
persons using them in social discourse to project background interpretations upon the concept. It is in this process that the social act is
generated and the peculiar meeting between the individual and the
greater society takes place.

FINDING 3 "Over the course of the exchange the assumption
seemed to operate that there was an answer to be obtained, and that if
the answer was not obvious, that its meaning could be determined by
active search, one part of which involved asking another question so as
to find out what the adviser 'had in mind' [p. 89]."

We shall refer to this as *searching.* That is to say, the students came
into the "counseling" with a sense of an answer which was presumed to
be there and which would be ascertained with a proper *search.* The
character of the stimulus event is anticipated prior to the moment when
the student encounters the stimulus.

Garfinkel is impressed by the "artful" nature of the sustained social
event. When a person is "set up" for an engagement, the general theme
of the engagement is carried through in terms of premises that give the
engagement meaning. *Again, this meaning is sustained by the actor's
capacity to continue to interpret the responses of the other as relevant
to that meaning—regardless of whether it really is.* In this finding, Garfinkel begins to display the extent to which a common social interaction
relies on conditions far removed from the persons involved but "brought
into" the situation to "fill it" and retain its continuity.

FINDING 4 "The identical utterance was capable of answering several different questions simultaneously, and of constituting an answer to
a compound question that in terms of the strict logic of propositions did
not permit either a yes or no or a single yes or no [p. 90]."

We shall refer to this as *compounding.* Garfinkel demonstrates that

---

[13] The picture of a parakeet pecking at its image in a mirror comes to mind here, but it is
a much too simple picture. While each participant in a social interaction loads the responses
of others with materials from his or her own personal background, the individual is
responding to much more than an immediate self-image.

318   people are often quite satisfied with what are, in the final analysis, totally illogical responses. In the "counseling" study a student might ask, "Should I marry my girl friend, or should I go to Europe and forget all about it. Or, maybe it would be better to go to work." The counselor might reply by saying, "My answer is, 'Yes.'" The student has asked a compound question and is satisfied with a simple response. Apparently the counselor's response is not being related to the student's question in any strictly rational or mechanical manner.

This is one of those findings common to sociology, insofar as it appears to be something that everyone has known all along. However, one of the peculiarities about things that we have known all along is that we often do not really know them. This finding seems to underscore a conception of people as rather irrational and certainly illogical. Garfinkel concedes that human beings are not logical in much of their social interaction. However, he sees most of this interaction as a response to quite rational concerns. That is, the individual does engage in "searches" for support of a particular position he or she has taken. The rational behavior of the person engaged in day-to-day social discourse is not, however, the same as scientifically rational behavior. In the final section of the work being discussed here, Garfinkel goes to great lengths to explain the ways in which a purely scientific rationality would destroy any sense of social relationship among people. For our purposes, however, it is sufficient to note that social behavior, as seen by Garfinkel, is not necessarily logical in its nature. Again, we see a kind of overloading of terms with meanings they cannot, in a strictly logical sense, actually have.

FINDING 5 "More subjects entertained the possibility of a trick than tested this possibility. All suspicious subjects were reluctant to act under the belief that there was a trick involved. Suspicions were reduced if the adviser's answers made 'good sense.' Suspicions were least likely to continue if the answers accorded with the subject's previous thought about the matter and with his preferred decisions [p. 91]."

We shall refer to this as *test resistance*, although the term does not do Garfinkel's observation justice. Garfinkel was interested in the fact that students rarely made tests of the situation they were in. Garfinkel suggests that evidently the students found their own constructions of the "sense" of the situation sufficient. It is important to underscore, once more, that the students were responding as much to their own creations as they were to the external and "real" situation. For as long as the students could sustain a correspondence between their comprehension of the situation and what they were doing, they refused to test the situation and accepted it for what it appeared to be.

This is the world "taken for granted." Garfinkel is interested in the extent to which most of us are unwilling to test certain kinds of rules or possibilities inherent within a particular moment or situation. In a different demonstration, Garfinkel had students go out as potential customers and show an interest in some item worth no more than two dollars. Then they were to bargain with the salesperson, beginning with a very low opening bid. Garfinkel found, first of all, that students found this difficult to do—particularly if the assignment called for the student to try to bargain only once. Where students were to make the effort three or more times, there was a greater tendency for the students to carry through with the assignment. Interestingly, the students found that by the third time they were able to enter a bargaining stance with sales-people and enjoy "dickering" with them over the price of an item. They even discovered, somewhat to their surprise, that more often than not they could get significant bargains by this process. For Garfinkel, how-ever, the significance of their efforts lies in more general possibilities. One of the qualities of whatever is taken for granted is that it does not get tested. Many rules operate, he suggests, not because they have withstood some test of time but rather because they simply have not been tested. "Indeed, the more important the rule, the greater is the likelihood that knowledge is based on avoided tests."[14]

Among the students who were being "counseled" the possibility that a trick was in progress was more likely to be considered than tested. Interestingly enough, the judgment as to whether deceit was involved rested on the congruence between the background expectations and interpretations of the student and the pattern of random responses being presented by the counselor. Garfinkel is suggesting here (though he does not pay much further attention to the possibility) that paranoid or suspicious qualities in an interaction arise out of incongruencies between expected backgrounds. That is, paranoia is not specifically a personality characteristic in many cases but comes, instead, out of qualities of the interaction between persons—with the most significant aspect of the interaction being the matching or mismatching of backgrounds.

FINDING 6 "Throughout there was a concern and search for pat-tern. Pattern, however, was perceived from the very beginning. Pattern was likely to be seen in the first evidence of the 'advice' [p. 91]."

We shall refer to this as *patterning*. The students in the counseling demonstration believed they were able to deal with the entire range of stimuli. They would indicate this with statements such as, "Ah, I see, now, how it *all* fits together." In other words, stimuli were not discrete "Yes" or "No" responses but were manipulated by the student into an organic pattern of stimuli.

This is a major feature of Garfinkel's work. It is an overriding prem-ise that pervades the whole of his thinking about the nature of social behavior.[15] Garfinkel is interested in the consequences of the fact that people come into social relationships with a preestablished sense of

---

[14] *Studies in Ethnomethodology*, p. 70.
[15] There is a strong temptation to draw parallels between the Gestalt school of psychology and Garfinkel's work—with Garfinkel representing an unusual form of Gestaltist sociology. The concept of pattern underlies both points of view. Unlike psychologists, however, Garfinkel is not especially interested in pattern as it affects the individual's purely sensory perception. He is interested in pattern as it relates to the ordered manner in which people conduct their ordinary social affairs.

320   pattern.[16] How does this pattern influence the interaction? What is its source? What are the consequences of even minor disturbances in the pattern? How can the nature of the pattern be ascertained by disrupting it?

We can gain an appreciation of the extent to which Garfinkel does not accept the taken-for-granted aspects of social behavior as we progress into some of his evaluations of the finding that social interaction is grounded in the "search for pattern." He comments, for example, that the subjects found it difficult to deal with the fact that they had been given random counseling. When they were informed that this was the situation, they shifted their interpretation of the counselor's comments from "advice" to "deceit." Again, keep in mind that during the period when the subjects were naive they had accepted the random advice as advice. *In other words, the character of the advice itself is not what determines whether it is acceptable as advice.* Some other condition or background factor determines this.

So the character of the advice received is not a function of the advice being given but is rather the conceptualization of the advice by the recipient. The random responses, seen as an event, provide documentation for an established pattern. Once the pattern is established, the documentation process takes place with some insistence. The underlying patterns may shift, but the constant process of documenting the pattern from the givens of the interaction remains as an integral part of the person's social concern.

FINDING 7 "Subjects assigned to the adviser as his advice the thought formulated in the subject's questions. For example, when a subject asked, 'Should I come to school every night after supper to do my studying?' and the experimenter said, 'My answer is no,' the subject in his comments said, 'He said I shouldn't come to school and study.' This was very common [p. 92]."

We shall refer to this as *projection.* This general concept is an old one in psychology, where it is commonly used to describe defensive behavior. For example, a disturbed person may project his or her disturbance on to others. This sometimes happens with a person who is inclined toward homosexuality but who, at the same time, fears homosexuality. He then accuses others of making advances toward him or otherwise acting homosexually. His homosexual fears have been projected. Garfinkel goes further. He suggests that such projection is not simply a defensive psychological device. Instead, it is a purely natural and common aspect of any human interaction. People are constantly projecting, as it were, those backgrounds that they bring into a given social moment.

[16] The idea of a preestablished pattern of ideas about an interaction sounds similar to the older social psychological concepts of attitudes and prejudices. In their older usage these terms either had a pejorative quality (it is "bad" to be prejudiced) or restricted application (one has attitudes about some relevant issue of the time, such as the election of a Catholic as president or the use of fluorides in drinking water). Garfinkel finds that the existing apparent patterns are a constant and necessary condition for *any* social interaction. In this sense, his work is a simple extension of already well-established concepts in the fields of social psychology, sociology, and cultural anthropology.

This seventh observation has a great number of implications. It **321** suggests, among other things, that: (1) the meaning of messages in social interchange cannot be isomorphic (show a one-to-one correspondence) unless the backgrounds of the participants are isomorphic, (2) distortion is a natural part of ordinary social events, (3) a message does not exist as an isolated event and cannot be given any value as such, (4) messages that carry no meaning in themselves can establish a meaning through the process of communication, and (5) understanding any message that is presented within a group (where such understanding is sought by some outside observer) calls for comprehensive knowledge of the social and cultural backgrounds of all members of the group, including how those backgrounds influence received messages. There are other implications in this observation that space does not permit us to consider. We urge the reader, however, to note how commonly this matter of "projection" occurs in day-to-day interactions with friends and associates.

It is also important to note here that people are not generally cognizant of the extent to which they are shaping and influencing the situation that is also shaping and influencing them. When students were informed, after the counseling sessions, that they had contributed a great deal to the "advice" they received, they were astounded.

FINDING 8 "Subjects made specific reference to various social structures in deciding the sensible and warranted character of the adviser's advice. Such references, however, were not made to any social structures whatever. In the eyes of the subject, if the adviser was to know and demonstrate to the subject that he knew what he was talking about, and if the subject was to consider seriously the adviser's descriptions of his circumstances as grounds of the subject's further thoughts and management of these circumstances, the subject did not permit the adviser, nor was the subject willing to entertain, *any* model of the social structures. References that the subject supplied, were to social structures which he treated as actually or potentially known in common with the adviser. And then, not to *any* social structure known in common, but to *normatively valued social structures* which the subject accepted as *conditions* that his decisions, with respect to his own sensible and realistic grasp of his circumstances and the 'good' character of the adviser's advice, had to satisfy. These social structures consisted of normative features of the social system *seen from within* which, for the subject, were definitive of his memberships in the various collectivities that were referred to [pp. 92–93]."[17]

This lengthy and, at first, obvious-sounding "finding" has some not so obvious and even lengthier implications. First of all, Garfinkel is probing into what constitutes the subjects' determination of the validity of information they are receiving from someone. However, rather than seeing it as a "psychological" or "personality" matter, Garfinkel finds that the individual's actions are a peculiar working out of institutional directives. The individuals begin to appear as people who are relating to others in terms of rules of which they are uncertain and are attempting

---

[17] Italics are Garfinkel's.

322 to define as they go along. However, they define the rules by referring to what they consider the central rule-making agencies, which they believe the others also accept. We shall refer to this as social *validation*. The important thing to note here is that the process of validating the situation rests, essentially, on a determination of the social character or identity of the counselor.

From this perspective, then, individuals become the representatives of a not very well defined institutional system, and *they attempt to establish the reality of that institution within their conversations with others*. In the case of the students and the counselor, the students attempted to make the counselor a proper or valid representative of the system of rules that were the foundation for the judgments and aspirations of the students. It is as though they were involved in some kind of game situation in which they knew that it was proper to play the game, but they could not be certain just what rules were involved and whether the other person also understood the rules. So, some parts of the interchange between the students and the counselor involved attempts by the students to make certain the counselor was properly representative of the game and knew about its rules—even though the students themselves were not certain of them. They then made use of replies from the counselor which enabled them to conclude they were correct in their feeling that the counselor was "with it" and could therefore be used to validate the norms or rules of which the students were uncertain.

This is a conception of people as creative agents who fashion within each social moment the affirming conditions, which then move on to become the "real" institutionalized complex of lifeways that they can turn to as justification for their particular actions. Though it sums up matters much too briefly, Garfinkel is suggesting here that what individuals shore up, when they engage in what is commonly thought of as ego-supportive behavior, is actually their conception of central institutional structures *within* which they see themselves significantly involved.

FINDING 9 "Through the work of documenting—i.e., by searching for and determining pattern, by treating the advisor's answers as motivated by the intended sense of the question, by waiting for later answers to clarify the sense of previous ones, by finding answers to unasked questions—the perceivedly normal values of what was being advised were established, tested, reviewed, retained, restored; in a word, managed. It is misleading, therefore, to think of the documentary method as a procedure whereby propositions are accorded membership in a scientific corpus. Rather the documentary method developed the advice so as to be continually 'membershipping' it [p. 94]."

This final observation and conclusion coming from the random counseling study by Garfinkel summarizes all that has gone before. In the course of conversation and ordinary discourse, people behave in terms of social norms and manners. However, this "puppet on a string" approach is much too simple for Garfinkel. People do not merely reflect some psychological-personality characteristic, nor do they simply respond mechanically to a given social-normative-cultural demand. Individuals, from an ethnomethodological perspective, are constantly in need of other people as agents through which they can continuously confirm their own uncertain and hopeful-fearful sense of what they represent within the community.

Garfinkel observed that students did not passively receive information and act on it. They "managed" the information they received. We shall, therefore, refer to this as *information management*.[18] We are all familiar with the gross management of information in Orwell's novel *1984*. It is apparent that people often distort information or otherwise use it for some special purpose other than its original intention. What is unique about Garfinkel's perspective is, again, his awareness of the extent to which this is a constant and natural feature of virtually any human interaction. Information management is something all of us engage in and it is probably something we must engage in throughout our lives.

Rationality, Science, and "Ordinary" Behavior

So it comes about, from this point of view, that individuals move as creative and actively "documenting" agents within any social setting. They reinterpret the comments and actions of others and then incorporate them within a preexisting body of conceptions of how the world is and, more specifically, how people are. Individuals become unwitting and uncertain propaganda agents. That is, whatever information they receive is employed to sustain the already established sense of moral order they bring into their interactions with others.

The "reasonableness" of people is not a function of what they are or even what they are doing. It is axiomatic for the kind of sociology that Garfinkel develops that it is actually quite impossible to know what people are or what they are doing! That is, it is impossible to know this without creating a "meaning" or imposing one on the situation. But created or imposed conceptions of what people are or are doing force us to consider the process of creation or imposition, and the question of what people *really* are begins to lose its salience. The "reasonableness," then, of what others are and are doing does not come directly from them or from their actions. It comes, instead, from the extent to which we can accept what they do as valid in terms of our diffused understanding of what is required of us as participants within the greater community.

After dealing with human behavior in commonplace situations, Garfinkel closes his work with a discussion of rationality, science, and "ordinary" behavior. It is a discussion that reviews the interpretations and observations that have gone before and relates them to one of the dominant forces of modern culture—science. In his discussion of science and common day-to-day social living, Garfinkel views both realms of action as data and not as methodologies. That is, science is something more than simply a method. It is a socially viable point of view and is competitive, as such, with other social doctrines. At this point science begins to press upon us a way of life and as a way to achieve rational

---

[18] There is an interesting parallel, here, with Goffman's notion that people are forced to manage the impressions they must present before others.

324 social relations. However, Garfinkel comes to the conclusion, after comparing science as a social fact with what takes place in common social interaction, that science cannot be an integral part of ordinary social behavior. To attempt to be social requires that specifically scientific thoughtways be set aside.

Because the issue of science and the place that science occupies in modern life are now approaching overwhelming dimensions, it is worth spending time on Garfinkel's view of this sector of human life. The discussion reveals, at one and the same time, the general character of Garfinkel's mode of understanding human social behavior and the pressing relevance of his concerns.

The term *rational* has come to have great influence within both the academic world and the world of everyday affairs. What is a rational person? How did our belief in rationality come to have its current massive support? Why do we seek to produce rational social orders and rational educational programs and rational models of war? Is there any difference between rational behavior in ordinary situations and rational behavior within the context of scientific investigation? If there is a difference between scientific rationality and the rationality of ordinary social events, then where does the difference appear? Finally, is there any necessary conflict or interference between rationality as it operates within the moral program of science and rationality as it operates within the moral order of human social relations?

Garfinkel concludes that there are significant differences between rationality in science and rationality in common affairs. He also concludes that the two forms of rationality are in serious conflict. He makes a plea at the end of his work that the relationship between science and human affairs should not be taken dogmatically as something given. It would be unwise to hold that science can give form and substance to human affairs. It cannot do this. He suggests, instead, that the imposition of a scientific rationality on ordinary daily life would probably result in a multiplication of the anomic or disorganizing features of human relations.

One of the distinguishing features of daily social interaction is the extent to which it cannot rely on a purely scientific rationality. Scientific rationality, for example, requires being neutral or even skeptical toward the idea that things are what they appear to be. In daily social activities, rational positions are almost the opposite of this. One must take a position that is not neutral. Things must be accepted for what they appear to be. Although doubt can be entertained, it is the exception rather than the rule. So, for example, it is a *social,* though not scientific, form of rationality to accept the belief that one's teacher is an expert or that the President is unusually dedicated to the affairs of the country. A scientific stance toward such aspects of the "social" realm would, by its very dedication to doubt and neutrality, tear at the social fiber and generate anomie and disorganization. Thus, Garfinkel claims that the proper study of the sociologist is the examination of how people generate the means (the folk methods) whereby doubt is minimized and a sense of things-as-they-are is sustained.

There are further implications in this statement by Garfinkel. The most significant, given the trend of our times, is that any kind of attempt to impose a rational-scientific mentality on people as a whole would defeat its purpose. The kind of rationality necessary to sustain social interaction simply is not the same kind of rationality that is necessary for the solution of scientific problems. In a day and age that subscribes so totally to science as a problem-solving device, we must be kept constantly on guard lest we abuse and misuse, through oversubscription, this most powerful of thoughtways. Garfinkel's studies, eccentric as they seem to some readers, have a profoundly humanistic theme at their center. How far can we go with science before we have done more damage to ourselves than good? There is no easy answer to this question. A review of *Studies in Ethnomethodology* will offer any serious student of these issues an introduction to the complexities that surround the dream of producing social behavior that is more scientifically rational than we have been able to achieve in the past.[19]

In concluding this all-too-brief introduction to one of the more controversial developments in modern sociological thought and writing, we would like to suggest that Garfinkel, for all of the detached and abstract character of his work, is rich in practical implications for those who wish to find them. We have received more than a few letters and comments from students and instructors in which we were informed that we had imposed too much impractical theorizing on the reader. Students want something more immediate and direct, something useful. The paradox of understanding, however, is that often the route to truly useful efforts calls for a thoughtful examination of what is going on. To the ordinary mind, the most practical way to get to the moon would seem to be to build a simple rocket and aim it in the right general direction and then set it off. We are all aware, today, that to accomplish such a task required the development of innumerable theories and observation in the fields of mathematics, physics, metallurgy, pressurized systems, waste control, communications, and so on, and so on.

It is the same with modern understandings of and work in the realm of human social and cultural affairs. If nothing else, Garfinkel warns us that projections, loadings, distortions, information management, and other irrational features of social communication are inherent, in all

---

[19] For those students who lack the patience or background to cope with Garfinkel's major works, there is an engaging alternative. One of Garfinkel's best-known students is the author Carlos Castaneda, the author of the famous series of novels involving the character of an old Yaqui Indian named Don Juan (*The Teachings of Don Juan: A Yaqui Way of Knowledge; A Separate Reality: Further Conversations with Don Juan; Journey to Ixtlan: The Lessons of Don Juan;* and so forth). These novels have been extremely popular and widely read, especially among college-age people. The thing that is interesting about the old "Yaqui Indian" is that he really talks more like a modern phenomenological or ethnomethodological sociologist than one might expect. This has led to some speculation that Don Juan is really a romanticized and fictionalized characterization of Castaneda's teacher—Harold Garfinkel. Whether this is true or not we are unable to say. We can, however, suggest that one can get at least a charming introduction to some of the major ideas behind Garfinkel's work by thoughtfully reading about the adventures of Castaneda and his friend "Don Juan."

326 probability, in any social discourse. Moreover, they cannot be removed. To be placed on one's guard, even when the circumstances are commonplace and ordinary, is to move toward a more practical understanding of these capricious and irrational forces or processes that can, if not understood, lead to gratuitous forms of injury and damage. But Garfinkel is not interested in the practical. The extent to which his work can be given practical value will have to be left to the student.

Problems and Issues

Garfinkel's theories help us realize that we are so much a part of whatever takes place in our day-to-day lives that we rarely have an opportunity to comprehend the extent to which much of what we do is constructed by ourselves, or by friends and others. Usually, events are constructed in an informal manner rather than formally. We are daily reconstructing and reestablishing social reality. We bring a great amount of background material into a social interaction, which is then incorporated into the moment. Whether this information is valid or false is not so important as whether it "works." Many groups rely on someone who takes on the role of "butt" or scapegoat in the group. By what procedures is such a person identified? What methods are employed to keep the person in the group and, at the same time, sustain his or her identity as the least able member of the group?

Ethnomethodology seeks to make us more aware of the devices we employ in creating the realities to which we respond. Often these realities are not "outside" us so much as they are "inside" us. Ethnomethodology, of course, raises a host of questions concerning the nature of reality. Particularly significant is the problem of the nature of social reality. How is it constructed for us, and how do we participate in its construction?

The question is not an academic one. How we develop particular conceptions of social reality can have a variety of effects. The example is given in the text of the extent to which asserting the right to bargain for an item in a store can have beneficial economic consequences for those who do it. On a deeper level, the way in which economics, as an institutionalized "method," has defined the economic behavior of the culture as a whole has also had consequences. One has to see the economic features of the society as more basic than the noneconomic features. American economists tend to emphasize commodities over values. Is this one reason for the recent problems that economists have encountered in trying to deal with such contemporary difficulties as inflation?

Garfinkel's study of counseling is both simple and devastating in its implications. What happens to us when we seek counseling—whether it is from a professional or from a friend? What are you doing when you "counsel" someone who has come to you for help? What are the implications of Garfinkel's counseling demonstration for those who would like to reduce social behavior to genetics?

Communication, Art, and Victims

**HUGH DALZIEL
DUNCAN**

. . . there is a peculiar kind of
anguish *in communication.*
Communication and Social
Order

BORN: 1909   DIED: 1975

Peculiarities in the Idea of Cause

18

Western culture developed the idea of *cause* to help people understand
the world around them. It was, and remains, an awkward idea. Philosophers find the notion of cause filled with controversial and inconsistent
features. It produces as many problems as it resolves. So messy is the
concept of cause that some writers have suggested the whole thing be
tossed out of any rational vocabulary. However, the idea lives on, and
we still attempt to understand the world by looking for causes and their
effects. If something happens, then it must have a cause. If there is a
cause, then it must have some effect.

What we are interested in here is not an examination of the metaphysical problems that arise from the concept of cause. Instead, we are
interested in some of the features of social behavior that come from our
concern with the "causes" of such behavior. One problem we get into
when we apply causal terms to the study of social acts is that we soon
find ourselves running down a path of infinite regressions of causes.

328   For example, we are told that a juvenile has stolen an automobile. What made him do that? That is, what *caused* him to do that? We answer that he wanted to be a big shot with his friends. Why did he want to be a big shot? Because our culture rewards aggression and assertion of self. Why does our culture reward aggression and assertion of self? Because individuals who are assertive and aggressive are useful to a cultural system engaged in a quest for profit and progress. Why did profit and progress become important? Because there were certain prior ideologies that were congenial to the development of such interests. Like a child's constant questioning, it can go on and on and on. Why? Because. Why? Because. There is no end to the causal implications that come from even the simplest social moments.

The problem of the infinite regression of causes also exists, of course, for the natural sciences. It has led to peculiar notions, such as the idea of a prime or ultimate cause that accounts for the ultimate effect of the universe around us. But this is not our concern here. What we are interested in is how the infinite regression can be *stopped* when dealing with social analysis or interpretation. When is it proper to go on asking why, and when is it necessary or acceptable to stop? How is the decisive moment reached when the decision rests, in the final analysis, on a leap into faith? Something must happen that permits people to conclude that only so much investigation of a situation is sufficient. Once this conclusion is reached, then other forms of action can take place.

In the natural sciences, the question of infinite regression is solved, at least in part, by the nature of technology. You do not have to go beyond the limits that are imposed by the thing you are trying to make work. Why did the transformer burn out? Because it was overloaded. The further problem of why it was overloaded may or may not be of interest. However, the causal explanation that it was overloaded is likely to be seen as satisfying because it is relevant to the question of why the transformer did not work. In other words, the mechanics of the transformer define the limits within which questioning is proper.

When we come to human social behavior, however, we run into a different problem. First, the causal circumstances are probably located in a history that cannot be directly manipulated or observed because it is part of the past. Second, social events are often the product of language or symbols and are, therefore, subject to interpretation rather than to rigorous causal explanations. Third, many causal factors work together to produce any particular social moment. Fourth, the limits or social boundaries of a person or group are not as well defined as are the limits or boundaries of a machine. Finally, the causal interpretation made of a particular social event is *always* subject to the criticism that it is a product of vested interests.

So, in the analysis of social behavior, the precise attribution of causal conditions becomes difficult—possibly beyond the capacity of human intellect. At the same time, the difficulty is apparently surmounted. That is, people do, in fact, ascribe causes to social happenings, and they do so with a sense of satisfaction and completeness. The situation confronting them has been explained. They accept the explanation and then act on it.

To act in terms of the explanation, of course, makes the explanation itself the significant point of departure for understanding the action. This is important if we are to comprehend some of the arguments that are developed later in this chapter. The accepted explanation becomes the foundation for action itself. It can be such an integral part of the action that we come to see the action as a reflection of the accepted explanation of events. For example, when the Nazis selected Jews as an explanation for what they perceived as problems, the consequent acting out of events, in all its tragic and massive horror, became intricately interwoven with the accepted explanation of events. *The explanation of what was happening was the force that brought about the happening itself.*

The theme we will develop in this chapter is that people are able to act by virtue of the fact that they have closed off further questioning about the act. They have concluded that what they are doing *is* the way to act. Any further questioning of the matter would cause hesitation. In order to act, one must be committed to act in faith or must somehow become committed. One's faith can be in science, health foods, capitalism, communism, beauty, or some other ideal; but faith, unquestioning and strong, is required. In their fundamental character, overlooking the social forms they espouse as real, the staunch deist and the rabid atheist are no different. The liberal Democrat and the conservative Republican are of the same basic stuff—they are all willing to act.

So, curiously enough, we must begin by developing an appreciation for the simple fact that people do things—they act. Against a paralyzing world that offers an infinite set of possibilities, they select a few that serve, and they become committed with great intensity. They kill, maim, insult, destroy themselves and others—all in the name of some principle of action.

It is much too simple to try to account for such behavior by saying it is learned. The concept of *learning* and its related concept of *socialization* have been popular ideas for handling the problem of why people behave. Simple and apparently obvious though these concepts are, they nonetheless are incapable of dealing with the problem of action. They can help account for *what* has been learned, but they do not necessarily account for the ways in which that learning will be put into action. That is, learning and socialization help account for the *form* of behavior but not for the *act* of behaving itself. One can, for example, learn and know the doctrines of Quakerism or Nazism without being disposed to behave in their terms. Whether an action will be engaged in depends, finally, on an "artful" judgment by the actor, who must evaluate the complexities of a communicative act and move within those complexities in a way which is *something more* than a mechanical or machinelike learned response.[1] It is this "something more" that interests Hugh Dalziel Duncan.

---

[1] The mechanical behavior of rats running mazes gives the learning process an apparent necessity that it does not have when we reach social-symbolic behavior among humans. The rat *has* to turn to the right or left to appease his hunger or avoid a shock. Some physical behavior has a nearly mechanical necessity about it. However, symbolic behavior is not mechanical—or, at least, mechanical metaphors are very crude ways to describe what happens when people interact symbolically.

330   Art and Social Action

For Duncan, the social order is a wobbling and uncertain process that goes careening through history on the wheels of communication. Where other sociologists have emphasized the orderly nature of society, Duncan emphasizes its disorderly nature. Where other sociologists have tried to ground social behavior in physical conditions, Duncan has tried to ground it in the symbolic act of communication. Where other sociologists have almost totally ignored the institution of art and the artfulness of institutions,[2] Duncan makes art the central force that moves through all other social institutions and agencies. Art is the "prime mover" of social action. People become committed to action by art, not by science. Even a commitment to science requires that the individual come to see the significance of science through artful presentations of its value. Science is not without its own rhetoric.[3]

For Duncan, art is essential for human social action. It varies among cultures, but it is common to all people. It is an integral aspect of the process of communication. Because we cannot understand human social structures without understanding something about the process of communication, we are forced to consider the nature of art, the functions of art, the relationship between art forms and human action. Art is not a secondary phenomenon, a luxury used by a culture or society when it has nothing else to do. Art is the essential nature of the culture. It *is* the culture.

A soap opera, for example, is not something that works just to amuse the frustrated housewife. The housewife may actually rely on the soap opera to gauge the nature of her own social existence. She may view the soap opera as a presentation of someone else's domestic problems, but she may also incorporate its value priorities into her own domestic problems. The soap opera and the "realities" of life are thus conjoined. It is not a mechanical connection. To the extent that the housewife acts out the concerns of the soap opera, art and life have come together. The woman's day-to-day existence is as much a reflection of art as art is a reflection of her life. But this description of Duncan's

---

[2] To a great degree, sociologists not only ignore art in their analysis of social behavior but even view art as something trivial or not essential to what is "really" going on. George Lundberg has expressed the most extreme form of this sentiment by suggesting that artists are actually very gifted liars. See George Lundberg, *Can Science Save Us?* 2d ed. (New York: McKay, 1961).

[3] Such rhetoric occurs whenever somebody engages in either open or disguised pleas for science as a proper life activity. Science is not its own justification. It must be sustained by rhetorical appeals just like any other form of social behavior. Indeed, the success of science rests, at least in part, on the extent to which it has provided some cultures with powerful weapons for imposing their ways of life on others. Science is justified by what it presumably can do for people, as a means of bringing about progress, freedom, wisdom, or understanding. Actually, any such accomplishments are debatable. The acceptance of science as a way of life rests, as it has always rested, on a recognition of its values without much further questioning of those values. Wherever this sort of thing occurs, rhetoric accounts for the commitment to that which is ultimately an arbitrary matter.

point of view is so banal that it nearly strips it of the profundity that is revealed only after one has read, and reread, Duncan's major writings.[4]

Symbolic Life

Duncan begins with the simple premise that the unique thing about human social order and disorder is the extent to which it rests on communication and the employment of symbols.[5] If we are to understand ourselves, we must understand what we do with, and what is done to us by, symbols. People are symbolic. To behave with dignity is to use dignity as a symbol of majesty and propriety. To be involved is to be involved with ideals of justice, truth, or beauty. Symbolic life is characteristic of human beings, and of humans alone among all life forms on this planet. Duncan suggests that we turn directly to the symbol and its properties in order to understand what is special to human nature. What happens when people are caught up in the act of communication?

One of the central properties of symbols, as Duncan sees them, is their capacity for extensive elaboration. Any event or any human quality can be made the subject of a symbolic development. This development can be so elaborate that it becomes impossible for any single individual to comprehend, even after a lifetime of study, the total symbolic portrayal of a given concern. We can take any realm of human activity we want to and use it to exemplify Duncan's argument.

Sex, for example, when thought of in terms of purely physiological considerations, is the relatively simple bringing together of sex organs for the mutual enjoyment of the participants. At one time, prior to the development of language, the act must have been simple enough so that one could carry it through without having much education in the matter.[6] Symbolically, however, sex is something quite different. It is the central

---

[4] Of the various social theorists we have studied, Duncan stands above most in his struggle to add to our understanding of social behavior, and for this we admire him. Among his major works are *Language and Literature in Society: A Sociological Essay on Theory and Method in the Interpretation of Linguistic Symbols with a Bibliographical Guide to the Sociology of Literature* (Chicago: University of Chicago Press, 1953); *The Rise of Chicago as a Literary Center: A Sociological Essay in American Culture* (New York: Bedminster Press, 1964); *Communication and Social Order* (New York: Bedminster Press, 1962); and *Symbols in Society* (New York: Oxford University Press, 1968). Of his many works, we most strongly recommend *Communication and Social Order*. It is a vexing book, ponderous in its style and badly flawed in many respects. It is, nonetheless, extremely sophisticated.

[5] Duncan associated himself with the central symbolic interactionist theorists in academic sociology. He identified with Charles Horton Cooley and George Herbert Mead and saw his work as an extension of their ideas. His greatest acknowledgement, however, was to the literary critic-teacher Kenneth Burke. Duncan often referred to Burke as "the master." The sophistication of Duncan's work can be attributed almost exclusively to the astonishingly subtle and varied arguments of Burke. Burke has influenced a growing number of modern social scientists—among them Erving Goffman and Harold Garfinkel.

[6] We are not claiming, of course, that monkeys or subhuman non-language-using creatures do not need some learning to be able to engage in intercourse. However, the learning is relatively simple when compared with the meanings that sex can acquire for symbolic beings.

332 theme of thousands of books and lectures and songs and dramas. It is the core concept for psychiatric treatises. It is the foundation for moral and ethical issues. It is seen as dirty and as the primal sin. It is glorified as beautiful and the way to achieve the full life.[7] It is a device for justifying the condemnation of numbers of people who do not perform their sexual actions properly. Sex has been elaborated to the point where it is used symbolically to sell cars. And cars thereby have become sexual in character. By the time sex has been symbolically elaborated, it has moved from a physiological condition to an abstract force that calls for its understanding as symbol or myth. For humans, intercourse occurs within the context of an art of sexuality. The purely physiological act is not irrelevant; it is simply insufficient. The human act is an artful act. And the character of this artfulness, Duncan insists, should be the proper concern of the sociologist.

Symbols, then, have as one of their special abilities the capacity for elaboration. Any event or feature of the world can be made an object of elaborate description. Symbolic elaboration is a quality of symbols and not of the real world. The elaborate descriptions given by sportswriters of such events as grown men walking around a cow pasture and swatting little white balls into holes with sticks are what make the events what they are. The game of golf becomes the game of golf not simply when it is played on the course but when it is talked about and symbolically described in an elaborated manner. In this context the game of golf becomes something more. It becomes a "sudden-death" playoff. It becomes a test of character and nerves. It becomes a symbolic complex that transcends, in character, the immediate act itself. It is not simply that words are necessary to describe the event. In using words to achieve a description, the words and the event become such integral aspects of each other that we cannot comprehend the one without understanding the other. The event becomes significant in its description. More interestingly, its symbolic description has the capacity to be elaborated.

Granting, then, that symbols have a capacity for elaboration, the next step in Duncan's reasoning is to observe that elaboration can, and generally does, progress to the point where it is impossible to meet the demands that grow out of the elaborated presentation of some aspect of character. Consider, for example, the incredibly elaborated presentations of the love relationship that should obtain between people in this society. Love, one of the central themes of popular and classical literature and drama, has a history of symbolic interpretation that goes back beyond the Bible. It gained its impetus in Western culture, however, with the ballads of the twelfth-century troubadors. Already subjected to an elaborated literature of love that came from Christian doctrine, the troubadors created songs and ballads that praised courtly forms of love. The idea then developed that one should express love by remaining true, chaste, distant, subservient, and constant. The sincerity of love should

---

[7] Writers from *Playboy* to Wilhelm Reich have suggested that sexual gratification is necessary for the good life. Reich believed that a truly profound orgasm was necessary if the individual was to have anything other than a stunted life.

be manifested by deeds of courage or sacrifice. Those who followed such practice would find a love that would be eternal and unfailingly ecstatic. It was an interesting notion. It was also an impossibly idealized statement of human relations.

The Process of Idealization

The concept of romantic love, derived from courtly love, still functions as the main subject of most popular music and literature. Keeping it in mind as an example, there are two features of the process of idealization that should be mentioned here. The first is that the development of impossible idealizations does *not* lead to the ultimate demise of the idealization. The second is that people elaborate on and change their idealizations.

Duncan develops the view that one of the inherent characteristics of idealizations is that they invariably reach the point where they set forth inhuman and impossible demands and aspirations. As these impossible conditions are elaborated as ideals to be pursued by people, a point is reached where it is absolutely inevitable that people will fail. The ideal cannot be met by any person or by any group. The ideal, however, is not rejected; instead it is made the source of still further elaborations that maintain the integrity of the ideal.

After a number of centuries during which couples have crashed against the impossible demands of romantic love, we still have romantic love as a fundamental theme for symbolic elaboration and idealization. It has not died as an ideal even though it cannot be achieved; it is a strong force in modern life despite the fact that it is probably more often a cause of marital misery than of marital happiness.[8]

So, one of the interesting things about idealizations is that they continue even though they are unworkable. Indeed, according to Duncan, the invariable character of idealizations is that they *are* unworkable! The ability of symbols to move beyond realities places people in situations where they come to promote unrealities as a way of life. They set off on a quest for such things as happiness, the super race, holy grace, true love, justice,[9] peace, success, scientific societies, transcendent understanding, and any of a number of other equally peculiar ambitions.

The first thing, then, about idealizations is that they continue to develop and be elaborated. The second thing about them is that they are impossible. People cannot match the demands of the idealizations that have developed around them. They are doomed to failure. Note, here, that the argument focuses on the character of symbols or language. Idealization is a consequence of the capacity to use and be used by

---

[8] It is amusing to hear a popular folk singer tell us, via a recording, that she is going to find happiness and true love by giving her heart forever to a poor man. There is nothing wrong with this, of course, but one wonders about the message. Could the singer herself really find happiness by living forever with a poor man?

[9] The famous lawyer Clarence Darrow said, "There is no such thing as justice—in or out of court." He recognized justice for what it is—an idealization.

334 language. It is a natural consequence of language itself. This point of view turns attention toward the structure and character of language— what it means to be involved with language—rather than toward physiological, genetic, or psychological factors. We should hasten to add that this point of view does not, of course, deny the significance of genetic and physiological factors. It simply maintains some awareness of an element in our lives that seems so ordinary that we tend to ignore it when trying to understand human actions. To ignore the nature and character of symbolic systems is, Duncan would argue, to ignore a powerful force in its own right.

We have argued so far that symbols possess the capacity for rapid and extensive elaboration. This, in turn, can lead to symbolic constructions of a highly idealized nature. Such symbolic definitions of the world create exaggerated ideals that move far beyond human capacities. People are motivated to seek the ideal, but are placed in situations where the ideal is impossible and failure is the necessary consequence. The inevitability of failure places people in a situation where they are forced to handle failure as a functional part of their character and society. It is essential that we comprehend the extent to which Duncan looks on this sense of failure as a property of the act of communication. It is not a psychological property and it is not a matter of our moral nature as fallible beings. It is instead a quality that emerges from the symbolic act. There is a difference between a subhuman primate failing to reach a banana and a human being failing to achieve the elaborated conception of what properly constitutes being a "real" person.

Symbols lead to the process of elaboration. Elaboration in turn leads to idealization. Idealization produces situations that promote a sense of failure or inability to achieve the ideal. Failure to reach the goals of symbolic idealization induces, in turn, a deep sense of incompetence, which manifests itself in the form of either recognized or unconscious guilt. The individual can never be truly certain that he or she is a "real" person, a "real" scholar,[10] a "real" American, a "real" Christian, or a "real" anything else which rests, in its final expression, on symbolically elaborated ideals.

The Killer of the Dream

Guilt, then, is a personal reaction to idealized and symbolically elaborated communal values. There is one response to the failure-guilt complex, and that is to locate the source of blame for the failure. The human tendency, it seems, is to act as though the locus for failure cannot be placed within the ideal itself. Something outside the ideal must be the cause. The dream was a perfect dream, but something killed it. People are driven by clouds of words to seek the killer of the dream, who must be made to pay for violating the ideal. Because the ideal was so grand

---

[10] It is certainly not uncommon for people with Phi Beta Kappa keys and other excellent qualifications to denigrate themselves as educated people.

and magnificent, the killer of the dream must be revealed to one and all **335** for the dreadful and rotten creature he is. He must be punished and must become the embodiment of suffering which will stand as atonement for the hideousness of what he has done. He has stood between the ideal and its fulfillment.

What we have referred to here as "the killer of the dream"[11] is a central concern in Duncan's work. He is vitally interested in the issue of victimization and the creation of the victim as an essential part of social behavior. People create idealizations and then, in failing to reach them, create victims to help account for the failure. They use the victim to support and further reinforce the value of the ideals that led to the victimization.

The grand exemplification of this process in the twentieth century was the dramatic and total victimization of the Jews in Germany. The nationalistic ideals of Germany were obviously frustrated by something or someone other than the German people. After all, the German people idealized themselves as a nation capable of accomplishments beyond those of ordinary mortal beings. They were the finest that European culture had to offer; and Europe was the finest that the world could offer. They had not failed in their effort and their longing, yet the ideals had not been met. Something or someone must be held accountable.[12]

The use of the Jews as scapegoats in the bloody elimination of millions of people was not merely a political device. To see it as such is to lack a comprehension of the political process itself. For Duncan, the employment of the "final solution" by Adolph Hitler was part of a grander drama. The political structure was not simply something sustained by the dramatic devices of Hitler's forces. The dramatic aspects of these events were such an integral part of the political structure that we cannot consider one without thinking about the other. Drama and politics are different sides of the same coin.[13]

Duncan uses the term *drama* as a central metaphor for further investigation of what people do to other people, and it leads him to see some interesting things. Foremost among these is the selection of human beings to experience intense and prolonged suffering. These are the ones who must pay for all sins. These are the ones who, in the drama of human existence, have threatened the "grander principles of social order." Of course this statement still leaves us with the nagging problem of determining, or somehow comprehending, what the nature of those principles might be. Duncan deals with this issue, but for the moment we shall set it aside. Right now we must complete the idea that begins with the observation that symbols promote the elaboration and idealization of any quality of human social interaction. This idealization brings

[11] The term *killer of the dream* is ours, not Duncan's.
[12] It is very important not to see this process as something limited to a few aberrant occasions, such as the historical tragedy that was Nazi Germany or the racism that even now exists in the United States. It is a pervasive feature of *any* social context.
[13] There is a suggestion here that any dramatization we witness contains within it some political content. A film such as *Easy Rider*, for example, has to be looked at differently when it is seen as an artistic consideration of the politics of being "hip."

336 about failure and guilt, which leads to a quest for the source of failure and which finds and then victimizes the source.

The Drama of the Victim

With the establishment of the victim as the source of failure, a high dramatization of the person's heinous nature can be elaborated. The person is villainized and criminalized by devices that transcend the specifics of villainy or criminal behavior. The person is brought into the enactment of the crime, which is then made the source of a drama in which the principles of social order are reaffirmed in the ordeal to which the victim is subjected.

With the dramatization of the clash between the principles of order and disorder and the ritualistic establishment of the victory of the principles of order, the cycle is complete. The ceremonies of victimization have upheld the ideals, and the act of victimization can itself become part of the history and drama that further justifies the ideal. The ritualistic condemnation of the victim serves in part as evidence of the value of the ideals that led to the person's victimization. The ideals may then be further elaborated. This, in turn, will lead to the search for other victims.

This interpretation of social behavior accounts for two rather peculiar features of human aggressive action: (1) It is, or can be, extremely intense, and (2) it can, and usually does, maintain a high degree of continuity—that is, it can be sustained over relatively long periods of time. It is common, for example, for feelings of hostility to be sustained by an individual throughout an entire lifetime and then passed on to following generations. Human aggressive or punitive behavior moves far beyond the simpler forms of aggressive behavior that characterize subhuman organisms. It is difficult, therefore, to account for it simply in terms of human physiological or biological capacities for aggression.

The Act of Communication

Certainly there are biological bases for aggression and violence that can be studied and understood in terms of prevailing knowledge of the genetic and organic nature of humans. But such studies cannot produce more than a knowledge of what is capable of initiating aggressive action. That which sustains and intensifies it will have to be viewed as a more complex matter, and one of the elements entering into that complexity is the symbolic-cultural nature of human beings. Among the world's creatures, we alone possess an ability to record, in language, a variety of feelings and experiences. We can communicate these feelings. The act of communication possesses both a continuity and an intensity that further augments our original physiologically grounded capacity for feeling.

Duncan, therefore, is led into a consideration of communication as it bears on human social action. He is especially interested in the moral issue of how people come to the conclusion that they have the right and the moral imperative to condemn others and subject them to intense and prolonged suffering. One form of his concern is to see this as a product of the chain of elaboration–idealization–failure–guilt–victimization–elaboration–idealization process.

Before we consider another form of Duncan's concern with the moral issue of victimization, it is worth noting that his ideas, when carried to their final implications, suggest that there is little that can be done with or for the human condition. Victimization is an integral part of the communication process itself. Subhuman organisms fight and kill each other, but they do not engage in prolonged and torturous displays of victimization of one another.[14] This is a human specialty. Communication, in the elaborated form that symbols permit, is also a human specialty.

The communication process, then, becomes the focal point for Duncan's theoretical concerns. He finds the communication process inherently possessed of the property of leading people into making victims of themselves and each other. There is no quick panacea for human ills in this point of view. In fact, it leads to what sounds like an impossible contradiction in terms. If we are to surmount the trap that communication draws us into, then we are going to have to reach the point where we can use communication to avoid the pitfalls of communication. This is the best that Duncan has to offer as a solution.

The other alternative, that we attempt to abandon communication, he correctly recognizes as unfeasible. To abandon communication is to abandon that which is worthwhile in the human enterprise—indeed, that which *is* the human enterprise. So we are left with an impasse. It is difficult to see, on the one hand, how communication can be the device that solves the problems of communication or, on the other, how we can abandon communication. There is deep pessimism in this theory.[15]

---

[14] Durkheim was also deeply concerned with victimization. See chapter 4—especially the sections dealing with punishment.

[15] This impasse might account, in part, for some of the weaknesses of Duncan's theoretical writings. He refuses, as a humanist, to accept the idea that people are doomed to an eternal cycle of redemption through the torture of fellow beings. Yet, at the same time, there is nothing in his writing that reveals a way out. When Duncan begins to feel the pinch of this, his writing takes on a sophomoric quality. He becomes a naive exhorter. He comprehends the extent to which his exhortation is rooted in a point of view which is not at all optimistic. He concludes his major work with the following suggestion for promoting better relations among human beings:

> Much uneasiness, even despair, pervades our search for a way of thinking about how society arises in, and continues to exist through, communication. This is caused by the spectacle of Hitler and the wide gap between what we know as social scientists about human motivation and what such monsters as Hitler can put into practice. They seem to grasp intuitively that social relations are determined by identification, which is reached through *staging* human relationships in community dramas modeled after horrible perversions of religious drama. *What drama of reason can we create to match these terrible dramas of unreason?* [Italics ours.] Can we develop theory and method in symbolic analysis which will tell us *how* to do what we *ought* to do, as citizens of a free

338   The redemption of the ideal through the victimization of the carriers of the evil principle is but one of many themes in a work which, in its entirety, moves far beyond this simple Christian metaphor. At the same time, the redemption theme provides an entry into the heart of Duncan's thought. Society, as Duncan looks at it, is as much a state of disorder as it is a state of order. It is certainly wrong, he argues, to look at society as a mechanical device with smoothly functioning roles and integrated parts that create a nearly robotlike system. Duncan concentrates on the confusion that exists among people. The question is not one of how social disorganization takes place within an otherwise organized community. The question, rather, is of how some kind of integration and continuity exists when there is so much possibility for confusion and disintegration.

In trying to deal with such an issue, Duncan turns his attention to how people come to accept and then act in terms of symbols that transcend the person in their power to evoke action. These transcendent symbols are sustained by artful devices. It is the artist who, in Duncan's thought, becomes the special agent of society. Art is the social effort par excellence.

Art and the Social Order

Duncan's attempt to locate social action within art—totally bypassing the rational efforts of science as a source of social order—makes him unique among social scientists of the nineteenth and twentieth centuries.[16] Duncan does not see art as simply the "reflection" of something more fun-

world? And can we do it soon enough? Throughout this book we have argued that until the wide gap between humanistic and scientific understanding is closed, there is small reason for optimism. We must return the study of man in society to a study of communications, for how we communicate determines how we relate as human beings. (*Communication and Social Order*, p. 438.)

In this statement Duncan reveals the overwhelming nature of the problem. Those who believe the communication process can be readily reformed should set themselves to the task of trying to change the meaning of even a single word. Duncan is calling for a study and revision of the entire communication process. The near impossibility of this is something he recognizes. At the same time, he does not, as a humanist, want to accept the possibility that people are being shoved into rhetorical cul-de-sacs from which they cannot return.

[16] It is certainly interesting to compare Duncan's point of view with that of George Lundberg, a spokesman for the empiricist sociology of today. Lundberg sees art as a whimsical form of entertainment and great artists as essentially liars of incomparable talent. Duncan, on the other hand, sees artists as people who induce the desire to act. More significantly, he views any social act as being so imbued with artfulness that art and social behavior cannot be separated from each other. Even the most commonplace happening is motivated and inspired by the artful conduct of the participants. Above all, these participants do not behave scientifically. It is impossible to imagine, for example, how a joke could be told scientifically. Despite this, there is a belief among many academic sociologists that scientific sociology is the only hope for achieving an effective social order. Duncan is convinced that this point of view is impossibly naive.

damental in the social order. Art is not, for example, a response to the economic conflicts that are taking place within society—as a Marxist might want us to believe. Nor does art "reflect" the political system. In fact, art does not "reflect" anything. Art *is* the device whereby the social moment is constantly created and re-created. Art and the social moment become one and the same event. Art does not reflect the social order and social motives. Art *is* the social order and art *is* the social motive.

Duncan might suggest, for example, that when a man tells a woman he loves her, his statement does not reflect his motives. Instead, his ability to construct an artfully symbolic relationship with the woman is, in fact, the motive itself. Certainly it is a motive which derives from the massive and artful presentation of this theme within the culture. But that does not make the lover a "reflection" of the theme. In his passionate avowals of undying fidelity and his rhetoric of romance he is re-creating the theme—functioning artfully, not mechanically. The lover, in his conceptions of his love, is influenced by artful presentations of the ways men and women are supposed to relate. But the influence is not simply a lore that is learned or observed for amusement. It is the influential experience which, in turn, is sustained by the lover's employment of it for the development of his own artfully managed love affairs.

Duncan looks on social behavior as a befuddled and uncertain kind of action that manages, somehow, to achieve a sense of certainty. People possess at least a sufficient sense of certainty to generate action; they do act. But what do they act in terms of? At the physical level, of course, they are impelled by the simple demands of biological drives. They must eat, sleep, seek shelter, and somehow meet the demands that life imposes. But social action moves far beyond this, providing a sense of propriety for a great variety of situations. How do you relate to people who stand "above" you in status? How do you relate to people who are "beneath" you? How do you relate to equals? How do you ascertain these matters of status? What signs do you seek? How will you transmit to others your own level of social identity? These and other similar issues are not a matter of physiological resolution. Nor are they a matter of logic or science. Nonetheless, people do act and interact, and they possess a sense of certainty about their actions.

Transcendent Principles

In an attempt to deal with this matter, Duncan suggests that one of the fundamental elements of social action is "transcendent principles." Transcendent principles are valued ideals that are accepted as reasonable without critical consideration. They are principles of action that enable us to sustain a sense of propriety about our acts, even as the acts force us into moments of total madness (viewed from the perspectives of logic). Nothing better illustrates the peculiar qualities of social conduct than the behavior of an American officer in Vietnam who is reputed to have said that it was necessary to destroy a particular village in order to

340   save it. He then ordered a barrage which, when the smoke cleared, left only splintered remnants of the village.

This single case pulls together much of what is of interest to Duncan as a social theorist. It reveals that while the individual is more than a little confused by events, his confusion is not sufficient to incapacitate him. Indeed, he does act! In our example the officer acted to the point where his action killed the "enemy." In an attempt to justify his action, he called on ill-defined, vaguely comprehended, and peculiarly alluded-to transcendent principles. He destroyed the village because it was the only way he could save it. Save it for what? For freedom? For democracy? From communism? From destruction by something even more evil than an artillery barrage? Our example provides a scale of understanding if we can come to see that a transcendent principle has as much (if not more) authority as an artillery barrage.

This incident is a powerful case in point, because it reveals a process that appears throughout the entire range of social action. The officer was performing a social act whereby he destroyed something in order to save it. The lethality of the barrage makes his behavior of special interest, perhaps, but it is not distinguished by its confusion. Duncan might suggest that the officer's behavior is a paradigm of what we all do much of the time.

Duncan finds statements like that made by the officer characteristic of the rhetoric of opposites.[17] The occurrence of opposed points of view within a single rhetorical context is, on the one hand, perfectly illogical and, on the other, a revelation of the power of transcendent principles of action. Nothing better reveals the nature of symbolic-social behavior than the rhetoric of opposites. Following are some examples of this rhetoric:

> "Technology is capable of solving the problems it creates." Source unknown.
> "The union of the mathematician with the poet, fervor with measure, passion with correctness, this surely is the ideal." William James, *Collected Essays and Reviews*.
> "If a man have a strong faith he can indulge in the luxury of skepticism." Nietzsche, *The Twilight of the Idols*.
> "The world must be made safe for democracy." Woodrow Wilson in his Address to Congress, asking for a declaration of war, April 2, 1917.
> "A man is rich in proportion to the number of things which he can afford to let alone." Henry David Thoreau, *Walden*.
> "The only thing we have to fear is fear itself." Franklin Delano Roosevelt, First Inaugural Address.

What is of interest to Duncan about such statements is that they themselves constitute the data of social action. They are moving appeals to action, but they make little or no rational sense. In part, they appeal

---

[17] As is the case with much of Duncan's work, the terminology and the general ideas being developed here go back to the literary critic Kenneth Burke. Burke should be thought of as the truly original and innovative genius behind this argument.

because they do *not* make sense. They are designed to bring about **341** affirmation by the community, to infuse the listener or reader with a sense of identification with the greater purposes of the society. The miracle of rhetoric is that it works.

When Woodrow Wilson says that the world must be made safe for democracy, he is appealing for the employment of a rather nondemocratic instrument—the American war machine. The statement itself is nondemocratic in character, and Wilson simply states it in an authoritarian manner. Whatever "voting" about the issue that was to take place in the struggle between nations took place with guns and not ballots. The world is still being made safe for democracy by the same nondemocratic procedures.[18]

The Artful Use of Rhetoric

Despite the irrationalities of the rhetoric of opposites, such statements do achieve the effects they seek. They get people to identify with social causes and to act. The form of the action varies. It can involve working devotedly to advance scientific knowledge; it can also involve expressing oneself as an "aware" and dedicated member of a hippie commune.[19] Underlying these forms of action is the artful use of rhetoric.

If we are to understand people and their societies, we must examine their rhetoric and the irrational appeals that are contained within that rhetoric. We must not dismiss rhetorical appeals as simple wordiness; we must instead note the appearance of rhetoric even when it is disguised. (For example, how can we cope with someone who tells us, with elaborate but subtle rhetorical appeals, that we must not allow ourselves to be taken in by rhetoric?)

Rhetoric, then, is seen by Duncan as a special form of language distinct from word play—as is the case with some kinds of poetry. While the making of rhymes, for example, may have a rhetorical effect—the advertising jingle is a case in point—it can also be the use of language for display. Scientific language, in contrast, is for neither display nor action. It is a language that prepares for action but does not motivate the action in and of itself. Science can provide information concerning the energy released by atomic fusion or fission. Rhetorical language, however, is the force that leads to the employment of that knowledge for the purpose of building bombs and aiming them toward human targets.

Duncan suggests, then, that science is always subordinate to the

---

[18] This is not, of course, any condemnation of democracy as an ideal for political action. We are interested here in the ways in which the concept of democracy can be used to justify policies that are not democratic.

[19] Our notion of rhetoric is that it often is used to create hateful, irrational states. However, it is, of course, also used to create gentleness of character. Hitler was a notoriously skilled orator. But so is Joan Baez. It is interesting to observe the extent to which the members of a "hip" group talk constantly about the ideals they should subscribe to and about the dramatic devices they use to confirm those ideals.

342　action language of rhetoric. In fact, science has achieved a value in our society only because it has proved useful to rhetoric. It is not the other way around. The pride of science is that it feels itself either above or in control of rhetoric. It is not. It cannot be. It will never be.[20] Science is always subordinate to the demands of rhetoric—and rhetoric is irrational by most of the criteria of scientific procedure.

As we have already emphasized, rhetoric is action language. It helps individuals identify with community principles, which are then believed in without critical examination. As we begin to understand the character of rhetoric and its role in the generation of social action, we can consider the question of the purpose of action. What interests does rhetorical language serve? Society does not urge people to do anything and everything. We have a moral order that we believe is proper and to which we subordinate ourselves and others. This sense of order is pervasive, and its guidelines move throughout the community. The principles that give form to the moral order transcend any specific group within the society and manifest themselves as acceptable to all. They are the "transcendent principles" referred to earlier. Duncan uses the term *transcendent principles* to refer to valued forms of behavior that are accepted by all rankings within a society and that form the basis of order for those rankings. As we have suggested, these principles are neither empirically valid nor necessarily logical. They are, however, always artful.

Following are some transcendent principles of social order that pervade our own social system. Romantic love, for example, is a principle of behavior almost universally accepted across all class rankings, from "lower class" to "upper class." It is a principle geared toward sustaining the family—an important integrating element in any communal structure. There is a steady rhetorical drumbeat in our society that sustains this transcendent principle of action, and most people get hooked into it.

Another example is the value given to the quality of "intelligence," which has a nearly sacred status in our society. As we define it, intelligence serves well the needs of a society integrated along the lines of a technological-industrial state.

It is interesting, in this light, to consider psychology not simply as a science of behavior but also as a legitimating agency for the promotion of various transcendent principles that are relatively arbitrary in their nature. Psychology is overtly a science and covertly a form of rhetoric. Like the church in earlier times, the behavioral sciences can provide an apparent sanctification of principles serving particular forms of social order. Intelligence is a case in point. Psychologists who engage in major battles over whether blacks have an I.Q. the same as, lower than, or higher than that of whites emphasize intelligence as a major criterion of the social acceptability of the individual and of whole classes of individuals.

So thoroughly acceptable is intelligence as a transcendent principle of order—the bright should be at the top and the stupid at the bottom—

---

[20] There is perhaps some hope in this. We cannot, as yet, produce eloquent and rhetorical computers who are taken in by their own ideals—HAL 9000 notwithstanding.

that any reader who has followed the discussion this far is probably **343** muttering, "What's the matter with that? What do you want, a nation of morons?"

It is a reasonable question, but it misses the point. The point is: Why intelligence?[21] Why is it considered so critically significant that millions of hours have been spent in the quest to measure it? Why is it so significant that a difference of several points in a test of somewhat dubious validity can be the basis for concluding that one whole race of people is superior or inferior to another? This is really a peculiar scientific issue. Other qualities might be given significance but are not. For example, why not develop extensive testing of esthetic concern and talent, which are qualities as universally vital to the organization of the society as is intelligence?[22] Two points are being made here: (1) intelligence has acquired the status of a transcendent principle whose value is acknowledged across the different groupings of our society, and (2) intelligence requires the support of a rhetorical program that sustains it as a value.

Money as Communication

Still another transcendent principle is money. It is valued and respected by people of high status and low status, by liberals and conservatives, by the good and the bad. The acquisition of money is a valued activity, and as long as it is acquired in legitimate or "nice" ways, it is a measure of one's value. Its value is *not* intrinsic to itself, however. At one time in our history the acquisition of money was looked on as a gross concern. This is no longer the case. One is now subjected to a rhetorical barrage underscoring the value and the acceptability of money. Even as we write, we are looking at a small ruler on the desk, a gift from a local merchant. A slogan printed on the front of it never fails to impress us. It says, "Time is money." This certainly has to be one of the most unusual slogans in the history of humanity. However, all we are interested in here is the development of the point that money is sustained by rhetorical devices, as are any other pervasive principles of action that help integrate a community.

From Duncan's point of view, the significant thing about money is the way it is related to the communication process. Money simplifies not only economic exchange but other forms of exchange as well. It is a way of communicating a great variety of conditions in an immediate and simple manner. It can communicate status, for example, as when we are told that someone makes $200,000 a year. It can communicate inequali-

[21] The artful consideration of the nature of intelligence should be contrasted with the scientific consideration of intelligence. Sherlock Holmes stands as a rhetorical device for the kind of character which is highly valued in an industrial age. Evil is destroyed by the application of brilliance rather than goodness of soul. Science cannot help being flattered by such an image and is motivated to establish it by its own devices.

[22] There are, of course, numerous tests of esthetic sensitivity. We are dealing here with the fact that esthetic concern is simply not a transcendent integrative principle in the way intelligence is.

344 ties, as when we are told that women make less than men for the same work. Above all, money is a form of communicating to each private individual the interests of the community at large. Citizens may not be able to determine, for example, what a new school will do in the way of educating children, but they can establish that it will cost a certain amount in taxes.

Money talks. We all know that, of course. But what is it saying? Duncan suggests that it says more than we might be inclined, at first, to suspect. It communicates, among other things, a set of presumptions about the psychological character of the person who possesses it. Being "better" in wealth, a person is likely to be seen as better in other respects as well—mentally healthier, more intelligent, alert, capable, industrious, and possessed of other virtues (including moral and religious virtues). Poverty is difficult not only because it is constraining but because it suggests moral failure. The communication is highly distorted, but that is beside the point. The point is that money does in fact communicate, regardless of whether the communication is distorted. To the extent that the communication is accepted as real, it is acted on, and the arbitrary moment is handled by the arbitrary nature of money itself.

> While money is no more efficient (as a symbol of social order) than kingship, ancestor worship, religion, or ownership of land or office, it has specific qualities and takes certain forms, which we must understand if we wish to understand modern society. Money changes hands in hidden and unrecognizable ways not possible to land, houses, clothes, offices, and rank. It can create effects at a distance—as we see in the ease with which we invest in remote and distant markets. There is a kind of anonymity or neutrality about money. . . . Money is highly abstract.[23]

The success of the marketplace as a center of social order and disorder derives in part from its capacity to communicate the value of things by ascribing to them an abstract monetary value. We come to see that a Rembrandt painting is important because it has been sold at auction for a million dollars. It is on a par with a modern small jet plane in value. A plane and a painting can be given an equivalence, *and that equivalence can be simply communicated.* Duncan suggests that the current mania within the academic behavioral sciences for quantification of the nonquantifiable probably has received much of its impetus from the impact that money has had on the communication process. He says, "The use of money pervades our daily life with weighing and calculating, with constant numerical determinations, and with the constant reduction of qualitative values to quantitative units."[24]

Transcendent principles, then, are commonly valued and accepted criteria of worth. Money, intelligence, and romantic love are such principles. These principles are so commonly accepted that they operate throughout the entire ranking system of the society. They are not chal-

[23] *Communication and Social Order*, p. 353.
[24] Ibid.

lenged either by the people who stand at the top of the ranking system **345**
or by those who stand at the bottom. They provide the axiomatic conditions, the unquestioning acceptance, which in part promotes the communication process itself. As the principles are challenged or are made
ineffective by time, the social order becomes disturbed.

> It is not the difference in rank between superior and inferior which disturbs
> a social system, but the inability . . . to communicate in terms of a common
> transcendent principle of social order.[25]

Social Communication

Social communication is the tenuous stuff on which social order rests.
Social disorder is a disruption of communication. But what constitutes
such a disruption? Communication becomes disrupted when there is a
breakdown in those principles that provide a sense of commonality
among the disparate members of the community. Because such a breakdown is always possible unless some effort is made to sustain the principles, many of the communication mechanisms of a society become
directed toward the end of propagandizing for these principles.

Therefore, church, government, education, and all the other central
agencies of social relations direct themselves, in one fashion or another,
to the task of sustaining the great communal principles. Seen from this
light, the great institutions of human society are gigantic rhetorical
forces. They are given the task of daily reaffirming and sustaining the
accepted values of monogamous love, political freedom, the market,
money, the value of knowledge, or whatever other principles provide a
sense of integrity for the community.[26]

The nature of social communication requires that commitments be
made, for the most part, to principles that have a very arbitrary quality
about them. This means, in turn, that the individual will be "worked
over" by communication devices that are not logical or factual but which,
instead, are geared to the end of getting people to act. Such devices are
essentially what we are talking about when we refer to rhetoric or rhetorical language. Rhetorical language is action language. It brings about
movement and commitment. It leads the individual to identify with a
cause or a point of view. It enables one to know how to act in the
uncertain social moment when there is no biological directive for action.

A contemporary case in point can be mentioned here. As we are
readying this material for publication, the nation finds itself in what is
almost universally referred to as an energy crisis. Duncan, were he alive,
might find this an example of the power of rhetoric. There are, after all,
a number of other ways of viewing the situation. One way of looking at

---

[25] Ibid., p. 391.
[26] Those familiar with the works of Emile Durkheim will find it worth their time to compare
this discussion with Durkheim's ideas concerning the "collective conscience."

346 it is to see it as a crisis in overconsumption. Few people have put the matter before the public in these terms and, at the moment, we know of no political figure who has dared to do so. Rather than question the "meaning" of our resources and our manner of using them, we accept as "real" that we must go on consuming them in ever greater and greater quantities. Indeed, we even refer to ourselves as "consumers." It is a peculiar concept, if you think about it to any degree. The point is, however, that we are so rhetorically committed to this conception of ourselves that we cannot resolve an issue which, if even modestly wise conservation practices were put into effect, would no longer exist. The power of rhetoric lies in the extent to which it is essentially not recognized. When we are aware of rhetoric, as in old-time melodramas, we can enjoy it but not be deeply moved by it. The energy crisis is difficult for many people to see as a rhetorical matter. This makes it all the more effective as a rhetorical force. The energy crisis is, from the point of view of a writer such as Duncan, a crisis in rhetoric. We cannot disengage ourselves from our conception of ourselves as "consumers." So long as this is the case, we shall not only continue to have an energy crisis, we shall probably continue to indulge in the systematic rape and pillage of this planet in our quest for more things to consume.

Duncan's View of the Self

Institutions, whatever their nature (family, education, government, or any other), must and do subject the individual to a continuous stream of rhetoric. Through this effort we as individuals are transformed into persons with definite social concerns and commitments to transcendent principles. We are also transformed into beings who constantly discuss with ourselves, as well as with others, the appropriateness of our character. We have not only an external audience whose allegiance we attempt to win with convincing arguments. We also have an "inner audience" that we try to win with dramatic and rhetorical devices. We do not simply talk to ourselves. A good bit of the time we spend pleading and haranguing ourselves. There is an internal as well as external drama. We are as artfully rhetorical within ourselves as we are with others.

This conception of people is not one usually offered by social thinkers in recent years. Rather than seeing people as animals driven by physiological impulses or as beings constrained by mechanical conformity to the roles of society, Duncan looks on people as creatures struggling to reconcile within themselves the conflicting demands for action they encounter. People are engaged constantly in the act of convincing themselves of the propriety of their actions, just as they try to convince others.

The significant feature of self, for Duncan, is its argumentative character. Society is threatened by disorder every day, and every day it counters this threat with a steady rhetorical appeal for order and for the acceptance of transcendent principles. The individual is also confronted with disorder. We are all faced with the possibility of questioning matters to the point where action becomes impossible. To be or not to be. To act or not to act. To maintain a viable and active character, we must each resolve the problem of action for ourselves. We generally do, but the procedure is a dramatic one. We become rhetorical with ourselves. In our soliloquies we use oratorical devices that are found in any political speech. Rhetoric is often thought of as inflammatory language leading to hate and used for rousing people who cannot think for themselves. However, kindness and love require rhetorical support as much as hate does. We have to talk ourselves into being kind. In many ways, the rhetoric of gentleness is more subtle and difficult than the rhetoric of hate. It is easy to talk people into hating some person or group; it is not always easy to persuade them to be kind.

For Duncan, we are anguished creatures caught up in the peculiar business of making rhetorically effective or ineffective speeches to ourselves and to others. In any event, whether we are speaking to others or to ourselves—whether we are trying to convince others or ourselves—the effort is as much artful as it is rational. The individual is not a machine, from Duncan's point of view, and he tries to show us not only the limitations but the possible dangers of a mechanistic view of society.

In Conclusion: Pornography and Spirit

Many students are uncomfortable reading Duncan. To locate the sources of human social endeavor in something as nebulous as symbols seems to deprive humanity of any "solid" foundation. People are, after all, physiological beings; they live in a natural order that imposes stern physical demands. It is a materialistic world we live in, and we should turn to it for an understanding of ourselves. From such a viewpoint, symbols are the haziest, lightest, and flimsiest of devices for coming to a realistic understanding of human communities. Yet if we leave symbols out of the picture we get a conception of humanity that is, if not grim, at least rather dull and uninspiring.

Crude pornography illustrates what happens when one strips away the status symbols and other artful-linguistic aspects of human social behavior. Many people who have attended a pornographic film report that it was surprisingly dull. After the initial shock of seeing some "raw" sex, the movie quickly got tedious. This tediousness comes from the film's lack of dramatic qualities. Dramatic qualities are developed through a variety of symbols that have relevance for the audience. In their most common form, symbols define various types of authority and those who might violate that authority. There is more to interest the viewer in a cowboy film than there is in the ordinary pornographic film.

But what about the "real" world? "Pornographic" approaches exist in the real world also. It might be argued, for example, that American medicine has come more and more, through the objectification of science, to see people as "meat." When this happens, patients are treated in a pornographic manner. Their symbolic character is considered to be irrelevant to the issues at hand. Duncan would argue, however, that people are symbolic as well as physiological, and a full treatment of any

348 patient would take the patient's social and symbolic character into account along with the physical illness. In fact, we have learned that many birth traumas of expectant mothers can be avoided simply by transforming the "rhetoric" of their hospitalization.[27]

Duncan's major work, *Communication and Social Order,* is an exasperating book to read. It is wordy, occasionally self-contradicting, and written in a style that lacks the clarity of some of the more scientific social writers and the dramatic and emotional quality of the best of the humanists. It is, nonetheless, a radical work in the extent to which it deals with the "cost" exacted by language and symbols in shaping our thoughts and concerns. No other work, to the best of our knowledge, reveals the extent to which symbols are behind our inclination to victimize each other. Nor does any other book make the reader as totally aware of the complexity and the delicacy of the problems facing us as we seek to achieve those ideals which forever seem to dangle just in front of our collective noses.

Problems and Issues

Duncan relies on the metaphor of drama, much as does Goffman. For Duncan, the most fruitful way to interpret human social activity is to see it in terms of what he calls the dramatic motive. Drama involves conflict between competing principles of good and evil. It involves exaggeration. It involves display and risk. To what extent do we seek to build these kinds of conditions into ordinary social moments? To what extent has this society dedicated itself to the promotion of drama? What role does drama play in our everyday lives?

Is it possible to have dramatic action without having some kind of victim—or potential victim—involved in the performance? The approach that Duncan takes to the interpretation of human affairs implies that sometime, in the pursuit of dramatic action, we get carried away by the drama and are led into more risky ventures then we might originally have been willing to undertake. Are there possible examples of this interpretation?

Is it possible, in a society as devoted as this one to reliance on dramatic entertainments, to ignore the place of drama in human affairs? Why is this sort of behavior so compelling? What functions does it serve? What is the relationship between language and drama?

Duncan, following the work of Kenneth Burke, concentrates on symbols as the paramount concern of the community. Especially important is the nature and character of symbolic language itself. We are driven, Duncan suggests, to try to give ever-more-specific meanings to the symbols that

---

[27] See Ronny E. Turner and Charles Edgley, "An Obstetrics Ethnology: The Birth of a Conception," paper read at the meetings of the Western Social Science Association, Denver, Colorado, 1975.

become increasingly important to us. The search for more specific meanings requires the development of more language. We are hoisted, as it were, by language itself into a futile kind of circular pursuit. Is it possible to abandon language? Can people move beyond the present system of communication that they have relied on for hundreds of thousands of years?

Duncan writes that art is a way of providing apparent resolutions to concepts that cannot be given specific meanings through logic or observation. Art helps provide us with the illusion of knowing relatively well what something means when, in fact, nobody can be certain of its meaning. The contradictions contained within many ideas can only be disguised or hidden. Often the contradictions manifest themselves even when we think we are being logical and specific. This was the point about the "proving of opposites." What are some more elaborate examples of the way in which a particular event can offer two diametrically opposed or logically contradictory interpretations of the same concept? In what ways have you experienced this in your personal life? Why is ambiguity and contradiction threatening to most people? Should it be?

Overview: A Coming Crisis in the Social Sciences?

19 Whatever people have become, whatever we mean by civilization, progress, or cultural evolution, whatever we achieve in the way of controlling nature, and whatever we imply when we talk of being better off—is a consequence of human social organization. To be human is, one way or another, to be a member of some kind of organization. We cannot think of any more elementary social fact than this. American society, with its extremely powerful individualistic ideology, and the pervasive and influential rhetoric that goes with such an ideology, has led all too many people to think that organization is either bad or unnecessary, or both. We cannot determine whether organization is good or bad. Its essential nature, however, is difficult to dispute. At the very least a minimal form of organization, that of the family, is necessary for the survival of the individual. If we move only a little further, we find that extraordinarily elaborate forms of organization become necessary. Today, the youth who drives a car (constructed by organized groups of workers numbering in the tens of thousands), who listens to electronically augmented music on a hi-fi system (all of which evolved out of a history embracing countless artists, engineers, and workers), and who is working toward a degree in law (a totally collective and organized activity) can, nonetheless, subscribe to a belief that the individual is everything and that social organization is not, ideally, necessary. Or there might be a grudging concession that social organizations are necessary, but hardly worth the effort of serious study.

Sociology has grown out of the recognition that social systems are as much a part of our fate as are the physical and biological systems that grant us life. There is nothing new in the recognition. Philosophers, humanists, priests, and generals have long been aware that people are social animals and that their strength is derived from their ability to organize themselves into larger systems. Society has been discussed and evaluated in philosophy, literature, and religion.

Modern social thought has moved toward more rational, systematic, or "scientific" modes of interpretation. As we observed in the chapter on Durkheim, social forces in earlier and simpler societies were dealt with in terms of myth and religious expression. Religion has been, and still is, one way of making evident the subtle and indirect forces of the community. The quest, now, in economics, sociology, and political science (and, to a lesser extent, in history and anthropology) is for a reasoned understanding—based on logic and data. The statistical approach to the study of society is fairly recent. The current effort to find some kind of mathematical logic that will uncover basic processes in human social behavior is an extreme extension of this faith in logic.

Whether we approach society from a mystical point of view, through myth, through ideology, through propaganda, or through rational understanding, it is something we must live with and it is something we must understand in some fashion if we are to survive. Sociology and the social sciences in general are essential. We have no choice with regard to whether we will or will not be involved with social theory. We can only choose to try to do the job well or poorly. We can either improve our understanding or regress. And history is replete with examples of what happens if we regress.

At the same time, the study of society poses some difficulties that make it particularly frustrating. On the one hand it appears that society is all too easy to study. It is not the kind of thing that draws the attention of the truly serious, greatly talented or intelligent student. Some time ago a study was conducted which showed that social science students generally scored slightly lower on measures of scholastic ability and general I.Q. It also revealed, however, that people who had undergone a deeply unsettling adverse social or economic experience were much more likely to recognize that social reality was, in itself, a proper and serious intellectual concern than those who had not.

The Study of Society: A Paradox

The study of society seems easy because almost anything you may say about it makes some kind of sense, and, paradoxically, anything you say about it can also be viewed as the purest nonsense. For example, we

352 have theorists in academic sociology who emphasize the extent to which human societies are stratified; such social differentiation makes for conflict and internal stress and exploitation. This, of course, was one of the central themes of Karl Marx. On the other hand, the writings of contemporary sociologists such as Robert K. Merton and Talcott Parsons emphasize the idea that society is composed of various functioning elements and these elements work together; they are structurally interrelated in such a manner as to sustain the entire organization. Such a point of view downplays conflict and endorses the extent to which cooperation is a part of human social systems. Like the particle–wave problem with light, it seems that either of these opposed positions is reasonable.

Almost any kind of metaphor is likely to work when we talk about something so remote from our direct comprehension as the social order. If so, then the analysis of society, in any manner, rational or irrational, is all too easy. We can speculate however we wish and we can always find examples to fit our speculations. We can argue and debate, but we can never hope to resolve any social issue in the same clear way we can solve an equation. The analysis of society becomes a pettifogging sort of game—a bit of fun, perhaps, but not something to be taken too seriously.

Sociology, then, is too easy. It is not disciplined. It is not for the tough-minded or those who wish to deal with truly challenging intellectual problems. But there is another barrier. People find sociology impossibly difficult. It is beyond rational consideration. Einstein's intellectual concerns involved, probably, no more than ten or twelve fundamental variables—space, energy, mass, time, and other similarly fundamental dimensions of reality. For any social issue, however, the number of complicating factors, events, dimensions, and variables is as large as anyone might wish to make it. Unfortunately, any one of those variables can have a significant role in the outcome of a historical happening. And so one concern of the social scientist is to select that which is singularly important or basic and eliminate the extraneous. This was a critical matter for Leslie White. It was true, he argued, that minor and unforeseen happenings could alter the course of history—the assassination of Kennedy or the misunderstanding of a Japanese word during peace negotiations that led to the atomic bombing of civilian populations—but, despite these particular moments, there were broader social and cultural processes at work that could be delineated and become the basis for simplifying the great variety and complexity of human social behavior. In this respect, the general concept of culture is to society in all of its complexity as the simple and general concept of mass is to the physical world in all of *its* complexity. The process of trying to find general and relatively universal elements of social reality becomes, in itself, an important intellectual task.

If, then, some people have avoided the study of social organization because it is, on the one hand, too easy and on the other, too difficult, it appears that sociology is damned if it moves in one direction and damned again if it moves in the other. Certainly sociology offers to the serious and involved student as much challenge as any other discipline or field can offer; and just as certainly, we cannot ignore the study of society whether it is too difficult or too simple. The major problems of **353** our time, without exception, are sociological problems and little more than sociological problems. Let us suggest just one illustrative case that, despite its obviously sociological nature, has not been seriously dealt with as such by any major political or economic commentator we know of.

Some Sociological Perspectives on the Energy Crisis

The United States, at the present time, is caught up in what is generally referred to as an energy crisis. The ramifications of this crisis are far beyond anything we can deal with in a detailed manner in a book of this kind. We intend to use the crisis only to illustrate the extent to which a sociological understanding helps shed light on a situation that at first appears to be strictly a matter of limited resources or supply-demand economics. The energy crisis is actually a matter of glaring difficulties in the ability of human beings to establish more efficient and effective forms of social organization. We shall use the energy crisis to demonstrate, though we are not trying to prove our point, that a sociological perspective is not only reasonable but essential if there is to be any hope for a solution to this and various other crises that confront humankind today. We shall endeavor to make the case for a sociological perspective by suggesting how a number of the writers who appear in this book might be used to obtain new views of the problem.

A Marxist point of view, for example, concentrates on the economic issues involved in the energy crisis. From this perspective the energy crisis comes out of the fact that corporate enterprise, in the quest for profit, has subordinated the interests of the community and the nation to the pressing demand for profit increments to ensure further investments in those enterprises that now dominate the oil and gas industries. The Marxists would point out that it has been to the economic advantage of the great oil companies to promote an astonishingly extravagant consumption of the nation's resources. The energy industry is not alone in this, however. They share guilt with a variety of other industries, all dominated by the quest for profit, regardless of the impact on human communities and the environmental resources of the planet. Given that the automobile industry, tourism, housing, supermarkets, and other such enterprises have been animated by the quest for profit, it is little wonder, the Marxists would claim, that we have an energy crisis. The Marxists would have to admit that the capitalistic venture has succeeded all too well in its effort to create a nation of consumers. Blind and passionate consumption has been the central thrust of the modern capitalistic society. Until the social and economic order can be turned toward the efficient utilization of resources, rather than the utilization of resources for the profit of large corporate enterprises, there can be little hope for any worthwhile solution to the energy crisis. Capitalism cannot function when resources are used in a conservative manner. There might be an interesting paradox in the suggestion that the most politically

354 conservative elements in American society today are promoting the most liberally profligate utilization of American labor, energy, and resources.

One of the major writers reviewed in this book is Max Weber. The relevance of Max Weber to an issue of this kind is difficult to summarize in a mere paragraph or two. However, we can suggest that Weber's approach offers a variety of possibilities for a deeper understanding of the energy crisis. Weber, let us recall, was interested in religion and he was interested in the rise of large, modern bureaucracies. It might seem far-fetched, at first, to suggest that many of the uses to which we put energy, as we seek to sustain what we call a proper standard of living, are more religious in character than we might at first think. The problem now, as it was for Weber, is to determine how we moved from a belief in conservation to a belief, in effect, that greed is a moral good. We are, by any meaning of the term, *morally* impelled to consume resources in this modern society of ours. It is the way we establish our worth before others and, in a more profound sense, before God. So it is that we have hordes of young people (and some not so young) who wander about, more or less aimlessly, in cars and on motorcycles and any other kind of vehicle they can find, as a way of presenting themselves to the world. Weber would have understood that such apparently vulgar and secular people as the members of motorcycle gangs are people of deep faith. They are cultists, but they are offshoots of a broader religious and cultural tradition that has come to believe that power is manifested through the machine. These people carry to an extreme the belief that the individual counts for everything and that freedom is the highest moral virtue. They set out, then, to pursue freedom and individuality on their machines. They are manifestations of a more pervasive set of cultural values which has impressed itself upon the people as a whole. Just as it is difficult to imagine any member of a motorcycle gang being meticulously concerned with conserving energy, it is equally difficult to think of anyone who comes from the more current transformations of the Protestant Ethic, seriously seeking to conserve energy. Individuality and freedom are not moral qualities that inspire the kind of thinking necessary to subordinate to the greater interests of the community and nation one's own desires to consume.

Weber was also interested in large bureaucracies. Any bureaucracy is concerned with its own particular goals and the maintenance of its own structure. The problem becomes not so much a concern with the survival needs of the individual—which are, after all, relatively modest—but with the survival needs of a corporate system. These needs can become enormous. The demands of the bureaucracy necessary to sustain the operations of a large modern airline far transcend the needs of any of the individual members of that bureaucracy. (What individual, for example, has a physiological need for a Boeing 747 or a Douglas DC-10?) Moreover, the needs of an airline transcend the needs of the communities served by the airlines. So it is, then, that the airlines must attempt, to the fullest extent possible, to generate a demand for the services they offer. The result is the development of a social and economic system that operates rationally in terms of the interests of the bureaucracy, but irrationally in terms of the interests of the greater community. Resources are consumed in efforts not related directly to any real survival and welfare needs of the people. At this point, Weber and Marx would tend to converge.

Among the writers we discussed was the great French social analyst Emile Durkheim. What can the works of Emile Durkheim tell us about today's complex and seemingly insoluble problems? He does not at first appear to be relevant. After all, Durkheim was interested in such esoteric matters as primitive religion, the workings of law in primitive and modern societies, suicide, and the division of labor. None of this appears to be particularly related to our modern difficulties. Modern society prides itself on its secular nature. There is little, anymore, which is considered sacred. Science has come to dominate our approach to the world. But must we, then, dismiss Durkheim's ideas because they do not have a direct bearing on the energy situation?

Durkheim is quite relevant—more relevant than we can show in this brief overview. A proper understanding of Durkheim leads to the conclusion that the energy crisis cannot, in the final analysis, be resolved by simple-minded quests to uncover more resources. For Durkheim, the individual is a member of society and, as such, is connected with forces greater than himself or herself. He referred to these forces, in a general way, as the *collective consciousness*. We are made to feel stronger and less vulnerable by the extent to which we identify with collective forces that are, *in fact*, stronger and less vulnerable than we are as individuals. To the extent we sense an identity with the power of the organizations to which we belong, we achieve an experience of unusual power. Durkheim developed this theme by noting the irrational aspects of punitive behavior among human beings. We punish in intense and elaborate ways that appear to go far beyond the character of the offense. There is an irrational element in such behavior which can be accounted for only if the social functions of the behavior are considered.

Durkheim might, if he were called on to comment on the current energy situation, note first of all the extent to which the utilization of our energy resources has been excessive. He might also note that just as the ability to punish is an indication of power, the ability to consume resources indicates power. Power, punishment, and energy are interrelated. The more modern form of society has moved from retributive punishment or direct exchange—an eye for an eye and a tooth for a tooth—to restitutive punishment, in which, usually, a monetary exchange is made for an injury. Energy, Durkheim might have argued, is much like money. It has a kind of exchange value. It can be used for restitution. It can help make up for injuries, insults, and damages. A banal example is seen in the fight for the station wagon in middle-class divorce cases.

Energy can be used to represent the moral order itself. Energy and social power are combined. Durkheim might suggest that in modern society the most powerful people are those who control or have access to the most powerful forms of energy. The frighteningly remote and mysterious people who have access to hydrogen bombs, nuclear power, and other high forms of energy are the dominant figures of our time.

356 Lesser mortals can come close to them only by their own access to energy—the more the better. Power has increasingly shifted from the actual punitive act to the potentially massive punishment that we find to be a normal aspect of advanced social orders. This potential is acquired, of course, through the control of energy. So the mechanism, the punitive act, remains much the same; only the form and the intensity have changed. Control over energy becomes a central sociological fact. The forces that precipitate human beings toward a greater demand for energy come from the character of the social structure itself. Nothing within the individual, per se, implies any such need for energy. A social structure has potentially unlimited needs for energy and an unlimited amount implies a quantity beyond human comprehension. There is *no* limit to the energy sought by a society. There is very little need for energy on the part of an individual. No better way of coming to an appreciation of Durkheim's vision probably exists than through this discussion of a practical problem which at first seems removed from Durkheim's interests. Those needs for energy that any particular individual believes are "natural," "necessary," "essential," or "normal" do not come from the individual but, instead, from the society of which that person is a member. If so, then energy consumption is a *sociological* problem of some magnitude, complexity, and subtlety.

For Pitirim Sorokin the modern energy crisis would be little more than another manifestation of a Sensate mentality. The Sensate mentality looks for worldly experiences. It seeks "kicks." The raw consumption of energy, whether in the form of a wild explosion, or in the form of powerful racers circling a loop at Indianapolis, is one of the quests of the Sensate mentality. Sorokin might look on this as a quest for energy for its own sake. The argument that we need energy to maintain some mystical "standard of living" or, even more inappropriately, for survival, would be viewed by Sorokin as a rhetorical subterfuge to hide the true force behind our quest for more energy—the Sensate cultural mentality.

One of the more engaging of Sorokin's ideas was the notion of "gigantism" or "dinosaurism." The argument was basically that a given trend continues until it becomes so excessive that its faults become obvious and eventually intolerable. At this point, the contradictions inherent in the effort become paralyzing and the trend is reversed. Sorokin believed that when the contradictions of Sensatism become painfully apparent, people will move toward a less Sensate form of culture, that of Ideationalism. There is a little hope in Sorokin's thinking. The energy crisis might be resolved by demonstrating to people the extent to which the excessive development of a Sensate society has created unworkable situations. However, since Sorokin believed such major transformations in the fabric of large societies took place over three or four centuries, we might find ourselves living with the crisis for quite a while before it would be resolved through the appearance of a new, more Ideational sociocultural system.

C. Wright Mills would have found the energy crisis simply an extension of his concern with power. Few other events in recent times would have offered him a better opportunity to discuss the extent to which business and government have become divorced from the concerns of the people. At the same time, the energy crisis has revealed the impotence of the people in general to deal with the crisis that confronts them. One of the more interesting moments in the present crisis was the rioting that took place in Levittown, Pennsylvania, when gasoline supplies became low. Mills might have found this especially noteworthy. He might have suggested that this was simply another manifestation of the extent to which the present white-collar working element in America is content with things as they are and shocked, when all is not going well, to discover they have little real power.

The present crisis, for Mills, would constitute a further entry into the investigation of power. Obviously power relationships are required which could, on the one hand, enhance the development and supply of energy and, on the other, promote the appropriate use and conservation of fuel and energy. At the moment, American leadership seems incapable of doing either. We know that we are taking considerable liberties here, but we seek only to suggest to readers how Mills's work might be applied to the present moment, and we believe it is relevant to the present. Granting this, we would like to suggest that an understanding of Mills's work generates an appreciation of the extent to which the so-called energy crisis might also be considered a crisis in power.

What might be a crisis in power for Mills would be a crisis in culture for Jules Henry. Henry concentrated his attention on how our present culture, once a positive force in human development, has now begun to work against the people who brought it into being. Henry would concentrate on those cultural forces which have led the American people to a point where they believe, with unquestioning faith, that they must continue to consume energy in the same way they always have. That is to say, Americans have come to believe that a continuing increase in energy consumption is a natural and necessary matter. It takes little reflection, however, to comprehend that an economy cannot continue to grow forever—although our culture espouses this as an essential and unquestionable economic matter. At some point the unchecked growth of anything will absorb the available environment within which the growth is taking place. In the first year of life, a typical infant grows from six to eighteen pounds in weight. Were it to continue growing at that rate, it would weigh more than the entire planet after merely a little more than fifty years of growth. Nature, at least, is wise in recognizing that growth is not something that can be promoted in perpetuity. But our culture prescribes constant growth, constant consumption, and constant exploitation of the earth's resources to promote "growth." It is as though, Henry observed bitterly, we must be kept as massively stupid as possible in order for the culture to continue on its course. The energy crisis would not have come as a surprise to Henry. It would have been only further evidence of how our culture has turned against the people it once served.

Erving Goffman dealt with the elementary theme of people as actors and human life as drama. In the course of this drama we appear before others and we engage in what Goffman referred to as "impression man-

358 agement." With ever-more-elaborate devices becoming available for impressing each other, people find themselves consuming more and more energy for purposes of display. Energy used essentially for the purpose of impressing others has become an important part of the total energy we consume. A large house, for example, with high ceilings and many rooms, few of which are used efficiently and constantly, is on the one hand impressive and, on the other, a tremendous drain on energy. Automobiles are not simply functional transportation devices. They are also devices for display. A car is all the more impressive to the extent it is powerful and showy. Such a car is also inefficient with respect to the mileage it can get from a given amount of gasoline. The point is that the discrepancy between a highly efficient automobile and a less efficient one is usually a discrepancy with regard to display and impression management.

This example of the fancy car is one we are all familiar with and we are all, to a greater or lesser extent, aware that we spend considerable amounts of energy simply for the purpose of putting on a show. The only difference between an ordinary understanding of this aspect of human life and Goffman's understanding of it is the degree to which Goffman pursues the implications of our need to impress others. Few of us really probe deeply into what it means to be a creature concerned with the dramatic forms of presentation of self.

A Goffmanian perspective has much to offer with respect to identifying the cause of our energy crisis. Is it really an energy crisis, or is it now becoming a crisis with respect to having sufficient energy to carry on those displays before others which we have found so impressive? Is it possible that young people, deprived of their machines and other energy-consuming devices, will simply wilt under the frustrations they encounter in trying to impress their peers? If so, what we might really be having at the moment is a "boredom crisis." The thought of losing energy, and control of the machines that such energy offers, is to encounter an intense fear of having to live under circumstances that would be intolerably boring. Of course impression management, powerful machines, energy-consuming houses, water-wasting swimming pools and golf courses, and other such status symbols are not restricted to the youth of our society. It is a fairly universal aspect of human behavior. It is certainly a universal feature of American society.

From Goffman to Hugh Dalziel Duncan is a short step in interpretive perspectives. Like Goffman, Duncan subscribes to a dramatic perspective. He felt that people are dramatic creatures. At the same time, people are also caught up in subtle language problems, which can have detrimental results for those not aware of what it might mean to be used by language. Duncan argued that language is used not only to describe events but also to initiate and give form to action. For human beings many aspects of action are inseparable from language. This argument is not especially easy to understand in all its ramifications, even though examples are common enough. Duncan would say that we are not only describing an event but we are also suggesting appropriate forms of action when we refer to our current difficulties as an energy crisis. The

very form of description leads to an effort to resolve the problem by **359**
looking for more fossil fuel deposits, alternate forms of energy, and
more efficient forms of distribution and supply.

This only appears to be a "natural" response. It is a highly arbitrary
definition of a situation. We could equally well call the current crisis a
crisis in overconsumption. It could be called a corporate profit crisis. It
could be called a growth-economy crisis. It could be called a variety of
other things and still refer to the complex situation that confronts Americans today. The selection of the term *energy crisis,* which has caught on
and which has been supported by the political and economic structure
of this society, has oriented action in a particular direction. We are being
hoisted, Duncan might suggest, by the vagaries of our own rhetoric.

Surely he would point to the peculiar practice in America of an
entire population referring to themselves, quite naturally, as consumers.
Here is a term that has definite implications for action. The American is
referred to as a "consumer." The typical American man or woman consciously, subconsciously, or unconsciously comes to think and act in
terms of consumption. At a conscious level this is seen in the preparation
of and the general use of magazines and journals with titles such as
Consumer Reports, Consumer's Guide, Consumer Behavior, and *Consumer Protection Reports.* At an unconscious level, this is seen in the
extent to which Americans consume food when they are not hungry.
Eating, in America, is as much a matter of eating for sport, because others
are eating, or because it tastes good, as it is a matter of eating to satisfy
the fundamental needs of hunger. Americans often consume without
knowing why they consume.

In much the same manner, Americans consume energy, often without any profound awareness of why they are doing what they do. They
are responding to what they know themselves to be—and they know,
from all that they have been told, that they are consumers.

Duncan sensitizes us to the problems of language. His point of view
is not especially optimistic with regard to change. Is it possible, for
example, to transform the American's self-concept of being a consumer
into something less infantile and economically ruinous? It is possible, of
course, but how long might it take? What structural changes in the
society would have to take place before we might rid ourselves of this
conception? What label might take the place of "consumer"? It is difficult
to believe that Americans will think of themselves in any other manner
unless some catastrophe forces them to reconsider what it means to
have an entire society calling itself "consumers."

We have, then, considered the energy crisis very briefly from the
perspectives of a number of the writers whose work has been presented
in this book. We have tried to reveal the extent to which these social
critics are relevant to practical concerns. People are generally aware that
the present crisis has economic and political overtones. We want to
suggest that there are also some sociological and anthropological and
even linguistic perspectives which open the question to still other avenues of investigation. We have tried to suggest that the so-called energy

360   crisis is actually a crisis in social organization. Our society, our economy, our cultural traditions have set us up to accept as inevitable, the "reality" that confronts us. It is something that, as Garfinkel might point out, is taken for granted. It seems to have an inevitable quality to it.

So people have gone off looking for ever more certain sources of energy and have not, at least so far as we know, given any serious consideration to the question of why and how they use the abundant energy already available to them. The closing off of available "realities" while seeing only one that is taken for granted is something that can be understood better through the study of works by people such as Harold Garfinkel.

We have not been trying to suggest, throughout this discussion, that energy is unnecessary or that life cannot be enhanced through access to energy. We are suggesting only that until we discover some cheap, clean, and relatively safe form of energy, we should accept the fact that energy, in whatever form it appears, requires a deeper understanding of its proper use than American leadership has been able to come up with at this time. We have suggested that such an understanding can be augmented through an intensive examination of sociological problems as well as the political, economic, and biological ones.

Concluding Comments

Despite the fact that people seem as socially troubled in the twentieth century as they were at any previous time, there is still the prevailing sentiment that the study of society is the easiest and the simplest of intellectual undertakings. This final chapter has been concerned with making it apparent that the accomplishment of effective and "truthful" sociology is almost beyond the capabilities of human beings. The social realm might, by virtue of qualities unique to it, resist the kinds of rational and naturalistic investigations that have proved so successful in the physical sciences.

We are concerned with more, however, than simply making the point that sociology is a difficult effort when taken seriously. We are also concerned with the general problem of defining or expressing what we are dealing with when we talk about "social" behavior or the "social system." We have suggested that social behavior resides in symbolic interchanges between people and that these interchanges are subject to a variety of interpretations. Interpretive behavior is itself a part of the social process. It is difficult to separate sociological theory (viewed broadly as various efforts to interpret society) from society itself. We become social when, in confrontation with another, we interchange points of view and interpretations of the significance of each other. These interpretations are extremely presumptuous and are based on collectively sustained ideas of what constitutes the "right" way of labeling and categorizing people.

In conclusion, let us say once again that we do not mean to imply that sociology is an ineffectual or impossible effort. Granting the massive obstacles confronting it, academic sociology has been surprisingly successful and worthwhile. However, we prefer not to give a false feeling that sociology is a "scientific" enterprise in the sense that it has come forth with social knowledge as substantial as the knowledge offered by the physical sciences. It has not done this—and it will not do it. It is better to discover at the very beginning that there are serious limitations to academic sociology and that we have to work within these limitations.

We have no choice, really, as to whether we are going to be sociologists. Each and every one of us, as we act within the community, must make a number of sociological assumptions and rely on them every day. We will label some people immoral and others moral because we believe in a particular theory of how social affairs should be arranged. We will condemn some people as not fit to belong to our group and will actively seek the membership of others because we have very definite theories about how such membership will influence the group. The importance of the group will be enhanced by other theories or presumptions that we have about how the group serves the society as a whole. Our sense of personal worth and what we are as human beings is related to the kinds of social theory we subscribe to and attempt to enforce. There is no way we can avoid being sociologists. We can only be ignorant or knowledgeable about the alternatives that face us. This book is predicated on the simple belief that it is better to be knowledgeable than ignorant about these alternatives.

As our social and economic systems grow larger and more complex, the effort to understand them becomes increasingly difficult. The future may well find the social sciences increasingly at odds both with those not trained in them and with each other—economists versus sociologists, anthropologists versus psychologists, "hard headed" scientists versus "soft thinking" humanists. It could prove to be a time of crisis. Hopefully, however, if the social sciences can continue to attract dedicated and serious students, this time of crisis might prove to be a period when fundamental controversies are resolved and humankind is at last able to order itself in a manner that provides greater opportunities for the expression of life than are now available.

Problems and Issues

In this chapter we discussed the possible ways in which the thinkers in this book might be drawn on to reveal interpretations of and approaches to the "energy crisis." We have a lot of other crises facing us in this society—pollution, racial differences, poverty, crime, divorce. You have really not gained any worthwhile knowledge from this book unless you can select one social problem that happens to interest you—women's rights, gay liberation, fascism, anti-intellectualism, whatever it might be—and can carefully follow through, attempting to draw on the perspectives of each writer in the book. Only then have you incorporated ideas in a way that brings them closer to being working ideas. We like to think that ideas should work for their keep just like anything else.

Glossary

This glossary contains terms we thought would be unfamiliar to the typical undergraduate. Often the definitions include concepts that are not likely to be found in the ordinary desk dictionary.

Abstracted Empiricism
A term used by C. Wright Mills to refer to factual studies that concentrate on some part of a process and, as a result, lose their grasp of the whole. For example, voting studies have demonstrated that wealthy Americans tend to vote Republican. These studies are empirically or factually sound. At the same time, the abstracted nature of such data leads us away from a consideration of the more complex political machinery that makes such facts significant. Mills used this term to criticize what he thought was one of the central limitations of empiricism as it exists in sociology—its tendency to destroy comprehension of the complex unity of human social action.

Altruism
Behavior revealing a concern with the welfare of others, unselfish conduct, subordination of one's interests to those of another. See *altruistic suicide*.

Altruistic Suicide
Suicide resulting from altruistic motives. Durkheim saw in altruistic forms of suicide a means of indirectly assessing the nature of the social bond. Collective sentiments have the capacity to enable the individual to overcome his or her own fears of death. Altruistic suicide is self-destruction in the interest of socially established goals. An example of such conduct would be the self-immolation of Buddhist monks in Vietnam.

Ambivalence
Having feelings or reactions of both a positive and negative kind toward some object, event, or condition. For example, intellectuals in America are probably viewed ambivalently by many people. On the one hand their knowledge is admired and recognized as the source of many cultural accomplishments. On the other hand, they are viewed with some suspicion and hostility as a threat to established values and tradition.

Analogue
A condition or event similar to some matter one wishes to understand and that, because of the similarity, can promote such understanding. For example, since the computer is, in many ways, analogous to the human brain one can understand some aspects of human thought by turning to the

362

computer. Most social theories rest ultimately on some kind of analogous reasoning. In some theories the biological organism is implicitly taken as an analogue for society; society is then seen as having a circulatory system, intelligence centers, digestive mechanisms, and so on.

Anomic Suicide
Suicide resulting from being placed in a situation where the regulative controls of the social order have been weakened or removed. Durkheim saw in the higher suicide rates found among divorced people evidence supporting the proposition that anomie is conducive to self-destruction. The divorced person, he argued, finds intolerable the anomic conditions existing after being freed from domestic responsibilities. See *anomie*.

Anomie
Literally, without name or identity; the condition of not knowing what one's social character is supposed to be. The subjective character of anomie is similar to the feeling that comes when one is supposed to go someplace but has no map to tell how to get there. This term was coined by Durkheim to identify situations in which individuals are, or feel, only loosely united with the community or social order.

Asceticism
A philosophical point of view which claims that individuals can improve themselves spiritually by denying their physical nature; a philosophy of self-denial and discipline of the flesh. According to Sorokin, asceticism is one of the distinguishing features of an Ideational society. Ascetic philosophy is virtually nonexistent in the overripe Sensate society. Ascetic conduct includes fasting, self-flagellation, exposure to temperature extremes, self-mutilation, self-degradation, and humiliation. It is difficult to determine, however, whether, in its subjective state, such ascetic exercise serves to mute the senses or to excite them.

Atavistic Stigma or Stigmata
Marks (stigmata) that identify people as reversions (atavisms) to primitive physical types. Lombroso thought that many criminals had a primitive physical appearance. American white racists believe that American blacks can never really be civilized because they are physically a primitive type and that, moreover, this is proved by the blacks' physical appearance—their atavistic stigmata. Physical anthropologists, we should note, have convincingly demonstrated that Caucasians share as many physical traits in common with the gorilla as do the members of any other race.

Autarchy
Self-sufficiency, independence. Henry uses the term *consumption autarchy* to refer to the capacity of an economy to consume all the goods it produces.

Biologism
As used in this text, the belief that the social nature of people is inherent within, and explainable in terms of, biological nature. In its crude form, biologism argues that our major institutions are a reflection of biologically

endowed instincts. If we followed this line of reasoning, the Bank of America would have to be seen as a genetic phenomenon arising from an acquisitive instinct found in all people. Another naive form of biologism is the argument that a superior society can be created by producing a biologically superior form of human. In a more sophisticated form the modern biologist argues, quite reasonably, that we must not ignore people's animal nature. This form of biologism concedes that some aspects of the social order are not simple manifestations of biological urges or drives. Social and biological forces interact with each other. Thus, Konrad Lorenz, after exploring the biological nature of aggression in subhuman animals, very tentatively explores the possibility that the lessons learned at such a level might be applied to the aggressive nature of human beings. Note, however, his use, in the following quotation, of both biological and sociological or anthropological concepts.

The ganging up on an individual diverging from the social norms characteristic of a group and the group's enthusiastic readiness to defend these social norms and rites are both good illustrations of the way in which culturally determined conditioned-stimulus situations release activities which are fundamentally instinctive. (*On Aggression,* translated by Marjorie Kerr Wilson [New York: Harcourt, Brace, 1966], p. 259.)

Sociologists for the most part have eschewed biological approaches to human behavior.

Bureaucracy
A large-scale organization, hierarchically structured, dedicated to efficiency in the pursuit of its goals, with duties prescribed by a written set of regulations, personnel selected on the basis of examinations, and power resting within the concept of an "office" rather than in the individual. A modern bureaucracy can be almost incomprehensibly large. Seymour Melman, for example, says:

The Department of Defense of the United States employs 3.7 million people, of whom 2,680,000 are in the uniformed forces. . . . The armed services use 340,000 buildings. The total property value of the installations and equipment exceeds $171 billion. (*Our Depleted Society* [New York: Holt, Rinehart and Winston, 1965], p. 15.)

Bureaucracies, because of their reliance on codified rules, are highly legalistic in nature. Bureaucratic modes of organization in modern societies tend to diminish the influence of traditionalistic and kinship systems of organization.

Celibacy
For an adult, the state of living without a sexual partner. Dictionaries define celibacy as being single or unmarried. Celibacy, however, appears to be declining among the unmarried of our time. Vows of celibacy refer to the intention to lead a life devoid of sexual experiences involving a partner.

Charisma

A Greek word meaning *divine gift*. As used by Weber, this term refers to the dramatic or exciting personal characteristics of the prophetic leader or demagogue that enable the person to retain power over a following. Charismatic power is located in the unique personal attraction of the leader. Because such power is neither long lasting—dying when the leader dies—nor dependable, one of the problems faced by any social organization is the need to achieve more stable modes of allocating power. Bureaucracy achieves greater stability in its power structure by placing power within an office or position rather than in the individual. Thus people of power within a bureaucracy are often those having very little personal attraction or "charismatic" quality.

Consumerism

A social movement seeking to augment the rights and powers of buyers in relation to sellers. Historically, consumerism began in the Middle Ages by those who attacked deceptive selling practices and promoted the concept of "just price" rather than charging what the market would bear. (James F. Engel, Roger D. Blackwell, and David T. Kollat, *Consumer Behavior* [Hinsdale, Ill.: Dryden Press, 1978], p. 587.

Continuum

A condition to which we can, in our imagination, assign any value as we move from its lowest to its highest extremes. A continuous variable differs from a discrete variable. The latter permits only particular values as one moves from its lowest to its highest extremes. For example, wealth is a discrete variable. Along the tremendous range from no wealth to the billion dollar worth of a Howard Hughes, one must move by a series of discrete steps resulting from the fact that wealth is an accumulation of pennies. One must go from $25.00 to $25.01—there is no stage in between. Time, on the other hand, is continuous. No matter how finely we divide a second, we can think of a still finer division.

Cultural Lag

The idea that the material aspects of culture progress more rapidly than the nonmaterial or symbolic aspects. The adherents of this point of view claim that many social problems of our time arise from the inability of our moral concepts to keep pace with our technological development. Thus, while we are surrounded by atomic technology and super computers, we still depend upon a legal and moral philosophy that met the needs of a pastoral people who lived two thousand years ago. Opponents of the culture lag theory argue that all aspects of culture, including the technological, are essentially symbolic in nature and that the distinction between material and nonmaterial features of culture is spurious.

Darwinism

The theory of evolution attributed to Charles Darwin. It holds that all species (plants or animals) developed from earlier forms by natural selection among chance mutations. Those forms survive that are best adapted to the environment. See *Social Darwinism*.

Dehumanize

According to Goffman, the act of divesting any person of the right to employ those props, symbols, costumes, or fronts which enable that person to impress others favorably. A subtle example of dehumanization was offered by a woman who explained that during the 1930s, when she was employed as a clerk in a department store, she was instructed by her superiors to outfit Negro customers with clothes that fitted poorly or were in bad taste. Our conception of humanity, however we define it, is associated with group membership. A particular action which might be seen as human when carried out by a group member can be viewed as less human when performed by someone outside the group. Sociologists have summarized this phenomenon with the phrase, "In-group virtues are out-group vices." So it happens that *we* are "ambitious," but *they* are "pushy." *We* are "intelligent," but *they* are "too smart for their own good." Dehumanization is a complex form of behavior, operating at a symbolic level, which requires, first of all, a set of devices for depriving some class of persons of their right to use positive forms of impression management, and second, a justificatory scheme for the enactment of such deprivation.

Demography

The study of the numbers of humans living at any time as affected by fertility, mortality, and migration. Because mortality rates have been dramatically reduced in recent years, fertility has been the major factor accounting for variable rates of population increase in different nations. Demographers have become especially concerned with factors influencing human fertility.

Determinism

The philosophy that, in principle at least, all actions, including those of people, are the result of causes over which the acting agent has no control. Thus, a rock falls because of the determining influences of gravitational force. A human being does something because of the numerous determining forces of the situation. A person engaging in some action, placed in the same situation again, would respond in the same manner. Advocates of this point of view claim that the idea of choice or volition is entirely a matter of illusion—that in actuality we have no choice. Just as we physiologically mature and enter senility because of biological processes over which we can exercise no control, so we behave in response to the very complex conditions in which we find ourselves and which are, in their entirety, fortuitous circumstances. Even whether or not we believe we have a choice is a matter of cultural and ideological determinants into which we are thrust by the accident of birth. Critics of a deterministic position argue that determinism requires the capacity to assign causes to events. Where such causes cannot be assigned, an indeterminate situation exists. When a situation is indeterminate, the future is uncertain. The uncertainty of the future offers us the opportunity to assign, in the present, the priorities we will give to future actions. This assignment of priorities is a decision-making effort and involves thoughtful choices. Thus, we can choose. The fact that a determinist cannot predict the choices that will be made is a limitation of deterministic philosophy. In summary, determinism is a conceit that arises from the feeling that people will someday understand the workings of the entire universe. Meanwhile, we must live with the fact that our understanding is not sufficient to tell us whether we will survive the present century.

Dialectic
An approach taken by Marx as a way of interpreting social change. The dialectic process is one in which a given society or economic system generates its own opposition and is forced, ultimately, to change. For example, the feudal system was sufficiently successful in organizing economic affairs to produce a capitalistic system, which then modified the feudal system that brought it into existence. The term is used in argumentation to refer to the way in which a thesis can generate an attack or antithesis. The result is a synthesis, which can become a new thesis for further argument.

Dichotomy
A twofold classification of some condition. For example, we can dichotomize people as rich or poor, strong or weak, bright or stupid, good or bad. The most famous dichotomy we can think of is that pertaining to the sexes.

Dust-Bowl Empiricism
A term coined during the thirties, when the southwestern areas of the United States had suffered monstrous dust storms. The term refers to arid factual studies which have had the top soil of thoughtful interpretation blown away, leaving behind the bedrock of numerous statistical or descriptive observations.

Dysfunctional
Any social action which disrupts the well-being of the greater social system. The prefix *dys* means *bad*; therefore, we are talking about a bad function. In medical terminology "dysfunction" refers to the incapacity of an impaired organ to maintain the welfare of the whole organism. The idea of dysfunction in social analysis implies that its user has a very good concept of what a healthy social system is. However, this would imply an ethical judgment because social structures are, as Durkheim pointed out, moral structures. But social scientists are hesitant to make ethical judgments. Thus, the concept of dysfunction places them in a bind. If they exorcise it from their terminology, then they become apologists for the status quo. If they include it, they can be accused of making hidden ethical judgments—which would contradict their commitment to ethical neutrality. It is difficult to find examples of dysfunctional features of a social structure with which all sociologists would agree. Rioting, for example, would seem to be dysfunctional. However, one might reasonably claim, as would sociologist Georg Simmel, that such behavior is functional.

Ecological
A perspective that concerns itself with the interaction between organic systems and their environments. Ecology concentrates on life systems as complex interactions producing delicate, mutually sustaining living patterns for a great variety of organisms. If this ecological system is disturbed at any

point within its structure, the established equilibrium is destroyed and the whole structure is affected. This can be illustrated by a story attributed to Charles Darwin. Old maids in a certain area keep cats. The cats reduce the number of mice in the fields. Mice feed on bees. The reduction in mice increases the bee population. The greater number of bees improves the pollination of the clover crop. Thus, there is a connection between old maids and clover crops. One of the critical limitations of contemporary science is that it cannot tell us right now what the ecological consequences of our present technology will be. Some ecologists are coming to the conclusion that we might see, in the near future, catastrophic changes in the earth's biosphere. These changes could be very abrupt.

Egoism
Having a concern with one's own interests rather than with those of others; a concern with self to the exclusion of a concern with others. Egoism should be contrasted with altruism. See *egoistic suicide.*

Egoistic Suicide
Suicide resulting from egoistic motives; suicide in which self-destruction is seen as serving the interests of the persons who kill themselves. Such suicide may take quite elaborate forms, and the individuals often show a curiousness and interest in the fact of their own death. Durkheim relates:

A calm melancholy, sometimes not unpleasant, marks his last moments. He analyzes himself to the last. Such is the case of the business man mentioned by Falret who goes to an isolated forest to die of hunger. During an agony of almost three weeks he had regularly kept a journal of his impressions. (*Suicide* [New York: Free Press, 1951], p. 281.)

Electra Complex See Oedipus complex

Empathy
The ability to feel or experience the subjective state of others; the capacity to enter the experience of another person. Social psychological studies have shown that students who can easily empathize with their teachers tend to make better grades than those who cannot empathize.

Empirical
Having a factual quality, based on facts and observations as opposed to logical or rational considerations. According to a well-known story, purely rational considerations led to the conclusion that the bumblebee is aerodynamically incapable of flying. Empirical considerations force us to conclude, to the contrary, that bumblebees do a very reasonable job of flying. Sociologists argue that much of what is wrong with our understanding of human social behavior arises from the fact that we have dealt with this subject on the basis of reasoning rather than observation. Sociology owes its distinction as a field pretty much to the commitment it has made to finding ways of factually determining the nature of human social behavior. However, because social behavior is both very complex and generally

symbolic in character, the application of purely empirical modes of investigation is an ideal difficult to meet. Sociologists functioning at their empirical best generally rely on offical records of various events, which are
then submitted to statistical analysis. Demography, usually conceded to be
the most empirical wing of the sociological enterprise, is of this character.

Epistemology

The study and examination of the means whereby one can establish true
or valid statements. The epistemologist is concerned with establishing the
limits that hold for human knowledge. The epistemologist keeps raising
the question: But how can you be *certain* that what you say is true?

Esthetic

Having the quality of beauty, considered pleasing to the senses, meeting
cultural definitions of what is thought to be symmetrical, well formed, and
artistically appealing. Until recently, at least, one could give the example
of a junkyard as a place lacking esthetic qualities.

Ethical

According to sociologists, behavior which conforms to the normative structure of the society in which the individual lives. Because sociology strives
to be a science, and because science is ethically neutral, sociologists try to
assume an ethically neutral stance. Professional ethics thus place sociologists in the unusual position of being unethical when they write or lecture
with an ethical bias.

Ethnomethodology

A term coined by Garfinkel to refer to the study of the methods employed
by people in everyday social relationships to sustain the relationships and
make them "real" or "valid" or "reasonable." (*Ethno* = folk; *method* =
methods; and *ology* = study of.)

Existentialism

A philosophical position of a highly varied nature grounded in the observation that mortal beings are contained and must exist within a universe
that appears to be neither for nor against them. Faced with the fact of
existence in an unconcerned world, individuals must elect the meanings
they will give life. Existentialism, as employed in this book, refers to a
philosophy of choice—that people have the possibility of making what they
will of life.

Exponent or *Exponential*

Referring to a figure indicating how often a number is to be multiplied by
itself. The exponent 3 in 2^3 means that 2 is to be multiplied by itself three
times, or (2) (2) (2). Reference to exponential forms of growth has to do
with the extremely rapid increases in values that come from repeated
raising of a value by a factor contained in an exponent. Thus, if the factor
in the exponent is 2, we would rapidly get very large terms by repeatedly
squaring any real number greater than 1 or less than −1. For example,
beginning with 2, we would have $2^2 = 4$; $4^2 = 16$; $16^2 = 256$; $256^2 = 65,536$;
and so on.

Generalized Other

According to Mead, to become fully socialized, a child must respond to others not simply as individuals but in terms of how these individuals are interrelated as a group or community of people. Ultimately we are influenced not simply by specific isolated others but by the way in which those others are related to each other—that is, by a "generalized" other.

Hedonistic

Subscribing to a philosophy of the pursuit of pleasure. The hedonistic calculus, a concept used to explain preference for criminal behavior, argues that if such behavior gives more pleasure than pain, it will be engaged in. A modern revival of hedonistic theory has appeared in the works of B. F. Skinner, a behavioristic psychologist at Harvard. According to Skinner, any organism will reveal a greater predisposition to repeat behavior which it has found rewarding. We can employ this knowledge to make an organism behave as we would like it to by rewarding it each time it performs according to our preference. Thus, we can get a dog to roll over by rewarding it quickly on any occasion when it rolls over by chance or even begins to look as if it might roll over. One of the difficulties in applying such a theory to human behavior is that we cannot always be certain just what it is we want to reward. If we give a novelist a great reward (reinforcement) for writing a wonderful novel, this does not mean he or she is supposed to sit down and write the same novel again. Sociological theory, concerned as it is with the structural relations between statuses or roles, is surprisingly devoid of a reliance on hedonistic principles in its approach to human conduct. Sociologically, people often appear to go about role performances in a cheerless and conformistic fashion. If they experience pleasure, it is because the role they are playing tells them to; they do not experience the role because of their desire for pleasure.

Heuristic

A device or concept which, though perhaps meaningless in itself, has the capacity to promote, advance, or stimulate understanding. We could label Riesman's concept of *other-direction* a heuristic concept. Though it is difficult to find its counterpart in the real world, the term sensitizes us to many aspects of institutional living as it takes place in modern society. Many mathematical models have heuristic qualities. Kenneth Boulding, economist and social philosopher, tells his students that mathematical models are wonderful, so long as you do not believe them. He means that one should use the model to comprehend the nature of the real world, while at the same time remaining acutely aware of the constricted and artificial nature of the model itself. Boulding is saying the mathematical model is best seen as a heuristic device.

Hierarchy or Hierarchical

Being arranged in a series of ascending orders of power or control, with each stage having greater power than those falling beneath it. The military is the typical example of a hierarchically arranged set of statuses with each level having authority over those beneath it.

The Holocaust

The mass murder of over 6 million people, mostly European Jews, by Nazi Germany during the 1940s.

Humanistic

Being concerned with humanism; revealing a strong interest in human thought and ideals as opposed to an interest in nature or religion.

Idealization

According to Duncan, idealization is a symbolic construction of an event or condition that moves it beyond reality. This can take place only because idealization is a consequence of symbolic elaborations. Goffman uses the term in a more restricted sense to refer to role-playing in which a person responds to some fantasy of how the role should be played rather than what the role does, in fact, demand.

Inner-Directed

Having the ability to retain a strong and contrary sense of moral purpose when placed in circumstances where it would appear reasonable to succumb to the norms of the natives. As Riesman noted, the inner-directed nature of the British colonial administrator in the tropics was exemplified by his habit of dressing in Western clothing for dinner.

Internecine

Referring to conflict which is mutually destructive; deadly rivalry; struggle which avails little to either side in the battle.

Latent Function

A consequence that was not anticipated or planned in the course of a social development. For example, if it is true that the institution of prostitution during the Victorian period helped hold the Victorian family together, then one of the latent functions of prostitution would be that it helps maintain the integrity of the family. Latent functions are the implicit, indirect, and "unofficial" reasons for the existence of some agency, corporation, institution, status, or position. Latent functions are contrasted with *manifest functions.*

Mana

A Polynesian term used generally by anthropologists to refer to an impersonal and diffused supernatural force which has magical powers. Thus, a tree that is very fruitful might be claimed to possess mana. A successful and healthy man might be said to have mana. According to Swanson, a belief in mana exists only in societies with a particular form of social structure.

Manifest Function

A consequence that was planned or anticipated in the course of a social development. The manifest function of an aircraft plant, for example, is simply to provide a safe and rapid means of transportation for the people in a society. Manifest functions are the simple, direct, and "official" reasons for the existence of some agency, corporation, institution, status, or position. Manifest functions should be contrasted with *latent functions*.

Metaphysical

Literally, *after physics*; speculative thought which attempts to move beyond the directly observable nature of the physical world. To be interested in the accelerative dynamics of falling bodies is a physical interest. To be interested in the question of whether God exists in the form of a perfectly symmetrical cube is a metaphysical interest. Science has abandoned metaphysical concerns on the grounds they cannot be responded to in a manner that produces consistent and reliable results.

Methodology

The study of method. Because of the problems encountered in trying to establish reliable knowledge about the social order, sociologists have shown an especially sensitive concern over the methods they employ. Most sociology departments of any size in American universities have at least one person, and sometimes several, whose special training is in the area of methodology. Sociologists subscribe to the belief that if their methods are sound, their conclusions will be acceptable. While concentrating on the means to be employed to establish factual results, sociologists sometimes lose sight of the ends to be accomplished by their findings. The fact that the study of method is a separate and specialized area of concern to sociologists suggests there is such a thing as a sociological method of research. In practice there are any number of procedures that, depending on the effect being sought by the particular writer, can equally well serve as means of setting forth convincing arguments. Because sociologists subscribe to the belief that only scientific results are acceptable to the field, the study of method has concentrated almost exclusively on the application of scientific procedures which have produced valid results in other fields. A uniquely sociological method or set of methods has yet to be found.

Milieu

A French term for environment or surroundings; a more elegant way of referring to environmental influences.

Monasticism

Preference for solitary living; a form of institutionalization of solitary existence by taking up residence in a monastery, where one lives a quiet, relatively solitary, and meditative life; a belief in the monastery as a way of life.

Monotheism

A belief in the existence of one God. We often hear Christian religious beliefs described as monotheistic. This is not correct. Christian theology contains a number of gods and godlike spirits. It is, therefore, a polytheistic religion. According to Guy Swanson, a sociologist at the University of Michigan, relatively few cultures contain purely monotheistic religions.

Motifs

As used in this text, themes or central ideas around which the different elements of a culture are organized; the unifying concepts of a culture. Henry, for example, sees our emphasis on self-indulgence and consumption as one of the dominant motifs in modern American culture. This motif becomes the central figure around which are formed our industrial interests, courtship patterns, educational practices, child-rearing habits, the character of our youth, and other features of our culture.

National Character

An elusive concept based on the idea that there is a correspondence between a cultural milieu and the personalities of the people brought up in that culture. The idea of a national character is a refinement of the folk awareness that people from different nationalities have different qualities—in addition to the obvious ones of language differences. In the cruder stereotypical forms that appear in common thought, German national character, for example, is viewed as militaristic, authoritarian, bureaucratic, romantically sentimental, and given to the enjoyment of heavy and fattening foods. The attempt to provide more factual bases for such thinking has proved difficult. Anthropological and sociological research has shown there is considerable variety in personality types within any cultural system. Such variety should be kept in mind when dealing with the concept of national character.

Naturalism

The philosophical position that whatever is experienced in nature is to be explained, accounted for, or understood in terms of nature; the philosophical position that supernaturalistic or extranaturalistic explanations are mythical, fictional, or silly. The natural sciences lean exclusively on this position—as their name suggests. One physicist put it rather baldly by arguing that there is no place for God in the laboratory. Another scientist is reputed to have claimed that God is a redundancy in any mathematical equation because He would have to appear on both sides of the equal sign. An extreme naturalistic position is less attractive in the human realm. However, sociology, to the extent it assumes a scientific perspective, is grounded in the belief that *any* human institution—*any* human social action—ultimately has its origins in purely natural phenomena. Despite occasional demurrers, such a position is logically and practically antithetical to a religious explanation of human conduct.

Oedipus Complex

A term coined by Freud to refer to the tendency of the maturing male to find his mother an attractive sexual object. The son is biologically impelled to commit incest. Society, of course, is opposed to such practice. The maturing male child thus finds himself biologically set against the demands of a constraining social order. A further feature of the Oedipus complex is the feeling of hostility developed for the father as the child becomes aware of his father as a block between himself and his mother. Thus, the son is led into a situation where he wishes to murder his father and make physical love to his mother. How the sexually maturing male child resolves these horrifying desires has an impact, according to Freud, on the course of his adult life. The term *Electra complex* was given to the same situation with the sexes reversed. Hence the sexually maturing female child would be physically attracted to her father and hostile toward her mother.

Ostracize

To ban, to make someone an outcast, to shut out from the group, to set up barriers that make normal interaction with members of the group impossible. Ostracism often implies that a person being ostracized has been a member of the group and is then found unacceptable and banned from further participation in the group's activities. Ostracism is highly varied, however, and may take many forms, including the exclusion of persons who were never a part of the group. Ostracism can also be partial in character. We know about a member of a country club who asked the golf pro if he could invite a friend to play a round of golf with him. When he told the club pro that his friend was a black professor, he was told the game of golf would be all right; however, his professional friend was not to go near the swimming pool.

Paranoia

A psychiatric term referring to systematic delusions of persecution that have reached the point where the individual is incapacitated in the performance of normal life routines. Paranoid individuals live according to the assumption that everyone is against them. If people are friendly, it is because they want to get close enough to take advantage. Paranoid persons are often quite dangerous insofar as they come to believe they have good justification for inflicting damage on those near to them—they must in order to protect themselves. At a national level such systematic delusions of persecution and misanthropy result in internecine struggles in which no one benefits and many suffer.

Para-Poetic

A term used by Henry to refer to the literary qualities of modern advertising. The term has two possible meanings. It might mean, on the one hand, literary expression similar to poetry. It might also mean abnormal or crippled poetic expression. Henry probably had the latter meaning in mind. It is likely that he left the term open to allow the reader his or her own interpretation. It is difficult to classify the literary nature of modern advertising, and possibly the term *para-poetic* achieves such classification while, at the same time, keeping us aware of the difficulty. How does one handle the literary quality of advertising jingles that are known by virtually every citizen of an entire nation? Certainly they cannot be claimed to lack literary impact. On the other hand, the motives that give them form are not literary in nature. It is poetry that is not poetry. It is literature that is not literature. It is an influential rhetoric which serves the most banal of human aspirations. It is, to use Henry's term, para-poetic.

Pathogenic

A medical term referring to anything that produces a disease or organic abnormality; in the context of this book, any event that leads to socially destructive behavior. In this sense, the term *pathogenic* is quite similar to the idea of *dysfunction* and has the same problems involved in its usage. Usually, whether we consider something pathogenic in a social sense involves a personal normative judgment.

Pathological

Of a diseased nature; organically dysfunctional. Sociologists, often fond of organic metaphors, sometimes refer to crime, marital discord, rioting, conflict, or other violations of humanistic ideals as "pathologies." Such metaphors should be treated with caution. They are invariably disguised value judgments. They permit the sociologist to retain a cloak of objectivity while using a term which is the equivalent of an epithet.

Pecuniary

As used here, showing an interest in money; relating events and people in terms of their monetary values.

Peer Group

Literally, a group of one's equals. Sociologists generally use the term to refer to equals in the sense of similar age levels. Thus, an eight-year-old's peer group would consist of other children of a similar age. However, the peer group of a college professor would consist of other professors who share similar levels of sophistication and prestige—regardless of differences in age.

Peyote

A mescal cactus of the southwestern United States and Mexico that yields a drug capable of inducing unusual subjective and introspective states of mind.

Pluralism

In its most general meaning, pluralism simply refers to the fact that something can exist in several forms. The term *pluralistic society* has become popular in recent years and has been applied especially to the American system, in which a variety of ethnic cultures have been able to share in the common expression of American ideals. We employed the term *industrial pluralism* in the text to refer to the American industrial system, in which a variety of industries are allowed to produce a common product. These products are supposed to be different because they come from different plants. Everyone is aware, however, that the differences that appear to exist come more from the office of an advertising agency than from the factory.

Polygamy

Literally, marriages in which one may have several spouses. In common usage this term is often used to refer to that situation in which a husband has multiple wives. This is more correctly called *polygyny*. The situation in which a woman has several husbands is referred to as *polyandry*.

Postulate

As used throughout this book, the assumption of a proposition without need of proof in order to further an argument; a statement regarded as self-evident and not in need of further verification. One of the postulates of structural-functional theory, for example, is that any social action must have social consequences and must, therefore, be capable of being interpreted in terms of its social functions. A basic postulate of naturalistic philosophy is that all natural events can be understood in terms of what we perceive in nature.

Pragmatic

Subscribing to the philosophy that knowledge should be evaluated in terms of its practical values; the idea that the world exists to be manipulated; the conviction that knowledge which promotes manipulation is good—the rest, being useless, is worthless; dedication to the belief that events and people should be related in terms of their usefulness.

Prognostication

An attempt to divine the future; a forecast; an estimate of the outcome of some course of action.

Proletariat

The industrial working class of the world; people who do not own any means of production other than their labor power—most of us.

Psychic

Having the capacity to go beyond natural constraints; transcending the boundaries of normal and natural mental processes. Persons who are psychic are said to be able to foretell the future, move objects by application of will, and have an awareness of what other people are thinking without having to resort to questioning and natural forms of communication.

Quantophrenia

A term coined by Sorokin referring to the fanatic desire we have today to measure anything and everything. It was Kelvin who said, in effect, that if something could not be measured, then it could not be known. Sorokin felt such a position was excessive to the point of madness.

Racism

(Institutional and informal) action, often backed by theories to justify the oppression of socially stigmatized groups and attribute their own status to inherited inferior traits rather than to the lack of opportunities and economic mobility in the society.

Replication

The act of repeating. As used here, this term refers to the practice of repeating investigations over and over in order to check the validity of initial results. The fact that a sociological study often can be replicated and maintain a consistency of results is, in itself, a strong argument for the possibility of a science of human relations.

Retreatist

As used by Merton, any individual who abandons both the goals and the means endorsed by a society as legitimate and worthwhile. The dropout is a retreatist.

Ritualist

As used by Merton, any individual who becomes involved in a socially sanctioned means activity to the detriment of attaining socially valued goals. Ritualism implies a "blind" reliance on established modes of attaining goals even after these have ceased being effective. The court-martial of Billy Mitchell offers a historical case in point. Traditionalistic officers were scornful of aircraft as an implement of war. Their desire to continue in the use of older and outdated methods moved them in the direction of being military ritualists.

Sensate

A term coined by Sorokin to refer to cultures in which emphasis is given to knowledge derived through the senses. Such cultures, according to Sorokin, have a number of common characteristics, such as sensual art forms, pragmatic philosophies, positivistic science, relative moral systems, situational ethics, and prestige systems based on external signs of worth.

Shaman

A term broadly used to refer to people who believe they can interfere directly in the workings of good and evil spirits; a medicine man.

Significant Other

The observation that we are not affected equally by all others with whom we come in contact. Some people are more significant to us and we seek to win their favor more seriously. (The significant other can also be an enemy whose respect for our punitive power is something that takes over our fantasies.)

Social Darwinism

A term that refers to the carrying of Darwin's theories into social and moral theory. Social Darwinism argues, essentially, that superior cultures are the product of adaptation to the demands of the struggle for survival. A superior culture is usually one of which an exponent of this theory is a member at the time.

Social Goals

Objectives that achieve a special significance because they are collectively held. When, for example, acting was considered a rather common way of making a living, few people felt any desire to become an actor. Today, the social significance given to acting makes it a prized social goal—an aspiration which many hold as a dream.

Sociometric

A means of recording patterns of social relationships within a group. A sociometric is typically a simple charting of friendships among people. For example, one might ask students in a classroom to write down the names of their three best friends. Given this information, one can then determine who is the most popular student in the class and who is the least popular. Lines of informal influence can be established from such data.

Status Panic
A term coined by Mills to refer to the problems faced by Americans in their quest for a sense of worth. Because the standards of worth in the American system, according to Mills, are ill defined, Americans, no matter how hard they work, can never be certain they are a success. No matter where you stand in the system, there is always someone who can be looked upon as being better. Moreover, because American culture emphasizes a competitive relation with others, one is then obligated to match the worth of the person who stands above one. The fact that this is a never-ending and uncertain enterprise induces a sense of panic—the constant feeling that one is on the edge of failing.

Status Quo
The existing order; the present way of getting things done; the established and accepted system of human relationships as it exists in the present.

Structural-Functionalism
As used here, a sociological school of thought (structural-functionalism is also found in the biological sciences and in other social sciences) that attempts to relate particular forms cf social action to the total social system within which the action occurs.

Sui Generis
Literally, *of its own kind*; something unique; a thing apart; having special qualities. This term was used by Durkheim in his attempt to establish the social order as something have qualities of its own. Just as life, though dependent on the physical order, is different from inert matter, so is society, though dependent on biological beings, different from biological matter. The term is a call for recognition of the special understanding that is required to comprehend the nature of social activities. A social system has dynamics of its own (sui generis); it is not a simple manifestation of individual human needs and character.

Supersensory
A term coined by Sorokin to refer to the capacity of the great thinker to transcend the limits imposed by the senses.

Symbiotic Ecology
Referring to mutually sustaining life systems. A symbiotic relation is one in which several life forms provide reciprocal benefits. A prosaic example of a symbiotic relation is a person and a dog. The dog, in return for its gratification of the human need for recognition and affection, is given shelter and food. In some areas of the United States the dog is also given psychiatric care. See *ecological*.

Symbolic Elaboration

The ability of symbols to enlarge upon almost any subject, including the symbols themselves. In thinking about this notion, it is important to recognize that such elaboration is a property of symbols and not intelligence, curiosity, or some other psychologistic variable.

Symbolic Interactionism

As used here, a theoretical point of view in the social sciences emphasizing the symbolic nature of human social relations; the idea that human interaction is essentially symbolic interaction; the belief that one's sense of self arises out of the capacity to view one's self as a meaningful entity apart from others—this in turn being based on our capacity to evaluate ourselves symbolically. A very simple demonstration of what the symbolic interactionist is trying to put across can be carried out with an ordinary television set. First, turn off the sound and watch the picture. Because this reduces the symbolic content of the picture drastically, the meaning of most of what is taking place is lost. Next, turn off the picture but retain the sound. The symbolic content carried by the physical action in the picture is now lost, but this is the smaller symbolic element. At the level of pure symbolic interaction we can retain a good sense of what is taking place. Human social interaction takes place at a symbolic level, and this makes it distinctive. When we interact with a person, we interact with that person in terms of the values that obtain through the symbolic meanings we attach to him or her. The symbolic interactionists, in the classical formulations of Mead, made much of the fact that not only do individuals have the capacity to interact at the symbolic level with others—they can also interact symbolically with themselves. Individuals can assume the role of others and then either praise or castigate themselves from the perspective of these other people. Symbolic interactionists see this as the most essential aspect of social control. Any biologically and mentally normal person is highly vulnerable to the symbolic evaluations that others make of him or her. We have no physically determinable and sensorily observable self. Therefore, what we are is what others make of us. We uncritically assume the symbolic evaluations of self that others give us. If enough people tell us we are bad, we come to accept this evaluation. Conversely, if enough people tell us we are good, we also accept this. Our self, therefore, is located in the external evaluations imposed upon us. For this reason, society and self are only different manifestations of the same process.

Symptomatic Behavior

A term coined by Goffman to refer to behavior that validates one's right to act out the content of a particular role. Such behavior is symptomatic of whether one "really" is what one is trying to appear to be. For example, a professor who has a deep British accent, everything else being equal, will be more acceptable to an audience than one who has a strong Arkansas accent. The British accent is viewed as symptomatic of a person of wit, dignity, and learning. A colleague of ours once said that he mistrusted the work of a certain man because he had seen him at a meeting and the man was deeply tanned. No *real* scholar would be tanned. As Veblen pointed out, a suntan is symptomatic of a frivolous life in an age of office workers.

Tautology

Circular reasoning; saying the same thing in different ways; redundancy; redefining a condition and then using the redefinition as an explanation. For example, it was once fashionable to define an immoral person as spiritually corrupt. Spiritual corruption was then used to explain immorality. All that was being done here was to claim that someone was immoral because he was immoral.

Testocracy

A term coined by Sorokin to refer to the tendency in modern Sensate cultures to rule people by subjecting them to various tests, such as those for I.Q., aptitude, and personality.

Tradition-Directed

A term coined by Riesman to refer to cultures in which individuals are strongly influenced by traditional as opposed to rational considerations.

Transcendent Principles

At the simplest level, transcendent principles of social order are those which, according to Duncan, are able to exert an influence or be accepted across various lines of social division. Money, for example, is an obvious transcendent principle—poor people and rich, young and old, male and female, bright and stupid, educated and ignorant subscribe with more or less the same intensity to the rigors of a money morality.

Transcendental

Going beyond the limits of normal human experience; transcending one's natural abilities; extending beyond normal physical awareness.

Tripartite

A threefold classification scheme. Riesman's three character types exemplify a tripartite classification.

Typology

A classification scheme; an examination of types.

Usury

The practice of lending money at very high rates of interest.

Utilitarian

Having utility or usefulness.

Utopia

An ideal community; a place in which people achieve their most noble conceptions of life; literally, no (*ou*) place (*topos*).

Value System

A structure or ordering of actions that are highly esteemed by a people; the assignment of worth to different activities in a manner that reveals an underlying common basis of evaluation of such activity. In this text, Sorokin's ideas most clearly illustrate a means of comprehending the nature of value systems. In a Sensate society the relative value of an activity is determined in terms of the extent to which it attains Sensate criteria of worth. In such a system chastity would be assigned little value; sending an astronaut to the moon would be assigned great value. These disparate activities are valued in terms of a system that ranks them according to the extent to which they can be ranked in terms of Sensate criteria of worth.

Volition

A concept implying that people have the capacity to exercise choice; will; decision making. See the discussion under *determinism*.

Weltanschauung

Literally, *world view*; a conception of life and the universe; a way of seeing the world.

Xenophobia

Having a fear (*phobia*) of that which is strange or foreign (*xenos*); a hatred of the foreigner.

INDEX